Legacies of the Stone Guest

Publications of the Wisconsin Center for Pushkin Studies

DAVID M. BETHEA
Series Editor

LEGACIES OF THE STONE GUEST

The Don Juan Legend in Russian Literature

Alexander Burry

THE UNIVERSITY OF WISCONSIN PRESS

The University of Wisconsin Press
728 State Street, Suite 443
Madison, Wisconsin 53706
uwpress.wisc.edu

Gray's Inn House, 127 Clerkenwell Road
London EC1R 5DB, United Kingdom
eurospanbookstore.com

Copyright © 2023
The Board of Regents of the University of Wisconsin System
All rights reserved. Except in the case of brief quotations embedded in critical articles and reviews, no part of this publication may be reproduced, stored in a retrieval system, transmitted in any format or by any means—digital, electronic, mechanical, photocopying, recording, or otherwise—or conveyed via the Internet or a website without written permission of the University of Wisconsin Press. Rights inquiries should be directed to rights@uwpress.wisc.edu.

Printed in the United States of America
This book may be available in a digital edition.

Library of Congress Cataloging-in-Publication Data

Names: Burry, Alexander, author.
Title: Legacies of the Stone Guest : the Don Juan legend in Russian literature / Alexander Burry.
Other titles: Publications of the Wisconsin Center for Pushkin Studies.
Description: Madison, Wisconsin : The University of Wisconsin Press, 2023. | Series: Publications of the Wisconsin Center for Pushkin Studies | Includes index.
Identifiers: LCCN 2022033682 | ISBN 9780299342104 (hardcover)
Subjects: LCSH: Pushkin, Aleksandr Sergeevich, 1799-1837. Kamennyĭ gost'—Influence. | Juan, Don (Legendary character)—In literature. | Russian literature—History and criticism. | Russian literature—Themes, motives.
Classification: LCC PG3343.K273 B87 2023 | DDC 891.72/3—dc23/eng/20220921
LC record available at https://lccn.loc.gov/2022033682

To Grace Yeh

Contents

Acknowledgments	ix
Introduction: Don Juan in Western Europe and Russia	3
1 The Artist-Seducer as Liberator: Pushkin's *Stone Guest*	29
2 Don Juan in Everyday Life: The Era of Realism	68
3 Don Juan in the Silver Age	104
4 Soviet and Post-Soviet Don Juans	144
Conclusion	185
Notes	195
Works Cited	219
Index	231

Acknowledgments

In writing this book, I have benefited from the help of many people. Above all, I am eternally grateful to Helena Goscilo, who supported me at every stage of the project, provided countless insightful suggestions on all the chapters, and generally served as a fount of knowledge and a source of feedback and inspiration throughout the process. Rolf Hellebust read a complete draft and provided exceptionally valuable ideas both for further contextualization of my analyses in other areas of Russian literature and for balancing my claims about Pushkin's originality with recognition of the momentous role played by his predecessors in shaping the Don Juan legend. Olga Livshin gave me continual encouragement, drew my attention to Liudmila Ulitskaya and other important writers, and also made many thought-provoking comments on a draft of the manuscript. I am also very grateful to the anonymous reviewers who made beneficial recommendations for useful additions and omissions. I thank Irene Masing-Delic, who critiqued an early draft of my analysis of Alexander Blok's works, and Anna Grotans, who helpfully corrected my translations of German scholarship.

The Ohio State University provided sabbatical and travel support that was instrumental in my research and writing. The Division of Arts and Humanities and the Department of Slavic and East European Languages and Cultures generously funded a subvention to assist in publication of this book. I also wish to thank everyone at the University of Wisconsin Press who assisted me in bringing this volume to publication, particularly the series editor David Bethea, who supported the project early on, Amber Rose Cederström, who provided wise and patient guidance as I went through the submission, review, and revision processes, Jessica Smith and the other editors who prepared my manuscript, and Jennifer Conn and the design team.

Portions of chapters 2 and 4 appeared in previous publications. I am grateful to the *Slavic and East European Journal* for allowing me to reprint "A Stony Vengeance: Donjuanism and Retribution in *Anna Karenina*," 57, no. 4 (Winter 2013): 544–60. I also thank the *Russian Review* for permission to reuse in chapter 4 my article "The Poet's Fatal Flaw: Venedikt Erofeev's Don Juan Subtext in *Walpurgis Night, or the Steps of the Commander*," *Russian Review* 64, no. 1 (January 2005): 62–76. In addition, I thank *Russian Literature* for allowing me to incorporate into the same chapter "Poetic Escape in Vladimir Kazakov's *Don Zhuan*," *Russian Literature* 68, nos. 3–4 (Oct. 1–Nov. 15, 2010): 275–90.

I would like to gratefully acknowledge my debt to my parents, Anthony and Veena Burry, who first introduced me to Russian and world culture and nurtured my fascination with literature and the arts in my childhood and beyond. I would also like to express my deep appreciation to my sons, Elliott, Jacob, and Leopold ("Poldi"), for their companionship and good cheer during my years of work on this project. Finally, I thank my wife, Grace Yeh, for her constant support. This book is dedicated to her with love and gratitude.

Legacies of the Stone Guest

Introduction
Don Juan in Western Europe and Russia

Don Juan: You can't see anything
　Under her black veil and widow's weeds.
　I caught one glimpse of a narrow heel.
Leporello: For you that's enough. Your imagination
　Will fill in all the blank spots in a minute;
　It works faster than a portrait painter
　And you don't care what it begins with,
　A forehead or a foot. (71)[1]

Дон Гуан: Ее совсем не видно
　Под этим вдовьим черным покрывалом,
　Чуть узенькую пятку я заметил.
Лепорелло: Довольно с вас. У вас воображенье
　В минуту дорисует остальное;
　Оно у нас проворней живописца,
　Вам все равно, с чего бы ни начать,
　С бровей ли, с ног ли. (143)[2]

EARLY IN ALEXANDER PUSHKIN'S *The Stone Guest* (*Kamennyi gost'*), as Don Juan begins his pursuit of Donna Anna, Leporello characterizes his master differently than do any servants in previous versions of the legend. By comparing Don Juan to a painter, the cynical Leporello indicates that his master does not require more than a body part to find a woman attractive and attempt to add her to his long list of conquests.[3] With typical ambiguity, though, Pushkin sets up two contrasting possible motivations in his hero. By depicting Don Juan as both an artist with a rich imagination and a seducer, he invites the reader or viewer to consider the indivisibility of these qualities in this character.[4] Pushkin thus provides a new interpretive angle on the legend, inaugurating a fresh approach to what was already an established narrative when he wrote the play in 1830. As I contend in this study, Pushkin's interpretation of the Don Juan legend along these lines, in this passage and others, proved to be decisive for subsequent Russian treatments of the legend.

Strictly speaking, Pushkin did not introduce Don Juan to Russia. Although the Don Juan theme, like many others derived from Western Europe, arrived relatively late in Russia, it could actually be found there over a century before *The Stone Guest* appeared. In the 1710s, during the time of Peter I, a Russian version of the play (of which only the fifth act is preserved) was performed. Translated from an anonymous Polish version of the French playwright Claude Deschamps, Sieur de Villiers's 1659 play *The Stone Guest, or the Criminal Son* (*Le Festin de Pierre, ou le Fils criminel*), it was titled *Don Pedro, Devoted Nobleman and Amarillis, His Daughter, or the Comedy of Don Jan and Don Pedro* (*Don Pedro, pochitannyi shliakhta i Amarillis, doch' ego, ili komediia o Done Iane i Don Pedro*).[5] The Don Juan theme reappeared at other points in the eighteenth century as well. The German composer Christoph Willibald Gluck's 1761 ballet *Don Juan, or the Stone Guest's Banquet*, based on a scenario by the imperial ballet-master in Vienna, Gasparo Angiolini, was performed in St. Petersburg in the 1780s, as was a 1781 ballet by the Italian composer Carlo Canobbio, who lived in the Russian capital at the time. Molière's seminal 1665 play was first produced in Petersburg by a French troupe in 1795 and garnered many performances in the 1810s, including some translated into Russian by the choreographer, ballet master, and translator Ivan Val'berkh in 1816 in St. Petersburg and 1818 in Moscow.[6]

Wolfgang Amadeus Mozart and Lorenzo Da Ponte's *Don Giovanni* (1787), in particular, created a sensation in Russia. It first appeared there in 1806 and was performed in Russian for the first time in 1828. Later, in the 1850s, a veritable cult developed around the opera. The Spanish diva Pauline Viardot-García purchased the original manuscript of *Don Giovanni* and, as Mark Everist explains, acted as "priestess" of this cult, displaying the manuscript as a shrine to Mozart to which luminaries such as Petr Tchaikovsky paid homage (177). Meanwhile, Lord Byron's unfinished novel in verse, *Don Juan* (1818–24), circulated through Russia immediately after its publication and influenced Pushkin in particular (though not in the creation of his own Don Juan).[7] Moreover, Byron's works and life alike, with their notorious Don Juan-like libertinage, inspired a series of imitators in Russia among both writers and nonwriters. In addition, the growth of Russian sympathy for Spain in its struggle against Napoleon in the Peninsular War (1807–14) was accompanied by a resurgence of interest in its language and culture, including the Don Juan legend, as both progressive and conservative writers and thinkers turned to Spanish themes for inspiration (Weiner 26–39). Thus, upper-class, educated, and artistically cultivated Russians would have been well aware of Don Juan and Donjuanism (*donzhuanstvo*, a term that has become part of the Russian vocabulary) had Pushkin never written his little tragedy.[8]

However, Pushkin's reworking of the Don Juan legend, as I argue, wielded an outsized influence on Russian writers and artists. Following the posthumous publication of *The Stone Guest* in 1839, the Don Juan theme flourished in both the nineteenth and twentieth centuries in Russia. Nineteenth-century writers as diverse as Nikolai Shcherbina, Evdokiia Rostopchina, Ivan Goncharov, Alexei K. Tolstoy, Lev Tolstoy, Alexei Bezhetsky, Alexander Mordvin-Shchodro, and Anton Chekhov all either created versions of the legend or included it as a prominent subtext in one or more of their works. Early in the following century, virtually every important Silver Age writer contributed at least one poem, play, or essay on the theme. Early twentieth-century writers on the Don Juan legend include Valery Briusov, Konstantin Bal'mont, Alexander Blok, Marina Tsvetaeva, Zinaida Gippius, Anna Akhmatova, and Sergei Esenin, as well as many figures in exile, such as Nikolai Otsup, Vladimir Nabokov, Georgy Adamovich, Vadim Andreev, and Igor' Severianin. Later, in the twentieth and early twenty-first centuries, the list of Russian writers on the Don Juan theme includes Samuil Aleshin, David Samoilov, Edvard Radzinsky, Vladimir Kazakov, Venedikt Erofeev, Viktor Sosnora, and Alexander Annin, among others. Not all of these writers were directly or primarily influenced by Pushkin (some looked to E. T. A. Hoffmann and other Western European writers for inspiration on Don Juan), but most had his play in mind to some extent. Pushkin's little tragedy is largely, though not completely, responsible for Don Juan's standing as a Russian archetype that has transcended literature and become part of the culture.

What particular aspects of the Don Juan legend appealed to Russian writers, and why did Pushkin's little tragedy engender so many subsequent versions? One key element of Pushkin's reworking of this European legend is his ability to tap into the theme of rebellion that undergirds the legend and suggest its relevance for Russian culture in various time periods. The Don Juan legend at its root posits a free, iconoclastic individual pitted against a restrictive, conformist society. Ian Watt, in his study of Don Juan and other European archetypes, notes that as with Faust and Don Quixote, the Don Juan legend in its written form was conceived in the Counter-Reformation period, which featured stringent opposition to the Renaissance individualism that had arisen in the preceding century. As Watt argues, "Faustus, Don Quixote, and Don Juan are all characterized by the positive, individualistic drives of the Renaissance; they wish to go their own way, regardless of others. But they find themselves in conflict, ideologically and politically, with the forces of the Counter-Reformation; and they are punished for it" (x).

This focus on an individual at odds with a repressive society, symbolized by the dichotomy of the rebellious libertine and the avenging stone statue, was particularly relevant for Pushkin and other Russian writers who lived and created their works within similarly restrictive environments. Pushkin's allusions in his play to the authoritarian Nikolaevan society in which he lived find reverberations in the Don Juan texts of subsequent Russian writers working in times of repression, upheaval, or both. They can be found in the works of Realists writing in a period of seismic shifts stemming from the movement of wealth from the aristocracy to merchants and members of other classes and the rise of the "woman question". They appear in works by Silver Age poets attempting to transform society through their writing in the period of apocalyptic expectation of violent cataclysm. And they also find their way into the works of late twentieth-century writers reacting to a repressive, stagnant Soviet society. The Commander figure, for several of these writers, takes on an apocalyptic aura, portending disaster in Russian society as a whole rather than simply serving as an instrument of vengeance on one libertine.

Thus, the appeal and influence of *The Stone Guest* in Russia testify in part to Pushkin's unique capacity to import distinctly foreign material and "Russianize" it. Numerous commentators have praised this aspect of his oeuvre. Most famously, Fyodor Dostoevsky, in his 1880 speech commemorating the unveiling of the Moscow monument to Pushkin, characterized the poet's (and Russia's) genius as the ability to absorb Western European art and recreate it in superior forms.[9] The novelist's list of his predecessor's opuses that purportedly accomplish this feat includes *The Stone Guest*: "Read 'Don Juan' once more, and were it not for Pushkin's name on it you would never guess that it had not been written by a Spaniard" (1292).[10] Dostoevsky's mythologizing of Pushkin in this speech clearly serves his own artistic and political purposes more than it objectively describes his predecessor's creation. Nevertheless, the novelist's depiction is characteristic of a peculiarly Russian reception of Pushkin.[11] One of the arguments I make in this study, though, is that *The Stone Guest* did not merely ensure a multitude of Don Juan progeny in the following two centuries, but also inspired diverse Russian writers and artists to extend the theme of Donjuanism into other literary avenues in an attempt to resolve or extend issues Pushkin raises in the play.

Thus, Pushkin's uncanny capacity to regenerate a European myth in this case goes far beyond his ability to represent qualities of other nations in his works, as Dostoevsky claims. He also displays a knack for unearthing surprising aspects of foreign works through ambiguous, open-ended treatments. We are left with many questions at the end of *The Stone Guest* that are resolved far more conclusively in other versions of the Don Juan legend. For instance, has Don Juan really been resurrected in his love for Donna Anna, as he insists, or is this proclamation a ruse, performed to trick yet another woman? Does Donna Anna merely faint at the approach of the Commander, or does she die, as some readers believe? What is the fate of the woman Pushkin adds to the legend, Don Juan's counterpart, Laura, and what is her significance, given the fact that she is abandoned after Scene 2? For that matter, what exactly happens to Don Juan himself at the end? The legend indicates that he goes to hell, but Pushkin's stage directions convey something more like "falling through," along with the statue: what does their exiting the scene together signify? And does Pushkin identify more with Don Juan (as a former young philanderer who kept a Don Juan list of his own), or with the Commander, as the groom of a much younger woman and a man who superstitiously feared his own imminent death? Does he identify with both equally? Other questions could conceivably be raised as well. Subsequent Russian writers who are influenced by *The Stone Guest*, as I will discuss in later chapters, often attempt to resolve these ambiguities.

Don Juan in the West

In order to contextualize *The Stone Guest* and the other Russian variants of the Don Juan theme that I analyze, I begin by examining some of the major Western European versions of the legend preceding Pushkin's little tragedy.[12] The first extant Don Juan work, *The Trickster of Seville and the Stone Guest* (*El Burlador de Sevilla y Convidado de Piedra*), was written by the Spanish monk and playwright Tirso de Molina (pseudonym of Gabriel Téllez) between 1612 and 1616. It first appeared in a collection of plays by Lope de Vega and other Spanish playwrights in 1630.[13] Although not all of the Russian writers on the Don Juan theme whose works I discuss read Tirso's play, it lays out a starting point for future versions, establishing the problems that subsequent writers contend with, regardless of their knowledge of this first written Don Juan work.[14] Moreover, *The Trickster of Seville* influenced the works that *did* impact Pushkin and other writers, directly or indirectly. I therefore devote a generous amount of space to describing its principal themes and motifs, along with its portrayal of the protagonist.

The dramatic action of Tirso's play revolves around a series of *burlas* (tricks) that Don Juan plays on unsuspecting women (and the men to whom they are attached). At the start of Act I, he enters the bedroom of the Duchess Isabela in the court of the King of Naples, disguised as her fiancé, Don Octavio. He is caught *in flagrante delicto* by the king, who orders him arrested, but the king's courtier and Don Juan's uncle, Don Pedro, helps him escape to Spain. Washed up on a beach after a shipwreck, Don Juan seduces a fisherwoman, Tisbea, only to abandon her at dawn. In Act II, he meets his friend the Marquis de la Mota, who is engaged to Ana of Ulloa. The Marquis asks Don Juan to substitute for him in paying a visit to his mistress, Beatriz, and gives him his cape to enable him to do so. Don Juan instead uses the cape to pay a visit to Ana, but is discovered by her father, Don Gonzalo, who forces him to fight a duel and is killed. After escaping Ana's house, Don Juan stops at a peasant wedding with his servant, Catalinón, usurps the groom Batricio's place, and seduces his bride, Aminta, promising that he will make her a noblewoman through marriage. In Act III, Don Juan and Catalinón find the monument of Don Gonzalo in a church in Seville, and Don Juan pulls the statue's beard and mockingly invites it to supper. To his surprise, the statue appears at his inn and, as part of the double invitation motif characteristic of the legend, demands Don Juan's word that he will visit him for supper the following evening. Don Juan goes back to the church at the appointed time, the statue grabs his hand, and they sink into hell together through Don Gonzalo's tomb. Just as the King of Naples and other characters are trying to unravel the chaos caused by Don Juan's tricks, Catalinón enters and announces his master's death.

As the first known version of the Don Juan legend, *The Trickster of Seville* establishes traits that recur in numerous subsequent works. I will examine some patterns set by this play and then trace them through other Western European versions. Because the following features recur in various Don Juan texts, including many Russian ones, each can be viewed as a dominant, which Roman Jakobson defines as a "focusing component of a work of art that rules, determines, and transforms the remaining components" (82). Some of these traits reappear in all or nearly all ensuing Don Juan works; others gradually disappear as the legend encounters new time periods and cultures.

One crucial dominant, at least for the first two hundred years of the legend, is the hero's nobility, which serves the practical function of affording him the money, leisure, time, and access needed for his endless pursuit of adventures and trysts with women of all classes. Tirso's Don Juan defines himself by his aristocracy, falsely offering the peasant girl Aminta the prospect of ennoblement through marriage to him. At the same time, however, he makes use of his noble privilege to undermine its rules and conventions. Thus, Don Juan's aristocratic status offers Tirso the opportunity to critique the noble class and his society as a whole. Don Juan's escapades, as he shows, are enabled by the complicity of other noblemen: in his first conquest of the play, of Isabela, it is his uncle, Don Pedro Tenorio, who helps him escape by her balcony and creates a series of deceptions that put in motion the ensuing action of the play.

Don Juan's demise at the hands of the Commander, an emissary from beyond the world of the living, signals the religious focus of the legend. As Watt notes, "Tirso's aim was to force his audience to face corrective conclusions from the pitiless punishment God meted out to Don Juan's soul" (118).[15] The libertine's refusal to follow society's rules ultimately entails rebellion against God. Writing in seventeenth-century Catholic Spain, Tirso explores the problem of God's grace, particularly the conundrum of how long one can postpone turning to it while leading a life of sin and still expect to receive salvation. The possibility of penitence is mentioned throughout the play, as several characters warn Don Juan that his evil deeds will anger God, and that he will be damned if he does not reform. Don Juan's refrain, "Tan largo me lo fiáis" (Plenty of time for that), indicates his sense of surety that he can repent and call on God's grace in the distant future. The cruel twist of the drama is that Don Juan turns out to have less time than he thinks for repentance, and his request for absolution, made as he feels the fire consuming his body, comes too late:

> *Don Juan*: Let me send for a priest at least; I want to confess and be absolved!
> *The Statue*: It cannot be. You thought of that too late. (97)[16]

Tirso, through the statue, conveys God's answer to Don Juan's refrain that he has plenty of time: "As a man sows, so shall he reap" (97). One may argue that perhaps Don Juan's greatest sin is not his seductions, his tricks, or even his killing of Don Gonzalo so much as his pride in presuming to decide his own time for repentance. "Believing that he will always have time to repent," Theresa Sears observes, "Don Juan usurps the divine prerogative to set the hour of humankind's demise" (98).

Tirso employs motifs of fire and burning throughout the play to convey the theme of damnation, which culminates in the image of the statue burning Don Juan with its handgrip:

> *The Statue*: Give me your hand. Never fear; give me your hand.
> *Don Juan*: Fear? Take it! . . . Ai, I'm burning alive. Burning, burning. (97)

This motif appears from the earliest points of the play and is not only alluded to by Don Juan. In the trickster's conversation with Tisbea after he is rescued from the shipwreck, both characters use fire and burning as metaphors to describe Don Juan's temperament and his passion for her:

> *Tisbea*: If you burn when you are so wet, what will you do when you're dry again? You promise a scorching flame; I hope to God you're not lying.
> *Don Juan*: Dear girl, God should have drowned me before I could be charred by you. Perhaps love was wise to drench me before I felt your scalding touch. But your fire is such that even in water I burn.
> *Tisbea*: So cold and yet burning?
> *Don Juan*: So much fire is in you. (59)[17]

Later, when Tisbea discovers Don Juan's trick (he leaves at dawn after having promised her his hand in marriage), she cries out "Fire! Fire! And madness! I'm burning!" (63).

On the other hand, Don Juan's comeuppance takes place through his invitation to the statue, which underscores his agency in his own downfall. The protagonist deliberately insults the Commander's image, perhaps provoked by the inscription on his gravestone: "Here the most loyal of knights expects God's vengeance on a traitor" (86). Whether subsequent writers keep Tirso's double invitation or reduce it to a single one, the invitations and consequent visits of the statue signify the incapacity of worldly society to bring down Don Juan, and to an extent a certain degree of powerlessness even of divine forces to stop him. Had Don Juan not invited the statue to supper, he would not have instigated the series of events that led to his damnation; presumably, he then could have gone on playing tricks and seducing women as long as he liked. Thus, Tirso—deliberately or unwittingly—indicates that the Don's downfall results at least to some extent from internal rather than solely external causes. Gradually, as the legend becomes secularized and the religious framework falls away, this notion of Don Juan summoning his own punishment is further emphasized, and he can be increasingly analyzed in psychological terms.

Don Juan's attack on all customs and institutions of his time in *The Trickster of Seville* involves a contrast of freedom and confinement that continues to appear in most ensuing versions of the legend.[18] As a libertine (*liber* = free), Don Juan rebels against the constraints that bind most people, and Tirso visualizes this freedom through his protagonist's constant motion from place to place. Don Juan moves from the King of Naples's castle, where he seduces Isabela disguised as her lover Duke Octavio, to the sea, and then to Seville. Moreover, he breaches confined spaces, whether actual (courts of kings, private dwellings, and in later versions, convents) or metaphorical (marital roles). He breaks these spaces down through immense sexual energy that impels him to commit all kinds of bold actions and requires constant movement, whether to permeate a new barrier or to escape the consequences of having done so. Don Juan is in motion throughout *The Trickster of Seville*, coming to a halt only when the statue of the Commander freezes him in its grip. Through Don Juan's two confrontations with Don Gonzalo—the first in Ana's room after Don Juan has attempted to seduce her, and the second with Gonzalo's statue—Eros (the libertine's sexual energy) comes into conflict with Thanatos (the force of death, as represented by the Commander). Already in this first version of the Don Juan tale, Tirso clearly opposes these two forces, as only an entity from beyond the realm of the living can overcome Don Juan's prodigious appetite for sex, movement, and life itself.

Throughout the play, Tirso creates a pattern of love triangles that becomes characteristic of the Don Juan plot, as the libertine's conquests are all paired with other men. Isabela is engaged to Octavio, Ana is betrothed to the Marquis de la Mota, and Don Juan seduces Aminta during her wedding to Batricio. Tisbea is less committed than the other women and seems to delight in refusing the admirers who surround her, but even she has a suitor, at least, in Anfriso, who remains a potential bridegroom for her at the end of the play. Although the resulting sense of rivalry becomes much more explicit in subsequent works, beginning with Molière (see below), Tirso sets the pattern of making Don Juan a rival of men, a libertine whose sexual impulses are awakened as much by the women's unavailability, and the challenge it represents, as by their desirability as women per se.[19] In this light, Don Juan's decision not to follow the Marquis's instructions and meet with his (available) mistress, but instead to pursue the forbidden seduction of his betrothed, is entirely in character.

Although Don Juan's primary motivation would seem to be sexual gratification, Leo Weinstein notes that, as Tirso's title indicates, trickery rather than erotic pleasure is the main driver of his conquests (13). As Don Juan frankly proclaims, "The trickster of Seville! This is what all Spain calls me. The man whose greatest pleasure is to play a woman for a fool and abscond with her honor" (70). His actions represent a form of male domination of females through trickery, a practice performed by the Marquis de la Mota as well. Don Juan's tricks can also be seen as a thumbing of his nose at the social order, which aimed to continue patrilinear heritage through sanctioned marriages. By substituting himself for approved suitors, Don Juan disrupts this continuity.

This contrast between Don Juan's real and ostensible motivations points to a paradoxical aspect of the legend, one that proves to be significant for several of the Russian versions I analyze. The focus of Don Juan's energy is presumably sexual, given his trademark activity of seduction, not to mention the popular understanding of a "Don Juan" as a man who is inordinately successful with women. However, both in the non-Russian works I discuss here and the Russian versions in the following chapters, we almost invariably discover that sexual pleasure is only the apparent purpose of Don Juan's seductions; something else always underlies them.

In connection with Don Juan's trickery, there is always a degree of artistry to his seductions, and he seems to enjoy the process of hoodwinking women at least as much as the actual intercourse. His artistry entails combining disguises with disarming language to persuade women to abandon their virtue. Although Shoshana Felman singles out Molière's hero for his use of words as performative acts, Don Juan's eloquence can already be seen in Tirso's version. As James

Mandrell observes about this play: "Don Juan's transgressions are not just cumulative, serial aggravations that add up to his punishment. They constitute a progressively complex exploration of the nature of language as it functions in the world: initially as Don Juan's tool in seduction and, finally, as the means of his undoing" (61). Don Juan's speech to Tisbea, as he awakens in her arms after being shipwrecked, offers one example of his flowery, seductive language and unending capacity to produce words to benefit himself in any situation: "If the sea gives me death, you give me life. But the sea really saved me only to be killed by you. Oh the sea tosses me from one torment to the other, for I no sooner pulled myself from the water than I met its siren—yourself. Why fill my ears with wax, since you kill me with your eyes? I was dying in the sea, but from today I shall die of love." (59)[20] With all his eloquence, ability to dissemble, and improvisational skill in these passages, Don Juan may be considered a brilliant actor as well. His capacity to take on various roles aids in his seduction of not only his love interests, but also the members of the audience, who despite their awareness of his villainy cannot help but marvel at his convincing and titillating deceptions.

From the beginning of the legend in its written form, then, Don Juan is presented as a master of the word, an actor, and thus a kind of artist. As my opening example shows, Pushkin in particular makes this connection explicit. Indeed, Don Juan's tricks themselves, in both their verbal and nonverbal components, involve an aesthetic inventiveness that is as striking as his sexual energy. He appears to crave opportunities for this artistry even more than the physical satisfaction of his lust for women.

Finally, Tirso's play sows the seeds of a certain ambiguity in the Don Juan plot that can be seen in all versions to some extent, and which Pushkin in particular exploits in his little tragedy. The viewer (or reader), confronted by a hero who pursues multiple women and engages in a series of escapades, cannot help wondering about the outcome of his quest. Will Don Juan really continue pursuing woman after woman, or will there be an end to his search? If so, will he repent? Will he meet a woman compelling enough to make all others superfluous? Or will he be punished for his transgressions? Are his protestations of love a mere ploy, or are they in fact sincere? These questions formed part of the suspense of Tirso's version and reappear continuously in subsequent Don Juan works.

The following major version of the legend, Molière's 1665 play *Don Juan, or the Stone Guest* (*Dom Juan ou Le Festin de Pierre*), may have been indirectly influenced by Tirso's play.[21] *The Trickster of Seville* was translated into Italian in the 1620s, and two Italian plays, Giacinto Andrea Cicognini's *The Stone Guest* (*Il convitato di pietra*, 1640s) and Onofrio Giliberto's *The Stone Guest* (*Il convitato di pietra*, 1652), served as sources for the first French plays, by Dorimon (pseudonym of Nicolas Drouin) and de Villiers, which in turn influenced Molière's drama.[22] The title character, as John Austen notes disparagingly, does not make an actual conquest in the action of the play and is therefore not a true libertine; rather, he is pursued from beginning to end by a scorned lover, Elvira, whom he has seduced in a cloister before the action of the play (154). However, Molière's hero is clearly a practiced seducer of women with a long history of victims, one who tricks men and women alike into doing his bidding. In this version, he is accompanied by a servant, Sganarelle, who performs the function of relating his master's exploits to the audience, along the lines of Catalinón in *The Trickster of Seville*.[23]

Beyond these basic parallels, however, both the plot and Don Juan's character differ strikingly from those of the Spanish play. To compensate for his lack of conquests, Don Juan is extremely garrulous and expatiates on his philosophy of life in long passages justifying his behavior to the moralizing Sganarelle. As Emilia Wilton-Godberfforde argues, Austen's critique "fails to appreciate that it is precisely the loquacious and mendacious aspect that Molière is interested in expanding and that therein rests the particular power and comedy of this new creation" (60). That Molière's protagonist functions verbally rather than through action has been noted by many critics. Felman likens Don Juan's performative acts (promising to marry women) with John Austin's performative utterances as explicated in *How to Do Things with Words*. As she puts it, "If we consider the play in terms of success or failure, it is no doubt significant that Don Juan's spectacular erotic success is accomplished by linguistic means alone" (28). Seduction takes place through the speaking body, and language itself represents seduction. This is particularly relevant to Pushkin's play, too, which foregrounds the use of poetry as a means of conquering women.

The hero's wordy passages in Molière's *Don Juan* also distinguish him from Tirso's protagonist because of their skepticism, typical of a seventeenth-century French nobleman. A good portion of his lengthy diatribes to Sganarelle involve the denial or disdain of God's punishment. Whereas Tirso's Don Juan appears to be a believer who accepts the existence of God, Molière's hero denies heaven, hell, and the afterlife, and he rationalizes away the supernatural events involving the statue.[24] In response to his servant's question of what he does believe in, he responds: "I believe that two and two make four, Sganarelle, and four and four make eight" (61). In keeping with his audience's expectations, Molière deemphasizes the role of the Commander from Tirso's play (by reducing the double invitation to a single one, as the statue sends Don Juan to hell at their first meeting rather than inviting him to a second supper). However, similarly to Tirso, Molière describes Don Juan's sensations in his final moments in terms of a fire that consumes him as he grips the hand of the statue: "Oh, God! I can go on no longer. An invisible flame is burning me. Through all my body runs a white hot fire" (91). This passage reinforces the religious imagery of Tirso's original play, something that will be lessened considerably in many subsequent versions, and especially in Pushkin's rendering, which secularizes the legend to the extent that religious references are completely absent from the description of Don Juan's downfall in the finale.

Mozart and Da Ponte's *Don Giovanni* (1787), the next major Don Juan version, written over a century later, was particularly vital for Pushkin's play. This opera has been considered by many commentators to be the greatest of all Don Juan works, mostly by virtue of its musical score, and has been highly influential on major writers and thinkers, such as Søren Kierkegaard, E. T. A. Hoffmann, and George Bernard Shaw. Weinstein calls it "a splendid synthesis of all the previous Don Juan versions worth borrowing from" (61), as Da Ponte weaves together features from Tirso (Donna Anna as a key character, the epitaph on the Commander's tomb), Molière (the character of Elvira as a heartbroken victim, the servant Sganarelle as a model for Leporello), the libretto Giovanni Bertati wrote for Giuseppi Gazzaniga's opera *Don Juan Tenorio* of the same year, and other intervening versions.

As in Molière's play, Don Giovanni does not conquer a single woman in the course of the opera; however, his force and energy as a seducer are apparent throughout, despite this fact and despite his lack of major arias. Early in the opera, Leporello's famous "catalogue aria," in which he lists his master's conquests by nationality and points to his wide-ranging taste in women (old and young, tall and short, etc.), testifies to Don Giovanni's skill in seduction. Most importantly, he seduces other characters and the audience alike through his power of desire and sexual energy, which can be felt throughout the opera, even when he is not on stage. Kierkegaard famously comments on this capacity of Don Giovanni in *Either/Or*, where he claims that the work offers an absolute unity of form and content, with the idea of the sensuous-erotic expressed in the perfect abstract form of music (he pays little attention to the libretto). For Kierkegaard, the title character embodies the third stage of the erotic in Mozart's operas, with Cherubino in *The Marriage of Figaro* modeling the awakening of the sensual, Papageno in *The Magic Flute* representing the awakening of desire after a dream, and Don Giovanni synthesizing these two stages: "Desire has its absolute object in the individual, it desires the individual absolutely" (68).

Some major alterations that Da Ponte, through Bertati, makes to earlier versions by Tirso and Molière point the way to Pushkin's own transformative version. Donna Anna's role, in this opera, increases greatly in importance from Tirso's play (Molière does not include this character). As the daughter of the Commendatore, she follows Don Giovanni throughout the opera, continually seeking revenge and forcing her betrothed, Octavio, to promise that he will exact this vengeance before he can marry her. Moreover, Mozart and Da Ponte, writing in the era of the Enlightenment and Neo-Classicism, and thus during a time of both skepticism and newfound appreciation of the pagan era, mix the Christian language of repentance with references to Classical antiquity, and thus dilute the Catholic message of Tirso's original play.[25] The Commendatore, on the other hand, takes on a more ominous role, because his music, heard in the very first notes of the overture, impresses itself on the minds of the listeners from the beginning. Mozart's music creates the notion of Don Giovanni's destiny being foreshadowed, something that becomes increasingly important for Pushkin. However, the statue lacks the same power of judgment that is felt in previous versions. As Bernard Williams argues, "He is indeed supernatural, but only in the sense of a realm of cause and effects which lie beyond the natural, not one that brings a new order of guilt and judgment" (114).

Along with Kierkegaard, another major figure influenced by this opera in the early nineteenth century was E. T. A. Hoffmann, whose 1813 story "Don Juan, or A Fabulous Adventure that Befell a Music Enthusiast on His Travels," inaugurated the Romantic view of Don Juan as an idealist. In this story, the unnamed protagonist discovers that a performance of *Don Giovanni* will take place at the country inn where he is staying. Absorbed in the opera, he fails to notice that the singer performing Donna Anna has joined him in his box and somehow manages to be there and onstage at the same time. Following the opera, he learns that the singer has died. Describing the opera in a letter to "Theodor" (the author), the protagonist claims that in this performance, he understood the depth of the masterpiece for the first time, and he offers a highly idiosyncratic interpretation of *Don Giovanni*.

Although "Don Juan" is not one of Hoffmann's major tales and, strictly speaking, may better fit the genre of criticism, its importance in shaping the course of the Don Juan narrative cannot be overstated. Weinstein writes: "It may be said that in its broad outlines the history of the Don Juan legend can be divided into two main parts, and the dividing line is Hoffmann's five-page letter" (67). Hoffmann interprets Don Giovanni as an ideal-seeker who has turned against God and humanity in his quest for the ideal woman. Anna turns out to be Giovanni's perfect counterpart—his foil, a woman in whom he awakens erotic passion. However, he encounters her too late and can only ruin her (in Hoffmann's interpretation, Giovanni consummates his seduction of Anna). Donna Anna's angry pursuit of Giovanni throughout the opera indicates the great impression he has left on her rather than simply the desire to avenge her father's killing.

This highly original, hybrid-genre interpretation of the legend has produced numerous followers in whose works, as Weinstein writes, "the second part of the traditional plot (the punishment of Don Juan by the statue) will decrease as the first part (Don Juan's amorous adventures) increases in importance" (77).[26] Hoffmann's interpretation of Don Juan as caught in a struggle between demonic and divine elements points the way to the Romantic interpretation of the figure as capable of being saved, gesturing toward his similarities to Faust. Several writers have either combined Faust with Don Juan or have written works about both figures.[27] The most prominent combined version is Christian Grabbe's 1828 play, *Don Juan and Faust*, in which both heroes fall in love with Donna Anna and each winds up going to hell. Grabbe preserves most of Don Juan's traditional qualities, but at times lends him attributes of the ever-striving Faust, as when the Don exclaims, "Happy is he who strives forever; yes, hail to him who hungers eternally!" (335).

The joining of the Faust subtext to the Don Juan legend raises the possibility that the protagonist can be saved, as Faust is, by the love of a woman. This notion shapes one of the most prominent Don Juan texts of the Romantic period, José Zorrilla's *Don Juan Tenorio* (1844), in which Doña Inés's love ends up saving the Don, who goes to paradise instead of hell after his death. This play has surpassed Tirso's original *Trickster of Seville* in popularity; it is performed every year on All Souls' Day (November 2) throughout the Spanish-speaking world and is considered the national drama of Spain.[28] Unlike Tirso, who underscores Don Juan's overconfidence in his right to endlessly defer responsibility and trust in God's mercy, Zorrilla portrays his libertine as issuing a challenge to the other world to manifest itself, through Don Juan's invitation to the statue. In effect, as Weinstein points out, Zorrilla justifies the "Tan largo me lo fiáis" philosophy of Tirso's Don Juan, since even a man who has killed thirty-four men and deceived seventy-three women still has the opportunity to gain salvation. Zorrilla's play serves as a culmination of the rehabilitation of Don Juan's image initiated by Hoffmann's story.[29] Its arch-Romantic attribution of positive qualities to a negative hero capitalizes on the tantalizing possibility, already inherent in earlier versions, that Don Juan's promise to one woman or another will actually prove to be genuine, and that he will find his ideal and conclude his quest.

Pushkin, then, writes *The Stone Guest* in the midst of the heightened atmosphere of Romanticism, in which the antihero has either found his ideal or been saved.[30] His little tragedy takes on many elements of this ethos by making the hero a poet and exploring the issue of his redemption. However, he approaches this possibility very differently from Hoffmann and other Romantics, offering an alternative, and ambivalent, approach to Don Juan's seductions and potential for redemption. In doing so, he opens up new directions for subsequent writers to explore, joining Mozart/Da Ponte and Hoffmann as exceptionally influential interpreters of the Don Juan theme.[31]

As with all of his reworkings of Western European imports, Pushkin thoroughly transforms the Don Juan legend in *The Stone Guest*. Taking the tradition of Tirso de Molina, Molière, and Mozart/Da Ponte as his starting point, he transports the myth into Russian Romanticism in large part by inscribing autobiographical features into it. Anna Akhmatova famously claims for Pushkin the discovery that "Don Juan is a poet" (92), and his hero indeed becomes a Romantic, elegiac poet, exiled from the capital and obsessed as much by past affairs and deathly specters as by the prospect of attaining elusive happiness through love. Typically of his little tragedy genre, Pushkin reduces the scale of the legend through the brevity of the play, a sharp reduction in the usual number of characters, and a focus on the dramatic denouement of the Don Juan story rather than the background. He also invents a new character, Laura, who in her free love, flightiness, and hedonism replicates Don Juan's own behavior. Lastly, the Commander plays the role of Donna Anna's husband, whom Don Juan has slain in a duel, rather than her father, as in *Don Giovanni*. The relationship between the two opponents therefore undergoes significant transformation, as the Commander represents a rival to Don Juan rather than merely an agent of justice and retribution.

Pushkin in many ways brings the inherent potential of the Don Juan theme in its original Spanish incarnation to fruition in his reworking of some of the dominants I described above in Tirso's play. The interrelation of poetry and Eros, for example, which can already be seen to some extent in the plays of Tirso and Molière, is especially significant in *The Stone Guest*, as the hero's seductions take place mostly through the poetic word. As David Herman and David Glenn Kropf have observed, Don Juan's seductions in the little tragedy testify to the poet's need for freedom and the ability to create a new self with each poetic recitation. Since Pushkin depicts both Don Juan and his female counterpart Laura engaging in this kind of artistic seduction, he also reinterprets the issue of gender and agency from previous Don Juan works, in which women play largely passive roles. Pushkin similarly represents Donna Anna's naïve curiosity as leading her to take a surprisingly active role in her own seduction: she asks questions and communicates an interest in the hero that distinguishes her from the female characters in previous Don Juan works. The idea of Don Juan possibly breaking the pattern of endless, serial seductions and arriving unexpectedly at a kind of rebirth through love may be not unique to

Pushkin among Romantic writers, but it testifies to his encoding of his own biography into his hero. As Akhmatova notes, though, Pushkin identifies with both Don Juan and the Commander: Don Juan is emblematic of the poet's younger self, and the Commander embodies his fears for the future, in which his younger wife might cuckold him or betray him after his death. For this reason, the ending of the play, so different from Mozart/Da Ponte's dramatic dispatching of Don Giovanni to hell, points to an uncanny identity between Don Juan and the statue. Pushkin's stage direction, "they fall through together" (provalivaiutsia), indicates a symbolic identity of ostensible opponents, a joining together, as it were, of younger and older versions of the same figure. Pushkin thus advances Tirso's pattern of love triangles to unprecedented importance, as Don Juan appears to represent a younger, liberating force for Donna Anna, freeing her from her deathly widow's rites; however, he ultimately functions similarly to the Commander, leading her to her downfall, just as, in a parallel situation in the past, he caused that of his former lover Inez, whose jealous husband, Pushkin hints, may have killed her upon discovery of her affair with Don Juan. Pushkin thereby acknowledges the dangers of Donjuanism even as he celebrates it as a possible path to more salutary interactions between the genders.

Approaching Don Juan Today

Our twenty-first-century vantage point offers various potential methodological approaches to studying and critiquing the Don Juan legend, and here I outline the ones I rely on in this study. Starting in the twentieth century, psychoanalytic critics took a great interest in Don Juan, opening up several promising directions for analysis of the works discussed here. Although Sigmund Freud did not undertake a study of Don Juan, several of his basic concepts are highly relevant to the topic. From its inception in Tirso's play, the narrative has included the murder of a father figure by a young man in pursuit of a woman, and it has concluded with Don Juan's punishment by an unexpectedly powerful paternal representative. Beyond Don Juan's disobedience to his actual father and uncle in some versions, his behavior, as several commentators have noted, represents a rebellious assault on all father figures—Anna's father, the king, God the Father, and the patriarchal society in which he lives.[32] The legend therefore lends itself to interpretation in terms of the Oedipal conflict. Freud's discussion, in *Totem and Taboo* and elsewhere, of the complex feelings of sons for fathers—a mixture of fear, jealousy, admiration, and love— resonates with the Don Juan theme particularly in its Russian instantiations, since one of Pushkin's innovations is that the Don Juan figure both identifies with and begrudgingly admires his opponent even as he expresses contempt for him. In addition, Freud's theory of the uncanny, by which what is old and familiar returns in a frightening guise, can be applied to the statue's appearance at the end of the Don Juan plot. Freud claims that "an uncanny effect is often and easily produced when the distinction between imagination and reality is effaced, as when something that we have hitherto regarded as imaginary appears before us in reality, or when a symbol takes over the full functions of the thing it symbolizes, and so on" (145). Such a sensation, I argue, becomes especially relevant in Pushkin's version of the Don Juan legend.

Freud's erstwhile disciple Otto Rank is the psychoanalytic thinker who has explored Donjuanism most deeply, writing a study titled *The Don Juan Legend* in 1924.[33] Rank starts from the premise that the Don Juan legend must be about more than just a seducer frivolously breaking women's hearts and that at its core, it ultimately centers on guilt and punishment rather than mere seduction, and invokes primal tales of father-son struggles. Rank interprets Don Juan's endless succession of women as a search for the "one irreplaceable mother," and he sees the rivals Don Juan kills one after the other as representatives of the father.[34] Noting the inseparability and at times interchangeability of Leporello and his master in *Don Giovanni*, he reads the servant as an alter ego of Don Juan, "the criticizing and anxiety-oriented conscience of the hero" (52). Leporello is eventually cast aside for the more powerful representative of the ego ideal, the Commander. The statue represents the motif of avenging death, rooted in folkloric tales of dead men coming back to kill their murderers. Where Rank departs most sharply from previous views of the legend, though, is in his understanding of Don Juan's punishment. He interprets the statue as maternal rather than paternal: "In the figure of the Stone Guest, who also represents the coffin, appears the mother herself, coming to fetch the son" (96). The Commander thus represents the wish fulfillment of a fantasy of returning to the womb, the initial source of pleasure, and completely possessing the mother.

Clearly, Rank appreciates the Don Juan theme more as an elaboration of older myths than as a story in its own right; like many psychoanalytic interpreters of literature and myth, he is more interested in universals than particulars, his impressive knowledge of various versions of the Don Juan legend notwithstanding. Rank's analysis of Don Juan's self-punishment as a means of returning to the womb is nothing if not intriguing. Questions arise, however, as one reads his work in relation to individual texts. For instance, although in Tirso's play Don Juan does disappear along with the Commander's tomb, in most versions, there is no womblike structure. Perhaps more significantly, the statue bears a distinctly paternal authority: the notion of a maternal punishment, while aligned with Rank's intellectual direction at the time, does not square with most Don Juan works themselves.

Jacques Lacan's psychoanalytic approach resonates particularly well with Donjuanism because of his focus on the nature of desire, and some critics have discussed the legend in light of Lacanian theory.[35] Mandrell has interpreted it in terms of Lacan's concept of the Name of the Father, an original and autonomous author of laws and a forbidding authority, whose precepts Don Juan consistently violates. In light of the various skirmishes between Don Juan and his opponents, the statue, as Mandrell puts it, "represents all of the various father-figures in the drama and functions as a symbolic father, in the role of what Jacques Lacan has called the 'paternal metaphor' or the 'name of the father'" (75).

Other Lacanian concepts can provide invaluable insights in analyzing Don Juan. Lacan's notion of desire, in particular, seems relevant in light of the degree and nature of Don Juan's attraction to women. Don Juan certainly expresses a stronger desire for women than does the typical heterosexual man, who at a certain point in life is content to marry and give up pursuing multiple women. For Lacan, desire appears in the space between need and demand: "Desire begins to take shape in the margin in which demand becomes separated from need" (*Écrits* 311). It comes because demand can never really articulate genuine need. Desire is also self-reproducing; it never comes to a complete stop. As Slavoj Žižek writes, "desire's *raison d'être* is not to realize its goal, to find full satisfaction, but to reproduce itself as desire" (39). What is demanded is never what is needed. The subject (Don Juan) assumes that the Other (any of the various women he pursues) has what he needs, but the Other herself is lacking as a subject. Thus, Don Juan never desires what he actually needs, and as a result, his individual conquests never satisfy him, no matter how many he makes. As Lacan writes, "If, in effect, the man finds satisfaction for his demand for love in the relation with the woman, in as much as the signifier of the phallus constitutes her as giving in love what she does not have—conversely, his own desire for the phallus will make its signifier emerge in its persistent divergence towards 'another woman' who may signify this phallus in various ways, either as a virgin or as a prostitute" (*Écrits* 290). Don Juan is fated to pursue woman after woman without finding satisfaction. Only death—through the statue—can bring his desire to an end.[36]

In light of Pushkin's emphasis on the triangular nature of love in his Don Juan retelling, French philosopher René Girard's theory of mediation of desire is also particularly relevant for this study. For Girard, love does not take place straightforwardly, through the development of independent desire for another person, but via a mediating third party. The jealousy and hatred one feels for a rival really comprise internal mediation, a third presence preventing the would-be lover from attaining his or her object: "True jealousy is infinitely more profound and complex [than just irritation at our desires being thwarted]; it always contains an element of fascination with the insolent rival" (12). He mentions Don Juan briefly in his study, referring to Molière's play. For Girard, Don Juan is far from autonomous and cannot perform his conquests without others. Seeing a pair of lovers in Act I, he is driven to jealousy by their passion, which compels him to try to end their engagement by transporting the bride-to-be by sea and seducing her. Although Girard does not cite *The Stone Guest*, Pushkin's little tragedy in fact confirms his theory of mediated desire to an even greater extent than Molière's play: Don Juan's pursuit of Donna Anna is inspired by her prayers for the soul of her dead husband, and he acknowledges feelings of jealousy and a longing to be buried in his rival's grave. Mediation of desire plays a crucial role in the kind of triangulation we see in some other Russian versions of the Don Juan legend as well.

Denis de Rougemont's classic study of romance in Western culture, which influenced Girard's triangular theory, provides another rich source for understanding the Don Juan theme. For de Rougemont, the seminal romance of Western culture is the myth of Tristan and Isolde, in which love is associated with suffering and death. De Rougemont traces this phenomenon to the Cathar heresy in France, characterizing it as a type of love based on passion and obstacles that, in contrast to marital love, can ultimately be satisfied only through death. This notion eventually spread through Western literature and even Hollywood film, shaping our contemporary views of erotic love. For de Rougemont, the myth becomes popularized and profaned over time, and the Don Juan legend essentially results from the degradation of the Tristan myth: "A modern Tristan lets himself turn into the antithetical Don Juan type—the man of successive love affairs. Alone the mythical Don Juan could evade this consummation. But he knew no Iseult, no unattainable passion, neither past nor future, nor sensual anguish" (285).

Yet the oppositions de Rougemont notes between the two myths—Tristan's fatal passion versus Don Juan's "perverse sensuality" (218), Tristan's One (Isolde) versus Don Giovanni's 1,003 Spanish women, the ideal woman versus the woman as object—also point to similarities between them, especially if one recalls the Romantic interpretation of the Don Juan theme. As with Tristan and Isolde, Don Juan's erotic pursuits thrive on obstacles that he must overcome. And the Don Juan tale similarly depends upon an interlinking of Eros and Thanatos. Just as Tristan and Isolde find fulfillment through death, the Don only seems to pursue affairs that involve some risk to his life; one of his attempted conquests (Donna Anna) is linked to the Commander, whom he has slain in a duel, and who eventually returns from the grave to kill him. Indeed, as we see in Pushkin's play, Don Juan's affairs are all connected in some way with death.[37]

Love and death are continually positioned next to each other, driving Don Juan and the Commander to their inexorable meeting. As Yuri Lotman writes, noting the identity between these two seeming opponents, "What they have in common is the aspiration to look beyond an inaccessible boundary" (*Pushkin* 314). Lev Tolstoy makes this linking of the erotic and the deathly explicit, in *Anna Karenina*, by comparing the eponymous heroine's lover Vronsky to a murderer standing over Anna's body after the consummation of their affair.

The issue of gender is crucial in many of the works I analyze and has often been used to discuss the Don Juan legend, which is, after all, at its core a story about (destructive) gender relations. Second-wave feminists such as Kate Millett and Shulamith Firestone theorized the patriarchy as a social system in which power is held mostly or completely by men. This power extends to sexuality, which is seen by Catharine MacKinnon as "the lynchpin of gender inequality" (533). Donjuanism often involves acts of aggression against women. Don Giovanni's first action in Mozart/Da Ponte's opera, for instance, is an attempted sexual assault against Donna Anna. His continual violence and seductions, in all variants of the legend, underscore patriarchal patterns of male-female sexual relations. They also reinforce the traditional view of women as sexually passive. As Hélène Cixous writes about male/female essentialism regarding sex, "Traditionally, the question of sexual difference is treated by coupling it with the opposition: activity/passivity" (64). Anticipating twentieth-century feminists, who would question the notion that the aggressive role in sexual relations is essentially masculine, Pushkin creates the female equivalent of Don Juan in Laura, who embraces her sexuality, chooses men instead of being chosen by them, and makes multiple conquests. Other Russian writers follow Pushkin in exploring nontraditional roles of women in relation to Don Juan, and as Don Juans themselves.

Considering the concept of hegemonic masculinity can be especially fruitful in shedding light on problems of gender in the Don Juan legend. Hegemonic masculinity, which R. W. Connell defines as "the configuration of gender practice which embodies the currently accepted answer to the problem of legitimacy of patriarchy, which guarantees (or is taken to guarantee) the dominant position of men and the subordination of women" (77), offers a way of categorizing Don Juan within his milieu according to the expectations his particular type of masculinity carries in terms of behavior toward women and other men. As Connell stresses, hegemonic masculinity is not universal and timeless, but historical and subject to change: "'Hegemonic masculinity' is not a fixed character type, always and everywhere the same. It is, rather, the masculinity that occupies the hegemonic position in a given pattern of gender relations, a position always contestable" (76). James Messerschmidt, too, emphasizes that masculinities are not essentialist, not fixed entities, but "configurations of practice that are accomplished in social action" (35).

Don Juan occupies a somewhat ambiguous position with regard to the hegemonic masculinity of Tirso's play, as he partakes of its benefits while at the same time violating some of its principles. Sears, in examining Don Juan's place in early seventeenth-century Spanish society, describes three masculine prototypes: the conquistador, the impoverished noble, and Don Quixote.[38] All three types valued and enforced the medieval chivalric code toward women but, at their worst, also promoted values of virility (often involving bloody revenge on opponents), the undervaluing of reason, and sexual repression of women. *The Trickster of Seville* provides as examples of hegemonic masculinity a nobleman who is engaged to marry a noblewoman but enjoys the privilege of taking his time marrying (Octavio), and one who consorts with a mistress and even prostitutes while already engaged (Marquis de la Mota). Their loyalty is to the king above all, and they are expected to defend the throne with their lives. They are also compelled to duel at the slightest provocation to their honor. Most importantly, they are required to ensure a kind of succession, the reproduction of noble society through women of their class. Some youthful pranks are permissible (Don Juan appeals to Don Pedro to think of his own youth as he escapes Isabela's bedroom), and at worst they are punished by exile, which, of course, permits the nobleman to pursue similar pranks in other places. Their masculinity is self-reinforcing, as J. Douglas Canfield notes: "The entire system is a conspiracy of males to keep them in power and to subjugate women, to keep women objects without consciousness, perhaps without consciousness of their role as complicit enforcers of the system because they have internalized its discipline" (53). This conspiracy is upheld by various symbolic gestures: the word-as-bond, oaths of allegiance, and vows of fidelity. If Don Juan defies this system, he is simultaneously generated by it, as its fixation on these values makes it all the easier for him to violate them.

Thus, Don Juan to an extent is sanctioned and indeed created by Spanish society and shares in its hegemonic masculinity, with its subordination of women as second-class citizens lacking control over their sexual lives and not even worthy of being listened to.[39] As Sears points out, Don Juan exemplifies a kind of complicity with the system he appears to scorn, taking advantage of the trappings of nobility (duels, titles, etc.) and using them for his own ends. His tricks are devastating to other noblemen, and an annoyance to the kings and their courts, but to some extent they are acceptable. They seem to exceed proper boundaries only when they create too much friction among the nobility: as a result of Don Juan's escape artistry, Octavio is blamed for ruining Isabela's honor, and the Marquis de la Mota is accused of killing Don Gonzalo.

Most of all, it is this latter action, Don Juan's slaying of a respected personage in the hierarchy of Spanish nobility, that brings about his downfall. This killing cannot be tolerated, whereas the seduction of numerous women can be, and is even expected. Moreover, Don Juan disrupts the "feudal patriarchal system of reproductive control" (Canfield 43) because his affairs with engaged women threaten to produce illegitimate children and disrupt planned marriages and political unions. Thus, Don Juan disobeys certain rules and in doing so turns masculine (and feminine) society against him. But for all his devaluation of women, other men, marriage, respect of elders, and just about all other standards of his society, parts of this behavior are already agreed upon by that society (particularly the devaluation of women). The same indulgence of the Don Juan figure can be seen in succeeding eras. The early nineteenth-century Russian aristocratic milieu in many ways resembled the environment Tirso describes. Pushkin, a self-styled Don Juan, repeatedly attempted to seduce married women with relative impunity; perhaps the most serious consequence of this behavior was his being sent from Odesa to Mikhailovskoe for his involvement with Elizaveta Vorontsova, the wife of his supervisor. Writing later in the century, Tolstoy—through *The Kreutzer Sonata's* Pozdnyshev—compares the men of his milieu to Don Juans who are readily tolerated in the drawing rooms of good families.

Pushkin, I argue, transforms Don Juan into a rebel who aspires to be a liberator of women. Noting Donna Anna's interest in conversing with him despite the inappropriateness of the setting of their first conversation (the monastery in which she prays for her dead husband), he encourages her to fulfill her inner impulses and explore her natural curiosity. Extrapolating from this incident, his elegiac reminiscences of Inez, and Don Carlos's remonstrances of Laura's flightiness before Don Juan's visit to her house, Pushkin's hero fights against men who in all three cases are tyrannical toward the women to whom they are attached. Unlike in Tirso's play, Pushkin's Don Juan is not primarily a trickster. He does disguise himself before Anna (first as a monk and later as a nobleman named Don Diego de Calvado), but he insists on ripping off these façades one by one and conquering her *as himself* rather than seducing her in the guise of someone else. In doing so, as I contend in chapter 1, he does not merely disrupt the traditional social order of his time, as Tirso's Don Juan does, but also undermines key principles of hegemonic masculinity.

Russian Don Juans

Several scholars have written on the Don Juan theme in Russian literature. German critic Frank Göbler's recent monograph, the only book-length study of the legend, surveys numerous Don Juan works, beginning with Pushkin's

Introduction   25

play, proceeding through later nineteenth-century and twentieth-century versions, and concluding with Alexander Annin's popular novel *Don Juan's Ring* (2010). Göbler thus offers a comprehensive discussion of the various Russian reworkings of the theme. My approach differs from his in several ways. For one, I seek to broaden the discussion of Russian Don Juans in relation to European prototypes, in part with my discussion of Tirso and other predecessors of Pushkin Göbler whose works touches on briefly at points. In addition, although I also proceed chronologically, I present my chapters more as essays on Donjuanism in different literary periods as exemplified by the authors I analyze. Rather than attempting to survey all major and minor writers who have dealt with the theme, as Göbler does, I start with a lengthy chapter on Pushkin and then focus on three or four figures in each period, interspersing occasional brief discussions of other notable Don Juan works.

Even more significantly, unlike Göbler, I do not restrict my discussions to works such as Pushkin's *Stone Guest* and the various Silver Age poems and plays that focus entirely on the Don Juan theme; rather, I examine these types of works along with others that either include the Don Juan legend as a secondary theme (Goncharov's *The Precipice*) or, in some cases, do not even mention it explicitly (Chekhov's "The Lady with the Little Dog" and Liudmila Ulitskaya's works), but implicitly portray Donjuanism in one or another character. Göbler correctly notes Pushkin's importance for the lengthy series of Russian Don Juan works (17, 257). However, I analyze ways in which the poet's particular interpretation spreads unexpectedly into works that do not make the Don Juan theme their singular focus. In some cases, I am interested specifically in how the Don Juan theme gets absorbed into larger works, and at times influences the course of Russian literature. This can be seen in my hypothesis, in chapter 2, that Pushkin's Donna Anna serves to initiate a new Russian archetype.

Robert Karpiak, a Canadian scholar, also explored the Don Juan theme throughout various periods of Russian culture in his dissertation on Don Juan in Slavic drama and several articles. His publications on versions of the Don Juan theme by Pushkin, Chekhov, Gumilev, and other Russian and Ukrainian writers offer valuable insights into the legend in Russia and beyond. As Karpiak correctly points out, some writers, including Alexei K. Tolstoy, were more influenced by Hoffmann's seminal contribution than they were by Pushkin's little tragedy. While I also briefly discuss those Russian Don Juan versions, my primary interest is in Pushkin's line of creative influence.[40]

In the first chapter, I examine the aforementioned ways in which Pushkin transforms the Don Juan theme from earlier versions by Tirso, Molière, and Mozart/Da Ponte. These range from his portrayal of Don Juan as a poet and his invention of the character of Laura to his abrupt, mysterious ending and the transformation of Donna Anna into the Commander's widow instead of his daughter. Pushkin also imports from his Western European models the idea of rebellion against convention, so vital to the Russian interpretation of the Don Juan legend, through his hero's deliberate transgressions against state and marital laws. I argue that his developments of the legend influence numerous subsequent transpositions of the theme. Chapter 1 concludes with a discussion of a musical reworking of Pushkin's *Stone Guest*: composer Alexander Dargomyzhsky's 1869 opera of the same title. Dargomyzhsky sets the play verbatim, using melodic recitative to try to approximate Pushkin's poetic intonations, but he also creatively interprets important aspects of the play, including the Commander's uncanny nature and the poet's ruminations on gender and marital roles (especially in the context of the "woman question" of the 1860s).

Chapter 2 examines how Realist writers integrated the Don Juan legend into their works. Here again I depart from Göbler and Karpiak, who focus on Alexei K. Tolstoy's Romantic rewriting of the legend. Instead, I trace the impact of Pushkin's little tragedy on Ivan Goncharov's *The Precipice* (1869), Lev Tolstoy's *Anna Karenina* (1877), and Anton Chekhov's "The Lady with the Little Dog" (1899), Realist works that incorporate the Don Juan theme into broader nineteenth-century social contexts and, in the case of Chekhov, build on both Pushkin's play and *Anna Karenina*. All three authors borrow Pushkin's conception of Don Juan and the triangular relationship he sets up between the hero, the Commander, and Donna Anna. Goncharov's hero Boris Raisky is an artist, seducer, and self-styled Don Juan who embodies some traits of Pushkin's hero. By showing his failure as an artist (and a Don Juan), Goncharov indicates the ineffectiveness of this type within a Realist aesthetic that privileges everyday action over Romantic heroism. Tolstoy begins his novel with an allusion to *Don Giovanni* in Stiva Oblonsky's opening dream, but I argue that he in fact incorporates elements of Pushkin's little tragedy into the novel on a deeper level, creating a configuration of relationships between Vronsky, Anna, and Karenin that parallels Pushkin's love triangle. In addition, he links the Don Juan legend to the notion of vengeance, and to a broader sense of impending apocalypse facing Russia. Following the Tolstoy discussion, I turn to Chekhov's story "The Lady with the Little Dog," interpreting it as a restructuring of Tolstoy's own reworking of Pushkin's triangular relationship in *Anna Karenina*, but this time to more comic effect.

The Don Juan legend flourished in Russian literature of the Silver Age. After short discussions of Bal'mont's poem and essay on the theme, I analyze works of Blok, Tsvetaeva, Gumilev, and Akhmatova. In the case of Blok, although "The Steps of the Commander" (1912) has received the most scholarly attention, I analyze not only this poem, but also the contemporaneous narrative poem *Retribution* (1910–21), in which, I argue, despite only including a brief Don Juan reference (comparing his father to this figure), Blok sets up a subtext involving the identity of Don Juan and the statue that recalls Pushkin's own similar creation of identity between these seeming opponents. In each poem, the confrontation of these figures prefigures the cataclysm Blok sensed was facing Russia. Following my discussion of Blok, I analyze Tsvetaeva's seven-poem 1917 cycle *Don Juan*, contending that it extends Pushkin's interest in gender relations and plays with traditional male-female binary oppositions by casting Don Juan as the weaker sex and having him confront his nemesis and female counterpart, Carmen. I then discuss Gumilev's 1913 play *Don Juan in Egypt* as a continuation of Pushkin's little tragedy in which Don Juan arises from the grave and seduces an American woman, leading Leporello, who has become a well-known Egyptologist, to wish he were Don Juan's servant again. I close the chapter with a discussion of Akhmatova's *Poem without a Hero* (1940–62), which synthesizes previous versions of the legend and contextualizes Donjuanism in relation to Stalinism.

In my fourth and final chapter, I discuss versions of the legend in the late twentieth and early twenty-first centuries. Although relatively little attention was paid to the Don Juan theme under Stalinism (as the Soviets were creating their own myth and enforcing its reproduction by writers), the figure takes on great importance for writers of the late Soviet period. I focus first on two works of the 1980s: Venedikt Erofeev's 1985 play *Walpurgis Night, or the Steps of the Commander*, and Vladimir Kazakov's 1983 cycle of four Don Juan plays. Erofeev, who indicates his Don Juan subtext in the second half of his title, recreates Pushkin's triangular relationship and also depicts poetic creation as a form of rebellion against confinement and tyranny through his hero Gurevich. Kazakov, by contrast, turns to a neo-Futurist and neo-Kharmsian form of absurdity to depict poetry as a means of escape not only from dangerous situations, but from sense and meaning themselves. I conclude the chapter with a discussion of Liudmila Ulitskaya, who creates Don Juan-like male figures in *Sonechka* (1992), *The Funeral Party* (1997), and *Sincerely Yours, Shurik* (2004). In works such as *Sonechka* and *Jacob's Ladder* (2015), she also features female counterparts who seduce multiple men, thus bringing the Laura phenomenon from Pushkin's play into contemporary literature. In the conclusion, I assess some broad patterns in the Don Juan theme in Russia, speculate on the reasons so many writers have found inspiration in Pushkin's little tragedy, and briefly examine its impact beyond Russia.

Thus, I explore diverse types of Don Juan texts, ranging from straightforward adaptations of the Don Juan theme such as the plays of Pushkin, Gumilev, and Kazakov to Dargomyzhsky's opera and the lyric poems of Blok and

Tsvetaeva. I also extend my reach to Erofeev's tragedy, in which the Don Juan theme serves as a secondary plotline to the *Faust* legend, and works that employ the Spanish legend more as a subtext—overt or hidden—fitting into a greater whole. Some of these subtexts consist of explicit and extensive references to the Don Juan legend, as in the various linkages of Raisky to the figure in *The Precipice* or the more fleeting references such as Stiva's recollection of a *Don Giovanni* aria in *Anna Karenina* and Blok's single allusion to his own father as a Don Juan in *Retribution*. Other Don Juan subtexts, such as those appearing in the works of Chekhov and Ulitskaya, may be less obvious but nevertheless yield important insights when viewed in connection to the Spanish legend.

Given this wide variety of subtexts, my study includes some unorthodox choices, and the reader may therefore wonder how many other literary figures could be included. Could the title character of *Eugene Onegin*, with his presumed long list of seductions and his trusty method of deliberately attracting women through his lack of interest in them, be considered a "Don Juan"? What about Mikhail Lermontov's Pechorin, who wanders from woman to woman in the course of *A Hero of Our Time*, or Nikolai Leskov's Sergei, a practiced seducer even before he meets Katerina in *Lady Macbeth of the Mtsensk District*?[41] In this regard, I would note that in this study, I am in effect trying to tell two stories. The first centers on how the Don Juan legend has been imported into Russia and interpreted by writers. The second, which overlaps with but is not identical to the first, is the story of the reception of one key text: *The Stone Guest*. Thus, in linking this play to Tolstoy's novel and Chekhov's story, which do not directly concentrate on the legend, I am describing what I see as the impact of Pushkin's play on nineteenth-century Russian culture, not just the Don Juan theme itself. And since I am focusing on Pushkin's influence, I am taking into consideration not only elements of the Don Juan tale per se but also elements of that play in particular, such as the triangular love affair involving an older and younger man, a young widow or unfaithful woman, and/or an uncanny statue-like entity. Thus, the goal is not to enumerate all the Don Juan-like figures in Russian literature, of which there are many, but to focus specifically on those who embody the particular characteristics of Pushkin's hero in *The Stone Guest*. Ultimately, Don Juan enriches Russian literature and culture not only through many eponymous works but also through the figure's intersection with other themes and character types and his assimilation into works with other foci. Pushkin's *Stone Guest* thus not only offers a fresh approach to the Don Juan legend but also extends it into unexpected areas. The Russian Don Juan exists at times as the primary subject but at other times as an unlikely guest in a surprising variety of narratives.

I

The Artist-Seducer as Liberator
Pushkin's Stone Guest

TIRSO DE MOLINA's original play on the Don Juan theme, as I have discussed, establishes clear patterns for future writers and artists. From Don Juan's licentiousness and trickery to the statue dispatching the libertine to hell, these patterns can be seen in various subsequent versions of the legend. Some of these elements are retained and others are deemphasized or lost as the play is refracted into Pushkin's little tragedy via intervening versions, particularly Mozart and Da Ponte's *Don Giovanni*. Pushkin, in turn, establishes a new paradigm in *The Stone Guest* that, as I argue in the course of this study, proves to be highly influential for subsequent Russian writers.

In this chapter, I explore the elements that, in my view, gave Pushkin's renewal of the Don Juan theme its extraordinary fecundity in nineteenth- and twentieth-century Russian culture. After a brief survey of the motifs that Pushkin reworks in this play, I focus in particular on his depiction of seduction as an act interwoven with artistic creativity, his exploration of gender roles, and his transformation of the traditional cause-and-effect logic of Don Juan's comeuppance. Before I analyze Pushkin's play, I will briefly explore the impact of Russian culture and society of the time on his approach to the Don Juan legend.

Given Pushkin's coming of age in a libertine culture that prized sexual freedom, his interest in the Don Juan theme is not surprising—nor is his emphasis on the connections between Eros and art. Pushkin's copious sexual experiences (he claimed to have had 113 loves) were intertwined with his poetry as he addressed numerous short lyrics to past and present lovers. As in eighteenth-century France, from which Russian libertinism was derived, sexual promiscuity was also closely tied to atheism and radical politics, and incendiary poems such as "Ode to Liberty" ("Vol'nost'," 1817) and "The Village" ("Derevnia," 1819) resulted in his exile to the southern part of the Russian empire in 1820.

Many participants in the 1825 Decembrist Revolt cited Pushkin's poetry as an inspiration in their quest for freedom, even though these poems tended to be moderately liberal rather than revolutionary. Pushkin's libertinage continued in exile, where he wrote *The Gabrieliad* (*Gavriliiada*) (1821),[1] a blasphemous parody of the Annunciation, and engaged in various types of scandalous behavior: his aforementioned affair in Odesa with Elizaveta Vorontsova, the wife of his supervisor, Governor-General Mikhail Vorontsov, resulted in the poet's transfer to his family estate of Mikhailovskoe in 1824.

Like others in his libertine cultural milieu, the youthful Pushkin exhibited a carefree, joking, mischievous approach to life that set him apart from more soberminded contemporaries. Joe Peschio demonstrates the importance in this period of the *shalost'*, roughly translated as "prank," which described both a verse genre used by Pushkin and other poets of the Lyceum and the Arzamas and Green Lamp societies, involving the incorporation of what Boris Eikhenbaum terms "domesticity" (domashnost') into literary genres, and a type of everyday behavior. As Peschio asserts, "a certain cynical spirit of play—a devotion to all manner of jokes, impertinence, erotica, impenetrably obscure allusions, intimate and inconsequential gestures, and Epicureanism—came to characterize the period 1810–1837" (6). As examples of Pushkin's own *shalosti*, Peschio cites his coarse public dressing-down of a senior official, wearing see-through pantaloons with no underwear at a regional governor's house, and writing "A Lesson to Tsars" on an engraving of a regicidal killer (9). Traces of this prank-oriented culture manifest themselves in *The Stone Guest*, whose hero, although he is not a trickster to nearly the same extent as Tirso's Don Juan, disguises himself as a monk and then pretends to be a nobleman named Don Diego de Calvado in his pursuit of Donna Anna. Don Juan's invitation to the Commander to stand guard during his tryst with his widow, of course, could be seen as the ultimate *shalost*.' The Decembrists, who by contrast with Pushkin and other libertines prized sobriety, high ideals, and friendship, maintained close relations with the poet but were careful not to involve him in their secret society because of his frivolous, dissolute behavior.[2] Thus, one could describe Pushkin as being at odds with both "serious" sides of the political spectrum: the liberal Decembrists, with whose political ideas he sympathized to an extent, and the reactionary autocratic government.[3] Pushkin's capacity to offend both sides, as Igor' Nemirovsky argues recently, stems not just from his debauched behavior, but from the sacrilegious character of his antics. Pushkin's misbehavior included the courting of schoolgirls in church and the writing of *The Gabrieliad* during Lent and Easter. "The combination of eroticism, libertinism, and liberal discourse," Nemirovsky asserts, "was irritating and unacceptable for both the government and the Decembrists" (50).[4]

Tsar Nikolai I's release of Pushkin from exile in 1826, the year he first considered writing a play on the Don Juan theme, signaled a transformation of his life from the poetic to the prosaic on several levels. Having lived as a libertine separate from the court, and having been away from the capital during his exile, Pushkin now found himself closely attached to St. Petersburg and the throne as a result of his restoration to the civil service and Nikolai's role as his personal censor. He served in the court beginning in 1831 as titular councilor of the National Archives and in 1833 was made a gentleman of the bedchamber, a position that he considered demeaning since it was usually occupied by younger men. At the same time, Pushkin was adjusting both to a changing literary culture that was becoming broader in readership and increasingly commercialized and to a reading public that was beginning to prefer prose to poetry. While he continued to write poetry in the 1830s, his attention turned increasingly to various prose genres. Moreover, having viewed literature primarily as a gentleman's pastime throughout much of the 1820s, he began in earnest to establish himself as a professional writer, and in particular to pursue journalism, which involved him in a fierce struggle with competitors such as Faddei Bulgarin, Nikolai Grech, and Nikolai Polevoi. His first journal, *The Literary Gazette* (*Literaturnaia gazeta*, 1830–31), coedited with his fellow poet and friend Anton Del'vig, failed in part due to a lack of subscribers, and in part because Pushkin's rivals made use of their government connections (which in Bulgarin's case included espionage) to prevent his journal from gaining the official permission he desired to print political articles (Todd 71).[5] Pushkin also contended with discouragement of his journalism from literary peers, such as Vasily Zhukovsky and Nikolai Gogol, who were relieved when his efforts to publish a newspaper failed in 1832, and his sister Olga Pavlishcheva, who like Zhukovsky and Gogol was concerned that he was sullying his genius with this commercial pursuit (Grigoryan 80–81). Ultimately, Pushkin never quite assimilated into the new journalistic milieu: his efforts in this venue were viewed, as William Mills Todd III puts it, "as a continuation of the earlier, nonprofessional approach to literary life" (64). But his journalistic ambitions represent an important aspect of his transition from gentleman-dilettante to professional writer.

These professional developments coincided with Pushkin's gradual exchange of libertinism for married life. Following unsuccessful courtships of Sofia Pushkina (his distant cousin) and Anna Olenina, he fell in love with the renowned beauty Natalia Goncharova, thirteen years his junior, at a ball in 1828. After his first proposal to her the following year yielded an indefinite answer because of her family's concerns about his political reputation, Pushkin proposed again in 1830 and was accepted. However, marriage brought new concerns, not the least of which were the societal intrigues surrounding his new wife, most notably the young French émigré Georges d'Anthès's flirtation with Natalia, which resulted in the duel that cost Pushkin his life. Having carried on affairs with several men's wives as a libertine in the 1820s, Pushkin thus experienced the reverse side of the equation as the husband of a much younger beauty, a family man who feared being cuckolded and reacted furiously to the spreading rumors.

The Stone Guest, written in November 1830 on the eve of Pushkin's marriage the following February, therefore occupies a transitional point in his life and career. Poetry was yielding to prose in his creative output, just as his "poetic," rebellious libertinism had given way to a more prosaic family life with marriage and children, and its attendant social and financial responsibilities. In this light, we can view *The Stone Guest* as a personal record of Pushkin's changing circumstances as he transforms from the carefree libertine of the 1820s to a pater familias and jealous husband in the 1830s, thus exchanging his former Don Juan role for that of the Commander. *The Stone Guest*, I argue, represents an attempt on Pushkin's part to reconcile these conflicting selves and come to terms with his past, present, and future.

In addition to its autobiographical relevance for Pushkin, the Don Juan theme is closely linked—as it is in so many literary works on the legendary seducer—with politics. In his 1824 poem "The Conversation of a Bookseller with a Poet" ("Razgovor knigoprodavtsa s poetom") and several letters to friends, Pushkin speaks of a materialistic "age of iron," in which the poet's need for free, spontaneous expression is being increasingly restricted. Although he initially expressed optimism about Nikolai's reign, he gradually became disillusioned with the new Tsar's reactionary, repressive regime.[6] As Boris Gasparov points out, Pushkin's pessimism following the failed Decembrist revolt led him to emphasize Don Juan's defeat by the Commander's statue, whereas in previous works such as *Ruslan and Liudmila* and *The Gabrieliad*, older authority figures had been successfully vanquished by youthful protagonists in similar situations involving love triangles. Ultimately, this "gradually developing master plot" culminates in *The Bronze Horseman*, with the decisive defeat of the young rebel Evgeny by the statue of Peter I. From this perspective, *The Stone Guest* represents a watershed moment in Pushkin's creative and political development: "The eighteenth-century comedy about a duped old suitor/husband and a triumphant young couple gradually turns into the story of Don Juan's defeat in which, finally, the Stone Guest assumes the commanding role" (Gasparov 58). Thus, *The Stone Guest* reflects Pushkin's growing doubts about the possibility of not just rebellion against the autocracy but even gradual political change within it.

Pushkin's Transformation of the Don Juan Legend

Although Pushkin knew several versions of the Don Juan legend, he announces his primary debt to Mozart and Da Ponte's opera in his epigraph, a quotation of Leporello's frightened attempt to obey his master and invite the Commendatore's statue to supper.[7] *Don Giovanni* was performed in Russian starting in 1828 and numerous times in Italian and German in Russia before that. Pushkin had heard performances of *Don Giovanni* in Odesa and St. Petersburg before writing *The Stone Guest*, and the play's epigraph positions the opera as both a model and a rival. Like Mozart/Da Ponte, Pushkin uses the name Leporello for the servant rather than Tirso's Catalinón or Molière's Sganarelle. Finally, *Don Giovanni*, as I explain later in the chapter, somewhat deemphasizes the theme of damnation that is crucial for Tirso. Thus, despite the imprint of other previous versions of the Don Juan tale on *The Stone Guest*, Pushkin's recasting of the legend takes Mozart and Da Ponte's opera as its starting point.

The unique "little tragedy" genre compelled Pushkin to reduce the plot, number of characters and scenes, and scale of the drama considerably from *Don Giovanni*. Although his hero, like previous Don Juans, is also a nobleman, the range of conquests, at least those referred to in the play itself, is limited to women of his own class.[8] However, his major innovations are inspired by far more than generic restrictions, and omissions from previous versions of the legend more often than not have greater significance than simply saving time.[9] Pushkin's most dramatic move in reworking the Don Juan legend is surely his transformation of the hero into a Romantic poet like himself. Don Juan seduces Donna Anna largely through poetic improvisations, reminisces in elegiac tones over a deceased lover, Inez, and has written the poetry on which Laura's songs are based. Moreover, in stark contrast to his predecessors, Pushkin's hero recalls previous conquests enough to mourn them (in the case of the deceased Inez) or revisit them (in the case of Laura). Although he has never met Anna before the action of the play, he is linked to her through his killing of her husband, Don Alvar de Solva, in a duel. In this sense, Don Juan finds no new women in *The Stone Guest*—all of them are connected to his past. Numerous additional conquests are alluded to in the conversations between Don Juan and Leporello, but only in passing, so as to remind the reader or viewer of the legendary libertine's biography. In this manner, Pushkin's Don Juan differs strikingly from Don Giovanni, all of whose attempted conquests are new women, while the one woman who pursues him from his past (Donna Elvira) is merely a source of annoyance.

Pushkin also transforms the heroine, Donna Anna, from the Commander's daughter in *Don Giovanni* into his widow, giving the plot an added dimension of sexual rivalry.[10] This new element can be seen most clearly in Don Juan's invitation to the Commander's statue not to supper, as in previous versions, but to guard the door of Anna's apartment during the Don's tryst with her. He thus turns the invitation's focus from blasphemy to cuckoldry. Moreover, the circumstances of the Commander's death create a different dynamic between Don Juan and Donna Anna from that of Mozart/Da Ponte's opera. In *Don Giovanni*, Anna is determined throughout to avenge her father's death; in the play, by contrast, Anna herself remarks that Don Juan's duel with the Commander was fought honorably.

Don Juan's fascination with the Commander, and his decision to pursue Donna Anna knowing that she was Don Alvar's widow, underscores the relevance of Girard's theory of mimetic desire to this play. Don Juan's desire for Anna is mediated through the Commander, whose hold over her appears to be so strong that Don Juan feels the need for his presence at the rendezvous. As I mention in the introduction, Don Juan's pursuit of Anna is inspired in large part by her prayers for her dead husband and possibly testifies to a desire to rival her husband by attaining the same devotion in life that the Commander receives in death. He expresses his jealousy of his rival rather straightforwardly during his visit to Anna's house, arousing her curiosity:

> *Don Juan*: I'm speechless with joy,
>   Thinking to myself that I am alone
>   With the lovely Donna Anna—here, not there,
>   Not by the grave of that happy departed one—
>   And I see you now no longer on your knees
>   Before your marble spouse.
> *Donna Anna*: Don Diego,
>   So you're jealous. My husband torments you
>   Even in his grave? (87)

> *Дон Гуан*: Наслаждаюсь молча,
>   Глубоко мыслью быть наедине
>   С прелестной Доной Анной. Здесь—не там,
>   Не при гробнице мертвого счастливца—
>   И вижу вас уже не на коленах
>   Пред мраморным супругом.
> *Дона Анна*: Дон Диего,
>   Так вы ревнивы—муж мой и во гробе
>   Вас мучит? (163)

The connection of Don Juan's pursuit of Anna with the identity of her husband dictates the aforementioned alteration of the legend, by which the libertine invites the statue to guard the door of Anna's house, thus insisting that his rival observe his victory.

Another notable addition to the legend is Pushkin's invention of a completely new character in Laura, a female counterpart to Don Juan who exhibits a great deal of his behavior.[11] This innovation is crucial as it represents Pushkin's introduction of the "feminine Don Juan" theme, and the notion that women can occupy this role as effectively as men.[12] As I argue, this evenhandedness in creating a female analogue of Don Juan indicates a larger theme of women's agency in their conquests and choices in love and marriage.[13]

Finally, Pushkin continues the process of secularization begun by Molière, particularly in the ending of *The Stone Guest*. This turn to the secular does not entail a complete elimination of the legend's religious underpinnings. Situating Scenes 1 and 3 of the play in St. Anthony monastery (which Leporello recognizes as the site where Don Juan earlier courted Inez), Pushkin retains the Christian environment, coloring, and phrases that would have been typical of the time period. Leporello's reference to the devil assisting Don Juan in his courtship is perhaps not as casual as it may seem in light of all the other mentions of God and the devil in the play. The monk, not recognizing Don Juan, refers to him as a "shameless, godless profligate." Don Carlos and Donna Anna also refer to him in similar terms.[14] Don Juan himself wishes for God to comfort Donna Anna as she has comforted him, and cries out "God in Heaven! Donna Anna!" when he sees the statue at the climax of the play. As Nemirovsky points out, Pushkin emphasizes his hero's sacrilegious actions, noting that Don Juan stresses that he does not repent of killing the Commander: "Don Juan's true goal turns out to be not the seduction of Donna Anna, but a sacrilegious challenge to the heavens" (223).

However, Pushkin omits the ending's traditional Christian content and thus changes the focus from divine punishment to psychological identity. Instead of sending Don Juan to hell, the Commander simply freezes him in his grip. The final stage direction of "they fall through" (provalivaiutsia) hints at not only a shared fate but also a mysterious identity between Don Juan and his nemesis.[15] In this manner, Pushkin removes the "moral" of the tale and switches the focus from the deserved punishment of a libertine—featured in the works of Tirso, Molière, and, to a lesser extent, Mozart/Da Ponte—to a focus on Don Juan's fascination with the titular figure. This is one of the ways in which Pushkin's conception of the legend differs from another key Romantic version, Hoffmann's 1813 story, which virtually ignores the role of the Commander in its focus on Don Juan and Donna Anna's relationship. The removal of the theme of vengeance and repentance (unlike in *Don Giovanni*, the statue in the little tragedy does not ask Don Juan to repent) testifies to Pushkin's unusual decision to withhold judgment of his hero's behavior and forgo any hint of moralizing.

Pushkin's Ambiguities

As I mentioned in the introduction, the Don Juan legend contains a great deal of potential ambiguity that Pushkin exploits in a fashion characteristic of his works. Dostoevsky, in his discussion of Pushkin's "The Queen of Spades," highlights the ambiguity that he sees as one of the poet's most distinguishing qualities. Pushkin, Dostoevsky points out, presents the Countess's ghostly appearance and the other strange events of the story in such a way that they can be interpreted as having either a natural or a supernatural origin. The reader is put in the position of being forced to choose which explanation seems most valid; Dostoevsky defines this irresolution as the "fantastic."[16] Ambiguity of various types can be seen in many other works of Pushkin as well. Akhmatova notes the divergent interpretations the little tragedies in particular involve, singling out *The Stone Guest*: "The complexity is so great at times that, when combined with the breathtaking conciseness, the sense is almost obscured, which invites various interpretations (for example, the denouement of *The Stone Guest*)" (91).

One of these points of ambiguity involves Pushkin's own links to his characters. Don Juan's poetic qualities clearly underscore the autobiographical elements of the retelling. In addition, Pushkin famously kept a Don Juan list of his own, in which his wife-to-be, Natalia Goncharova, represented his 113th love; he also cryptically wrote down an incomplete list of thirty first names in Elizaveta Ushakova's album.[17] Moreover, Pushkin's shift of the traditional Seville setting to the Spanish capital of Madrid hints at his own exile from the Russian capital of St. Petersburg.[18] Don Juan's return from exile recalls his creator's stay in various parts of Southern Imperial Russia, his estate in Mikhailovskoe, and his quarantining in Boldino during the writing of the play. Finally, Don Juan's courtship of both a married woman (Inez) and a widow (Donna Anna) reflects his author's own proclivities. Pushkin engaged in numerous flirtations and affairs with married women, including the wife of his older friend and mentor Nikolai Karamzin, and from a young age repeatedly found himself attracted to widows, such as the pregnant Marie Smith, to whom he wrote the poem "To the Young Widow" ("K molodoi vdove," 1817) in his last year at the Lyceum.

However, as Akhmatova points out, Pushkin inscribes himself into the Commander as well. The more mature Pushkin, who was engaged to the much younger Natalia Goncharova when he wrote *The Stone Guest*, worried that she would betray him after his death and, like the Commander, jealously protected his wife during their marriage. In his April 5, 1830, letter to Natalia's mother the day before he proposed and was accepted, and half a year before he wrote the little tragedy, he expressed the following concerns: "Surrounded as she will be with admiration, with homage, with enticements, will this calmness last? . . . God is my witness that I am ready to die for her, but that I should die to leave a dazzling widow, free to choose a new husband tomorrow—this idea is hell" (406).[19] As the drama of d'Anthès attempting to seduce his wife gradually unfolded, Pushkin became increasingly melancholy and sullen; he could be characterized as statue-like, watching menacingly as his younger would-be rival taunted him with his attention to Natalia. This conflict between Pushkin's younger and older selves creates an ambiguity regarding the poet's self-representation in the play. The poet experiences a shift in identity from his past to the present. As David Bethea notes about Pushkin's identity at this point, "This is not Don Juan, the man who claimed that his wife was his '113th love,' but the man who correctly suspects that one day in the not so distant future he will be nothing more than a dragonfly caught on the rapier of a younger, more desirable opponent" (121). Pushkin's dual self-portrait symbolically expresses itself in the brief, fateful confrontation between Don Juan and the Commander, in which the two opponents fuse together as the statue grips the libertine's hand. In this sense Donjuanism becomes a search for identity that reflects Pushkin's own struggle as a poet dependent on everchanging audiences, and as a formerly young, lighthearted seducer attempting a transition to the role of stable family man.

The question of Don Juan's sincerity toward Donna Anna is also left ambiguous. Vissarion Belinsky, analyzing Don Juan's words to her less than a decade after the play's publication, asks: "Is this the language of cunning flattery or the voice of the heart? We find that it's both at the same time" (634). As Gasparov notes, Don Juan's words as he is dying, "I am undone—it's finished—Donna Anna!" (94) / "Ia gibnu—koncheno—o Donna Anna!" (171), keep the mystery carefully hidden: "His last words, with which the drama ends, offer a note of ambiguity: is it indeed possible that Don Guan fell in love for the first time? What were his feelings in the last moment? And could he have given an account of them?" (54). To some extent, again, this ambiguity is characteristic of the legend itself, but Pushkin heightens it, perhaps reflecting his own ambivalent feelings toward marriage. No matter how convincing Don Juan's words are to Donna Anna (and to the reader), one may still be tempted to exclaim, along with her:

> And I should believe
> That Don Juan really loves for the first time,
> That he doesn't want to add me to his victims! (92)

> И я поверю,
> Чтоб Дон Гуан влюбился в первый раз,
> Чтоб не искал во мне он жертвы новой! (169)

If we believe Anna's words, then we may doubt the sincerity of Don Juan's claim of rebirth.

In fact, however, most Russian critics have interpreted Don Juan's love of Anna to be genuine.[20] Akhmatova, for example, argues that Don Juan's last line proves that he has been reborn in love for her but tragically receives death instead of salvation (100). Dmitry Ustiuzhanin, similarly, claims that Don Juan has been completely transformed by Donna Anna and "dies like a knight with Donna Anna's name on his lips" (83). The tragedy of the play, according to him, is that Don Juan dies for his past sins precisely when he awakens and becomes a deeper human being. For Stanislav Rassadin, Don Juan's monologue in Scene 3 as he prepares to meet Donna Anna shows the awakening of a great love in him. Anna represents a new life (in contrast to Laura, who represents the old one) as new questions arise that complicate issues of life and death and resist easy answers (224). As Lotman writes, "Pushkin paradoxically combines sincerity and the capacity to experience a 'first love' every time" (*Pushkin* 312).[21] Not all critics are convinced, however. Dmitry Blagoi, for instance, calls Don Juan a "professional seducer" and notes that sincere love for Anna would contradict the very archetype: "If Pushkin's Don Juan was capable of loving one woman forever, he would stop being Don Juan" (*Tvorcheskii put' Pushkina* 653).[22] Responding to this objection, Rassadin makes the counterargument that Pushkin would not give Don Juan his level of language, style, and imagery if he were not sincere (213), and overall, most critics see the hero's rebirth in love as genuine, but the ambiguous situation remains. As I claim in subsequent chapters, writers who follow up on Pushkin's transposition of the Don Juan legend tend to resolve this particular ambiguity by interpreting the hero as experiencing authentic love.

Don Juan's very motivation for his seductions is also ambiguous. On the one hand, he appears to share the energy and sheer love of the temporal world evinced by Tirso's, Molière's, and Mozart/Da Ponte's heroes and, for many critics, opposes the forces of life and love to the deadly, immobile world of the Commander, Don Carlos, and other forces that would contain him. Ustiuzhanin, for instance, remarks that "Don Juan throws a direct challenge to the world of sanctimony and hypocrisy" when he invites the statue to guard Anna's door (70). And for David Herman, "When Juan makes love to Laura in the presence of Carlos's corpse, another of Pushkin's additions, he demonstrates an implicit faith that every act of creativity makes a mockery of death and its authority" (17).

At the same time, Don Juan demonstrates an attraction to deathly forces in a manner that recalls de Rougemont's Western Romantic myth, with its interconnection of erotic passion and death. Composing the play in quarantine at Boldino, Pushkin felt himself to be surrounded by death, which was connected to a feeling of excitement at the risk, judging by such contemporaneous lyrics as "All, all that threatens ruin" ("Vse, vse, chto gibel'iu grozit," 1830) (Lotman, *Pushkin* 142). As several commentators have noted, Pushkin passes this quality along to his hero in a macabre fashion.[23] Don Juan kills Don Carlos in a duel as he is about to possess Laura sexually, and then he makes love to her himself right beside the dead body; he also courts Donna Anna at the cemetery where she is mourning the husband he has killed and invites the stone representation of Don Alvar to attend their tryst. For Lotman, "Don Juan's death is actually the suicide of a man who has transformed his striving to cross all boundaries of the basis for life and thrown himself into the abyss" (*Pushkin* 314). Don Juan's reminiscences of Inez, as he recalls her "deathly lips" (pomertvelykh gubakh), are described by Sergei Davydov as "bordering on necrophilia" (96). One can debate whether Don Juan's actions are meant to defeat the forces of Thanatos, as several critics argue, or testify to his attraction to them.

Art as Seduction

For Akhmatova, Pushkin's discovery that Don Juan is a poet decisively transforms him from earlier prototypes of the hero: Molière's rationalist and skeptic and Mozart/Da Ponte's rich libertine, enjoying his own wealth. To be sure, Akhmatova is not the first to notice Pushkin's emphasis on Don Juan as a poet: decades earlier, Dmitry Darsky wrote that "Don Juan is a poet, and he receives passion like an inspired master" (56). However, her essay proves to be seminal in establishing this approach as an important critical angle on Pushkin's play, and several commentators have followed her lead in exploring the poetic effect and style of Don Juan's "verses." Rassadin, for instance, begins his chapter on *The Stone Guest* with a discussion of Don Juan's two poetic replies to Anna on the marble of the Commander's gravestone. In the first, the libertine speaks sentimentally of women in general, and in the second, he converses more about an individual woman, describing her beauty from the point of view of a lover (202–4). Rassadin describes these contrasting statements in terms of a competition between dueling poets that encapsulates Pushkin's portrayal of his hero as a developing artist, transformed from preceding versions of Don Juan as someone who knows only lust to a man who also evinces a "spiritual thirst" (212).

Beyond its apparent reflections on Don Juan's status as a poet, though, the play is in some respects a meditation on art, particularly its linkage to seduction. Pushkin's desire to comment on artistic processes surely goes a long way toward explaining his inclusion, for the first time, of Laura as a female counterpart to Don Juan. Laura is portrayed as an artist who has just reached new heights in the performance of her role.

> *First Guest*: I swear, Laura, that you've never acted
> With such perfection as you did today.
> How well you understood your character!
> *Second Guest*: How powerfully you developed your role!
> *Third Guest*: And with what art!
> *Laura*: Yes, today every word,
> Every gesture came out well for me.
> I gave myself up freely to inspiration.
> The words poured out of me as if they were brought forth,
> Not by slavish memory, but by the heart . . . (72)

> *Первый*: Клянусь тебе, Лаура, никогда
> С такими ты совершенством не играла.
> Как роль свою ты верно поняла!
> *Второй*: Как развила ее! С какой силой!
> *Третий*: С каким искусством!
> *Лаура*: Да, мне удавалось
> Сегодня каждое движенье, слово.
> Я только предавалась вдохновенью.
> Слова лились как будто их рождала
> Не память рабская, но сердце . . . (144)

She then proceeds to sing to the assembled guests, thus performing in a second artistic capacity. The first guest explicitly links her art with love:

> *First Guest*: Among life's pleasures
> Music yields to none save love;
> But love itself is melody . . .

> *Первый*: Из наслаждений жизни
> Одной любви Музыка уступает;
> Но и любовь мелодия . . . (145)

And Laura's artistic success is then implicitly linked with sexual seduction:

First Guest: Even now your eyes are shining yet,
Your cheeks still burn, the ecstasy
Has not yet gone from you. (144)

Первый: Да и теперь глаза твои блестят
И щеки разгорелись, не проходит
В тебе восторг. (144)

Pushkin clearly intends for Laura to exemplify the connection of art and seduction, the artist's task of seducing his or her audience. This passage suggests that the linkage of art and love is a major theme of the play, and that we should approach Don Juan's interactions with Anna in this light as well.

Two critics, in particular, have discussed *The Stone Guest* as a meta-artistic work. David Glenn Kropf describes Don Juan's conquests (in Pushkin's play as well as *Don Giovanni*) using Gilles Deleuze and Felix Guattari's term hecceity, or "thisness," that which gives an entity its particular character. Hecceity is a concept that encapsulates the libertine's continual pursuit of freedom and signifies a mode of individuation that defines a person in terms of the movements and forces exerted on him or her at a specific time in a determined milieu. Each of Don Juan's new names, disguises (as a monk and a nobleman of a different name), conquests, and poetic improvisations comprises a new hecceity. As Kropf claims, "Don Juan does more than offer a song or poem improvised on a given theme: he offers his whole being, which he improvises in terms of a particular woman" (11). This improvisation requires changes, and results in a self-recreation, with Don Juan becoming anew and therefore always sincere in his love for the given woman. Don Juan's series of becomings is opposed by social forces arrayed against him that threaten to apprehend the libertine and confront him with his previous criminal behavior, thus identifying the Don Juan of the present in terms of his actions in the past.[24] "The 'place of residence' that a state bureaucracy would use to fix and stabilize an individual," Kropf writes, "changes with the libertines every night: a new object of desire, a new space and time, a new hecceity" (32).[25] Society defines each of Don Juan's becomings as a crime, a violation of order, and as far as conquests go, evidence of his insincerity. By extending his hand to freeze the libertine, the Commander preserves the sanctity of the marriage even after death, linking the Don Juan of the present, who has been reborn through love, to the Don Juan of the past (who killed him in a duel) and bringing an end to his repeated becomings. Thus, if Don Juan embodies Lacan's notion of self-reproducing desire, which never comes to a stop but moves incessantly from object to object, then this series of seductions can also be analyzed in terms of artistic "conquests," or continual remakings of oneself.

Analyzing *The Stone Guest* from a different angle (in light of the fragment "The Guests Were Arriving at the Dacha"), David Herman comes to similar conclusions, interpreting the play as the opposition of Don Juan's intertwined forces of poetry, seduction, and mobility and the statue's immobilizing force. He notes that for Pushkin, seduction and poetry are two fundamentally similar activities, as the poet must "seduce" his audience.[26] Herman writes,

> Pushkin as a poet was confronted by the challenge to move inert audiences, as poetry was going out of fashion in 1830 and being replaced by prose, and this required poetic mobility. This mobility is passed along to his hero in *The Stone Guest*. In imagining the lures of his next object of affection, Don Juan makes of love a primordially *artistic* act. (9; Herman's emphasis)

In the end, Don Juan's poetic gifts prove too powerful for his own good, as his invocation of the statue, his bringing of it to life, results in his own downfall: "Juan dies in the end not because he has killed," as Herman puts it, "but because he has given life" (19). The statue's grip of his hand freezes him in immobility.

These critics focus on Don Juan's process of self-discovery, but his artistic seduction has a transformative effect on the objects of his attraction as well. Keeping these critical observations on Don Juan as an artist in mind, I will switch focus by examining the way this quality enables him to uncover other people's inner essence. Poetic seduction allows Don Juan not only to reinvent himself in a new guise but also to draw out and affect other human beings. His rebirth in love, expressed through poetic seduction, thus represents a rebirth for Anna too. Before I explore this rebirth, I will examine Pushkin in relation to the question of women's roles, in society and in literature.

Anticipating the "Woman Question"

The Don Juan legend's foregrounding of the hero's repeated seductions of women, along with frequent duels to dispatch their husbands, fiancés, rival suitors, and fathers, establishes a kind of hypermasculinity that pervades all variants. Although Pushkin increases the hero's sympathetic qualities by transforming him into a poetic figure, his Don Juan still shares the essential immorality, from the Christian perspective, of his predecessors in Tirso, Molière, Mozart/Da Ponte, and others. Even if he recalls earlier conquests, such as Inez, with sadness, he does not hesitate to move on to the next one at Leporello's reminder that there were other women after Inez, and there will be more in the future; nor does he flinch from fighting a duel with Don Carlos. This immorality is thoroughly grounded in vices that are seen as typical and even socially acceptable in men but not women. Don Juan represents a grotesque embodiment of the ruthless seduction and violence that are generally essentialized as masculine qualities. Even if the hero of *The Stone Guest* may be on the precipice of reform at the play's conclusion, Pushkin certainly maintains the idea of Don Juan as a representation of these masculine traits and presents them as entirely appropriate, both for seventeenth-century Spain and for Russia in the 1820s–'30s. Pushkin portrays Don Juan as violating while also partaking of the benefits of hegemonic masculinity with the ambiguity characteristic of his own era.

At the same time, though, Pushkin complicates the legend's portrayal of gender relations. One of his most radical and influential transformations in *The Stone Guest* involves his reexamination of women in relation to the act of seduction. By using the legend as a starting point to examine female as well as male sexuality in the little tragedy—as in several of his other works—Pushkin explores the possibilities of greater inclusivity of women inherent in the legend, along with the attendant anxieties for men, and opens up ways of rethinking female roles in sexuality, art, and communication.

Pushkin's fascination with the female as well as the male experience of sexuality, and his notion of seduction as a battle between equal opponents, derives in part from certain of his Western European readings, going back as far as Ovid. Lotman connects Pushkin's self-image as a "fugitive poet" (poet-beglets) or "poet in exile" (poet-izgnannik) in the early 1820s to his identification with Ovid, a fellow poet in exile who was similarly banished to the edge of the empire by a tyrant, and who lived not far from Pushkin in Tomis (present-day Constanţa, Romania) (Lotman, *Pushkin* 66). Ovid also shapes Pushkin's ethos of sensual pleasure and libertinism through his *Art of Love*.[27] The Roman poet, writing in middle age, addresses an audience of females as well as males, offering advice to both genders on the laws of attraction, and treating women as active sexual "consumers" rather than mere passive recipients of male attention. Ovid's treatise contains "The Art of Beauty," a short poem offering women advice on preserving their beauty as they age and, following his extensive advice to men, begins a late chapter with the description "Arms for the Amazons now: turnabout is fair play," which, along with tips on grooming (dress, hair, teeth, makeup, etc.), includes a warning against Don Juan types: "What they are telling you, they have told to girls by the thousand" (166).

Several of Pushkin's readings closer to his own time also explore the notions of seduction as a battle of the sexes and women as active agents in their destinies. From Pierre Choderlos de Laclos's *Dangerous Liaisons* (1782), Pushkin absorbed the notion of love as intrigue: seduction as an act of intricate plotting and manipulation of people and circumstances. In the novel, the Marquise de Merteuil announces her competition with the Vicomte de Valmont to better him in the game of seduction and manipulation: "What have you ever done that I have not outdone a thousand times? You have seduced, even ruined, numerous women. But what problems did you have to conquer? What obstacles did you have to overcome?" (178). Valmont's response to her challenge establishes an identity between them, as he admits that she has made more "converts" than he. His seduction of Mme. De Tourvel testifies to his prioritization, like the Don Juan of Tirso's play, of the accomplishment of a bold and difficult feat that will gain him renown in society over sexual pleasure per se, and Tourvel's trip to a convent only adds luster to the act of seducing her. Pushkin's Anna suspects that Don Juan is playing a similar game and merely wants to make her an illustrious addition to his list of conquests. Like Ovid earlier, and Pushkin later, Laclos likens seduction both to an art and to warfare. Valmont, insisting on his "purity of method" in seducing Tourvel, claims: "I have not diverged at all from the true principles of this art, which we have often noticed is so very similar to the art of warfare" (311).[28]

A third important influence on Pushkin in this regard is Germaine de Staël, whose heroine Delphine from the eponymously titled 1802 novel represents the third, after Samuel Richardson's Clarissa and Jean-Jacques Rousseau's Julie, whom he mentions as Tatiana's models in *Eugene Onegin*.[29] Although Delphine frequently laments the limited options available to women in prerevolutionary France,[30] she finds ways to act in accord with her convictions, refusing a marriage to her unattractive suitor M. de Valorbe since she is in love with Léonce de Mondeville. Delphine's championing of her own and other women's rights to marry men of their own choosing, as Olga Hasty notes, marked the start of de Staël's advocacy for divorce rights: "Clustered around Delphine's narrative is an entire constellation of stories that tell of women's entrapments in appalling mismatches and that document the destructiveness of the ironclad conventions of a callous, hypocritical society" (*Pushkin's Tatiana* 53). In light of the misery Pushkin hints at in the marriages between Anna and Don Alvar and Inez and her husband in *The Stone Guest*, one can view de Staël's advocacy of divorce, and her protest against the confinement of women *and* men in unhappy marriages, as a call for freedom that impacted the Russian poet's thinking.

Through Pushkin's focus in the play on seduction as dialogue rather than one-sided domination, Donjuanism in nineteenth-century Russia unexpectedly dovetails with the so-called woman question (zhenskii vopros). This reevaluation of the role of women does not emerge as a central political issue until the 1850s and '60s and is inspired to a great extent by the novels of George Sand. In my view, though, Pushkin is no less preoccupied with it than Nikolai Chernyshevsky, Mikhail Mikhailov, and other later proponents of women's emancipation, even if his interest is mostly confined to his personal and work lives and exists independently of any utopian programs for liberation. Although I do not claim Pushkin as a direct ideological predecessor to these thinkers, he anticipates some of their concerns through his intuition of the complexity of women's behavior in relation to men and his growing awareness of their changing roles already in the 1820s and '30s. At the same time, he also anticipates modern-day Anglo-American and French feminists such as Kate Millett and Hélène Cixous, who critique the essentialization of both male and female qualities as well as men's and women's purported respective active and passive sexuality in relation to each other.

To be sure, Pushkin's understanding of women as expressed in his letters, reminiscences of friends, and other such documents does not put him ahead of his time. Petr Guber's 1923 study of Pushkin's Don Juan list reveals a rather typical brand of misogyny in the poet, who exhibited a *domostroi*-like attitude toward his wife, lovers, and women in general. Lotman draws parallels between Pushkin's desire to create a good housewife out of Natalia and Tolstoy's later efforts with his own wife, Sofia Andreevna Behrs, to "educate a young lady into a housewife" along the lines detailed in his descriptions of ideal family life in his works (*Pushkin* 161–62). Indeed, Pushkin's attempts to arrange his family life anticipate Jules Michelet's thesis, in his 1858 treatise *L'amour*, that a man has to create his own woman. In his letters, Pushkin repeatedly advises Natalia not to engage in coquetry at balls and remonstrates with her that "modesty is the best adornment for your sex" (*Letters* 763). And although Pushkin participated in long-lasting friendships with women such as Vera Viazemskaya (wife of fellow poet and close friend Petr Viazemsky), for whom he did not entertain romantic feelings, there is no denying an oft-displayed tendency to look down on women's spiritual, aesthetic capabilities.[31] As Guber remarks, Pushkin did not even suspect that the woman question would ever arise (30).

If Pushkin displays relations to women and a family ideal that would influence some rather conservative figures, though, he also anticipates some issues that would be explored by the radicals of the 1860s. At several points in his life and career, Pushkin was confronted by indubitable evidence not only of women's artistic talents, but also of their "masculine" behavior and identity. Perhaps the most famous example of such a phenomenon, albeit toward the end of his life, six years after writing *The Stone Guest*, was Nadezhda Durova's memoirs. Durova, who disguised herself as a man to fight in the Napoleonic Wars, wrote a quasi-fictional memoir of her experiences entitled *The Cavalry Maiden*, a fragment of which Pushkin published in his journal *The Contemporary* in 1836. Mary Zirin sums up the importance of Durova's memoir as follows: "*The Cavalry Maiden* speaks for all the women who have ever led a life of action outside the accepted female sphere, and particularly for the 'Amazons'" (44). Pushkin's interest in and commitment to these excerpts is obvious in his comment about passing them through censorship in May, 1836: "without them I am sunk" (*Letters* 764).[32] As Andreas Schönle points out, however, Durova was somewhat unsuccessful in negotiating the divide between her birth and chosen gender identities. In her memoir, she uses a male pseudonym and male voice, and she insists on being referred to as a man; however, she also uses female morphemes and a masculine form (Durov) of her real name rather than a male pseudonym. Despite her efforts to dispel traditional stereotypes of female weakness, she tells a comical tale in her memoir of her failures, weakness, and fatigue, thus reinforcing them. Ultimately, Durova was unable to successfully redefine her gender and resorted to extreme self-repression and isolation after her retirement from the army. However, her efforts to explore gender identity, especially in connection with writing, undoubtedly bore fruit for Russian intellectuals and writers as they opened up the exploration of this topic and merged with Pushkin's own interest in these questions.

Pushkin's comments to Durova show his fascination with gender, and in particular with the blurring of lines between what is deemed masculine and feminine behavior. In his correspondence with her, he acknowledges that she wrote the memoirs posing as a man. Pushkin's advice, apparently, was practical. Following the delays in the publication of her memoirs, Durova wrote an impatient letter to Pushkin. In his response, Pushkin complimented her on her frankness, praising "the genuine stamp of your fiery and impatient character" (*Letters* 773), and patiently explained to her the difficulty of fulfilling her request that he show the memoirs directly to the tsar to speed up the publication process. He also accepted her assumed masculine identity, addressing her as Alexander Andreevich Alexandrov, despite knowing that she was a woman.

However, Pushkin was even more fascinated by women's assumption of traditionally male sexual roles, and this comes across almost as an obsession in his personal correspondence. In teasing letters to Evpraxiia Nikolaevna Vul'f, who was his lover briefly in 1829 and a longtime friend, he repeatedly interrogates her about her seductions: "Are you in Riga? Have you made some conquests? Will you get married soon? Have you found some uhlans?" (230–31). Pushkin seems to be aware of women's capacity not just for Don Juan-like serial conquests, but for the enjoyment of those conquests for their own sake. Thus, Pushkin displays a mixture of views on women's roles and capacities in his society.

If Pushkin's attitude toward women in his personal life was often conservative and patriarchal, his fictional descriptions of women acknowledge a great variety of behavior and roles. This is most famously true of *Eugene Onegin*'s heroine, Tatiana, who astonishes many readers with her growth in art and life. Hasty aptly describes Tatiana's rejection of Onegin as "a self-assertive statement of moral and . . . creative ideals at which she had arrived herself" (*Pushkin's Tatiana* 7).[33] Significantly, Tatiana initiates the relationship with Onegin, writing him first. The questioning of what we would today call essentialist views of women can also be seen in numerous other works by Pushkin. In *Poltava*, for instance, the relationship between Mazepa and Maria can be profitably interpreted through the prism of Shakespeare's influence on Pushkin. As Catherine O'Neil explains, Pushkin, in his interpretation of *Othello*, was particularly interested in Desdemona as a rebel: "Despite Desdemona's seeming passivity and resigned submission to Othello's murderous delusion, she is also a brave and reckless woman, especially in the first two acts of the play, and it is to this part of her that Pushkin responds most" (131). Through Maria, Pushkin replicates Desdemona's relatively aggressive role in courtship, as his heroine rebels against her parents in order to marry a much older man. *The Stone Guest*, I argue, represents another example of works that feature strong, rebellious women, and it contains numerous parallels to *Poltava* in particular. For instance, like Desdemona, Maria devours her husband's tales of military exploits and is attracted to his art of storytelling; along similar lines, Laura performs songs with lyrics by Don Juan. Seduction takes place on the artistic, verbal level as much as, if not more than, in the realm of physical attraction.

To a great extent, then, *The Stone Guest* can be read alongside *Eugene Onegin*, *Poltava*, and other works by Pushkin that explore women's choices and women's roles as artists. Thus the play serves as an early foreshadowing of the "woman question" that began to flourish in Russia two decades after Pushkin's death. Pushkin's exploration of gender roles in these works, in fact, merges with other literary trends that were in turn influencing Russians to rethink male and female sexual relations. The novels of George Sand made this theme explicit and in turn decisively influenced many major Russian writers. Even before *The Stone Guest* was posthumously published in 1839, Sand's novels, with their treatment of gender and family, were widely read by Russians, including Pushkin himself, and eventually contributed to widespread changes in gender roles in society and literature alike.[34]

Gender Roles in *The Stone Guest*

Pushkin's female characters in *The Stone Guest* evince strikingly greater complexity than those of previous Don Juan works. The poet depicts women initiating affairs, choosing partners, and expressing themselves artistically—that is, performing traditionally masculine roles. Laura admits unapologetically that she has betrayed Don Juan in his absence and performs songs based on his lyrics. Anna, by contrast, would seem to be a virtuous woman who falls victim to Don Juan's seduction and trickery. However, it is she who first initiates contact with Don Juan, who is disguised as a monk, pushes him to reveal his secret, and yields rather easily to him even as he peels off layers of disguise, thus participating actively in the process of seduction. In short, Donjuanism in Pushkin's play turns out to be more of a shared role between the genders than a purely masculine one. Moreover, Don Juan is no longer simply a seducer of women, but also a would-be liberator. All three of his named conquests are attached to older, oppressive Commander-like figures. Inez has died at the hands of a stern husband, presumably for betraying him with Don Juan;[35] Anna was given in arranged marriage to a much older husband and struggles to maintain her duties as a widow in the face of Don Juan's pursuit of her; Laura, before Don Juan's brief reappearance, is in a relationship with the older, gloomy Don Carlos, who exhorts her to put aside the pleasures of her youth and think more soberly of her future. In all three cases, Don Juan offers these women an opportunity to exchange their entrapment for a more joyful, life-affirming experience.

Although Pushkin's Don Juan is known by reputation as a seducer of multiple women, only Inez, Laura, and Anna are explicitly mentioned in the play; the genre dictates some whittling down of his history of conquests, whose great extent would be known to the audience from earlier versions in any case. At first glance, these women seem to differ considerably from each other, but Pushkin creates several key parallels among them. For instance, all three are linked by their similar psychological and physical features and their attachment to stern, gloomy older men. These links appear all the more deliberate and striking given the brevity of Pushkin's little tragedy.

Pushkin's invented character, Laura, is perhaps the most prominent of the three female characters since she clearly serves as a female counterpart to Don Juan. When Don Juan reproaches her for infidelity, for instance, she points out that she is only behaving the way he does:

Don Juan: Tell the truth,
   How many times have you cheated on me
   While I was gone?
Laura: What about you, skirt-chaser?
Don Juan: Tell me. . . . No, we'll talk later. (79)

> *Дон Гуан*: А признайся,
>   А сколько раз ты изменила мне
>   В моем отсутствии?
> *Лаура*: А ты, повеса?
> *Дон Гуан*: Скажи... Нет, после переговорим. (152)

Don Juan's very question presupposes his awareness that she is cheating. (The question itself, of course, is inconceivable in any previous instantiations of the flighty libertine, as is his very return to Laura upon his arrival in Madrid.) Her half-playful, half-defiant comeback, clearly, reveals not only her desire to behave the way Don Juan does, but a sense that it is as natural for her as for him. Don Juan's response, interestingly, indicates his own urge to interrogate her on this topic; thus, Pushkin implies a discussion about male and female roles that, presumably, should take place in the future.[36]

Laura's identity with Don Juan is shown not only through her serial seductions, but also by her artistry. Her vocal performances make the idea of seductive art quite explicit. Following her songs, the guests (all male) note her "shining eyes," "blushing cheeks," and "ecstasy," which create an image with clear sexual undertones, in a passage I referred to earlier in the chapter.

> *First Guest*: True.
>   Even now your eyes are shining yet,
>   Your cheeks still burn, the ecstasy
>   Has not gone from you. Laura, do not let
>   It cool and die in silence; sing, Laura,
>   Sing something. (72)

> *Первый гость*: Да и теперь глаза твои блестят
>   И щеки разгорелись, не проходит
>   В тебе восторг. Лаура, не давай
>   Остыть ему бесплодно; спой, Лаура,
>   Спой что-инбудь. (144)

Since Laura's songs are based on Don Juan's own lyrics, her performance can be interpreted as a kind of co-seduction. Perhaps this is in part what incites Laura's current lover, Don Carlos, to anger as he realizes that he has in effect been seduced not only by the object of his love, but at the same time, indirectly, by his sworn enemy (through his poetry). Just as Laura seduces through the musical arts, however, she also does so through poetry, similarly to her mentor. Her response to Carlos's admonitions that she is young now but will grow older and lose her charms itself functions as a kind of poetic seduction.

> *Don Carlos*: You're young now . . . and you'll still be young
>   For five or six more years. You'll draw
>   The men around you six more years.
>   To pay you court and give you presents,
>   To sing you serenades at night,
>   And for your sake to kill each other
>   In darkness at the crossroads. But when
>   The time comes that your eyes have sunk,
>   Their lids grown wrinkled and discolored,
>   And your hair is streaked with gray,
>   And men start calling you "old woman,"
>   Then—what will you say?
> *Laura*: Then? Why should
>   I think of that? What talk is this?
>   Or do you always have such thoughts?
>   Come to the balcony. How calm the sky is,
>   The air is warm and still, the night is fragrant
>   With scents of lime and laurel, the moon
>   Shines radiant in the deep dark blue,
>   And the watchman cries, "Aa-all's well!" . . .
>   And far off, to the north—in Paris—
>   Perhaps the day is dark with clouds,
>   Cold rain is falling, the wind howls,
>   But what is that to us? Look, Carlos,
>   I'm ordering you to smile . . .
>   There you go! (75–76)

> *Дон Карлос*: Ты молода . . . и будешь молода
>   Еще лет пять иль шесть. Вокруг тебя
>   Еще лет шесть они толпиться будут,
>   Тебя ласкать, лелеять, и дарить,
>   И серенадами ночными тешить,
>   И за тебя друг друга убивать
>   На перекрестках ночью. Но когда
>   Пора пройдет, когда твои глаза
>   Впадут и веки, сморщась, почернеют
>   И седина в косе твоей мелькнет,

И будут называть тебя старухой,
Тогда—что скажешь ты?
Лаура: Тогда? Зачем
Об этом думать? Что за разговор?
Иль у тебя всегда такие мысли?
Приди—открой балкон. Как небо тихо;
Недвижим теплый воздух, ночь лимоном
И лавром пахнет, яркая луна
Блестит на синеве густой и темной,
И сторожа кричат протяжно: «Ясно!...»
А далеко, на севере—в Париже—
Быть может, небо тучами покрыто,
Холодный дождь идет и ветер дует.
А нам какое дело? Слушай, Карлос,
Я требую, чтоб улыбнулся ты...
—Ну то-то ж! (148)

Laura turns Carlos's attention instead to the calm sky, warm night, and fragrance of lemon and laurel, contrasting the pleasant southern (Spanish) air to cold, gray Paris. Here Pushkin anticipates Don Juan's overcoming of Anna's weak objections to his insistent declarations of love. Carlos, seduced by Laura and diverted from his stern moralizing, calls her a "sweet demon" (*milyi demon*). Later, Anna uses similar language with Don Juan, referring to his reputation as a "sheer demon" (*sushchii demon*). Thus, through Laura, Pushkin underscores the similarity of male and female behavior, demonstrating that women are just as capable of poetic seduction and creative self-reinvention as are men.

As Gasparov has pointed out, Pushkin's relationship with Karolina Sobańska finds a distinct reflection in Don Juan's efforts to seduce Donna Anna (49–50). However, the letters to the Polish countess make their way into his portrait of the dynamics between Don Carlos and Laura as well. In Pushkin's February 2, 1830, letter, he responds to Sobańska's reproach for not loving her seven years earlier, remarking, "Happiness is so little made for me that I did not recognize it when it was before me" (*Letters* 376). Such a statement recalls Don Juan's fears of losing happiness as a matter of timing. Pushkin's reference to her baptizing him and even converting him into a Catholic suggests the kind of rebirth Don Juan refers to in his speech to Anna. Other parts of the letter, however, recall Don Carlos, as he tries to persuade Sobańska of beauty's ephemerality: "But you are going to fade; this beauty is soon going to fall like an avalanche. Your soul will remain standing for a while longer, amid so many fallen charms—and then it will depart from them, and perhaps never will it meet mine, its timid slave, in the infinity of eternity" (376–77). In light of Akhmatova's argument that Pushkin distributes his attributes across both protagonists of *The Stone Guest*, one might continue this parallel, as Ustiuzhanin does, by pointing out Pushkin's similarities to Don Carlos (who is possibly the Commander's brother, after all). Thus Pushkin puts himself into the role not only of Don Juan but of both his stern opponents in the play.

However, Laura functions as far more than simply a female version of Don Juan or a contrast to the two more "virtuous" women in the play, as she is generally interpreted. Pushkin also uses her to illuminate those women through her parallels with them based on aspects such as their inner conflicts, burgeoning sexuality, and struggles against entrapment. Thus, as some critics have noted, Anna is far from the naïve and inexperienced foil to Laura that she may seem to be. To be sure, unlike Laura, Donna Anna cannot be considered a female Don Juan: she presumably has no experience with any men besides Don Alvar and is apparently sincere in her efforts to mourn her deceased husband according to the proper ritual. However, Don Juan awakens submerged impulses in her. For Blagoi, Anna's grieving for her husband hides coquetry and a thirst for a passion she has never experienced (*Tvorcheskii put' Pushkina* 648). Others have noted the relative ease with which Anna agrees to her seducer's requests, going so far as to invite him to her home. In their first interactions, as Nancy Anderson points out, Anna in fact initiates a dialogue with Don Juan by apologizing for disturbing him (in a gesture that is disingenuous since it only increases the "disturbance"; 171–72).

> *Donna Anna*: He's here again. Father,
>   I have disturbed you in your meditations—
>   Forgive me.
> *Don Juan*: I should ask forgiveness
>   Of you, señora. Perhaps my presence stops you
>   From freely pouring out your sorrow.
> *Donna Anna*: No, Father, my sorrow stays within,
>   When you are here, my prayers can rise
>   To heaven peacefully—I ask
>   That you join your voice with them. (80)

> *Дона Анна*: Опять он здесь. Отец мой,
>   Я развлекла вас в ваших помышленьях—
>   Простите.
> *Дон Гуан*: Я просить прощенья должен
>   У вас, сеньора. Может, я мешаю
>   Печали вашей вольно изливаться.

Дона Анна: Нет, мой отец, печаль моя во мне,
При вас мои моленья могут к небу
Смиренно возноситься—я прошу
И вас свой голос с ними съеднинть. (154)

The image of their prayers rising together recalls Laura's act of joining her music with Juan's poetry in the previous scene, again suggesting a duet.[37]

To be sure, Don Juan is only able to gain Anna's audience by disguising himself as a monk, but it is significant that she does not attempt to escape even as she notes that his speeches seem "strange" for a monk. This sets a pattern for the two scenes between them: Don Juan's gradual peeling away of disguises results not in her leaving, but in her invitation for further interaction. Upon his admission that he is not a monk but a nobleman, Don Diego de Calvado, she seems unconcerned about having her prayer disturbed and appears more worried that she will be seen with him as he speaks to her of love at the cemetery. She later actively encourages him to reveal the deepest layer of his disguise (that he is in fact Don Juan). The worse Don Juan's admissions become from a moral standpoint, the closer he comes to seducing her; following his confession that he is her husband's killer, she agrees to grant him a kiss and another rendezvous. Anna's protests against Don Juan's seduction seem so disingenuous as to only invite their continuation.[38] Her fears in Scene 4 that as a widow, she will not be able to entertain him are obviously groundless; her question of how he could be jealous of the Commander even seems flirtatious.

In this manner, Pushkin emphasizes Anna's active role in relation to Don Juan. Her boldness and initiative belie the notion that she is a naïve victim of Don Juan's seductive techniques and underline her role as a willing and eager participant, engaged in what Kropf terms her own series of "becomings": "While clearly not as active a libertine as, say, Laura, Donna Anna is not entirely a victim of Don Juan's seductive strategies" (28–29). Don Juan is first attracted, in effect, by her veil, out of which a "narrow heel" (uzen'kuiu p'iatku) appears, in the passage I referenced at the beginning of my introduction. This seductive glimpse of her feminine form induces Don Juan to try to uncover the rest of her image.[39] However, Anna performs the same act of unveiling in relation to him, questioning him about the evil deed on his conscience (his killing of Don Alvar). Pushkin views seduction not simply as an act of trickery and violence, as in previous Don Juan versions. He portrays it more as a dialogue, a cooperative process, and reveals this quality as much through Anna as through Laura. And as Boris Gorodetsky points out, this dialogue results in a kind of rebirth for Anna as well as Don Juan, since her obligations to the force of the grave, and of death, are overcome by the desire to live life anew (292–93).

Pushkin fleshes out Inez much less than he does the other two women. At first glance, her only role seems to be to underscore Don Juan's capacity for reminiscence, and therefore his similarity with Pushkin himself as a Romantic poet. However, because of the parallels Pushkin draws between her and the other two women, Inez also helps shape his larger portrait of male-female relations. For example, Don Juan mentions the "strange pleasure" (strannaia priiatnost') of her gaze, which recalls his description of Anna as a "strange widow" (strannaia vdova) for mourning her husband despite her youth and beauty. Pushkin's use of the word "strange," his focus on Don Juan's seeming obsession with both women, and his attraction to their deathly associations in each case indicate his interest in mystery and uncanny forces. Don Juan, significantly, has courted Inez from the same place—St. Anthony's Monastery—where he meets Anna.[40]

Pushkin also binds Inez to the other women through a "Spanish" motif. Unlike the Don Giovanni of Leporello's famous catalogue in Mozart/Da Ponte's opera, who loves women of all countries, Don Juan actually has a "type": he prefers dark-eyed Spanish women to the Northern "wax dolls" (kukly voskovye) whom he describes so disparagingly to Leporello at the beginning of the play. All three women are identified with these features (Anna's curly black tresses, Inez's dark eyes) or a predilection for the Southern climate and mentality (Laura, in the above-cited remonstrance of Carlos).

Most significantly, though, Inez endures the same kind of stifling relationship as the other women. Don Juan recalls Inez's death, possibly at the hands of her jealous husband, whom he characterizes as a "worthless wretch, and stern" (negodiai surovyi). In this manner, he describes Inez's husband similarly to Anna's Commander, who is "stern of spirit" (dukh imel surovyi), jealously keeping his wife locked inside and in effect depriving her of life. The same could be said of Don Carlos, who advises Laura to curb her youthful impulses to enjoy life and think of a future when her beauty will have faded. All three women are therefore attached to gloomy, foreboding older men who attempt to prevent them from engaging in creative self-exploration. Marriage and love relationships become prison houses, confining all three women, in Anna's case even after her husband's death. The monk, as a symbolic father, plays a similar role, acknowledging Anna's beauty but encouraging her to shut herself in the cemetery for prayer.

In this sense, Don Juan conspires with all three women, with at least their partial permission, to overcome their stultifying relationships.[41] Interestingly, Pushkin presents both Donna Anna and Inez as disembodied in some way: they are only visible through one feature, as Don Juan sees only Anna's heel, and recalls only Inez's eyes. Don Juan in effect pursues them not just for his own pleasure, but to free them from being mere parts of a whole and to entice them to reveal their entire physical and psychological selves. This pattern appears with Inez, whose overprotective husband forces Don Juan to spend three months courting her, and Anna, whose image—as Leporello points out—Don Juan is left to reconstruct from a glimpse of a single body part. It is even the case with Laura, whose true nature Don Juan "unveils" when he compels her to admit that she has consorted freely with other men in his absence. Thus, when Leporello accuses Don Juan of wanting to observe a widow's tears as he plans to woo Anna, he is mistaken in attributing motives of sadism to his master. To see Anna's tears involves a revelation of her true feelings, and the enactment of a continual dialectic of disguise, by which Anna and Don Juan *each* force the other into successive revelations of identity, personality, and feeling.

In short, Donjuanism in Pushkin's play turns out to be more of a shared role between the genders than a purely masculine one. Moreover, Don Juan is no longer simply a destroyer of women, but also a would-be liberator. In all three cases, he offers these women an opportunity to exchange their entrapment for a more joyful, life-affirming affair. However, his own attraction to deathly forces ensures not only his destruction, but possibly that of two of these women as well. Although Pushkin leaves the cause of Inez's death ambiguous, she is presumably murdered by her husband as a result of her affair with Don Juan. While it is not entirely clear exactly what happens with Anna, who faints at the Commander's entrance, critics such as Blagoi interpret her collapse as signaling her death; the Commander's vengeance, in this love triangle, is aimed at her as well as Don Juan (*Sotsiologiia tvorchestva Pushkina* 221). The tragedy of the play, perhaps, consists not only of Don Juan's destruction at the hands of his rival just as he has ostensibly been reborn in love for Anna. It is also that he ultimately fails in his efforts to help the women break out of deathly enslavement within their relationships.

For Pushkin, then, Donjuanism signifies more than seduction, even when it serves as an act of poetic creation. It offers possibilities of dialogue between men and women and a recognition that both genders can and even should engage in this activity of self-discovery and discovery of others. Pushkin was frightened to see the reflection of his own Donjuanism in women, of course, and the play thus serves in part as a reflection of his fearful premonitions of betrayal at the hands of his fiancée. But his artistic transformation of this anxiety through the attribution of Don Juan–like characteristics to his female characters, particularly Laura and Anna, paves the way for a deeper examination of women's nature and roles, and the shared terrain between men and women.

The Uncanny and Identity in *The Stone Guest*

The uneasiness Pushkin expresses regarding male and female roles, and their possible interchangeability, is part of a larger attempt to redraw the moral and ethical parameters of Donjuanism. If the moral crux of the Don Juan legend, as seen first in Tirso's play, is the protagonist's justified punishment for violation of the social and religious order, then Pushkin questions and reworks this issue of the direct cause-and-effect nature of retribution, transforming the notion of straightforward, Christian, morally satisfying vengeance on a libertine into a much more complex, inscrutable process.

In doing so, Pushkin makes an important revision to Mozart and Da Ponte's telling of the tale. *Don Giovanni* appears to affirm the certainty of divine vengeance, and the connection between eroticism and retribution, thus maintaining Tirso's moral center. Mozart included "Il Dissoluto Punito" ("The Rake Punished") as the opera's subtitle, and the statue of the Commendatore clearly acts as a symbol of divine justice, dragging Don Giovanni to hell after he refuses to repent. Mozart illustrates the inevitability of retribution musically as well, connecting the scene in which Don Giovanni kills the Commendatore in Act I with the appearance of the statue in the Act II finale by repeating segments of the earlier number. Da Ponte's libretto features the language of sin and repentance typical of the legend:

> *Commandant*: Penitence can still save you
>   Or face the final sentence.
> *Don Giovanni* (trying in vain to get free):
>   No, I despise repentance.
>   Off with you! Leave my sight! (103)

Giovanni's reaction to the flames of hell is similarly given in Christian terms:

> *Don Giovanni*: Limbs all aflame yet shivering . . .
>   Heart pierced with unknown agony . . .
>   Round me a void is quivering . . .
>   Can this be hell indeed? (104)

The concluding ensemble, in which the surviving characters sing, "the death of the perfidious always matches their life," also seems to confirm the inevitability of Don Giovanni's punishment and its Christian moral context. Moreover, Mozart/Da Ponte's foregrounding of Donna Anna's role from that of Tirso's play further unifies the opera around the theme of revenge, as she is driven by her anger at Don Giovanni for killing her father in a duel.

At the same time, Mozart and Da Ponte's presentation of this theme of vengeance weakens the original moral message considerably, leaving the justice of the retribution against Don Giovanni in doubt. It is unclear whether the Commendatore's revenge is proportional to the protagonist's crimes: since Don Giovanni does not actually seduce anyone successfully in the opera itself, the punishment is largely based on deeds that preceded the operatic narrative. For many listeners, the last number of the finale—left out of nineteenth-century performances of the opera—does not offer a satisfying moral. In addition, Da Ponte removes a great deal of the Christian content from previous versions, along with the accompanying focus on just retribution for sin, in part by mixing Christian and pagan motifs.[42] *Don Giovanni*, in short, maintains a Christian scaffolding but makes this framework less authoritative than it is in Tirso's play.

In *The Stone Guest*, Pushkin further complicates the relationship between sin and retribution in comparison with that of *Don Giovanni*. If Mozart/Da Ponte's denouement still focuses on the traditionally central issues of repentance and damnation, Pushkin completely divests the legend of its original Christian moral foundation. Unlike the Commendatore in *Don Giovanni*, who sends the protagonist down to the fires of hell, Pushkin's statue simply freezes Don Juan in his stony grip. Pushkin effectively eliminates any notion of justified retribution or cause and effect that characterized Tirso's play and *Don Giovanni*. Whereas Don Giovanni is forced to fight a duel with the Commendatore, Donna Anna's father, as he flees her quarters after attempting to seduce her, Pushkin's Don Juan has killed the Commander honorably in a duel (as Donna Anna herself points out) and has done so before ever meeting his wife. In addition, as Svetlana Evdokimova notes, Pushkin's finale contrasts sharply with Mozart/Da Ponte's in that it lacks a reconciliation scene (the final ensemble of *Don Giovanni*) that would give the audience some sense that vengeance had been properly carried out (134).

The aforementioned autobiographical aspects of the play cast further doubt on Don Juan's culpability and the justice of his punishment. Pushkin's likening of sexual seduction with artistic performance, as Kropf and Herman show, conveys his views on the poet's need for mobility and continually changing identities and his frustration with the restrictive society of Nikolaevan Russia. The irrepressible Don Juan traverses geographic boundaries (he refuses to remain in exile), moving from seduction to seduction and identity to identity. Unlike Don Giovanni's seductions, then, those of Pushkin's hero are far from merely erotic in nature: they indicate broader (and more sympathetic) aspects of his character. Moreover, given Pushkin's engagement to Natalia Goncharova at the time he was writing this play, many critics see evidence that Don Juan has similarly been reborn upon meeting Donna Anna, viewing his expression of love for her as a sincere awakening. This circumstance transforms his traditional justified retribution into a cruel, tragic fate. Although critics such as Jakobson and Akhmatova interpret vengeance as the statue's motive, many others find, rather, a complete absence of justified retribution. For this reason, Rassadin titles his chapter on *The Stone Guest* "Punishment without Crime" (Nakazanie bez prestupleniia), and does not think of Don Juan's fate as embodying vengeance: "The principal innovation of Pushkin's rethinking of the Don Juan theme is that there is simply no vengeance, if, of course, we understand it specifically as just vengeance, paying back good for good and bad for bad. Because in the given instance, vengeance would be inhumane" (241).

Through his alteration of the legend's traditional ending, Pushkin highlights the absence of divine order (where Mozart and Da Ponte reestablish it) and displays vengeance without cause. With its omission of the legend's traditional cause-and-effect moral message, *The Stone Guest* becomes more of a meditation on the return of the dead and of inexplicable destruction. Pushkin turns his focus to the eerie working-out of the secret, inexplicable, and personal fate of Don Juan in relation to the statue, to the return of the familiar and horrifying. In this sense, Don Juan's confrontation with the stone Commander exemplifies Freud's notion of the "uncanny," in which horror results not from an object's unfamiliarity, but from one's recognition of its familiarity. For Freud, "the uncanny is something which is secretly familiar, which has undergone repression and then returned from it" ("The Uncanny" 146). Don Juan evinces a curiosity to explore this secret that compels him to perform his blasphemous invitation. Rather than uncovering secrets from his own past, however, he seeks to cross the boundary of what is permissible in an effort to discover his linkage with the statue.

For this reason, the ending of the play, so different from Mozart/Da Ponte's dramatic dispatching of Don Giovanni to hell, points to an uncanny identity between Don Juan and the statue, a phenomenon that becomes crucial to future writers who recast the love triangle of *The Stone Guest* in their works. The jealousy Don Juan feels toward the Commander and his statue underscores a sense of identity with him that becomes increasingly apparent in the course of the play. As Jenny Stelleman remarks, "in no other version of the legend does Guan identify with the Stone Guest to such an extent" (505). Significantly, both of them are "guests," as Don Juan appears first as an uninvited guest in his homeland, then at Laura's house, and finally at Donna Anna's; in addition, Don Juan wishes to become marble, like the statue (Stelleman 504–5; 498). Don Juan issues his invitation to the statue right after receiving one himself, from Anna, to visit her the following evening. As Stelleman claims, the source of the identification can be traced to Don Juan's fascination with the statue's difference from his human form, and his recognition of this division in himself between his actual, human reality and the legend surrounding him: "the legend of Don Juan is, to Don Guan, a similar 'kamen" or stone: the realization (developed in the course of the play and intensified in scene IV) that the legend circulating about him detracts from his own unique Self and is in fact taking control of his Self" (505).

In keeping with this analysis of the hero's identification with the Commander, I would emphasize that Don Juan is not merely trying to imitate Don Alvar but also trying to *become* him. And this is where Pushkin's stage direction becomes very important, superseding Don Juan's consciousness and understanding of himself. The "falling through together," I would argue, indicates a symbolic identity of ostensible opponents, a joining together, as it were, of younger and older versions of the same figure.[43] Like Pushkin's encoding of himself into both male rivals, his stage direction hints at a merging together or even identification of the two with each other. Don Juan's duel with the Commander has immobilized his enemy, who is now represented by an immovable, inanimate statue. His invitation brings the statue to life, and the now mobile statue in turn paralyzes the Don with his grip. Pushkin thus gives prominence to Tirso's pattern of love triangles, as Don Juan appears to represent a younger, liberating force for Donna Anna, freeing her from her deathly widow's rites, but also functions similarly to the Commander, leading her to her downfall, just as he may have done to Inez. Significantly, Anna faints twice in Scene 4, each time at the "appearance" of one of the antagonists: when Don Juan reveals himself to be not Don Diego but Don Juan, and when the Commander enters. Though a would-be liberator of women, Don Juan in fact causes the destruction of two of the characters with whom he is involved and perhaps subjects Laura to risk as well, by fighting a duel with Carlos right in front of her. His attraction to life-affirming forces is countered by a fascination with death, which can be seen in his attraction to women with deathly features (Inez's lips, Anna's mourning veil) and in his fascination with the statue of a dead man. Paradoxically, even as Don Juan urges women toward greater freedom, in doing so he brings greater danger to them. Pushkin, worried on the eve of his marriage that he will have to confront a younger version of himself, shows an awareness of the essential similarity between seeming opposites: the young libertine will eventually become an avenging statue, and the avenging statue is a former young libertine. Thus, the melding together of the two figures signifies a symbolic unity between them.

Pushkin is not the first, perhaps, to express the horror of the familiar in the statue. *Don Giovanni*, indeed, famously uses musical means to express this terror, through the D-minor music that repeats from the Overture to the duel in Act I and, in its most dramatic form, with the statue's appearance in the finale.[44] However, the sense of surprising identity between two opponents appears to be Pushkin's invention, guided by the autobiographical elements cited above. This identity, as it turns out, is one of the elements that proves most fruitful for subsequent artists, and I will explore it in the following chapters. But I conclude this one with a discussion of Dargomyzhsky's 1869 opera *The Stone Guest*, one of the earliest examples of Pushkin's impact on future interpretations of the Don Juan figure. In its extension of several of the elements Pushkin brings to the legend—the sense of the uncanny, mostly through a recurrent motif Dargomyzhsky composes for the statue, as well as the exploration of female "masculine" behavior—Dargomyzhsky helps solidify Pushkin's innovations as canonical for Russian interpretations of the Don Juan theme. Because his operatic transposition was intended to replicate the little tragedy as accurately as possible, and because it represents a musical continuation of Pushkin's Romanticism, a discussion of it seems fitting as a conclusion for this chapter.

A Musical Transition: Dargomyzhsky's *The Stone Guest*

In the decades following his untimely death in a duel, Pushkin's reputation experienced something of a lull. After the strong reactions to his death, perhaps most notably Lermontov's "Death of a Poet" ("Smert' poeta," 1837), it took until the unveiling of the Pushkin monument in Moscow in 1880, with its various accompanying speeches, for the poet to attain universal recognition as Russia's central literary and cultural figure. Although Apollon Grigor'ev remarked in 1854 that "Pushkin is our everything" (Pushkin—nashe vse), the poet's reputation had actually reached a nadir in that decade. The 1850s and '60s saw a critical battle between nihilists such as Chernyshevsky and Dmitry Pisarev, who exalted the Gogolian school over Pushkin, and Pushkin sympathizers such as Grigor'ev, Alexander Druzhinin, and Mikhail Longinov, who considered Pushkin an ideal artist and called for monuments as a public means of showing respect for him. As Marcus Levitt notes, one of the major ways Pushkin's prominence was maintained in an era that featured relatively little literary criticism of his works was through the efforts of Russian composers, who created an operatic and lieder repertoire based on his texts (67). Dargomyzhsky, as the first composer to set one of Pushkin's little tragedies to music, was thus in the forefront of an effort to monumentalize the poet even before actual statues began to appear. This opera occupies a somewhat transitional aesthetic position, displaying qualities of Romanticism and Realism simultaneously: the composer's music is primarily Romantic in style, but his particular approach to Pushkin's text embodies a Realist trend in Russian opera.

Dargomyzhsky's role in this revival of interest in Pushkin during the 1860s took the form of an extraordinary musical experiment: a near-verbatim transposition of *The Stone Guest* into the libretto of his opera. This project was undertaken as an attempt to replicate Pushkin's written words with maximum precision and—through melodic recitative reflecting its spoken patterns as closely as possible—recreate how the lines of dialogue might have sounded as well. Through this manner of conveying Pushkin's text, Dargomyzhsky strove for a kind of musical realism. His lack of set pieces and minimal repetition of melodies (the music only repeats when the text does) also contribute to this realism. At the same time, the transposition into a musical medium and operatic genre by necessity considerably alters the play. Moreover, Dargomyzhsky's Realist aesthetic, its stated commitment to representing the "sound" of Pushkin's play as accurately as possible notwithstanding, in fact transforms the little tragedy in meaningful ways that go far beyond the pragmatic aspects of transposing a work from one medium into another.

As a radical experiment in musical Realism, Dargomyzhsky's project achieved a legendary status in its own right. Its unique response to the age-old question of the proper relationship between music and literature turned out to be highly consequential for Russian opera. *The Stone Guest* notoriously inspired fierce polemics rather than sober analysis in its early reception. Dargomyzhsky's near-verbatim transposition of Pushkin's play, with its continuous melodic recitative and near-absence of set pieces, led to misunderstandings of his musical style and approach to Pushkin's text. Opponents of the opera, and of the style identified with five composers known as the "Mighty Handful" (moguchaia kuchka), with whom Dargomyzhsky was affiliated, considered it an ill-fated experiment that overprivileged the role of text in relation to music. Tchaikovsky, most damningly, called *The Stone Guest* "an opera without music," that is, consisting solely of recitative (149).

Although this impassioned debate ultimately engendered productive discussion of the task, purpose, and possibilities of Russian opera, the participants' eagerness to follow their first impressions (and the *kuchkists*' own propaganda) without closely examining the opera itself, as Richard Taruskin has shown, obscured accurate understanding of its complex nature for many years. Following scant attention to Dargomyzhsky's opera in the first half of the twentieth century, critics in recent decades have analyzed its music-text interaction more closely. In doing so, they have helped untangle the myth created by Dargomyzhsky's followers and opponents alike, and shed light on the opera's actual nature. Taruskin, for instance, noting *The Stone Guest*'s fundamentally lyric qualities, aptly describes it as a "through-composed romance" (269), a highly lyrical type of melodic recitative. Avram Gozenpud points out that Dargomyzhsky includes more moments of reflectiveness and lyricism than Pushkin does, and that he renders Pushkin's spontaneous, flighty characters, Don Juan and Laura, considerably more meditative and sorrowful than in the play (288–94). Ekaterina Ruch'evskaia demonstrates that Dargomyzhsky's use of melodic accents and musical rhythm in many ways drastically departs from Pushkin's poetry, eliding the play's meter and rhythm.

Although the *kuchkists* considered Pushkin's little tragedies ideal source texts for operatic Realism because of their brevity,[45] which allowed a composer to transpose them into opera nearly verbatim, the plays represent intriguing objects of transposition for other reasons as well. Their laconic quality obviates the need for condensation that lengthier literary works demand, but Pushkin's sparse directions and narrative gaps offer tantalizing possibilities for expansion on the part of the composer as well. Both Dargomyzhsky and Nikolai Rimsky-Korsakov, in his *Mozart and Salieri*, supply ingenious set pieces for Pushkin's unspecified musical numbers in the respective plays. However, the tragedies' ambiguities—that is, plot events, gestures, and characterizations that seem incomplete or remain unresolved—demand even greater "coauthoring" by prospective composers. Thus, *The Stone Guest*'s elliptical quality, I would argue, encourages the kind of rethinking and development of Pushkin's conception that Dargomyzhsky undertakes in his opera.

My discussion of Dargomyzhsky's *Stone Guest* focuses on how he develops such ambiguous aspects of Pushkin's play. The composer picks up on and extends Pushkin's use of the uncanny in relation to the rivalry between Don Juan and the Commander; he also develops these conflicts to create greater psychological realism. The climactic, whole-tone statue motif represents Dargomyzhsky's vision of his place in musical history, reflecting both his anticipation of his own death and his rivalry not only with Pushkin, but also with Mozart (the original Don Juan opera composer) and Mikhail Glinka (the first composer, in *Ruslan and Liudmila*, to use the whole-tone scale in opera). Thus, memory operates on several levels in the opera: musical (rare but significant motifs), transpositional (from Pushkin), and rivalrous. At the same time, Dargomyzhsky, in the context of the 1860s' exploration of the woman question, extends Pushkin's ruminations on gender and marital roles through Laura's songs and Anna's vocal lines. Laura's inserted songs, in particular, which Dargomyzhsky fills in, extend Pushkin's examination of Laura's psychology, conflict, and performance of masculinity.

Dargomyzhsky and His Commander

Dargomyzhsky's famous whole-tone leitmotif suggests a constant, looming threat of death. Its fullest expression comes at the end of the opera, when the Commander arrives. This motif is an ascending and descending whole-tone scale associated with the statue's entrance. It is announced first in the trombones before it explodes into one of the few orchestral tutti passages in the opera. Used earlier in Glinka's *Ruslan and Liudmila*, it became known as the "Chernomor scale" that evoked the evil, the ominous, and the supernatural. This motif, however, appears in various other scenes, most fully when Don Juan and Leporello issue the invitation to the statue, but also in Don Juan's recollections of his duels with the Commander and Don Carlos and in his revelation of his true identity to Donna Anna. A hint of it can even be heard in Laura's music during her second song.

In this manner, Dargomyzhsky uses repetition to create a sense of the uncanny in his music. By the time we hear the Commander's motif, it is both familiar and unexpected. It thus recalls Freud's definition of the uncanny as evoking horror not from an object's unfamiliarity, but from one's recognition of something that is secretly known but has been repressed.

The sense of the uncanny, however, arguably extends beyond the boundaries of the score as Dargomyzhsky evokes three predecessors, each of whom he views as a rival: Mozart, Glinka, and Pushkin himself. Pushkin's ending is shocking in its abruptness, especially in relation to earlier versions of the Don Juan theme by Tirso, Molière, Mozart/Da Ponte, and others. However, Dargomyzhsky's *Stone Guest* also recalls two earlier opera composers. The most obvious, perhaps, is Mozart, whose inimitable D-minor music accompanying the statue's appearance and punishment of Don Giovanni was so familiar to music lovers in Russia. In addition, the use of the whole-tone scale in particular, which adds an ominous effect by weakening the sense of a tonal center, recalls Glinka's *Ruslan and Liudmila*. An audience familiar with previous Russian (and Don Juan) operas might reasonably have expected some frightening effect; thus Dargomyzhsky's finale is terrifying, yet also anticipated.

By incorporating elements of the Commander's motif into so many passages, Dargomyzhsky actively highlights Pushkin's continual comingling of Eros and Thanatos in the play, as all sexual encounters take place in the proximity of death (the Commander's grave, Carlos's dead body, and a widow's house). Musically, the Commander's motif represents not the threat of vengeance, but a more general, universal fatality hanging over all of the action. As such, it reflects the composer's own anticipation of death: perhaps identifying with Pushkin, preoccupied with the possibility of his own death, he referred to the opera as his "swan song."[46] However, it also alters Pushkin's autobiographical conception of a reformed Don Juan who, having finally experienced genuine love for the first time, is tragically destroyed on the precipice of happiness. Dargomyzhsky's characters, even more obsessed with memory and death than Pushkin's, seem doomed from the start, as underscored by the musical accompaniment and the statue motif in particular.

Gender in Dargomyzhsky's *The Stone Guest*

Despite the opera's focus on the hero, Dargomyzhsky also extensively explores the same ambiguity surrounding women as artists and seducers as in Pushkin's little tragedy. The most obvious example of this connection between women artists and Eros is his insertion of lyrics and music for Laura's songs in Scene II. On one level, this is a pragmatic move, as Pushkin gives no specifications about what songs Laura performs, leaving these choices to the imagination of the composer, director, or reader. Yet, these songs also reflect Pushkin's and Dargomyzhsky's respective interests in changing women's roles in nineteenth-century Russia.

Dargomyzhsky, of course, would have been well aware of the "woman question," with its advancement of the cause of equal social, marital, and professional rights for women. Moreover, his personal relations with women showed a great degree of egalitarianism and mutual respect. In the private rehearsals of *The Stone Guest* during its ongoing composition, singer Alexandra Purgold-Molas, who performed the roles of both Anna and Laura, made an indelible impression on the *kuchkists*, who nicknamed her "Laura" and referred to her as a coauthor of the opera (Gozenpud 296–97). As noted above, Pushkin himself explores this topic in several works. In *The Stone Guest*, this exploration is clearest in the figure of Laura, who seduces men not only sexually but also through her acting and music, and thus closely parallels Don Juan.

The pieces Dargomyzhsky writes to fill in Laura's songs are titled "Granada is Covered by Fog" ("Odelas' tumanom Granada") and "I'm Here, Inezilia" ("Ia zdes', Inezilia"). Since these songs are based on Don Juan's own lyrics, as I mentioned earlier, her performance can be interpreted as a kind of co-seduction of her guests. I will focus on the second of these two songs, which was originally a separate setting by Dargomyzhsky of Pushkin's poem "I'm Here, Inezilia," written only a week before *The Stone Guest*.

I'm here, Inezilia.
I'm under your window.
Seville is wrapped
in darkness and sleep.

Full of boldness,
my cape around me.
With guitar and sabre
I'm under your window.

Do you sleep? My guitar
will wake you up.
If the old man awakes,
I'll lay him down with my sword.

Hang your ropes of silk
from the window.
Why do you wait?
Is some rival there?

Я здесь, Инезилья,
Я здесь, под окном.
Объята Севилья
И мраком и сном.

Исполнен отвагой,
Окутан плащом,
С гитарой и шпагой
Я здесь, под окном.

Ты спишь ли? Гитарой
Тебя разбужу.
Проснется ли старый,
Мечом уложу.

Шелковые петли
К окошку привесь . . .
Что медлишь? . . . Уж нет ли
Соперника здесь? . . .

Since these lyrics are both Pushkin's and Don Juan's, Dargomyzhsky in effect imagines what the hero might have written. Inezilia, the object of Don Juan's affection, is a Spanish diminutive of Inez. This fact, combined with the reference to her "old man" feeling the sword if he awakes, accentuates Don Juan's continuing feelings for his deceased lover (as well as Laura's for Don Juan).

The playfulness of the expression (literally, "make him lie down again with my sword") accentuates Don Juan's verbal artistry, aligning the act of seduction with poetry. Further, the mention of a "rival" anticipates the following scene, in which Don Juan will appear at Laura's house and find Don Carlos in his way (Ruch'evskaia 144). In connection with Pushkin's love-death linkage, one can hear premonitions of the whole-tone motif. Here it is in the bassoon line, which in this passage is diatonic, not whole tone, but contains most of the same pitches and has similar rhythm and contours. The piece clearly displays Laura's fascination with masculine behavior. Her performance allows her to temporarily adopt her mentor's identity and gender and imagine what it is like to romance a woman. This imitation of Don Juan extends beyond the song, as Laura threatens Carlos with bodily harm and, after the party, seduces him despite his solemn warning against her frivolity. Dargomyzhsky clarifies that Laura has learned how to be Don Juan from the master himself, actively interpreting Pushkin through his added material. The composer's operatic filling-in of Pushkin's lacuna depicts Laura "performing" masculinity and linking her seduction to artistic performances, just as Don Juan does. The composer extends the poet's exploration of the possibility of reversing gender roles in art and sexuality.

Similarly, Dargomyzhsky's music for Anna reflects Pushkin's dual portrayal of her as a grieving widow and a coquettish if inexperienced young woman. Throughout Anna's vocal part, Dargomyzhsky uses musical means to emphasize her desire, agency, and collaboration with Don Juan. At several points, Don Juan and Dona Anna take over each other's music. During the rendezvous at Anna's house in Act III, her and Don Juan's vocal lines merge slightly, sometimes starting and ending with the same notes. Anna's leitmotif, which originally represents a widow's fidelity to her husband, is transformed into a more lush, passionate, chromatic line that resembles Don Juan's earlier music. In this manner, Dargomyzhsky interprets Don Juan's comparative ease in seducing Anna as evidence of her secret desires, communicated through a subtle transformation of the music accompanying her vocal lines.

Like the portraits of Laura and the Commander, these points of the opera showcase Dargomyzhsky's keen understanding of the play's ambiguous undercurrents and his ability to recognize and develop its relevance for his own personal circumstances and his era, with its increasing commitment to gender equality. As such, the apparent closeness of the opera to its source should not obscure Dargomyzhsky's innovations not only as a composer, but also as an interpreter of texts.

Although Dargomyzhsky's opera, with its melodic recitative, lack of set pieces, and minimal repetition, was considered an experiment in Realism, the term applies to the treatment of Pushkin's text rather than the opera's musical style. Musically, it can be considered part of the Romantic period, and as a setting of Pushkin, it heightens such elements as Don Juan's isolation as a hero, his romance with Anna, and the terror of the statue in ways that fit in with the Romantic rather than Realist aesthetic. In the following chapter, I analyze works by Ivan Goncharov, Lev Tolstoy, and Anton Chekhov that adapt the Don Juan subtext more to the mundane, everyday life on which Realist aesthetics focused.

2

Don Juan in Everyday Life
The Era of Realism

LIKE FAUST, Don Juan bears a special kinship to Romanticism. His rebellion against social and religious norms, in particular, enabled Romantic writers to refashion him into a lone, powerful, demonic genius on a quest for elusive knowledge and salvation. Don Juan's multiple conquests, reinterpreted as a search for an ideal rather than an unending series of ephemeral adventures, effectively transformed him from Mozart/Da Ponte's eighteenth-century libertine to the Romantic idealist of Hoffmann's 1813 story. It allowed Grabbe to combine elements of the Spanish legend with the Faust tale, creating a play in which Faust and Don Juan are rivals for the love of Donna Anna, the ideal woman. Along similar lines, Zorrilla's 1844 play concludes with Don Juan being redeemed from heaven by one of his deceased conquests, much as Goethe's Faust is saved through Gretchen's intercession. In this manner, Romantic writers in particular exposed a paradox that goes back perhaps as far as Tirso's first written version of the Don Juan legend: the moral imperative of showing the otherworldly punishment of sin threatens to be undermined by the reader's fascination with the hero's character and exploits.

Pushkin, as I discussed in the previous chapter, occupies a unique role in the Romantic evolution of the Don Juan legend. Aside from Byron's novel in verse, he was most likely unaware of contemporary Western European additions to the Don Juan literary catalogue.[1] Nevertheless, he took part in the period's reimagining of the pleasure-seeking libertine in a highly personal and innovative manner. Given Russian writers' unusual degree of responsiveness to one another, and to Pushkin in particular, it is not surprising that *The Stone Guest* created a remarkably fruitful field of possibilities for development by Realist writers who succeeded him. While the little tragedy continued the Romantic reevaluation of Don Juan, it simultaneously suggested directions for a

Realist approach to the theme, thus making Pushkin a transitional figure in the broader history of the legend.

Pushkin's interpretation of Don Juan as a poet and artist, his ruminations on gender and marital roles, and his creation of an uncanny relationship between rivals in a love triangle, in particular, were to varying degrees picked up on and developed by the writers I discuss in this chapter. His Realist successors further investigate these paths of inquiry, especially through their focus on contemporary questions of gender and politics. They also diffuse the Don Juan figure in their narratives by selecting particular elements that interest them, combining him with other archetypal figures, and treating the legend with irony by portraying Donjuanism as out of place or even clichéd in their time.[2] I trace the adaptation of these themes and motifs from the Don Juan legend in three late-nineteenth-century prose works: Ivan Goncharov's *The Precipice* (1869), Lev Tolstoy's *Anna Karenina* (1877), and Anton Chekhov's "The Lady with the Little Dog" (1899).

Romantic and Realist Don Juans

Not all nineteenth-century Russian writers on the Don Juan theme followed Pushkin's lead, partly because *The Stone Guest* (along with the poet's other little tragedies) was not perceived as particularly influential or performable in the two or three decades following Pushkin's death, and partly because of the comparative popularity of other Don Juan versions at this time. These included *Don Giovanni*, around which a cult had developed, and Hoffmann's story. Karpiak claims that "Russian Don Juan literature was decidedly in favour of the German example and consequently the majority of the Russian interpretations of the Don Juan myth in the nineteenth and early twentieth centuries are directly based on the Hoffmannian model of the hero" ("The Crisis of Idealism" 137).

Alexei K. Tolstoy's 1862 drama *Don Juan* heads a line of Russian works that show greater indebtedness to Hoffmann's story than to Pushkin's play, although the latter appears to influence it to some extent. Tolstoy's play is written mostly in blank iambic pentameter, the meter Pushkin used in *The Stone Guest*, and his hero's attraction to Anna's deathliness recalls the aforementioned fascination of Pushkin's Don Juan with death. Also, like Pushkin, Tolstoy places Don Juan at the precipice of happiness ("Oh, I will go mad with happiness" / O, ia s uma soidu ot schast'ia! ; 132) before he is cruelly deprived of it.[3] Don Juan acknowledges too late that he has fallen in love and, believing in Anna's goodness, declares that he believes in God, but he is killed by the statue nevertheless.[4]

These similarities with *The Stone Guest*, however, belie a more fundamental reliance on German sources. This influence can be seen immediately in the epigraph from Hoffmann and the "Prologue in Heaven" beginning the play, which recalls Goethe's prologue in *Faust*. Karpiak argues that, whereas Pushkin's version shares basic points with the established line of Don Juan versions by Tirso, Molière, and Mozart/Da Ponte, Tolstoy follows Hoffmann in making Don Juan a Romantic idealist rather than the Spanish trickster who is Pushkin's prototype. Tolstoy's presentation of the hero in the prologue ("How deeply he ponders, and how thoughtful he is at times!" / Kak razmyshliaet on gluboko, i kak zadumchiv on poroi! and "He is called to great feats and kind deeds" / On prizvan k podvigam i blagostnym delam; 46) portrays him as preoccupied by lofty goals of some sort, whereas Pushkin's Don Juan is sneaking back into Madrid simply because he misses his countrywomen. Don Juan's pursuit of Anna in Tolstoy's drama, far from revolving around simple seduction, functions as a kind of metaphysical test: will she turn out to be worthy of his romantic love? Moreover, as Margaret Dalton points out, as in Hoffmann's story, Tolstoy's Anna becomes the equal of the hero (131). Also as in the German work, the tragedy in Tolstoy is that Don Juan is incapable of seeing Anna's divinity and perfection until it is too late. Tolstoy's Hoffmann-inflected version of the Don Juan legend, as Karpiak shows, influenced the Don Juan versions of future Russian playwrights Alexander Mordvin-Shchodro (1896), A. N. Bezhetsky (1896), and Boris Zaitsev (1924), who similarly produced idealist heroes on a quest for a perfect feminine counterpart while in different ways rationalizing the supernatural punishment so as to remove elements that would conflict with the Realist aesthetic.[5] This lineage would seem to give Russian Donjuanism a decidedly Western ancestry, indicating a kind of reworking of the Hoffmannesque conception.

In this chapter, however, I propose that there is a concurrent Realist line of development that, rather than straightforwardly rewriting the Don Juan narrative, incorporates motifs from the legend into fiction that contains various other themes and subtexts. This line in fact tends to rework the legend through the prism of Pushkin's little tragedy rather than Western versions of the legend. The works of Goncharov, Lev Tolstoy, and Chekhov integrate the Don Juan theme into broader discussions of Realist preoccupations with such issues as the woman question, the superfluous man, and the general decline of the aristocratic class. In doing so, they transform the narrative into Realist art rather than simply continuing the Romantic line of interpretation. Whereas the aforementioned playwrights, as Karpiak remarks, fail to rework the Don Juan theme productively in their adaptations of Hoffmann's and Alexei K. Tolstoy's Romantic idealism into a Realist framework, the authors I focus on find ingenious ways to reconceptualize Pushkin's linking of art and seduction, and his tantalizingly ambiguous portrait of a man who may or may not have reformed through genuine love.[6]

Although archetypal figures such as Don Juan would appear better suited to the Romantic ethos than the Realist focus on everyday life, Russian Realist writers in fact often relied upon such figures for inspiration. Ivan Turgenev's "Hamlet of the Shchigrovsky District" from *Notes of a Hunter* and Nikolai Leskov's *Lady Macbeth of the Mtsensk District*, to take two well-known examples, each adapt Shakespearean characters into the realistic, contemporary milieu of provincial life. In fact, Pushkin's hero proved particularly adaptable in some ways to this Realist conception, because the poet's aforementioned focus on the seducer as artist, gender relations, and identity between apparently opposing figures translated easily from a Romantic framework to the ordinary, everyday life and psychologically three-dimensional heroes found in Realist writing.

The interest the Don Juan theme held for the Realist writers I analyze can be linked to momentous transformations taking place in Russian society and culture of the mid-to-late nineteenth century. Realist writers were working during the rise of the "woman question" in the 1850s and '60s, and displayed reactions to it in their works that ranged from supportive to dismissive. Chernyshevsky's 1863 novel *What Is to Be Done?*, with its program for the emancipation of women, played a central role in this movement, both in literature and in society, as thousands of Russian youth modeled themselves on the revolutionary heroes and heroine of the novel.[7] Connections can easily be made between the woman question and the Don Juan legend, which highlights a noxious form of masculinity involving the victimization of numerous women. At the same time, particularly in light of *The Stone Guest*, which features three unfaithful women, the Don Juan theme also brings to the fore the topic of female infidelity, and in the case of Laura, women who engage in serial relationships. This issue recalls Chernyshevsky's famous encouragement of his wife, Olga Sokratovna, to indulge her desires for other men, both during their marriage and in his absence after his arrest and imprisonment, and his dictum that the millennia-long double standard of the acceptance of husbands engaging in affairs while wives are castigated for them must be reversed: "after a stick has been bent for a long time, one has to keep it bent the other way for a long time in order to eventually straighten it out" (qtd. in Paperno, *Chernyshevsky and the Age of Realism* 111). The questioning of traditional women's roles in marriage and the workplace by Chernyshevsky, Mikhailov, Nikolai Dobroliubov, and women feminists such as Anna Filosofova, Nadezhda Stasova, and Maria Trubnikova had a great impact on other Realist writers. In two of the works I discuss in this chapter, Tolstoy and Chekhov each describe women who stray from stultifying marriages in an attempt to remedy not only a sexually unsatisfying relationship but also a dull life lacking in meaning and fulfillment.

The Don Juan legend also resonated with the ongoing decline of the aristocracy in wealth and prestige, which similarly preoccupied Realist writers. As I note in the introduction, Tirso's original written version of the legend critiques the noble class, particularly its male representatives. His Don Juan makes use of his noble status and privileges to undermine the order of his society, seducing married and engaged women and dueling with their husbands and fiancés. However, his destructive behavior is enabled by a complicit noble class, weak and ineffectual monarchs, and a gender code that renders women helpless and powerless. As I discuss in this chapter, Goncharov and Tolstoy in turn critique a nineteenth-century Russian aristocracy that was experiencing significant decline during the mid-nineteenth century, not only economically, but also in terms of their sense of purpose. The "superfluous man" type depicted by Turgenev, Goncharov, and other writers represents figures who, while talented, lack an outlet for their abilities. Raisky, the hero of *The Precipice*, surely fits this mold just as well as Goncharov's more famous Oblomov, and the novelist demonstrates that his hero's Donjuanism closely corresponds to his sense of superfluity and inability to succeed in his artistic vocation. Tolstoy, too, documents the decline of the aristocracy in *Anna Karenina*, partly in connection with Donjuanism. Perhaps the novel's main representative of the decline of the aristocracy, Stiva Oblonsky, who spends money on all sorts of luxuries despite being heavily in debt and, to his friend Levin's chagrin, sells his wife Dolly's forest to the merchant Riabinin for far less than its real value, may also be seen as a Don Juan figure, continuing to engage in affairs even after Dolly's discovery of his dalliance with their governess threatens his marriage. If for Pushkin, Donjuanism bears distinctly positive qualities associated with artistic creation, dialogue, and even rebirth, Realist writers view it instead in terms of the decay of Russian society caused by the selfish and destructive privileging of individual desires over the collective good. Thus, the foci of Realist writers dovetailed in surprising ways with the Don Juan theme, inspiring the authors I discuss to include the legendary seducer in their works.

In Defense of Don Juan: Goncharov's *The Precipice*

Goncharov finished his novel *The Precipice* in 1869, the year Dargomyzhsky died, with his own Don Juan project not quite complete. In contrast to the composer's replication of Pushkin's play in its entirety, Goncharov intersperses numerous Don Juan references with the myth of Pygmalion, which similarly features a statue coming to life. At the same time, he also combines Don Juan with other well-known Russian types of the nineteenth century, including the superfluous man and the nihilist "man of the '60s." In this section, I examine how Goncharov uses these other archetypes to transform Don Juan as a Russian figure. Following Pushkin's scheme, Goncharov creates a love triangle between a young woman, an artistic seducer, and a nihilist, in which the male opponents display remarkable similarities through their common desire to mold their would-be seducee.

The Precipice, the last of a trilogy of novels that also includes *An Ordinary Story* (*Obyknovennaia istoriia*, 1847) and *Oblomov* (1859), took Goncharov twenty years to complete, from 1849 to 1869. Its period of creation therefore spans the novelist's work on *Oblomov*, and in the political arena, the rise of nihilist ideology in the 1850s and '60s. Far more politically charged than Goncharov's other works, *The Precipice* is considered an anti-nihilist novel.[8] Despite its popularity with the reading public when it came out, it is considered significantly weaker than *Oblomov*, Goncharov's acknowledged masterpiece. Leftwing critics of the early 1870s panned *The Precipice* for its conservative tendencies (as did Soviet critics later, for similar reasons); [9] less ideologically biased critics have pointed out its melodramatic excesses and patchwork structure, among other aesthetic problems.[10] For my purposes, the novel's focus on art is of special importance. More than in any of his other works, Goncharov explores issues that, thanks to Pushkin, had become central to the Don Juan legend in Russia: the theme of becoming an artist, the intersection of art and seduction, and the relationship between art and life.

Goncharov's interest in the phenomenon of Donjuanism can already be seen in his early work "Ivan Savich Podzhabrin" (1848), a comic story with clear elements of vaudeville. Ivan Savich, a young civil servant, moves from one amorous adventure to another, continually repeating his refrain: "Life's short, as a philosopher said: you need to live it up" (Zhizn' korotka, skazal odin filosof: nado zhuirovat' eiu).[11] In the course of the story, he switches the objects of his seduction from a neighboring lady whose husband is away on a business trip to a maid and her lady, a baroness, and finally another neighbor who—together with her godfather—tries to rope him into a marriage that he escapes by moving to another apartment. The story, like *Oblomov*, includes a comical master-servant relationship; in this respect it also parallels Mozart and Da Ponte's Don Giovanni-Leporello pairing, as Ivan Savich's longsuffering servant, Avdei (who has his own comical refrain, continually responding to his master's impatient queries with "I don't know" [Ne mogu znat']), is forced to assist him in his sexual escapades. In another humorous passage that recalls *Don Giovanni*, Ivan Savich disguises himself as a fellow servant to woo the maid Masha, after which he drops his disguise to romance her mistress.[12]

The Precipice, by contrast, more closely recalls Pushkin in its focus on the relationship between Eros and art. However, there is a major difference in the way Goncharov depicts his Don Juan: in *The Precipice* the somewhat inclusive, mutually liberating relations of Pushkin's play give way to a greater emphasis on patriarchal attitudes toward women. The hero, Boris Raisky, is a talented novelist, painter, sculptor, and pianist, but also a dilettante who fails to complete works in any of his chosen media. Like his more lethargic predecessor, Oblomov, Raisky can be characterized as an impractical dreamer (the root of his name, "rai," is the Russian word for "paradise"). Following early, unsuccessful efforts to woo his second cousin, Sofia Belovodova, he travels from St. Petersburg to his provincial estate, Malinovka, managed by an old-fashioned, morally upright great aunt, Tatiana Markovna, affectionately known as "Grandmother." There, he falls in love with his much younger, distant cousin Vera, who returns his passion with coldness and bears a mysterious secret that Raisky sets out to uncover. Eventually he learns that Vera is in love with a nihilist named Mark Volokhov, who seduces her, leaving her shattered with remorse. Vera is comforted by Grandmother, who recounts her own, similar fall from innocence at a young age. She eventually marries a third competitor for her love, Ivan Tushin, an enlightened landowner neighbor. The novel concludes with Raisky leaving the estate for Rome, where he plans to continue his artistic pursuits, this time in the field of sculpture.

At first glance, Raisky typifies the "superfluous man" (lishnii chelovek). Neither an officer nor a civil servant, he has accomplished nothing of merit by the age of thirty-five. As he himself tells Vera, this malady is characteristic of the nation as a whole: "I should like to devote the remainder of my life to some extraordinary, enormous labor, but I do not seem capable of it—I am not prepared. We Russians have no real work to do!" (236).[13] In this sense he represents an artistically inclined version of the paradigm of heroes such as Turgenev's Rudin, Lavretsky, and the unnamed hero of "Diary of a Superfluous Man," as well as Goncharov's own Oblomov. The latter was famously interpreted by radical critic Dobroliubov as a literary apotheosis of the idleness, poetic but futile reveries, and stagnation of the typical Russian landowner. The traits of superfluous men, especially if the designation is retroactively applied to the eponymous hero of Pushkin's *Eugene Onegin*, Pechorin of Lermontov's *A Hero of Our Time*, and Chatsky of Alexander Griboedov's *Woe From Wit*, often coincide with those of the Byronic hero, with his jadedness, scandalous relations with women, and revolutionary tendencies. Along with aspects of both of these related archetypes, Goncharov also stresses Raisky's Don Juan-like qualities, which are at times connected to those of superfluous man and Byronic figures. Sofia explicitly compares Raisky to Chatsky, and Raisky defends himself by connecting the Donjuanism he is accused of with Byronism.

This defense encapsulates the tension between Raisky's behavior as perceived by others and his attempt to justify his Donjuanism by linking it to his artistic activities and world view. Raisky's behavior with women, to be sure, links him to the legendary seducer of multiple women. His main objects of passion, Sofia and Vera, are clearly two in a long list of attempted or successful seductions (in his youth, he was engaged to a girl named Natasha, who died of an illness). Multiple characters note this quality. Vera links his Donjuanism with the trickster qualities of the archetypal figure as well: "You're a fox—you're soft and sly. You lure your victims into the trap gently, cleverly, elegantly . . ." (321). Raisky defends himself against such accusations by justifying his pursuit of women as artistic in nature. In the first chapter of the novel, his friend Ivan Ayanov refers to him dismissively as a Don Juan, alluding to his courtship of Belovodova. Raisky responds defensively, characterizing his erotic desires as aesthetic rather than the empty, aimless motives Ayanov attributes to him: "One can get married once, twice, three times. Can't I enjoy the beauty of a woman the way I'd enjoy beauty in a statue? Don Juan's enjoyment of that need was primarily aesthetic, though it was also crude. A son of his times, education, mores, he was merely carried away beyond the proper limits of such devotion—that's all there is to it." (26) Another friend, the painter Kirilov, urges Raisky to devote himself more fully to art and to put aside his Don Juan–like pursuits: "Abandon your social rounds, your stupidities, your womanizing . . . close the curtains on the windows and shut yourself in for three or four months," he implores him (88).

However, for Raisky, the erotic and artistic represent two intertwined paths to beauty, or what Oleg Postnov refers to as "aesthetic Donjuanism" (185). Raisky insists that he is not merely womanizing but responding to artistic inspiration. In fact, his haphazard, impulsive approach to art resembles his amorous tendencies: "He rushed from one sensation to another, grasped phenomena, guarded impressions, and detained them almost by force, demanding food not for his imagination alone, but searching for something else, always trying to find something that would satisfy him" (83). Raisky generally evaluates women as material for his art, and in doing so, he objectifies them, treating them as the foci of his desire and material for his work rather than human beings on an equal level. In his conversations with Sofia, he does not so much try to learn more about her as find out her secrets for artistic purposes: "he was burning with the desire to find simply 'the woman' in her, to get at what was hidden beneath that tranquil, immobile shell of beauty" (31). Similarly, with Vera, he continually evaluates her in terms of inner layers that can reveal the truth he needs to create a novel (and later a statue) with her as the subject. Responding to the peasant girl Marina's story of her troubles with Savely, he views it as raw material for a drama and even wants to allow it to play itself out rather than solving the problem. Conversely, he is horrified at Grandmother's neighboring landlady Polina Kritskaya's attempts to seduce him because she is, as he puts it, "not even fit for a novel" (147). Here one can see both Raisky's aesthetic snobbery and his disdain for the notion of women playing the role of Don Juan. If Pushkin acknowledges and even celebrates the capacity of women to choose partners and seduce men, or at least to play an active role in their own seduction, Goncharov's hero accepts the patriarchal notion of women as passive objects of men's attention and rejects any sort of gender equality.

The intertwining of the erotic and artistic urges, however, links Raisky closely to Pushkin's hero, whose speeches embody a type of poetic, improvisatory seduction. Goncharov builds on Pushkin's transformation of Don Juan as a lover reborn through his passion for Donna Anna. Moreover, Raisky's sense of himself as an internal exile, his restless travels, his changeability, and his affirmation of genuine love for each woman are clear markers of Donjuanism as mediated through Pushkin.

Thus, in his conversations with Vera, Raisky repeatedly attempts to prove the uniqueness of his appreciation of her, much as Pushkin's Don Juan does in relation to Donna Anna. Evoking the aforementioned exchange with Ayanov, Vera reproaches Raisky with following "the path of Don Juan," to which Raisky responds: "The genuine Don Juan is pure and beautiful; he is a humane, subtle artist, a chef d'oeuvre among men. There are, of course, few like him, and I'm sure that an artist was wasted in Byron's *Don Juan*" (282). Raisky's declaration of his desire to marry Vera, however, is met with complete skepticism, as seen in the following conversation between them:

> "Tell me how many times you've said those very same words. Haven't you said them to every woman at every encounter?"
>
> "What is it you want to say with these questions, Vera? Perhaps I've said this to many, but never so sincerely." (282)

This conversation recalls the exchange in *The Stone Guest* in which Don Juan tries to persuade Donna Anna, who suspects that he has tried this approach before, that his intentions are sincere:

Donna Anna: How many poor women
  Have you ruined?
Don Juan: Not a single one of them
  Did I love till now. (91–92)

Дона Анна: Сколько бедных женщин
  Вы погубили?
Дон Жуан: Ни одной доныне
  Из них я не любил. (169)

Goncharov not only adapts Pushkin's poetic language of seduction to his Realist, novelistic context but also underscores the connection between Don Juan's passion and his artistic creation. In Pushkin's play, Don Juan's captivation with Anna is first inspired by a glimpse of her narrow heel, leading Leporello to compare him to a portrait painter. Like Pushkin's Don Juan, Raisky experiences love in conjunction with imagination and creativity. Thus, Goncharov takes as a starting point one of Pushkin's departures from Mozart/Da Ponte's *Don Giovanni*, following the poet by interpreting Don Juan as an artist rather than simply a lustful seducer. The legendary Don Juan's dismissive regard for marriage is attributed instead to Volokhov, who seduces Vera but refuses to marry her because of his typical nihilist disdain for social conventions.[14]

Raisky's Don Juan-like wooing of women, however, is simultaneously linked to the Pygmalion legend from Book Ten of Ovid's *Metamorphoses*, in which Pygmalion carves a pure, virginal ivory statue, falls in love with it, and—through Venus's intercession—brings it to life as a flesh-and-blood woman named Galatea. In *The Precipice*, this theme appears early in the novel in Raisky's pursuit of Sofia Belovodova, as he seems more concerned with penetrating her tranquil armor and exciting her passion than physically seducing her. He tells her: "My desire is to awaken you. You are sleeping, not living" (37). He has a dream-like vision of a woman's figure with Sofia's face, resembling a "white, cold statue" (282). In his painting of her portrait, he hears a voice telling him to breathe life into art and changes her facial features. We find out that the same had been true of Raisky's earliest love, Natasha, whom he had tried to make into his ideal. In fact, Raisky had been bored by her, and his confidence that she was attached to him was, as the narrator puts it, "the beginning of the degeneration of his happiness" (81). Only by a Pygmalion-like shaping of her into an ideal woman is he able to maintain an interest in her.[15] In this manner, Goncharov significantly alters Pushkin's portrait of the Don Juan figure to make him much more patriarchal in his attitudes. If Pushkin depicts Don

Juan as a collaborator of sorts with women (he supplies the lyrics for the songs Laura performs for her guests) who appreciates them for their inner nature, Goncharov portrays Raisky as a Don Juan who sees women only as raw material for him to transform.

The pattern of "shaping" women continues when Raisky leaves Petersburg for his country estate. In defending his love for Vera as unique, Raisky refers to Sofia as a cold, beautiful, lifeless statue that only Pygmalion could love. However, he applies the same metaphor to Vera several times, referring to her as a "statue" and bemoaning her "marble indifference" (227). Seeing her waiting for Volokhov at the precipice, he envisions her transformation, under the influence of her love for the nihilist: "She stood on her pedestal, not as a statue of white marble; rather she stood there as an irresistibly captivating, lively woman" (344). Raisky recalls that he had the same vision of Sofia, but by now Vera has completely replaced her as an object of beauty and artistic perfection. Following his discovery of Volokhov's seduction of her, Vera continues to serve as the inspiration for his novel, which he refers to as his "statue," and dedicates to women (416–17). Raisky's interest in Vera recalls Girard's concept of mediated desire, as it appears to derive as much from his rival's hold over her as from her own qualities. However, following his dream of a statue, Raisky is inspired to go to Rome, and forswears his novel-in-progress, intending instead to produce a sculpture of Vera there. As Ilya Kliger notes, from the novel's beginning to its conclusion Raisky largely remains unchanged, "retracing again and again the same path from artistic inspiration to abandonment of the project and from erotic infatuation to boredom" (667).

Although Volokhov, as the nihilist who seduces Vera, would seem to function solely as the hero's opponent, Goncharov in fact structures his relationship to her to somewhat resemble Raisky's by connecting Volokhov to both the Don Juan and the Pygmalion themes. Volokhov "doubles" Raisky as a Don Juan, using political rather than aesthetic ideology to seduce her.[16] By persuading Vera to abandon her traditions, rules, and convictions—accepting his own attitude toward love as something fleeting and temporary—he in effect combines nihilist opposition to romantic love with Don Juan's traditional notion of love as impermanent and view of women as objects to be seduced and then abandoned. Goncharov applies the Pygmalion myth to Volokhov in this manner as well. For Volokhov, Vera is also a type of "statue" in the sense of unformed material, except that instead of merging love with art, he tries to transform her politically. Goncharov makes this similarity explicit late in the novel in the narrator's description of Volokhov's thoughts: "And for him too, as for Raisky, she was a kind of beautiful statue" (341). Thus, Goncharov reveals the common ground between the two myths, underscoring a broader fascination, shared with Pushkin, with the idea of stone taking on a living form, especially in response to a human summons. Moreover, he recalls Pushkin's symbolic fusion of opponents in the statue's grip of Don Juan's hand and the stage direction "they fall through together." Just as both Don Juan and the Commander ultimately represent lethal forces for Anna, who either faints or dies at the statue's appearance, invoked by Don Juan, Raisky and Volokhov similarly both "freeze" Vera by trapping her in the role of marble figure to be enlivened by an artist (in the case of Raisky) or as raw material to mold with nihilist propaganda (in the case of Volokhov).

Here, as part of the anti-nihilist aspect of *The Precipice*, Goncharov seems to parody Chernyshevsky's love triangle in *What is To Be Done?* The heroine's name, perhaps, recalls Vera Pavlovna, the emancipated woman of *What is To Be Done?* But whereas the "new men" of Chernyshevsky's novel, Dmitry Lopukhov and Alexander Kirsanov, each help Vera Pavlovna advance and find self-fulfillment and equality in a male-dominated society (through a fictitious marriage to help her escape an arranged marriage and by helping her gain access to medical courses, respectively), Goncharov's male characters repress Vera through successful or unsuccessful attempts at seduction.

Both the Don Juan and the Pygmalion legends thus also relate to the woman question, although this issue does not seem to have preoccupied Goncharov as much as it did other Russian writers of the 1860s. Just as Pygmalion brings the statue Galatea to life, Pushkin's Don Juan similarly lifts Donna Anna from a state of widowhood and preoccupation with death into awareness of her sexuality, thus metaphorically breathing life into her. Both figures engage in an artistic act of seduction, creating living, sexual beings. But the act of creation is also an act of coercion, as the male figures control women through creativity, passion, and seductive power. Galatea cannot come to life without Pygmalion sculpting her and summoning her to life through prayers. Similarly, Don Juan of *The Stone Guest* and Raisky and Volokhov of *The Precipice* decide when to seduce and abandon women according to their personal whims. For too long, as Hélène Cixous argues, women have been in a state of sleep, passive creatures waiting for men to awaken them: "She sleeps, she is intact, eternal, absolutely powerless. He has no doubt that she has been waiting for him forever. The secret of her beauty, kept for him: she has the perfection of something finished. Or not begun" (66). Like Don Juan, Raisky and Volokhov seek complete control over the women they attempt to seduce, fashioning them according to their own desires.

In different ways, however, Pushkin and Goncharov each highlight the futility of this impulse. In *The Stone Guest*, Don Juan's old flame Laura frankly admits to having cheated on him with other men; in *The Precipice*, Sofia and

Vera similarly resist Raisky's attempts to recreate them in his ideal image and seduce them. In all of these cases, women respond differently than expected, asserting their own desires and drives. Like Pushkin, Goncharov uses the Don Juan legend to explore feminine sexuality and agency in women's own relationships. This exploration is particularly prominent in two other female characters of the novel. Polina Kritskaya plays a Don Juan-like role herself, seducing men not through actual sex but simply by attracting them sexually, with no intention of following through. During Raisky's visit to Grandmother as an adolescent, Kritskaya kisses him and tells him he will have many conquests in the future, beginning with her. Raisky's friend Leonty's wife, Uliana Andreevna, woos Raisky with much more serious intentions. He resists at first, but ends up being seduced by her.

Goncharov thus transforms the Don Juan legend—from the archetype of a heartless seducer and trickster who reaps an appropriate punishment and also from Pushkin's reworking of Mozart/Da Ponte's protagonist into a Romantic poet. Raisky is an artistic Don Juan whose desire for erotic gratification is inextricable from his spiritual ideals, which can be achieved only through the creation of art inspired by female beauty. The linking of Donjuanism with Raisky's Pygmalion-like desires to transform women reinforces Goncharov's change of emphasis from seduction to artistry. At the same time, his doubling of Raisky and Volokhov recalls the violence of the legend, as Volokhov's seduction is described unequivocally as a destructive force leading to Vera's spiritual and ideological disillusionment.

Pushkin, in his little tragedy, suggests that Don Juan can be either a creative, life-affirming force or one that is destructive and death-seeking—or perhaps both at once. His hero's appearances serve as invitations for Laura and Donna Anna, respectively, to abandon the gloomy, foreboding Don Carlos and the widow's obligation of mourning. At the same time, Don Juan's fascination with death pervades all his interactions with women, from his elegiac memories of the pensive, mournful Inez to the fateful encounter with the statue during his tryst with Donna Anna. Goncharov interprets this force negatively: Donjuanism in *The Precipice* leads either to violence or aesthetic failure. Whereas in *The Stone Guest* women play a more collaborative role in both art and romance, Goncharov portrays seduction as a one-sided means to artistic creation. Moreover, Raisky's perpetual quests for aesthetic revelation through women, far from allowing him to achieve fulfillment, lead to artistic and personal dead-ends. His painting of Sofia Belovodova appears to Kirilov, a genuine, singularly devoted artist, to be the image of a prostitute rather than a lofty ideal. His novel—which parallels the one that Goncharov actually writes—never comes to fruition. Instead, Raisky gives up on it and decides to go to Rome and sculpt

Vera. Based on his previous artistic failures, the reader is left with little doubt that this quest will come to nothing as well. Donjuanism, for Goncharov, thus represents not only dangerous, unchecked eroticism and violence but also yet another path to superfluity. Like Pushkin, then, Goncharov enters into a uniquely Russian exploration of the meaning of Donjuanism, and in doing so raises broader questions involving the interrelationship of art, seduction, and gender.

The remaining writers I discuss in this chapter, Tolstoy and Chekhov, differ from Goncharov in two important ways. First, the works I analyze, Tolstoy's *Anna Karenina* and Chekhov's "The Lady with the Little Dog," do not focus on the Don Juan legend as directly as *The Precipice*. Tolstoy alludes to it in his opening chapter, in which Stiva recalls an aria from *Don Giovanni*, and Chekhov does not refer to his hero, Dmitry Gurov, explicitly as a Don Juan figure. However, I find an underlying rewriting of *The Stone Guest* in both the novel and the story as each writer incorporates motifs from the little tragedy into the structure of his work. Specifically, both writers recreate Pushkin's love triangle of Don Juan, Donna Anna, and the Commander in the context of a Realist plotline involving everyday life. Moreover, as I will argue, Tolstoy's and Chekhov's respective portraits of Pushkin's Anna character ultimately contribute to the establishment of a new female "type" in Russian Realist literature, giving the Don Juan legend unanticipated ramifications for literary history. The very indirectness of Tolstoy's and Chekhov's use of the theme, perhaps, allows them to discover surprising ways in which Donjuanism relates to other currents in Realism.

Don Juan and Erotic Anxiety in Tolstoy

Similarly to Goncharov, Tolstoy explores the intersection of art, seduction, and the woman question through the Don Juan legend in *Anna Karenina*. However, in contrast to Goncharov's meditations on the impotence of the artist in his depiction of Raisky, Tolstoy, while continuing to investigate the relationship between the erotic and the aesthetic, focuses more on the moral implications of the theme for his nineteenth-century aristocratic milieu. For Tolstoy, unlike for Goncharov, Donjuanism does not just embody superfluity but also signals a moral downfall for Russia and is connected to an apocalyptic sense of the self-destruction that he feared the nation was about to undergo.

Tolstoy alludes to the Don Juan theme almost immediately in *Anna Karenina*, which famously opens with Stiva Oblonsky, banished to the couch for betraying his wife with a French governess, awakening from a dream. He recalls a party: "Yes, Alabin was giving a dinner on glass tables, yes—and the tables were singing *Il mio tesoro*, except it wasn't *Il mio tesoro*, but something better, and there were some little decanters and they were women" (2).[17] Stiva's initial recollection of an aria from *Don Giovanni* opens up a number of interpretive possibilities, as it points to his own Don Juan-like behavior, Tolstoy's broader interest in the role of opera in Russian aristocratic society, and this particular aria's eerie resonance with the novel's epigraph, "Vengeance is mine; I will repay" (1).[18] "Il mio tesoro," sung in Act II of the opera by Don Ottavio, Donna Anna's fiancé, announces the vengeance he is about to seek on her behalf: "Tell her I go to serve her, Tell her I shall avenge her! To him who made her suffer, Justice and death I bear!" (92).[19] The Don Juan theme, with its interconnected themes of sensuality and vengeance, thus echoes Tolstoy's epigraph, and simultaneously prefaces the main plotline involving the heroine, whose life and death revolve around these themes.

Stiva's dream, with its reference to "Il mio tesoro," would seem to indicate Tolstoy's moral disapprobation of Donjuanism, especially in light of his obsessive focus on adultery in *Anna Karenina* and elsewhere. Observing Tolstoy's frequent linkage of Stiva to his fellow libertines Vronsky (before his relationship with Anna) and Vasenka Veslovsky reinforces this conclusion. Moreover, the way Tolstoy structures the novel, at least in the early chapters, to an extent reflects the comic-tragic ambiguity of Mozart and Da Ponte's opera. Stiva's primarily comic adultery plot, resulting in his reconciliation with Dolly, is followed by Anna's adultery, which entails far more serious consequences for her marriage and leads to her tragic fate. The latter parts of the novel, like *Don Giovanni*, similarly mix tragedy and comedy, using the same characters. Rather than simply ending with Anna's suicide, Tolstoy follows it with an eighth part in which Stiva receives his coveted railway position.[20]

I would argue that Tolstoy's fleeting reference to *Don Giovanni*, however, is in fact the first of several Don Juan motifs focusing on the relationship between sexuality and retribution that can be found in *Anna Karenina*. Tolstoy, in my view, reads the Don Juan theme both through Pushkin's reworking of it in his little tragedy and through *Don Giovanni*.[21] Although he makes no explicit textual references to *The Stone Guest*, the portion of *Anna Karenina* involving the heroine displays significant parallels to Pushkin's play. Tolstoy's heroine deceives a stodgy older husband, just as her namesake, the widow Donna Anna, is about to betray the Commander's memory at the end of *The Stone Guest*. Following Pushkin's plot further, *Anna Karenina* features a love triangle between Anna, the rigid, Commander-like Karenin, and the younger, womanizing Vronsky, who experiences a serious romance for the first time in his life, as Pushkin's serial seducer claims to do. Thus the allusion to "Il mio tesoro" serves to introduce the general theme of Donjuanism, but it also prefaces a deeper, more complex investigation of it as a specific phenomenon in relation to *The Stone Guest* that takes place elsewhere in the novel.

Tolstoy's approach to the Don Juan theme in *Anna Karenina* therefore goes beyond the simple condemnation of debauchery that one might expect from him, venturing into a complex intertextual exploration. Further, the novelist's references to these particular texts are somewhat surprising in view of his notorious critique of both opera and drama as genres. Tolstoy judged opera in particular to be a false genre, which in its very combination of different art forms ran counter to his aesthetic principles.[22] However, Tolstoy actually loved *Don Giovanni* more than any of Mozart's other works, delighting especially in the duel between Giovanni and the Commendatore, the peasant wedding, and the appearance of the statue in the finale (Gusev and Gol'denveizer 22–23). Tolstoy praised Pushkin's little tragedy highly as well. In a June 5, 1856, letter to his sister Masha, he reports after reading the play: "I was so delighted that I wanted to write at once to Turgenev about my impressions" (58). Moreover, the letter indicates that—a decade and a half before beginning *Anna Karenina*—he was already thinking of *The Stone Guest* in relation to Mozart and Da Ponte's opera, as he concludes by asking Masha to send him a grand piano and music for four hands, including *Don Giovanni*.[23]

In the extensive critical literature on Pushkinian subtexts in *Anna Karenina*,[24] the poet's little tragedies have received scant mention.[25] However, in light of this letter and Tolstoy's rereading of Pushkin in the early 1870s, which undoubtedly included these plays, one may reasonably consider *The Stone Guest* a second Don Juan subtext, alongside *Don Giovanni*. Moreover, the aforementioned plot parallels in *Anna Karenina* revolve around some of the very elements that Pushkin transformed most extensively from Mozart/Da Ponte's version of the Don Juan legend. Therefore, although there is no concrete evidence that Tolstoy was referring to *The Stone Guest*, I argue that he likely had this little tragedy in mind as well as the opera.[26] Tolstoy uses Mozart and Da Ponte's and Pushkin's varying treatments of Don Juan as a starting point for his own focus on the interconnection of illicit sexual love and inexorable vengeance.

If the moral crux of the Don Juan legend is the protagonist's justified punishment for violation of the social and religious order, then Mozart/Da Ponte, Pushkin, and Tolstoy each successively question and rework this issue of the direct cause-and-effect nature of retribution, gradually transforming the notion of straightforward, Christian, morally satisfying vengeance on a libertine into a more complex, inscrutable process. *Don Giovanni* affirms the directness of divine vengeance and the connection between eroticism and retribution, dramatized in the finale when the protagonist meets with his inevitable punishment for a sinful life. Moreover, Mozart and Da Ponte's use of Donna Anna (included in Tirso's play but not Molière's) further unifies the opera around the theme of revenge, as she is driven by her anger toward Don Giovanni for killing her father in a duel.[27] This emphasis is reflected in Tolstoy's novel, as vengeance—beginning with the epigraph—becomes one of the main themes of *Anna Karenina*. Nevertheless, as discussed in the previous chapter, Mozart and Da Ponte in many ways also weaken this sense of deserved vengeance. The concluding ensemble, in which the surviving characters sing, "the death of the perfidious always matches their life," actually confirms their banality in comparison to the towering figure of Don Giovanni as much as any satisfactory moral lesson. Pushkin, in *The Stone Guest*, further complicates the relationship between sin and retribution found in *Don Giovanni*, divesting the legend of its original Christian moral foundation. In the mysterious ending, he removes whatever notion of justified retribution, or cause and effect, was retained in the opera, making his hero's punishment even harder to justify than his predecessor's. Pushkin's autobiographical allusions further work to vitiate any sense of divine justice in Don Juan's destruction.

In the analysis that follows, I discuss how such aspects of *The Stone Guest* as the protagonists' appearance and behavior, the triangular relationship of Don Juan, the statue, and Donna Anna, and especially Pushkin's portrayal of vengeance reappear in *Anna Karenina*, shaping the plotline involving Anna, Vronsky, and Karenin. This adaptation of motifs from the play is far from straightforward. In the course of recasting Pushkin's Romantic plot and characters into a Realist, psychological novel, Tolstoy disseminates motifs from the play rather than applying them exclusively to one character or another. Although Anna generally recalls her namesake, she also to some extent plays the role of Don Juan. Indeed, as Pushkin demonstrates, Donna Anna herself, who plays an unusually active role in her own seduction, takes on some characteristics of her seducer, and this unusually active role seems to have influenced Tolstoy.

The relationship between Anna and Vronsky is patterned in important ways on the dynamic Pushkin creates between Don Juan and Donna Anna. The poet's daughter Maria Gartung, whom Tolstoy met in 1868, is said to have inspired Anna's physical features. However, there are key resemblances between his protagonist and Donna Anna as well. Don Juan refers to Donna Anna's "long black tresses" (80) and "ringlets" (82), which resemble Anna Karenina's own curly black hair. Tolstoy also recreates the mourning Donna Anna's black veil. His heroine's lively gray eyes are partially concealed by her long lashes, and she is described several times as wearing an actual veil, for instance when meeting Vronsky in Part III to tell him that Karenin knows of their affair.

The veiling of the heroines is more than a mere physical trait; it also signifies a parallel of character. Anna Karenina, like her Pushkinian predecessor, is unable to conceal or control her liveliness and sexual energy. In both cases, this energy seems to have been stifled in part through arranged marriage to an older man. Upon seeing Anna for the first time at the railroad station, Vronsky is struck by the irrepressible liveliness that involuntarily emanates from her: "It was as if an abundance of something so overflowed her being that it expressed itself independently of her will, now in the radiance of her glance, now in her smile. She had deliberately extinguished the light in her eyes, but it shone against her will in her barely perceptible smile" (63). This brief encounter tantalizes Vronsky, compelling him to pursue Anna first by dancing with her at the ball, then by following her back to St. Petersburg, much as Don Juan's glimpse of Donna Anna's heel is enough to spark his imagination in *The Stone Guest*.

At the same time, both Pushkin and Tolstoy assign an unusual degree of agency to the female protagonist in her own downfall. In each work, the younger man opens up an unfamiliar world of sexuality and self-determination to the woman he seduces; neither Donna Anna nor Anna Karenina is sufficiently equipped to deal with this newfound freedom. Both heroines struggle with guilt over their betrayal, and in both cases, their compunction is overcome by growing desire. As I discuss in chapter 1, despite Donna Anna's efforts to conform to societal expectations of a widow's behavior, she is eventually persuaded rather easily by Don Juan to arrange a rendezvous, and even grants him a kiss right before the statue appears. Anna Karenina, too, becomes increasingly drawn to Vronsky throughout their courtship, even as she appears to postpone the consummation of their affair, which takes place almost a year after they meet.

Tolstoy further develops this motif of female-driven seduction, as Anna undermines her reprimands of Vronsky's behavior with gestures and expressions that in fact encourage him. At Princess Betsy's salon, Anna, ostensibly chastising Vronsky for hurting Kitty, expresses something completely different through nonverbal cues: "'That only proves that you have no heart,' she said. But her eyes said that she knew he had a heart, and that was why she was afraid of him" (141). Ultimately, this conflict between words and gestures convinces Vronsky that he should continue pursuing her:

> She did her utmost to focus her mind in order to say what ought to be said, but in place of that she brought her love-filled gaze to rest on him and did not answer.
>
> "There it is!" he thought jubilantly. "Just when I was beginning to despair, and thought there was no end in sight—there we are! She loves me! She is admitting it!" (142)

Thus, Anna in many respects drives the affair; she wordlessly signals her interest in Vronsky, knowing that these signals will supersede her more appropriate verbal statements. In light of her active role in the seduction, Girard's concept of mediated desire plays a role less in Vronsky's pursuit of her than in her pursuit of him, as she sets the affair in motion not at the train station where they meet, but at the ball at which she reluctantly appears. Despite this initial reluctance, Anna becomes Kitty's rival for Vronsky at the ball, attracting him despite her ostensible efforts to cede the central role to her younger friend. Kitty's enchantment with Anna quickly turns to horror as she realizes that Vronsky has fallen for her. Anna's attraction to Vronsky may stem to an extent from Kitty's interest in him, and her envy of Kitty's youth and period of courtship—a ritual that she was deprived of by her arranged marriage to Karenin.

Vronsky, for his part, clearly displays characteristics of the Don Juan type.[28] He has had many lovers in the past, as his old friend Serpukhovskoi notes in Part III, and takes pleasure in turning the heads of young ladies such as Kitty. His bold but patient seduction of Anna recalls Don Juan's success with Donna Anna. During the courtship phase, he displays a typical libertine's "total command of the special code that constitutes the 'wordless language of love'— gestures, expressions, and actions that presumably communicate emotions and states of mind" (Goscilo, "Tolstoy, Laclos, and the Libertine" 401). This role is, of course, perfectly acceptable as a type of masculinity in Vronsky's circle, although it clashes with the perceptions of Kitty's family; Princess Shcherbatskaya thinks that Vronsky's attention to her daughter signifies a desire for marriage.

At times, though, Vronsky comes across less as a Don Juan than as an actor playing one. He appears to be a character continually in search of a role, trying out the parts of rake, military man of honor, bohemian artist, and husband and father, among others, at various points of the novel.[29] In this sense, Vronsky, like Goncharov's Raisky, represents a linking of traits of Donjuanism and the superfluous man type. In particular, Tolstoy adapts Pushkin's portrait of Don Juan as a poet-seducer in order to stress the debasement of these qualities— considered fashionable during the Romantic period—in his own time. Don Juan in *The Stone Guest* is a consummate improviser who can tailor his poetic performances to each unique audience, and always expresses himself eloquently. In Vronsky, though, Tolstoy transforms Pushkin's original poet and improviser into an imitative painter who can only mimic Renaissance styles. Vronsky therefore contrasts both with Tolstoy's ideal, genuine artist, the painter Mikhailov, who is able to create the artistically convincing portrait of Anna that her lover cannot, and with Pushkin's poetically resourceful Don Juan.

Moreover, Vronsky lacks precisely Don Juan's artistry of language. If for Pushkin poetry and seductive language are interlinked, Tolstoy's libertine becomes an imitative artist of the word as well as the brush. His seduction of Anna is characterized not so much by inventive poetic phrases as by clichés. Following the consummation of their affair, Tolstoy emphasizes Vronsky's inability to find the right words, or to understand Anna properly:

> "I can never forget that which is my whole life. For a minute of this happiness . . ."
> "What happiness!" she said with loathing and horror, and the horror was ineluctably transmitted to him. "I beg you, not a word, not a word more." (152)

In such passages, Vronsky relies on the same type of language that Pushkin's Don Juan uses to seduce Donna Anna: "What's death? For one sweet instant together / Willingly I'd give up my life" (92) / Chto znachit smert'? Za sladkii mig svidan'ia / Bezropotno otdam ia zhizn' (169). The very romantic phrasing that is so convincing in Don Juan's mouth, though, comes across as banal from Vronsky, who still does not fully grasp the significance of his actions. Tolstoy's seducer is an awkward, would-be Don Juan, imitating without his predecessor's fluidity or originality. Nevertheless, unlike Goncharov, who seems to doubt the depth or permanence of Raisky's love for Vera, Tolstoy makes clear that Vronsky feelings for Anna are genuine, thus agreeing with commentators who have interpreted Don Juan's claim of rebirth in love as sincere.

Tolstoy's particular interest in the problem of vengeance brought about by sexual transgressions dictates a focus not just on Vronsky as a Don Juan imitator, but also on his interactions with Karenin in relation to Anna. Karenin functions as a Commander-like figure of vengeance and moral chastisement: his last name, with its root "kara" signifying punishment and retribution, supports this association. Tolstoy continually refers to Karenin's features as deathly or motionless and in other ways likens him to the statue. Whereas Pushkin depicts a statue brought to life through the supernatural, Tolstoy, within a Realist context, plays with the boundary between the animate and inanimate, and the mobile and the rigid, in Karenin. He underscores the impression of this character's rigidity in Vronsky's awkward exchange with Karenin, using the image of a stone: "Vronsky's composure and self-confidence now came up against the glacial self-confidence of Alexey Alexandrovich like a scythe on stone [kosa na kamen']" (108). Elsewhere, Tolstoy notes Karenin's "tightly pursed" lips (150), his "bloodless, pinched face" and "lackluster, staring eyes" (360), as well as his cold, stern speech with Anna and other characters.

Even more significantly, Karenin plays the role of an insulted and ridiculed husband who, like Pushkin's Commander, nevertheless acquires newfound dignity and power when least expected. The scene of Anna's illness following childbirth, in which she asks Karenin to join her and Vronsky at her bedside, features several important parallels with the Don Juan legend, and Pushkin's play in particular. Initially in the course of Anna's affair with Vronsky, Karenin serves as a figure of ridicule, like the Commander. Anna mocks Karenin's expression to Vronsky, and Vronsky wonders why Karenin does not challenge him to a duel. This mockery recalls the Commander's unprepossessing appearance and position as described by Don Juan in *The Stone Guest* in comparison with his statue:

The man himself was small and puny,
If he were here and stood on tiptoe,
His fingertip couldn't reach to his own nose.
When we went out beyond the Escurial,
He stuck himself on my sword and died
Like a dragonfly upon a pin—but still
He was proud and bold, and stern of spirit. . . . (79–80)

А сам покойник мал был и щедушен,
Здесь став на цыпочки не мог бы руку
До своего он носу дотянуть.
Когда за Ескурьялом мы сошлись,
Наткнулся мне на шпагу он и замер
Как на булавке стрекоза—а был
Он горд и смел—и дух имел суровый . . . (153)

Just as Don Juan is forced to admire certain of his opponent's qualities at the end of the above excerpt, though, Vronsky feels himself to be lowered in relation to Karenin after the latter's unexpected Christian behavior at Anna's bedside. After admitting that he had sought revenge on Anna and Vronsky, Karenin explains that he wants to forgive his enemies, and is even willing to endure humiliation: "You can trample me into the mud, make me the laughingstock of society, but I will not abandon her, will never utter a word of reproach to you" (417). However, this selfless response is precisely what "defeats" Vronsky[30]: "The deceived husband, who until now had seemed like a pathetic creature, an unexpected and slightly comic obstacle to his happiness, had suddenly been summoned by Anna herself, elevated to an awe-inspiring height, and had shown himself at this height to be neither vindictive nor false nor ridiculous, but kind, straightforward, and dignified. Vronsky could not help but feel this. The roles had suddenly been reversed. Vronsky felt Karenin's towering stature and his own humiliation, Karenin's righteousness and his own falsehood" (418). Tolstoy focuses on the psychological effects of Karenin's Christian epiphany, as Vronsky is eventually driven to a suicide attempt by his rival's magnanimity. As the above passage shows, however, the Realist texture is replete with Pushkinian motifs. Vronsky's references to Karenin's formerly "pathetic" and "comic" qualities, in contrast to his present metaphorical stature, recall Don Juan's descriptions of the Commander's monument. Moreover, Vronsky's notion of this version of Karenin as "summoned by Anna herself, elevated to an awe-inspiring height" parallels the Commander's impressive stature and strength as a statue—both in the graveyard and in his final appearance at Donna Anna's house—compared to his less impressive living form. And just as the statue in effect rises to defeat his formerly triumphant rival, in Tolstoy's novel, Vronsky is "replaced" by Karenin, temporarily, as the latter becomes caretaker to his wife and her newborn daughter, rendering Vronsky superfluous during Anna's recovery.

Like Pushkin, Tolstoy depicts a "substitute duel" in this scene. Pushkin's statue, which Don Juan mockingly invites to guard the door during his tryst with Donna Anna, avenges his foe not with a "rematch" of their duel but with his stony grip. In Tolstoy's novel, both Karenin and Vronsky consider the possibility of dueling; Karenin ponders it before rejecting it as an option, and Vronsky is surprised that he does not receive a challenge from Anna's husband. Instead, there is a struggle of wills. Karenin, summoned by Anna to join the two lovers, decisively defeats the man who has won his wife's affection. Tolstoy transforms Pushkin's play of revenge, with the vanquished unexpectedly gaining the upper hand, into a psychological situation in which Karenin's very humility is precisely what proves to be a weapon (although he does not intend it this way) against both Vronsky and Anna. Tolstoy's narrative, of course, extends long past this parallel plot situation. In effect, he provides a continuation, in which Vronsky again gains the upper hand by reestablishing his self-esteem and power over Anna following his failed suicide attempt.

In addition, this passage reproduces the aforementioned triangular quality of Pushkin's final scene, in which the putative opponents Don Juan and the Commander, centering on a common love object, merge and acquire aspects of each other's identity. In *Anna Karenina*, this unity of seeming opposites is underscored by Anna's comment about Karenin and Vronsky, "what a strange, terrible fate, that they both are Alexey, isn't it?" (414). Critics have noted the significant parallels that Tolstoy shows between the two male characters. As Edward Wasiolek points out, Vronsky's ambitions to rise in the military, if realized, would make him another Karenin, insisting on regularity, routine, and a solid position in society, all of which clash with Anna's passionate, rebellious internal impulses (142). Although Vronsky provides a temporary respite from the immobilizing, overregularized life Anna seeks to escape, eventually he desires a kind of stability that frustrates her and turns out to be just as unsatisfactory. Tolstoy, noting Pushkin's ambiguity and the identity between seemingly opposed characters in the play, creates a Realist version of this encounter, transposing it into a hidden psychological similarity that Anna senses between her "two Alexeis."[31] For Anna, both Karenin and Vronsky focus on practical concerns rather than engaging in the kind of genuine, emotionally satisfying interaction she requires.

For Tolstoy, however, Pushkin's triangular structure serves as a starting point rather than a mechanical scheme to follow. In fact, he does not restrict Anna to the role of her namesake, but attributes traits of Pushkin's Don Juan to her as well. Like Pushkin, for instance, Tolstoy concerns himself with the interaction of art and Eros. In his Part VII description of Mikhailov's painting of Anna, he demonstrates her seductiveness not, as in *The Stone Guest*, through poetic activity, but through her representation in a work of art. Before Levin even meets Anna, he is struck by the painting of her, which, combined with their ensuing conversation, entrances him to such an extent as to incur Kitty's jealousy and to temper his own prejudice against "fallen women": having referred to them earlier as "vermin," he now comes to feel pity and compassion for Anna.

Perhaps more importantly, though, Pushkin's and Tolstoy's protagonists share a fascination with death and an obsession with the relationship between their sexuality and the forces of destiny. De Rougemont's paradigm of romantic love, in which proximity to or even desire for death serves as a goad for passion, applies to an extent to both Don Juan and Anna Karenina. Mozart and Da Ponte's Don Giovanni represents a force of life, as he celebrates worldly pleasures right before he is visited by the Commendatore: "Women, I drink to you! Good wine, I bless you! These are the glories of Humanity" (101). Pushkin, by contrast, puts sexuality in proximity to death throughout *The Stone Guest*. Tolstoy, similarly, associates Anna's sexual passion with death, beginning with her interpretation of the peasant being killed by a train at the time of her first meeting with Vronsky as a bad omen. Nowhere is this juxtaposition more apparent than in her consummation of the affair with Vronsky, which is described in violent, deathly terms: "He meanwhile was feeling what a murderer must feel when he looks at the body he has robbed of life" (151–52). And deathliness is associated no less with Karenin. As Karenin hears his wife's confession of infidelity, as the narrator describes it, "his whole face suddenly acquired the imposing immobility of a corpse" (216). Tolstoy's depiction of Anna's intermingling of fascination with death and fear of it recalls Pushkin's depiction of Don Juan in his little tragedy, which, for some critics, dramatizes the death of a poet at the hands of a society that freezes his motion and stifles his creativity.[32] Insofar as Anna tries to fashion a new identity for herself and determine her own erotic and marital situation, the same can be said of her frustrating relations with both Karenin and Vronsky.

Tolstoy's heroine is not only obsessed with the idea of her own death but, like Don Juan, summons it herself. Don Juan's invitation to the statue, of course, constitutes one of the distinct motifs of the legend and plays a crucial role in many retellings, but Pushkin's version is particularly enigmatic because of Don Juan's request that the Commander guard his tryst with Anna. Don Juan's fascination with the statue, indeed, hastens his own destruction just as he claims he is about to achieve the supreme happiness of experiencing true passion for the first time.[33]

Tolstoy, needless to say, emphasizes the element of self-destructiveness even more than Pushkin does: Anna not only "invites" her own death but also commits suicide. However, both characters are essentially engaged in a process of discovering the working-out of a mysterious retributive force in relation to their sexual transgressions, regardless of their degree of agency. Don Juan's mixture of bewilderment and terrified realization upon feeling the statue's grip ("Oh, it's heavy, The stony grip of his right hand! Leave me alone, let go—let go of me ... I am undone—it's finished—Donna Anna!" [94] / o tiazhelo / Pozhat'e kamennoi ego desnitsy! / Ostav' menia, pusti-pusti mne ruku ... / Ia gibnu—koncheno—o Donna Anna! [171]) resonates with Anna Karenina's horror at the onrushing wheels: "'Where am I? What am I doing? Why?' She wanted to get to her feet, to hurl herself out of the way; but something huge and inexorable hit her on the head and pulled her along by her back. 'Lord, forgive me for everything!' she murmured, feeling the impossibility of struggling." (771) Like Pushkin, whose characters seem to fall together suddenly and unexpectedly in his finale, Tolstoy suggests a type of vengeance that acts as an invisible and unpredictable force, waiting to strike at some unknown point in the future. In this manner, Tolstoy transfers key attributes and sensations of Don Juan to Anna Karenina, who has played the role of Pushkin's Donna Anna throughout much of the narrative. At the end of their lives, each transgressor—Juan and Anna—experiences an uncanny realization that the dreaded fate has arrived. Mozart and Da Ponte's opera, with its weakening of the straightforward causal relationship between Giovanni's deeds and his punishment, questions the certainty and justice of vengeance. Pushkin and Tolstoy in turn make this indirectness and unpredictability of retribution a central theme and the focus of their respective texts. As in Mozart and Da Ponte's and Pushkin's Don Juan retellings, the instrument of vengeance in *Anna Karenina* turns out to be an inanimate object that inexorably paralyzes human freedom, creativity, and passion, whether it be the statue's stone or the unstoppable cast-iron wheels of the train that cuts off Anna's life.[34]

Tolstoy's description of Anna's Don Juan-like rebellion and demise reflects his stance on the woman question. Anna's attempt to experience genuine love in place of a stultifying, unsatisfactory marriage reflects the urges of both Pushkin's Donna Anna and his Don Juan, who declares that he has fallen in love for the first time. This pursuit can be linked to her efforts to find fulfillment in the occupations she engages in, such as her readings on agriculture and architecture, her writing of a children's book, and her charitable endeavor of raising Hannah, the daughter of Vronsky's English trainer who had deserted his family, and coaching his sons in Russian as they prepare for high school. Donjuanism, in the sense of rebellion from social restrictions, thus intersects with the woman question. In all of these cases, Tolstoy portrays Anna's arrangements as lacking in genuineness in some way. Describing Anna's life with Vronsky on his estate through Dolly's eyes, he paints a picture of an ersatz marriage, lacking in legitimacy or naturalness.[35] Similarly, Tolstoy implies that Anna's intellectual and professional activities constitute a meager substitute for the affection she feels is lacking from Vronsky and the stability she had experienced earlier in her legitimate marriage. If Pushkin's play suggests the possibility of women escaping from imprisoning relationships, then Tolstoy argues that such an escape leads only to boredom, frustration, and eventually, suicide. In this manner, he conveys a dismissive attitude toward proponents of the woman question, with their aspirations for greater freedom and agency for women in their selection of marital partners, expression of sexual impulses, and professional opportunities.[36]

Besides its relation to the woman question, the Don Juan legend also bears political implications for *Anna Karenina* more broadly related to Russia's future, albeit in a more indirect manner than in *Don Giovanni* and *The Stone Guest*. In some Don Juan versions, the protagonist represents rebellion against established social and religious orders. Don Giovanni's defiant refusal to repent in the final scene, for instance, acquires political overtones by virtue of the fact that Mozart and Da Ponte's opera was composed on the eve of the French Revolution. The same is true of his Act I cry, "Viva la libertà," which ostensibly refers to his own freedom, but which audiences would have also interpreted as an allusion to revolutionary politics. Pushkin, as I discuss in chapter 1, develops these political implications further, as his autobiographical Don Juan reflects the plight of the poet, especially in light of other writings.

In *Anna Karenina*, Tolstoy, rather than directly transferring Don Juan's rebellion to his plot, focuses on a broader sense of political anxiety. He finds Pushkin's model of inexorable vengeance particularly apt for describing his own age of expanding railroads, a buildup to what he viewed as a senseless war in the Balkans, and his growing dissatisfaction with the Russian government, military, society, and church. If Pushkin uses the figure of a statue coming to life to portend destruction, Tolstoy transforms stone into iron, creating an equally implacable image of the train as an embodiment of retribution that affects Russia on a political as well as personal level. Robert Louis Jackson, tracing Tolstoy's apocalyptic vision to the beginning of the novel, connects the train's grotesque destruction of the heroine to a broader severing of "crucial linkages" in Russian society: "The dismemberment of Anna, of course, is only the final representation of this tragedy, just as the 'disfigured corpse' of the guard at the railroad station is the first harbinger of Anna's death and of the general theme of family, social and economic breakdown in Russian life" (350–51). However, the tragic cataclysm in *Anna Karenina* extends beyond the heroine's suicide. Tolstoy uses the same symbol of vengeance, the train, to prefigure the likely death of Vronsky and other volunteers headed to the Serbian front in Part VIII.

In light of this relation between the personal and the political suggested by the Don Juan subtext, Tolstoy's epigraph appears to signal an all-powerful force issuing vengeance that cannot be left to humans. It also affirms an essential unknowability about the workings of this retribution. Given the numerous sexual misdeeds of other characters such as Stiva and Princess Betsy that—unlike Anna's—are left unpunished in *Anna Karenina*, Vladimir Alexandrov is right to remark that the novel's conclusion "acknowledges God's inscrutability from the limited human perspective" (70). Tolstoy's own remarks on the epigraph confirm this inscrutability. Mikhail Sukhotin reports a 1907 conversation in which the novelist referred to his desire "to convey the idea that the evil that man does has as its consequence only bitterness, which comes not from man, but from God, and which Anna Karenina, too, experienced" (Qtd. from Eikhenbaum 142). Anna's punishment is generated not so much by her peers (or even herself, despite her suicide) as by a mysterious, unexplained process and an inhuman agency.

The Don Juan theme in *Anna Karenina* thus sheds light on the critical debate regarding the culpability of Tolstoy's heroine in her own demise. Several critics have posited Anna's immaturity, narcissism, and obsession with symbols as the primary cause of her self-destruction.[37] While this view of the novel's tragedy as largely psychological in origin is persuasive in many respects, it does not account for the sense of an uncanny, apocalyptic force that pervades the entire novel from the epigraph. Stiva's fleeting dream of Mozart and Da Ponte's apocalyptic aria, following closely upon the epigraph's theme of the Lord's vengeance, combines with other motifs of chaos to suggest not only the personal fate in store for Anna, but also that of a nation potentially on the verge of self-destructive acts of military aggression. Regardless of Anna's psychological makeup and flawed decisions, her destiny is symbolically tied to larger cataclysmic currents as well. Tolstoy's use of the Don Juan theme as a "doubling" of the epigraph's focus on inexplicable, inhuman retribution reinforces this impression of all-embracing disaster.

Reading *Anna Karenina* through *The Stone Guest* as well as *Don Giovanni* thus sheds light on Tolstoy's efforts to link his adultery plot to broader questions involving Russia's future. The novelist's exploration of the Don Juan plot and theme, in conjunction with his multi-referential epigraph, makes for an extremely dense intertextual dialogue in *Anna Karenina*. Far from alluding to Donjuanism simply to censure erotic license, he also employs it to illuminate the mysterious connection between sin and retribution, and to convey apocalyptic anxieties pertaining to his nation as a whole.

Ultimately, Donjuanism—seen first and foremost in characters like Vronsky, Oblonsky, and Veslovsky—migrates in the narrative to Anna herself, in the form of her gesture of individual rebellion against the status quo. At the point of her suicide, as she sees the train approaching and "realized what she had to do" (770), she sees the result of her individualism and, like Don Juan, comes to understand the consequences of her rebellion against the norm. Anna's transgression, like those of Pushkin's hero, represents a failed rebellion against societal and religious (internalized) forces beyond her control. In a broader sense, Anna's experience of Donjuanism through her choice of a serious romantic relationship outside marriage and the consequent rebellion against her society that this choice entails sheds light on Tolstoy's lifelong examination of the fate of the individual who places self over collective.

Tolstoy's use of the Don Juan theme in *Anna Karenina*, then, is surprisingly indirect, even indeterminate, in light of his lifelong moral castigation of libertinage. A decade later, however, in *The Kreutzer Sonata*, he makes a direct reference to the phenomenon, casting it in precisely the moralizing terms we would expect in a post-conversion work: "Out of a thousand men who marry (not only among us but unfortunately also among the masses) there's hardly a one who hasn't already been married ten, a hundred, or even, like Don Juan, a thousand times, before his wedding" (146). In this brief reference, Tolstoy's antihero observes that Donjuanism is now so common that it lacks any of the possible heroism it may have had in earlier versions, where it served as a rebellion and exposé of a repressive, hypocritical, and ineffectual society. Here, Donjuanism has been so thoroughly integrated into social behavior that it is utterly conventional and, indeed, barely noticeable; as a ritual for young men, it thus represents a kind of unthinking conformity to the norm. Pozdnyshev, in his extraordinarily literal equation of the sexual act with marriage, hints at a parallel linking of the two often made by the traditional Don Juan: to gain access to women, he often connives by promising them marriage. Here, however, the deception is worse because instead of one isolated person (or even a type of man) tricking women, Donjuanism has become a universal form of deceit (and self-deception) practiced by all of society at large, with the total complicity of women. For Pozdnyshev, who can see male-female relations only in terms of animalistic sexuality, all men are Don Juans, and all women—as soon as they reach the inevitable stage of corruption—are fully aware of this fact. If, in *Anna Karenina*, Tolstoy only hints at what he sees as the dangerous link between art and seduction, in *The Kreutzer Sonata* this connection—celebrated by Pushkin in his play—becomes the main pretext for the novella's tragic outcome. In Pozdnyshev's feverish mind, Beethoven's sonata, with its spellbinding and unpredictable power, serves as a vehicle to encourage adulterous relations between his wife, a woman in the full bloom of her second youth, and the violinist Trukhachevsky, who exudes sensual enjoyment of music, food, and women.

Donjuanism, according to Pozdnyshev, also becomes a veritable struggle for power between the sexes. As he points out, women respond to the male objectification of them as sexual objects by using this very quality to ensnare them. "'Ah, you want us to be mere objects of sensuality—all right, as objects of sensuality we'll enslave you,' say the women." In the process, according to Pozdnyshev, women gain control of the economy as well.

"Go around the shops in any big town. There are goods worth millions and you cannot estimate the human labor expended on them, and look whether in nine-tenths of these shops there is anything for men. All the luxuries of life are demanded and maintained by women.

Count all the factories. An enormous proportion of them produce useless ornaments, carriages, furniture, and trinkets for women. Millions of people, generations of slaves, perish at hard labor in factories merely to satisfy women's caprice. Women, like queens, keep nine-tenths of mankind in bondage to heavy labor. And all because they've been debased and deprived of equal rights with men. They revenge themselves by acting on our sensuality and catch us in their nets. Yes, it all comes to that." (150)[38]

The parenthetical comment on Don Juan in *The Kreutzer Sonata* is thus closely linked to Tolstoy's appraisal of class relations in his late period as well. Donjuanism, with all its multiplicity and proliferation, represents one of many means by which the upper classes corrupt the lower classes. By linking sexuality with "stimuli" that tend to reinforce each other—as in his 1890 essay "Why Do Men Stupefy Themselves?"—Tolstoy suggests that the sexuality of Donjuanism is connected to other vices and that even the peasantry, whom Tolstoy views as purer than the aristocracy, is corrupted by this sexual disease as much as by the drinking, smoking, and other vices of the upper classes. Donjuanism becomes a symbol of the sexuality that Pozdnyshev (and Tolstoy himself) views as the foundation of a degraded social and economic order. If Tolstoyanism proclaims the need for unification of men and women in a chaste brotherhood, then Donjuanism embodies the roots of the human separation and disorder that Tolstoy hopes to repair.

To an extent, Chekhov also describes a "cure" to Donjuanism in his most famous short story, "The Lady with the Little Dog," but along very different lines. Far from Tolstoy's castigation of promiscuity in *Anna Karenina, The Kreutzer Sonata*, and so many other works, Chekhov consciously reworks his predecessor's approach into a more nonjudgmental attitude toward adultery. While "The Lady with the Little Dog" lacks Tolstoy's apocalyptic vision and focuses more on the comic aspects of the Don Juan theme, it nevertheless takes a similar approach to Donjuanism, reflecting, not surprisingly, the influence of Pushkin.

Donna Anna and Don Dmitry: Chekhov's "Lady with the Little Dog"

Unlike *The Precipice* and *Anna Karenina*, Chekhov's masterpiece in the short story genre contains no direct references to the Don Juan theme; nor is there any explicit evidence that he had the little tragedy in mind while writing the story. Nevertheless, several scholars have viewed the protagonist, Dmitry Gurov, as a variation on the eternal Don Juan type. Noting both this parallel and the story's relationship to Tolstoy's novel, Donald Rayfield writes: "'The Lady with the Little Dog' seems to defend adultery and to explode Tolstoy's *Anna Karenina*: of all Chekhov's works it upset Tolstoy most. Gurov is a very ambiguous hero: he is Don Juan in love" (501). Michael Finke, too, refers to Gurov as seducing Anna Sergeevna "like an accomplished Don Juan" (145).

To my knowledge, though, Vladimir Kataev is the only critic who links "The Lady with the Little Dog" specifically to *The Stone Guest*. According to Kataev,

Chekhov transfers Pushkin's plot of a libertine who unexpectedly falls in love for the first time into a more mundane context that, unlike *The Stone Guest*'s tragic finale, ends without resolution: the lovers realize that "the most complex and difficult part was only just beginning" (183).[39] Kataev also notes Pushkin's and Chekhov's similar circumstances at the time of writing their respective works. Following extended periods of seducing women in their youth, both writers had fallen in love and were about to get married, Pushkin to Natalia Goncharova and Chekhov to Moscow Art Theater actress and colleague Olga Knipper. Both writers were separated from their fiancées at the time they were writing their respective works (Pushkin was quarantined in Boldino, and Chekhov was attempting to treat his tuberculosis in Yalta). Kataev also cleverly observes that Don Juan ("Guan" in Pushkin's spelling) and Dmitry Gurov even share the same initials.[40]

This intertextual relationship, however, is arguably even more complex than a straightforward series of parallels between the two works, as Chekhov recasts Pushkin's triangular relationship between Don Juan, Anna, and the Commander through the prism of Tolstoy's novel. Many of the same connections critics have noted between "The Lady with the Little Dog" and *Anna Karenina*, its most prominent subtext, apply to Pushkin's play as well. Given Chekhov's intertextual reliance on *Anna Karenina* as well as, in some critics' view, *The Kreutzer Sonata*, it is not surprising that his adultery plot highlights many of the same elements of Pushkin's rewriting of the Don Juan narrative that Tolstoy had explored. Chekhov's serial seducer, like Pushkin's Don Juan and Tolstoy's Vronsky, is unexpectedly transformed by his encounter with a woman, also named Anna, who is similarly trapped in a loveless marriage with an unattractive, oppressive man. The statue's role—so crucial to the archetypal Don Juan plot—would seem at first glance to be minimized in Chekhov's story, as Anna's husband, von Dideritz, is reduced to an obsequious lackey. However, even this character, in Chekhov's presentation, constitutes a comical reflection of Pushkin's tragic avenger. The story's oft-discussed intertextual relationship with *Anna Karenina* therefore encapsulates the aforementioned Don Juan plot that I argue is embedded in Tolstoy's novel, reopening and examining the same questions, but with markedly different conclusions. Via Tolstoy's novel, Chekhov's story ingeniously recasts the central conflicts and characterizations of Pushkin's play about Don Juan within a more everyday context.

Before I examine the Don Juan subtext of "The Lady with the Little Dog" in greater detail, some background on the autobiographical relevance of Chekhov's own relation to the Don Juan theme for Chekhov should be considered. Donjuanism is clearly an important theme in Chekhov's oeuvre, judging from his numerous characters who engage in serial love relationships.[41] The eponymous, married hero of the play *Platonov* (1878) is explicitly referred to as a Don Juan. Having attracted the love of two women, the landowner Anna Petrovna and Sofia Yegorovna, the wife of Anna Petrovna's stepson, he declares: "I've ruined innocent, defenseless women, not out of passion, Spanish-style but out of stupidity, Russian-style" (92). Platonov continually expresses his sense of boredom, despair, and unfulfillment, both in his profession as a schoolmaster and in his family life, and this existential angst appears to lead to a new kind of Donjuanism that, though predicated on his love of women (kissing the medical student Anna Grekova, he proclaims: "I love all women! You're all so soft and beautiful!"; 94), really serves as a distraction from his feeling of emptiness.[42]

Although Chekhov's tendency to create Don Juan-like characters appears to be autobiographical, his actual erotic life is more shrouded in mystery than Pushkin's or Tolstoy's: he seems to have allowed rumors of his many encounters with women to proliferate, but they are not well substantiated, and he was reticent to speak of his sexuality. His misogyny, on the other hand, is well documented. As Virginia Llewellyn Smith has demonstrated, Chekhov viewed female sexuality as a threat to men's happiness and portrays women as dangerous enchantresses and vampires. His treatment of women who engage in extramarital relationships is particularly harsh. As Smith notes, "few writers have been so uncompromising in their attitude to erring womanhood" (30). "The Lady with the Little Dog," however, departs from this tendency. Although Gurov reflects Chekhov's private nature and combination of condescension toward and fear of women, the narrator clearly sympathizes as much with Anna Sergeevna's search for happiness through infidelity as with Gurov's similar quest. At first glance, Gurov's attitude to women would seem to replicate the author's own: Chekhov describes his hero finally finding a genuine relationship just as he himself, at the same age, was falling in love with Knipper. Nevertheless, besides some obvious and major differences (Gurov is married with children and works in a bank), Chekhov's protagonist differs from his creator in the very act of Donjuanism. Chekhov establishes Gurov as a character who resembles the image he created for himself—of easy and frequent conquests—rather than the actual writer, who appears to have long tired of mistresses by the late 1890s.

The bare outlines of Pushkin's Don Juan plot that I describe in "The Lady with the Little Dog" might be passed off as a coincidence, but the connections resonate even further. As a serial seducer, for example, Gurov recalls both Pushkin's Don Juan and Tolstoy's Vronsky in surprising ways and adds another layer to the phenomenon of artistry in seduction. As in *The Stone Guest*, seduction is directly linked to both artistic abilities and a search for redemption. Like Pushkin's Don Juan, Gurov is an artist by nature, having trained as an opera singer and studied literature before becoming a banker, and has possibly sublimated these creative urges into his womanizing. Although Gurov seduces women in part simply because he enjoys their company, they also provide a kind of gateway to the eternal, especially in Yalta, where the exotic location—despite its banality—nevertheless offers a vision of that which will survive all humans.

> The leaves on the trees did not stir, the cicadas were chattering, and the monotonous, muffled noise of the sea coming up from down below spoke of rest and of the eternal sleep which awaits us. It had made that noise down below when neither Yalta nor Oreanda existed, it was making that noise now, and would continue to make that noise in that same hushed and indifferent way when we are no longer here. And in that permanence, in that complete indifference to the life and death of each one of us, is perhaps concealed a guarantee of our eternal salvation, a guarantee of the constant movement of life on earth and of endless perfection. (173)

The courtship and relationship of Anna Sergeevna and Gurov in important respects parallel those of Anna Karenina and Vronsky. Anna Sergeevna's reaction after she and Gurov consummate their affair, for instance, distinctly recalls the similar point in Anna's relationship with Vronsky, in which he visualizes himself as a murderer. Anna Sergeevna's comments to Gurov about her position as an adulteress recall her namesake's shame, rooted in the same Christian expectations of marital fidelity: "How can I justify myself? I am a bad and wretched woman, I despise myself; justification is the last thing on my mind" (171). Unlike Vronsky, however, who is inspired to a greater sense of purpose by Anna's reaction, Gurov experiences only pity, annoyance, and boredom listening to Anna Sergeevna's self-recriminations. In this sense, Gurov represents the deep-rooted misogyny underlying the Don Juan myth. In Gurov's case, the traditional Don Juan-like seduction of a stream of women with no intention of staying with them for any length of time is motivated by a paradoxical combination of love and scorn for the gender. Although Gurov feels more comfortable with women than with men, this comfort is accompanied by disgust, since he considers women the "lesser species." If Tolstoy's own oft-critiqued misogyny does not seem to be overtly reflected in Vronsky, in Chekhov's story, such attitudes permeate the Don Juan figure himself. Gurov also views some women as "predatory" in their lovemaking and expresses his disgust for such women in a wonderfully evocative metaphor: "their beauty would arouse hatred in him and the lace on their underwear would seem like fishscales" (171). Only love for an individual woman, Chekhov implies through his depiction of Gurov's transformation, can heal this misogyny and allow for some degree of mutual respect.

The statue motif, as I have mentioned earlier, tends to be less emphasized in Realist works than in texts composed in other periods. Given the supernatural quality of this motif, this deemphasis makes sense. In *The Precipice*, for example, Goncharov focuses almost entirely on the Don Juan character, and the idea of vengeance does not play a role in the novel. In *Anna Karenina*, by contrast, the idea of vengeance—as indicated explicitly in the epigraph—is quite central, and in addition to frequent references to Karenin's statue-like appearance, this notion of supernatural retribution is transferred from a human/stone hybrid to the iron train that embodies the idea of apocalyptic, indiscriminate destruction. However, Karenin, Anna (with her desire to punish Vronsky for his alleged lack of passion for her), and the train all encompass elements of Pushkin's Commander, so it is impossible to find a concrete replication of this aspect of the legend, as we do in both Pushkin's and Dargomyzhsky's versions of *The Stone Guest*. Chekhov, in turn, would at first glance seem to minimize the presence of a statue figure embodying retribution to an even greater extent than do Tolstoy and Goncharov.

However, looking more closely at the story, one can find traces of the statue, diffused as in Tolstoy's novel, even though Chekhov deemphasizes the idea of vengeance in favor of another important attribute of the Commander: his imprisoning, immobilizing essence. Anna Sergeevna's scornful denigration of her husband as a lackey belies his true force in her life: he entraps her in a provincial town, behind gates that remind Gurov of a prison. This circumscription of a wife by a husband recalls *The Stone Guest*, in which Don Juan accuses the dead Commander of hiding his treasure (Donna Anna) from the world (just as Carlos attempts to do to Laura, and presumably Inez's husband to her). In this sense, Chekhov transforms Pushkin's and Tolstoy's preoccupation with inexorable, deathly powers into a kind of banal force, a "death in life," a sucking-dry of all lifegiving essence. Like the Commander and Karenin, von Dideritz represents a sterile companion for a younger woman whose life energy cannot be shuttered inside her.[43] Even at the end of the story, von Dideritz (along with Gurov's wife) continues to play this imprisoning role from afar when both Gurov and Anna are described as "two migratory birds, a male and a female, who had been caught and made to live in separate cages" (183). Of course, he does not intentionally restrict Anna Sergeevna, as the Commander does his wife in Pushkin's play, but he in effect fulfills the same function. Chekhov implicitly critiques the morality of his time for creating these cages.

Another implicit reference to the statue may be a moment involving Gurov himself in the story's final scene. Seeing his reflection in the mirror, shaken by the signs of his aging, he experiences an uncanny moment of seeing something familiar but heretofore unknown about himself. This revelation prompts a degree of insight into his love for Anna and his own imprisoned state in life. In this sense, the scene recalls the aforementioned interlocking quality between Don Juan and the statue, which reflect different sides of Pushkin, different times in his life. They are part of the same continuum of aging: the young seducer becomes the old cuckold. This identity, of course, gets extended in Tolstoy's novel, in which the two rivals for Anna seem to be opposites but turn out to have a lot in common. In one image, Chekhov condenses this mixture of opposition and sameness. Gurov, a man who behaves as though he were still young, still playing the role of a seducer, comes face to face with his older, present, actual self. As such, he transforms from a lover into a potential husband, just as Don Juan is transformed, at least according to him, from a flighty seducer into a romantic lover by the end of *The Stone Guest*.

Thus Chekhov takes the statue, bifurcates it, and creates two images based on two important features of the Commander: his actual power despite apparent weakness (von Dideritz is a lackey, but he has the power to imprison Anna in their marriage) and the sense of identity between rivals who are ostensible opposites. In light of the small-scale tone of Chekhov's revelations, by contrast to Tolstoy's, it is only appropriate that the statue be represented less in dramatic, deathly, quasi-supernatural events than in small but significant psychological revelations along the lines of Gurov's inexplicably changing feelings toward Anna in the last part of the story.

Chekhov's intertextual references to two "Anna" characters, Pushkin's Donna Anna and Anna Karenina, in this rewriting of the Don Juan narrative have an additional effect of helping establish and illuminate an Anna type in Russian literature.[44] This type contrasts markedly with two other familiar female types: the wise Sofia (often Sonia) depicted in works of Denis Fonvizin, Griboedov, Dostoevsky, and Chekhov himself in *Uncle Vanya*, and the eternally suffering "poor Liza" type depicted by Karamzin, Pushkin, and Dostoevsky. The Anna type, by contrast, represents a much more independent character, one who is more in touch with her desires (sexual and otherwise). All of the Anna characters I discuss embody some or all of these characteristics, from the young but previously married Donna Anna to Anna Karenina and Anna Sergeevna, all of whom submit (or are about to submit) to their desire for sexual pleasure in violation of received morality. This heroine also recalls another Anna who shares the name and patronymic of Chekhov's heroine: Anna Sergeevna Odintsova of Turgenev's *Fathers and Children*. Chekhov's Anna Sergeevna resembles Odintsova in key ways. Her "little dog," or "lapdog," a plaything, marks her as being independent and in control. The root of "alone" or "lonely" (odin), evoked by "Odintsova," applies to Chekhov's heroine as well. Turgenev's Odintsova, despite her two marriages and relative agency in her own life, is restricted by her own fear of uncovering the "animalistic" self, as Jane Costlow puts it, which an affair with Bazarov would force her to do.

This female character type, then, embodies a kind of tension between freedom and restriction. Tolstoy's and Chekhov's Annas pursue affairs as a response to stifling marriages. Anna Karenina's difficulty obtaining a divorce from Karenin, perhaps, similarly hints at the hardships Gurov and Anna Sergeevna will face in the continuation of the open-ended story's action. The ending of "The Lady with the Little Dog" is ambiguous: it is unclear whether Gurov and Anna will remain "like two migratory birds," forced to meet secretly, conceal their true feelings for each other, and remain in false marriages. The last lines about "a new, wonderful life" do not necessarily clarify the future. This pattern recalls the conundrum of Donna Anna in *The Stone Guest*, whose perceived duties as a widow conflict with urges for sexual freedom that are activated by Don Juan. Thus, the Anna type consists of a series of would-be liberated women who experience some form of frustration because of a combination of psychological conflict and societal restrictions and who pursue the love they desire with great ambivalence. If the Sonias and Lizas confirm the stereotype of Russian women as suffering, self-sacrificial, and single-mindedly devoted to men, the Anna line, beginning with Pushkin's rewriting of the Don Juan legend, questions this accepted ideal. It acknowledges women's desire to find new life experiences and the unanswered questions raised by their rebellion against the status quo.

Chekhov, like Tolstoy, transports the essential triangular rivalry and the notion of a Don Juan figure falling in love from Pushkin's play into a Realist narrative. But in doing so, he goes far beyond simply isolating this device from its surrounding themes. Ultimately, for Chekhov as for Pushkin, Donjuanism involves a combination of creation and recovery of the self. In *The Stone Guest*, Pushkin's hero operates via disguises at several points of the play. He returns to Madrid in disguise and speaks first to the monk, then to Donna Anna at the Commander's cemetery, each time pretending to be someone else. But the climax of the play comes as he throws off his disguise and reveals his "true self" while simultaneously announcing that his "true self" has actually changed. Don Juan no longer casually seduces women, but has fallen in love. Pushkin depicts both the shedding of disguise and the announcement of a new, reborn person in what Kropf—borrowing from Deleuze and Guattari—refers to as hecceities, self-reinventions.

"The Lady with the Dog" features a similar focus on the self. But what Chekhov depicts is an unfulfilled desire to reconcile divided parts of a person. Gurov, we recall, sacrifices his earlier intellectual and artistic interests and performs the most mundane work, surrounded by a wife and friends who disgust him with their banality. Anna Sergeevna represents an alternative to this life, though one that cannot be fully embraced yet. It is an ideal love that is perhaps unreachable, a work in progress. The tragedy of *The Stone Guest*, perhaps, is that Don Juan is destroyed just as he is reborn and on the threshold of achieving happiness. In "The Lady with the Little Dog," the tragedy lies rather in Gurov and Anna Sergeevna's difficulty—perhaps the impossibility—of reconciling their desires with reality and resolving the conundrum of the "two lives, public and private" that they are forced to experience. Don Juan in Pushkin and Anna and Vronsky in Tolstoy are able to throw off their disguises and present themselves, at least to some degree, openly. Whether Gurov and Anna Sergeevna will be able to exchange their double lives for a single, unified, happy, public life is left ambiguous. Chekhov proposes that real, genuine, mutual relations can overcome Donjuanism, but he pessimistically declines to affirm that they can lead to full-fledged happiness for both parties in a rigid society that values stability and propriety over genuine feeling. And insofar as their affair in a very general way reflects Chekhov's own search for a romantic love that he could reconcile with his private nature and fear of intrusion into his personal life, it is unclear whether he found an answer to this conundrum.

Thus, as a key subtext for several important late nineteenth-century Russian figures, the Don Juan theme transforms the Realist ethos and is transformed by it. Just as Pushkin's alterations to the Don Juan theme intimately reflect his sexual, marital, poetic, and professional concerns at the time when he wrote the play, the treatment of the Don Juan theme by Tolstoy and Chekhov in particular reveals some of their deepest anxieties on the broader "woman question" and the relation of female sexuality and self-determination to their personal lives. Pushkin's transformation of the Don Juan legend in *The Stone Guest* from a tale of supernatural vengeance wreaked on a notorious libertine to an exploration of poetic and erotic identity generates a series of Don Juan figures in the Realist period who forsake their life of seductions for more conventional relationships. This transformation is reflected in the absorption of Pushkin's Romantic poet-seducer into more complex Realist characters limned in prose. And introducing this figure into the everyday framework of this literary period diffuses Don Juan's traditional identity. Although the triangular sexual rivalry Pushkin creates through Don Juan, Donna Anna, and the Commander is replicated in all of these works, by the time it makes its way to *Anna Karenina* and "The Lady with the Little Dog," the archetypal figure ceases to be referred to as such. Later, in early twentieth-century modernist literature, Don Juan's "archetypicality" is reestablished when the legendary figure reemerges in the works of various Silver Age poets.

3

Don Juan in the Silver Age

BEFORE THE TWENTIETH CENTURY, most writers explored the Don Juan theme through relatively lengthy narratives. The episodic nature of the plot, beginning with Tirso's play, encourages this expansiveness, as writers depict Don Juan's persistent refusal to reform, his serial seductions, the continuing frustration of rivals and authorities who attempt unsuccessfully to bring him to justice, and his gradual path either to supernatural punishment or, in the rare case of writers such as Zorrilla, to redemption. The Russian Realist writers discussed in the previous chapter, not surprisingly, given the prominence of the novel as a genre in this era, tend to explore the Spanish legend via lengthy prose works, dispersing elements of the Don Juan story through capacious narratives focused on other plots, and interweaving elements of Pushkin's terse retelling freely with other archetypes to examine the way Donjuanism intersected with daily life.

In the Silver Age, by contrast, writers tended to choose shorter genres such as poetry, brief plays, and essays for their Don Juan variants. The subject also became remarkably widespread, as nearly every major poet turned to the Don Juan legend. These poets include—in roughly chronological order of their works—Valery Briusov, Konstantin Bal'mont, Alexander Blok, Nikolai Gumilev, Marina Tsvetaeva, Zinaida Gippius, and Anna Akhmatova. Rather than attempt to survey all iterations of this topic in this period, I focus on four writers—Blok, Tsvetaeva, Gumilev, and Akhmatova—whose work develops motifs I have discussed in previous chapters. In all four cases, these poets intertextually connect the Don Juan legend to their own poetic personae by reprising aspects of Pushkin's autobiographical approach in *The Stone Guest*.

The flourishing interest of Silver Age writers in the Don Juan theme can be linked in large part to the widespread reevaluation of Eros in early twentieth-century Russian culture. This period witnessed unusually frank discourse about sex, intense erotic experimentation, tolerance for extramarital affairs, and exploration of sexual fluidity and nontraditional gender roles. Writers often engaged in unorthodox relationships, such as the love triangles between Blok, his wife Liubov' Dmitrievna, and Andrei Bely; between Briusov, Nina Petrovskaya, and Bely; and later, between Vladimir Mayakovsky and Osip and Lilia Brik. Such unorthodox relationships comprised efforts on the part of these poets not only to achieve greater sexual fulfillment but also to refashion the world around them. In the Symbolist practice of *zhiznetvorchestvo*, or "life creation," poets saw their task as the merging of life and art into a world-changing unity. To an extent, this impulse can be traced back to the efforts of Pushkin and other Romantic writers to encode their life experience into art, and in turn to use art to shape society.[1] However, Silver Age writers brought a new intensity to this project, leaning on the philosophical writings of Vladimir Solov'ev to participate in a reshaping of the world through poetic, social, and erotic means. They strove to make reality a domain of the ideal and beautiful by bringing the realm of the beyond into this world. As Irina Paperno puts it, *zhiznetvorchestvo* represents a synthesis of Romantic and Realist notions: "While romanticism saw the other world as the 'true' world, Symbolism adopted the realistic notion of the ultimate 'truth,' or reality, and superior aesthetic value of this world and of life" (*Creating Life* 22).

The Don Juan legend, particularly as recast by Pushkin, with its emphasis on a love triangle, naturally resonated with writers who were trying to redefine sexuality in various ways. It offered a great deal of potential for creating alternative approaches to love and for inspiring rebellion against social and religious conventions. Moreover, Pushkin's creation of a female character in Laura who explores her own sexuality freely models the kind of independence that, as I discuss below, characterizes Tsvetaeva's and Akhmatova's descriptions in particular of women choosing partners on an equal basis with men, or even taking the upper hand.

At the same time, *zhiznetvorchestvo* sometimes involved experimentation that rejected sexuality altogether. Olga Matich argues that fin-de-siècle writers were seeking to transcend their mortality by rejecting procreation: "the transfiguration of life," she writes, "could be accomplished only in an economy of desire that proscribed coitus" (5). If the Symbolists in particular, as Jenifer Presto also argues, frequently pitted art against life, in the sense of sexuality and procreation, then where does the Don Juan theme fit in? Often, incorporating this theme into art involved transformations of the notion of gender. In her 1926 poem "Don Juan's Answer" ("Otvet Don-Zhuana"), Gippius identifies directly with Don Juan by employing a masculine poetic speaker. As Presto notes in her analysis of the poem, "Gippius, much like Don Juan, moves from lover to lover, traversing almost as many geographic as personal boundaries" (171). As I discuss below, Tsvetaeva and Akhmatova, though retaining a feminine poetic voice, also find ways to identify with the legendary figure. Thus, Don Juan, with his virility and extreme appetite for sexual activity, paradoxically could appeal to poets who were interested in eliminating procreation as well as those who celebrated exuberant, prolific sexuality. Either way, the legend inspired writers to rethink traditional gender assumptions. Tsvetaeva, as I argue, voids Don Juan of his traditional sexuality as part of this reexamination.

At the same time, Silver Age writers tended toward an apocalyptic view of the world, particularly under the influence of Solov'ev, whose *Short Tale of the Antichrist* (*Kratkaia povest' ob Antikhriste*, 1900) predicted an invasion of Russia from the East followed by the eventual triumph of the Antichrist. This apocalyptic sensibility was reinforced by the intense political upheavals of the early twentieth century, such as the 1905 and 1917 Russian revolutions and World War I, which led them to view humanity as facing imminent all-embracing cataclysm. Indeed, their erotic experimentation was integrally connected to an attempt to transform the world in an apocalyptic light. Blok in particular wrote in this vein, warning repeatedly of dark days ahead and viewing himself as a prophet of a coming upheaval that would finally bring salvation to a spiritually suffering Russia. Three of the poems I analyze below—Blok's "The Steps of the Commander" and *Retribution*, and Akhmatova's *Poem without a Hero*—can be understood as reflecting or reacting to this period of revolutionary upheaval. Blok, in both poems, uses the Don Juan myth to evoke a broader sense of retribution in light of the contemporary political upheaval; Akhmatova describes Donjuanism as a sin (on her part and that of her contemporaries) that has called forth the horrors of Stalinism as a form of vengeance.

In keeping with the principles of *zhiznetvorchestvo*, Silver Age Don Juan works also take a distinctly autobiographical approach to the theme. This pattern recalls Pushkin, different parts of whose erotic career can be mapped onto Don Juan and the Commander. For the Realists I discussed in the previous chapter, this identification recedes to an extent, partly because of the premium they place on an avowedly objective portrayal of reality, and the autobiographical links are less conspicuous. In *The Stone Guest*, the connections between author and hero are quite apparent from the beginning of the play, when Pushkin refers to Don Juan's exile not from the traditional Seville but Madrid, which as the capital of Spain evokes the imperial Russian capital of St. Petersburg from which Pushkin had been exiled. Such links are less overt in the works of the Realists Goncharov, Tolstoy, and Chekhov. Although we can speak of autobiographical links, as between Gurov's and Chekhov's own Donjuanism and misogyny, we can also easily read the works without feeling compelled to make this connection.

In the Silver Age, by contrast, autobiographical links reassert themselves. Much of this renewed role of autobiography in literature has to do with the return of poetry, with frequent close identification of the author and speaker, as the leading genre after the decline of the novel following its culmination in *Anna Karenina* and *The Brothers Karamazov* in the 1870s. Poets such as Briusov, Bal'mont, Blok, Gumilev, and others who wrote Don Juan texts deliberately and self-consciously conveyed this connection between the heroes and their own authorial personae. Thus, the history of the Don Juan theme in the Silver Age, like so many other aspects, recalled Pushkin's foregrounding of autobiographical traits and stressed many of the motifs and themes he added to the Western legend.

This reliance on Pushkin, though, is by no means universal. If we consider the Don Juan legend in the broader context of Europe as a whole, we see a variety of interpretations. The most famous Western European Don Juan narrative during this period was George Bernard Shaw's *Man and Superman* (1903). This play's third act features a section titled "Don Juan in Hell," in which John Tanner (who, as his name indicates, is a descendant of Tirso's Don Juan Tenorio) dreams of conversing with the Devil, the statue, and Donna Ana in hell. Shaw turns for inspiration not to Pushkin, but to Mozart: "Don Juan in Hell" opens with the sound of the overture to *Don Giovanni*. Shaw's originality consists, among other things, in adding a new dimension to the Don Juan narrative by imagining the aftermath of the libertine's trip to hell. As I discuss below, Gumilev undertakes a similar project in his short play on the theme, though most likely without knowledge of Shaw's drama. For Shaw, the Don Juan theme serves as a pretext for a broader examination of male-female relations in which Tanner (voicing Shaw's ideas) claims that women, not men, are the true drivers of the act of seduction.

Russian writers on the Don Juan theme, too, turned to a variety of texts for inspiration. As mentioned in the previous chapter, Mordvin-Shchodro and Bezhetsky each produced Don Juan plays in 1896 that featured idealist heroes on a quest for a feminine counterpart along the lines established by Hoffmann in his 1813 story and continued in Alexei K. Tolstoy's play. Other fin-de-siècle writers also explored the Don Juan legend along European lines. Bal'mont's 1904 essay "The Don Juan Type in World Literature" ("Tip Don-Zhuana v mirovoi literature") focuses on European writers and singles out José de Espronceda's poem *The Student of Salamanca* (1840), Stanisław Przybyszewski's novel *Homo Sapiens* (1896), and Gabriele D'Annunzio's novel *The Pleasure* (1889) as exemplars of contemporary trends. Without mentioning Pushkin, Alexei K. Tolstoy, or any other prominent nineteenth-century Russian writers, the essay traces the theme back to the first Don Juan writer, Tirso.[2] In each of the three works Bal'mont cites, he notes the tragic debasing of the hero, arguing that Don Juan no longer has the sympathetic qualities attributed to him by writers such as Hoffmann. "The old Romantic Don Juan," he writes, "has irrevocably died, along with the temporal conditions that created his living and literary type" (542).[3] At this point, for Bal'mont, Don Juan is of interest despite his debasement because he embodies a "secret symbolic image" that will never die. Because he pursues everything to the limit, remains a seeker into the beyond, and has access to spirits from the other world, Bal'mont explains, he holds great importance for the age of Symbolism: "Don Juan is as multifaceted, as inexhaustible, as our soul, and, like our soul, he passes through the whole world, from pole to pole, and reaching the limits of these poles, feels melancholy and looks beyond" (544). Thus, according to Bal'mont, despite the revulsion Don Juan inspires with his deeds, he remains significant as an artistic image.

Bal'mont's incomplete poem "Don-Zhuan," written as part of his 1898 cycle "Silence" ("Tishina"), embodies some of the ideas expressed in his essay. Don Juan is depicted as unsatisfied with his lover Ines at the very beginning:

La luna Ilena . . . The full moon . . .
Pale Ines kisses like a gipsy.
Te amo . . . amo . . . Again, quiet . . .
But Don Juan's stubborn gaze is gloomy.

La luna Ilena . . . Полная Луна . . .
Иньес, бледна, целует, как гитана.
Te amo . . . amo . . . Снова тишина . . .
Но мрачен взор упорный Дон-Жуана. (497)

Bal'mont portrays Don Juan as disillusioned not only in love, but by people in general.

Words will lie—for a thought there can be no deception—
The love of people is absurd to him.
He's seen everything, he's understood too soon
The meaning of his visionary dream.

Слова солгут—для мысли нет обмана, —
Любовь людей—она ему смешна.
Он видел все, он понял слишком рано
Значение мечтательного сна. (497)

Because of his disillusionment, Don Juan is dead set on revenge, which will affect women and men alike. Bal'mont portrays Don Juan as both a world traveler, crossing oceans and steppes, and a toxic force: "And thousands of hearts / Will be enslaved by the breath of poison" (I tysiachi serdets / Porabotit dykhaniem otravy; 498).

Not all Silver Age writers agreed with Bal'mont's conclusions, however. For Tsvetaeva, as I discuss, Don Juan is far from a malevolent figure and is not even depicted in the act of seducing and destroying women, as he does in the three works Bal'mont cites. Moreover, unlike Bal'mont, several Silver Age figures found the psychic struggle depicted in Pushkin's *The Stone Guest* more relevant than the multiple seductions of traditional Don Juans. Blok and Akhmatova in particular rework Pushkin's dual autobiographical portrait in surprising ways. I begin with a discussion of Blok's Donjuanism in life and in two of his major poems. In the following two discussions of Don Juan works by Tsvetaeva and Gumilev, I explore how each poet, in varying ways, counters Blok's vision of Donjuanism thematically and stylistically. I conclude with a later work, Akhmatova's 1940–62 *Poem without a Hero*, which synthesizes several strands of Silver Age interpretation of the Don Juan legend.

Blok as Don Juan and the Commander

In Blok's personal life and poetry alike, one may speak of the same opposition that Akhmatova and others have found in Pushkin: the combination of Don Juan and the Commander in one figure. In light of Blok's frequent doubling of himself, it makes sense to think of him as a fusion of opposites. Below I examine the intersection of the two opponents within Blok and then analyze the projection of these two personae into the protagonists of his works.

Blok followed in the footsteps of Pushkin and other real-life Don Juan figures in terms of making multiple conquests, the most prominent of whom were the actresses Valentina Shcheglova and Natalia Volokhova and the singer Liubov' Delmas.[4] Avril Pyman describes these relationships as a cycle of abortive affairs in which Blok's fleeting infatuation with various women would lead them to fall in love with him and either plan to leave their husbands for him or demand that he dedicate all his verse to them (116). Blok himself analyzed these affairs as no more than repetitions of the same thing compared to his love for his wife, Liubov' Dmitrievna Mendeleeva: "I have had not 100 women—200—300 (or more?), but only two: one is Liuba; the other—all the rest" (*Zapisnye knizhki* 303).

However, because so many of Blok's sexual partners were prostitutes he met on nightlong walks through St. Petersburg, both he and his poetic persona also invoke the flâneur figure described by Walter Benjamin and featured by other Russian writers such as Dostoevsky (especially in *White Nights* and other early St. Petersburg works). This aspect of Blok's sexual activity made for a more passive type of Donjuanism: the typical Don Juan figure wanders from country to country, often owing to exile, and this mobility creates the sense of adventure, of episodic, serial activity that characterizes so many narratives of the legend. But in contrast to the legendary Don Juan, who typically seduces women as he meets them, Blok's flâneur simply *sees* an endless number of women, an act that feeds his poetic imagination, just as Pushkin's Don Juan is inspired by the sight of Donna Anna's foot and only "seduces" prostitutes.[5] The risk of failure, then, is completely eliminated in the demimonde, and the wandering—restricted to Petersburg—takes on a more predictable character than in the legendary Don Juan's international peregrinations.[6]

Blok's unusual relationship with his wife positions the prostitutes with whom he consorted within the broader Don Juan theme. Since Blok viewed Liubov' Dmitrievna from the early years of their relationship as a manifestation of the Beautiful Lady, a symbol of the Eternal Feminine, he was reluctant to consummate their marriage and delayed doing so for several years.[7] Blok's visits with prostitutes, already quite different from traditional Don Juan seductions, therefore serve in part as substitutes for marital relations, or even a kind of "safety valve" that helped him maintain his desired lack of sexual relations with his wife and preserve his ideal, mystical worship of the Beautiful Lady. His neo-Romantic interpretation of Donjuanism as bound up in a search for an ideal woman thus links him to early nineteenth-century writers on the theme such as Hoffmann, Zorrilla, and Pushkin.

This search for the ideal woman surely stems from Blok's early initiation into love by Ksenia Sadovskaya, a Ukrainian grass widow twice his age with whom he began an affair at the Bad Nauheim spa in 1897 and continued the relationship until 1901. As Pyman explains, Blok's sad realization later in life that ideal love may be impossible can be traced back to the fact that Liubov' Dmitrievna was not actually his first love: "He had felt things for Sadovskaya and given her words which should have been given to one woman only" (97–98). This affected his love for other women as well, as his involvement with Shcheglova in spring 1910 suggests: "It was in part to this infatuation that Blok owed the final realization of his inability to form any further profound ties with a woman, and the crystallization of the theme of retribution which enabled him to write the superb but baleful 'Steps of the Commander'" (98).

In contrast to Hoffmann's addition to the legend of an ideal woman, Donna Anna of the *Don Giovanni* performance, Blok's poetic persona makes no false promises to women, but rather undergoes a kind of self-deceit as he experiences a continual betrayal of his ideal through his encounters with prostitutes.

Don Juan thus progresses from a conqueror for the sake of his own pleasure (Tirso, Molière, Mozart/Da Ponte) to a quester for an ideal (Hoffmann, Zorrilla, to some extent Pushkin), to a failed seeker whose encounters are not really conquests and who already has his ideal but cannot consummate it. Despite the progression, the serial, episodic structure remains.

Like Pushkin, though, Blok can be seen not only as a Don Juan, but also as a Commander figure. Many of Blok's contemporaries, including Akhmatova, Bely, and Elizaveta Kuzmina-Karavaeva (a poet who eventually took vows as a nun and became known in Paris as "Mother Maria"), described his physical appearance as Commander-like. Sergei Gorodetsky, recalling Blok's poetic recitations, wrote: "He would go slowly to the table with the candles, look around at everyone with his stony eyes and would himself turn to stone until the silence became complete" (qtd. in Mochulsky 174).[8] Blok, moreover, was involved in a notorious love triangle with Bely and Liubov' Dmitrievna in which he played the role of cuckold, just as the Commander does.[9] In this sense, he reflects the very identity of opposites Akhmatova describes in Pushkin. In light of the links one can find between Blok's poetry and Pushkin's Don Juan play, he seems to have been aware of this ambiguity; thus both his persona and career continue the Russian fascination with the identity of two seeming opposites, in contrast to the clear distinction Tirso, Molière, and Mozart/Da Ponte make between the antagonists.[10] In the next part of the chapter, I interpret Blok's concept of Donjuanism through the most direct example of his exploration of this theme, the 1910–12 lyric poem "The Steps of the Commander" ("Shagi komandora"). I then consider his incomplete narrative poem *Retribution* (*Vozmezdie*) in relation to the Don Juan theme.

Blok's "The Steps of the Commander"

Blok's ten-stanza lyric poem "The Steps of the Commander" is easily the best known of the various Silver Age lyric poems on the Don Juan subject. Like the Realist works I discussed in the previous chapter, it recalls not just the Don Juan theme in general, but specific aspects of Pushkin's *Stone Guest*. The title, for starters, similarly refers to the Commander rather than Don Juan. However, in place of the "stoniness" that obsesses Pushkin, Blok focuses on the statue's steps and movement (and the contrast of silence with sounds).[11] I discuss this and other allusions to Pushkin's little tragedy in this section, paying special attention to what could be considered hybrid generic characteristics in the poem. I argue that in "The Steps of the Commander," Blok, while removing some of Pushkin's ambiguity (his Don Juan, like Tolstoy's erstwhile libertine Vronsky, is unequivocally in love with Anna), recreates his predecessor's identification between opponents, as well as his own aforementioned combination of features of Don Juan and the Commander in his personal life, as the two characters merge together symbolically in the poem.

"The Steps of the Commander" certainly has all the characteristics of a lyric poem and indeed is part of a cycle of such poems, also called *Retribution* (*Vozmezdie*, like the narrative poem [*poema*] of the same title that he was simultaneously working on). And as G. N. Gorchakov notes, Blok's disruption of time, space, and sequence in the poem scatters our sense of a logical narrative (331). At the same time, however, various aspects of the poem recall a stage for a play, or even an opera, in light of Blok's vocalic sounds and deliberate repetitions, along with the interspersed spoken lines "You invited me to supper / I've come. Are you ready . . . ?" (Ty zval menia na uzhin / Ia prishel. A ty gotov . . . ?).[12]

The very first couplet underscores the poem's stage-like qualities. The heavy, thick curtain in the first lines, for instance, is a dual, ambiguous image. Although it is a curtain in a luxurious bedroom (v pyshnoi spal'ne), it also evokes a stage curtain, likewise heavy and thick. As Margarita Fainberg notes about the beginning of the poem, "The theatrical curtain—and it is theatrical—is a curtain-symbol, in which [can be found] the dust of the wings, and the weight of memories, and theatrical passions, actresses, and a series of Don Juans, and the memory of that 1899 amateur performance in which the young Blok and Liuba Mendeleeva played Pushkin's "Stone Guest" . . . —and everything that followed. . . ." (213). In this light, Blok appears to be staging his own past life and psychic battles.

The second couplet, which describes the sleeping servants and the sound of the crowing cock, also resembles a stage description. The eighth stanza, which seems to serve the same function, even recalls the second, as it repeats some of the same material ("in the luxurious bedroom" / v pyshnoi spal'ne) while giving it different qualities ("frightening at daybreak" / strashno v chas rassveta), where earlier it was "cold and empty" (kholodno i pusto). Similarly, "The servants sleep, and the night is pale" (Slugi spiat, i noch' bledna) recalls "The servants sleep, and it's the dead of night" (Slugi spiat, i noch' glukha) in the same stanzas. Both repetitions are deliberately arranged to echo each other, like operatic motifs with slight variations. And the Commander stepping out of his car, entering the house, and challenging Don Juan similarly recall what a director might describe as the next action and dialogue of a drama.

These "stage directions," however, are unsettlingly incongruent, with strange, unearthly, illogical, apparently disordered images that suggest a dream rather than the concrete reality of a play.[13] For instance, in the first stanza, the crowing of the rooster takes place at night rather than in the morning, and it comes from a "blissful, foreign, distant land" (iz strany blazhennoi, neznakomoi, dal'nei). Thus, Blok juxtaposes two different times and places: the present location, where it is night, and an unspecified realm where it is dawn. This line also anticipates the conclusion of the poem, the "hour of dawn" (chas rassveta). And what could make this crowing sound seem blissful? Perhaps the end of a dream, indicating morning, a new day, and survival of death or other horrors. However, it also seems logical to interpret the crowing cock as a symbol of betrayal, as in Jesus's prophetic words to Peter: "Before the rooster crows today, you will betray me three times."[14] After all, the poem is about betrayal, and Blok felt guilty for betraying his "Beautiful Lady," a symbol of the loftiest purity. But then what would be "blissful" about this betrayal, especially considering the outcome of this event: "Peter went outside and wept bitterly" when he remembers Christ's words, which have come true? The horror of daybreak ("strashno v chas rassveta"), moreover, seems both incongruent and somehow anticlimactic at the same time. Finally, the description of Anna is ambivalent: is she sleeping ("Donna Anna sleeps, crossing her arms on her heart" / Donna Anna spit, skrestiv na serdtse ruki) or dead ("Anna, Anna, are you sleeping sweetly in the grave?" / Anna, Anna, sladko l' spat' v mogile?)?[15] Thus, if there is a "drama" taking place, it is a psychic drama rather than a play, despite the stage elements.[16]

Moreover, the poem seems to focus on the aural more than the visual dimension. As several commentators have noted, "The Steps of the Commander" is structured around vocalic repetitions: Konstantin Mochulsky describes the use of "o" as the motif of darkness and the Commander and the "a" (through the repetitions of "Anna") as a motif of light and Donna Anna (318). If Pushkin focuses on the immobility of the Commander as part of his myth of an immobile statue going into motion, then Blok turns the emphasis to the Commander's sound, as reflected in the title's reference to footsteps.[17] There are many of what could be called internal rhymes, rhymes within a line or in the beginnings or middles of consecutive lines. Some of these could be explained simply as the linking of adjectives ("heavy, thick" / tiazhkii, plotnyi), but many are quite insistent ("Don Juan who has known fear" / strakh poznavshii Don-Zhuan; "whose features have frozen in the mirror" / ch'i cherty zhestokie zastyli). In the climactic point of the poem, Blok's repetition of the "a" sound nine times in the couplet "Maiden of Light! Where are you, Donna Anna? /Anna! Anna! —Silence" (Deva Sveta! Gde ty, donna Anna? /Anna! Anna! —Tishina) reinforces the poem's focus on her, linking her to the persona of the "Beautiful Lady" that Blok develops throughout much of his poetic career.

The poem's theatrical qualities hint at *The Stone Guest*, but the relationship between the two works is deeper than that. In his exploration of how Blok transforms Pushkin's statue myth, Adrian Wanner enumerates the various parallels between "Steps of the Commander" and Pushkin's little tragedy, noting the "rueful Don Juan and tantalizingly vanishing Donna Anna" whom they share (241). As he also points out, the words of Blok's Commander, "You invited me to supper. / I've come. Are you ready?" (Ty zval menia na uzhin. Ia prishel. A ty gotov?) recall Don Juan in *The Stone Guest*: "I invited you" (Ia zval tebia). The last words of Blok's hero, "Where are you, Donna Anna? Anna! Anna!" (Gde ty, Donna Anna? Anna! Anna!), recall Pushkin's Don Juan's anguished cry to his beloved at the end of the play. Significantly, Wanner notes that all three protagonists become "statue-like" in some way: Anna is in a deathlike sleep, and Don Juan becomes transfixed, like a statue, as he awaits the Commander's arrival: "Whose cruel features have frozen, reflected in mirrors?" (Ch'i cherty zhestokie zastyli, V zerkalakh otrazheny? ; 241–42).

This similarity underscores what is perhaps Blok's most important borrowing from Pushkin: the identity between seeming opponents. What is most striking at the end of *The Stone Guest* is not so much Don Juan's punishment as his symbolic unity with the Commander. Blok recreates this identity in part through ambiguous apostrophizing. It is not clear who calls Donna Anna two times: it could be the poet himself, Don Juan, or the Commander. One gets the sense that either Don Juan or the Commander could equally be referring to Anna as the "Maiden of Light," and both could see her as their means of salvation. It is also significant that the Commander's aforementioned words to Don Juan are not answered. Given the Commander's lack of physical presence (we hear a car horn and steps, but do not *see* him approach), is it possible that he is only a projection of Don Juan's mind, a symbol of his conscience? The first reference to the Commander invokes an incorporeal representation of death rather than the solid, palpable figure of traditional narratives of the legend (including Pushkin's). Earlier in his career, Blok's "beautiful lady" is often similarly described as felt or sensed rather than seen, as in, among many other lyric poems, "I Foresee You" ("Predchuvstvuiu Tebia . . . ," 1901). In "The Steps of the Commander," Anna is the figure who is relatively concrete, as the physical image of her sleeping with her arms crossed is not surrounded by any mist or an intangible appearance, unlike the Commander. In previous instantiations, Don Juan—having defied human laws for his whole career as a seducer of multiple women—now transgresses into the world of the dead, the world beyond the grave, through his sacrilegious invitation of the statue to dinner. Blok's hero, by contrast, invites not so much a dead man as an instantiation of his fate, accompanied by the disillusionment with his ideals that characterizes much of the poet's work of this period:

Life is empty, mad, and fathomless!
Come out and fight, old fate!

Жизнь пуста, безумна и бездонна!
Выходи на битву, старый рок!

Thus, Blok's earlier more hopeful challenge to an unearthly feminine vision to appear from beyond the mist is replaced by a challenge to an equally incorporeal male figure, known as a rival but also a representation of his destiny, apprehended for a long time. Don Juan's challenge is answered concretely, but in *aural* fashion, as the Commander's horn from his car resounds. The horn, moreover, conveys desire; it is "victorious and amorous" (pobedno i vliublenno). This sound image simultaneously conveys battle and intimacy. It signals a victory that has *already* taken place ("victoriously"), and the word for horn (*rozhok*, from *rog*) indicates a bugle announcing battle. The word also hints at sexual intimacy as it connotes a sharp object, but the diminutive of it—pleasurable to a sexual partner, but threatening to a male rival. Most concretely, however, the *rozhok* is also a car horn. It is thus an incongruous image emphasizing the placement of an old legend within the present day, but also the act of transportation or picking up of a romantic companion (who, unbeknownst to him, is in that ambiguous state between sleep and death). Looking at these images through Pushkin's play, with its symbolic joining of Don Juan and the Commander in the last stage direction, however, allows us to see the combination of attributes in each figure, as the sexual desire, for instance, pertains to both Don Juan and the Commander. Because one can hear the word for "fate" (rok) as well in this image (*rog* devoices to *rok*), Blok also links sex to fate, or death.

However, Blok changes the transgression, and therefore the purpose of revenge, from that of Pushkin's play. In *The Stone Guest*, the reason behind Don Juan's punishment is not entirely clarified. It could be for his slaying of the Commander in a duel, his brazen invitation of the statue to guard the door during his tryst with Donna Anna, his act of seducing the Commander's wife, or his past libertinism. The purpose of inviting the statue, for some critics of the play, is to defeat the forces of death, to test his fate, and to attempt to triumph over the forces that would deprive him of the ultimate happiness (true love); the fact that the statue does succeed in defeating Don Juan as he is on the verge of happiness, for critics like Rassadin, is what makes the play a tragedy. Blok's Don Juan, however, seems to unequivocally call forth his own punishment. Blok saw his Donjuanism as something demonic, unnatural, and degenerate. So he takes Pushkin's Don Juan, whom he interprets as being on the cusp of reform and happiness, and turns him into a "traitor," something worse than Pushkin's Don Juan. In Blok's interpretation, Pushkin's hero, having found his ideal in Anna, is ready to fight the forces of death for her, to defeat the past and ensure his happiness, and is tragically, cruelly defeated.[18] But Blok's betrayer of his ideal deserves only defeat, and there is a sense that he is inviting Fate to mete it out. There is no chance of happiness because, having found his ideal (the Beautiful Lady), he has already ruined her (and she, likewise, has betrayed him and her higher calling). Blok's Don Juan, following up on the possibility Pushkin indicates of his hero's rebirth, has found his worthy, ideal love, and his last hope for redemption, but in "The Steps of the Commander," this love is dead and will only arise at Don Juan's death.

While Pushkin's Don Juan claims that he hopes for rebirth through Anna until the very end, Blok's hero appears to lack such expectations. Anna is already sleeping (or possibly dead), and this causes despair rather than hope. For Gorchakov, the Commander's words addressed to Don Juan "are you ready?" (ty gotov?) imply a question as to whether Don Juan is ready for resurrection or renewal: the response of silence seems to indicate that he is not, as his soul is already dead (344–45). As Mochulsky puts it, "Blok sees the legend of Don Juan as a tragedy of conscience. Having been unfaithful to the Maiden of Light, the hero falls into the power of dark forces" (317). The realization of the poem, written after a period of great disillusionment for Blok following his *Poems about a Beautiful Lady* (*Stikhi o prekrasnoi dame*), and his turn to political topics and revolution in 1906, is that destruction is the only possibility: hence, "life is empty, senseless, and fathomless" (zhizn' pusta, bezumna i bezdonna), with the wordplay of "bezdonna" indicating both "fathomless" and "without the Donna [Anna])." Walter Vickery comments that the poem embodies a type of retribution for Blok's "sex guilt syndrome," a sense of despair in his inability to overcome the schism between spiritual love and sexuality in his own relationships ("Hamlet and Don Juan in Blok," 474). Blok in effect reproduces Pushkin's identification of opposites, "playing" both roles here: he functions both as Don Juan, going to meet his Fate, and the Commander, dispensing his own punishment. The poem represents a drama of psychic self-punishment, in which the poet acts as both the avenger and the punished.

Blok's portrayal of Anna, similarly, both takes Pushkin as its starting point and departs from his predecessor's portrayal. Donna Anna's fate in Pushkin is ambiguous: she appears to faint as the statue appears, and some readers interpret this loss of consciousness as her death. Don Juan is preoccupied with her, and he calls out to her with his last words before descending to hell, though the statue admonishes him to set her aside. This ambiguity as to Anna's fate is continued in Blok, who portrays her as either sleeping or dead. But the poem ends with Anna rising at the hour of Don Juan's death, a passage Blok chooses to emphasize with italics and repetition: ("*Donna Anna will rise at your hour of death. Anna will rise at the hour of death*" / *Donna Anna v smertnyi chas tvoi vstanet. Anna vstanet v smertnyi chas*). Why does Anna rise? And is it from death (resurrection) or sleep (awakening)? How could this scene be connected to Pushkin's play, in which it is not exactly clear whether Anna faints or dies? Does it mean that the poem is not completely tragic, that Anna (the "Beautiful Lady," the poetic ideal) will survive Don Juan's (and the poet's) death after all? Does she deserve this chance at redemption because, unlike Don Juan, she is not completely corrupt?

The sense of expectation pervading the poem calls forth a distinct sense of apocalypse, as in so many of Blok's lyric poems. Along with its focus on punishment and failure to achieve redemption, the poem more broadly uses Don Juan topoi to portend greater disaster than just the hero's fate. The Commander's "heavy steps" (tiazhelye shagi) themselves suggest impending cataclysm. As Wanner notes, they recall *The Bronze Horseman*'s "heavy-sonorous riding" (tiazhelozvonkoe skakan'e) and "heavy clatter" (tiazhelyi topot; 242). Thus, Blok recalls Pushkin's own apocalyptic vision of the 1824 flood, a disaster that left several hundred people dead. Like Tolstoy in *Anna Karenina*, Blok focuses on the role of technology in his depiction of apocalypse, even mentioning the Commander's car. S. F. Dmitrienko points out that Blok's use of the word "motor" (car) is jarring, and reflects his frequent use of machine motifs, which symbolize the ruin of human beings (55). As Nathalie Labrecque suggests, Donna Anna, who may be liberated with Don Juan's death, personifies Russia itself; thus, Anna rising at the hour of Don Juan's death represents a kind of release of the "true Russia" by the revolution Blok was awaiting (96). In this sense, Blok's title points to impending cataclysm, and his poetic drama outlines the revolution that he thought would cleanse the old, corrupt Russia.

Donjuanism in *Retribution*

As with other poets of the time, such as Bal'mont and Gumilev, whose creative expressions of this theme appear in multiple genres, Blok's exploration required further working out in another form. The Don Juan theme is reprised in *Retribution* (*Vozmezdie*), the narrative poem that Blok started working on around the same time as "The Steps of the Commander" but never finished. Incomplete literary works should be handled carefully, but in this case, it seems appropriate to make the comparison with *Retribution* since, as I argue below, Blok's description of his father in particular contains echoes of the Don Juan theme as explored in Pushkin's *Stone Guest*. As in "The Steps of the Commander," there is an intermingling of oppositions, as characters take on both Don Juan and Commander attributes.

The death of Blok's father, Alexander L'vovich, in 1909 closely preceded his first work on both *Retribution* and "The Steps of the Commander" in 1910, and *Retribution*, as Mochulsky notes, represents an effort on Blok's part to exorcise his father's ghost (257). Blok had a complicated relationship with his father, to say the least. He grew up without him, in the maternal Beketov family, and his mother divorced his father and remarried in 1889. Blok saw his father only rarely, during annual visits Alexander L'vovich made to Petersburg from Warsaw, where he was a law professor. Blok dreaded these visits, but at the same time felt a strange affinity with his father. In keeping with the degeneration theory that dominated scientific and cultural thought in fin-de-siècle Europe, Blok viewed his inability to establish a satisfying relationship with a woman that integrated love and lust as a hereditary taint. He sensed himself to be cursed with a cruel sensuality that he had inherited from his father, and called himself "a degenerate from the Blok family." As Pyman notes, "The record of his worldly love affairs, his seductions in the demimonde and in the realm of art and literature, was a series of Don Juan-like disappointments: the excitement of the chase, the triumph of conquest, then boredom, a sense of letdown, of cold, cruel sobriety" (79).[19] But while Alexander L'vovich accepted his cruel lust as an integral part of his character, Blok saw his own "demonic sensuality" as unnatural. This sense of degeneration affected his decision not to have children. "Let one of the Blok lines at least end with me—there is little good in them," he remarked.[20] The similarities between Blok and his father touch upon the artistic realm as well: although Alexander L'vovich was an unsuccessful poet, he was an accomplished pianist who particularly loved Beethoven and Schumann, as detailed in *Retribution*. As Mochulsky describes it, father and son exhibited "the same split in perception of the world, the same anxiety and dreaminess, the same musical-lyrical instinct, sense of doom, and poisoning with irony" (18–19).

Blok's simultaneous identification with and alienation from his father evoke Oedipal theory, which can be used to characterize both Blok's relationship with his father and its instantiation in the *poema*. *Retribution* contains passages that seem to join the Don Juan legend with the Freudian myth of Oedipal father-son relations. In keeping with the primordial ambivalence expressed in *Totem and Taboo*, throughout Blok's description of his father in the *poema*, hatred and fear mix with love and admiration. Ultimately, the Oedipal conflict and its working out involve the desire to become a father oneself. This can be seen in Freud's description, in an early piece on the Oedipal conflict, of rescue fantasies directed toward the father. These fantasies "aim at expressing the subject's wish to have his father as a son—that is, to have a son who is like his father" ("A Very Special Type of Choice" 394).

In keeping with Blok's preoccupation with his father at this time, especially as a key to understanding his own character and destiny, the Don Juan subtext in *Retribution* revolves around Alexander L'vovich. The subtext begins with Blok's brief allusion to Don Juan in his account of how his father met the Beketovs and married his mother, Alexandra Beketova, in Chapter 1 of the *poema*. Blok describes his father as a guest at Anna Vrevskaya's (Anna Filosofova's) salon. Alexander L'vovich is noticed by Dostoevsky, who whispers to the host that he resembles Byron. Other Byron references follow as the ladies at the salon agree with Dostoevsky's assessment:

> And the ladies were in ecstasy:
> "He's Byron, so, a demon"—Well, so?
> He simply resembled a proud Lord
> His face had a haughty expression
> And somehow also, what I want to call
> A heavy flame of sadness.

> И дамы были в восхищеньи:
> "Он—Байрон, значит—демон . . ."—Что ж?
> Он впрямь был с гордым лордом схож
> Лица надменным выражением
> И чем-то, что хочу назвать
> Тяжелым пламенем печали. (467)

Blok's father attracts the attention of the youngest Beketov daughter, Alexandra, with his handsome appearance, and when he is invited to their home, he captivates them with "lively and fiery conversation" (Zhivoi i plamennoi besedoi / Plenil; 468). His interest in the younger daughter becomes obvious, but he puts off making a marriage proposal: "He delays, and he himself doesn't know / Why he delays, what for?" (On medlit; sam ne znaet, / Zachem on medlit, dlia chego). At this point, Blok, noting that another man in such a position would have fled, describes him explicitly as a Don Juan:

> Another groom in his place
> Would have taken to his heels long ago,
> But my hero was too honest
> And could not deceive her:
> He was not proud of that strange custom,
> And he was given to know
> That to conduct himself as a demon and Don Juan
> In that age was ridiculous . . .

Другой жених на этом месте
Давно отряс бы прах от ног,
Но мой герой был слишком честен
И обмануть ее не мог:
Он не гордился нравом странным,
И было знать ему дано,
Что демоном и Дон-Жуаном
В тот век вести себя—смешно . . . (471)

Blok presents his father, then, as a "would-be Don Juan" or reformed Don Juan. He links him continually to Byron (the writer of one of the most well-known Don Juan works) and describes his behavior as demonic but depicts his father as behaving properly at the critical moment and marrying Alexandra. The first chapter closes with Blok in his mother's arms at the time of the March 1, 1881, assassination of Tsar Alexander II: "And a baby lies in her arms" (I na rukakh lezhit rebenok; 472).

Although Blok links his father principally with Byron, Lermontov's Demon, and Don Juan, there are also echoes of Pushkin's statue—as part of his dualist interpretation of the legend, following his predecessor—in his description of Alexander L'vovich and the Beketovs in Chapter 1. Describing his father's effect on his mother, Blok writes: "And he turned her childhood home into / A prison (although not in the least / Did this home resemble a prison)" (I dom ee rodnoi v t'iurmu / On prevratil (khotia nimalo / S t'iurmoi ne skhodstvoval sei dom) (469). This description applies to an extent to Don Juan, a predator who traps his prey; at the same time, it also aptly describes the Don's opponents in *The Stone Guest*: both Don Carlos, who attempts to tame Laura's promiscuity, and Don Alvar, who entraps Anna at home during his life and in mourning after his death. Blok's father has the effect of immobilizing his future bride, who is so captivated by her Commander-like fiancé that she is unable even to flirt—that is, to carry on relations that would establish some equal ground between a man and a woman.

This passing reference to Blok's father as not behaving like a Don Juan, perhaps, would not justify extended analysis if the same subtext did not also emerge in a different part of the *poema*. In the third chapter, Blok narrates elements of the theme again, but this time through a description of the hero (a stand-in for Blok himself) going to his father's funeral and then visiting his apartment. Although Blok does not make the Don Juan theme explicit again here, he includes various details that, among other intertextual resonances, hint at the Don Juan/Commander interactions in Pushkin's little tragedy. Blok describes himself as flooded with memories of his father that almost seem to bring him back from the grave. "And he couldn't shake the evil thought: 'Perhaps he's still alive! . . . '" (I zluiu mysl' ne otognat': 'On zhiv eshche! . . . '; 477).[21] In one of these recollections, Alexander L'vovich is compared to a guest, recalling the statue's dramatic entrance at the end of *The Stone Guest*: "His father came to him like a guest / Bent over . . ." (Otets khodil k nemu kak gost'/Sogbennyi . . . ; 480). During the burial, Blok notes the lead cover on the coffin, which he interprets as necessary so that his father cannot rise, cannot be resurrected. He looks in the grave, however, as though hoping (or perhaps fearing) to find something out of the ordinary, and takes a ring off his father's finger.[22] Thus, Blok preserves a sense of ambivalence between life and death, recalling the statue of the Don Juan legend in his portrayal of his father's death, as if wondering whether a motionless corpse can be set into motion.

Blok follows the funeral with a description of his protagonist looking through his father's study in great detail, a passage that recalls Tatiana's thorough examination of Onegin's house and library in Pushkin's *Eugene Onegin*, for the similar purpose of fathoming a seemingly larger-than-life figure. If Blok describes his father as a Byron in Chapter 1, the description in Chapter 3 is more mixed. He compares him at one point to a weakened Faust, and at another to Harpagon, the protagonist of Molière's *The Miser*, who hoards money and wants to marry the much younger woman with whom his son is in love. The elements of rivalry over a woman and withholding of money do not apply directly, but Blok's father, a pathological miser, could certainly be seen as "hoarding" affection, and thereby estranging his son. Here in this scene, the son is pondering the mystery of the father as Don Juan ponders the mystery of the statue in Pushkin, comparing the Commander's small size in life to his larger-than-life depiction as a statue.

Possibly the most interesting point in this passage, in view of the Don Juan theme, is Blok's description of himself as a young boy mischievously sticking a pin into his father's elbow; the memory of his father's scream rouses him back to consciousness.

The son remembers: in the nursery, on the couch
His father sits, smoking and angry;
And he, senselessly mischievous,
Circling in front of his father in the smoke . . .
Suddenly (what an evil, stupid child!)—
As if a demon is egging him on,
Headlong, he pricks his father
Near his elbow with a pin . . .
And his father, bewildered, pale from the pain,
Emits a wild scream . . . (480)

Сын помнит: в детской, на диване
Сидит отец, куря и злясь;
А он, безумно расшалясь,
Вертится пред отцом в тумане . . .
Вдруг (злое, глуппое дитя!)—
Как будто бес его толкает,
И он стремглав отцу вонзает
Булавку около локтя . . .
Растерян, побледнев от боли,
Тот дико вскрикнул . . .

This passage recalls the object (the "pin"/*bulavka*) that Pushkin's Don Juan uses to describe the Commander while standing near his statue at the cemetery: "He died / Like a dragonfly upon a pin" (Zamer / Kak na bulavke strekoza). Don Juan's astonishingly demeaning image emphasizes the Commander's puniness in real life (and his own strength and relatively large size). This insulting comparison is not just a description of the Commander, however, but also a prelude to Don Juan's challenge to him (it comes before he attempts to seduce his widow and invites him to guard the door during their tryst).

It is impossible to say for certain whether Blok has this scene in mind here, but there is definitely something of a similar challenge both in the child's mischievous provocation of his father and in the adult Blok's act of examining his father's possessions after his death. Both the living and dead fathers are Commander-like: the father of his boyhood seems to have been distant, larger-than-life, and even threatening, recalling the Lacanian Name of the Father. And just as in *The Stone Guest*, Don Juan's demeaning description of Don Alvar is accompanied by grudging admiration and recognition of his more impressive status in death, other sides are revealed about Alexander L'vovich as well. Blok describes his father playing the piano ("His embittered hands awakened the sounds of Schumann" / I Shumana budili zvuki / Ego ozloblennye ruki; 483), and thus as capable of some sort of "genius," depth, and otherworldly feeling.[23] This focus on his father as a musician also recalls the intense importance of music in general in the poet's life and sense of history, as elaborated in his essay "The Intelligentsia and Revolution" and elsewhere (Blok spoke of his inspiration in musical terms and described himself as no longer hearing music when, after writing *The Twelve* and "The Scythians" early in 1918, he found himself unable to compose poetry). Thus his father's piano playing is linked to Blok as a creator. The awakening of his father's deep artistic feeling parallels his own process as a poet and functions as a discovery or recollection of who he is and how his father's proclivities shaped him—one of the topics that inspired *Retribution*. This point of the *poema* thus focuses on a major theme of the Don Juan legend: a young man's attempt to come to terms with an older man with whom he has an unusually close connection, in keeping with the Oedipal conflict, involving some combination of enmity and identity.

This Don Juan subtext merges with various points of the *poema* in which Blok refers to statues and statue-like qualities, such as immobility and heaviness. He makes reference to the statesman Konstantin Pobedonostsev, who played a Commander-like, stultifying role in Russian history and whose "iron hand" (rukoi zheleznoi) recalls the statue.[24] Pobedonostsev's two hands each recall Don Juan motifs from Pushkin: the iron hand (like Pushkin's "iron age") freezes motion, as does the other, bony hand (representing death, and the stiffness of the Commander, who of course punishes Don Juan with the grip of his hand). By referencing Pobedonostsev, Blok hints at the connection between the Commander and Tsarist oppression, in turn recalling allusions to political rebellion in the Don Juan works of Pushkin and Mozart/Da Ponte.

The statue/Commander theme also appears in the reference to the Copernicus statue in Warsaw, which depicts the Polish scientist holding a compass and armillary sphere. Copernicus serves as an apt symbol of revolution but also recalls, in this context, the vengeful Commander of the Don Juan legend. This parallel functions on several levels. The revolving motion of the sphere Copernicus holds evokes his revolutionary scientific discovery that the earth is rotating around the sun rather than vice versa, a revelation that in turn reveals the uncanny in that it points to an unexpected, unfamiliar relationship between the sun and the earth. Of course, statues in general embody an interplay of motion and immobility, as Jakobson discusses in his article on Pushkin's treatment of the phenomenon. This is particularly true when the figure is holding a moving object, such as Copernicus's sphere. As a scientific discoverer, Copernicus embodies the uncanny interplay of revolution and authority characteristic of Don Juan and the statue, in which the young seducer and rebel against the established order becomes the old cuckold and authority: the scientist overthrows the old understanding of the solar system, and his theory eventually solidifies into established scientific authority. For Blok, moreover, Copernicus also hints at political revolution and future vengeance, as the statue serves symbolically (until the independence of Poland in 1918, at least) as a foreign captive in the Russian empire.

Following his description of his visit to his father's house, Blok enlarges the scope of his *poema*, meditating on both the Russian people and Poland as figures of vengeance. The poet-hero, like Don Juan, is in effect in exile, wandering throughout Warsaw after burying his father. At the same time, Blok includes features of the statue in his description of the poet as well, including motifs of mortality and petrification that are associated with the Commander: "there is no light in his empty pupils" (v pustykh zenitsakh net siian'ia), "his stone heart is dead" (serdtse kamennoe glukho), "will bury the dead body" (mertvoe zasyplet telo; 485). At the same time, he poses the possibility of his own redemption. Contrary to Blok's expressed hope that his "degenerate" line would die out with him, he planned to posit a future resurrection of both the narrator and the Russian nation in the third, incomplete chapter, through the impregnation of a Polish peasant woman and the birth of a son. This resurrection can be seen as a kind of redemption of the past world, the "frightening world" (strashnyi mir) that justified historical retribution through revolution, with the redeeming peasant class sitting in judgment of the old world, including Blok himself. Irene Masing-Delic connects Blok's perception of his syphilis to this sense of himself as part of the old world of "brothel civilization" ("Black Blood, White Roses"). In this light, Blok planned to describe his redemption despite the Donjuanism he inherited from his father through dedication to his homeland and siring a child. In *Retribution*, father-son relations are thus linked to history and to the apocalyptic destruction of the Bolshevik revolution. Alexander L'vovich, representing the Commander, becomes the object against which his son, Blok, rebels. But just as revolution breeds new order and authority, Blok's Don Juan will eventually become a Commander and father himself. This proleptic vision recalls Pushkin's understanding of himself as a future Commander as he sets out on a path to marry and potentially be cuckolded.

Ultimately, to the extent that a Don Juan theme can be perceived in *Retribution*, the *poema* underscores by contrast a significant pattern in the legend. Following Tirso's play, in which father figures play an important role, they start to drop out of some versions of the legend, which begins to feature a lack of paternity in relation to the hero. Pushkin's transformation of Don Alvar from Anna's father to her husband is one such important move. This lacuna, arguably, symbolically leads to a search for a father figure, and the resulting fatal conflict. Pushkin's symbolic joining of Don Juan and the statue in his final stage direction links the two together in a mutual search for one another: Don Juan's fascination with the Commander in real life as well as with the monument and the contrast between the two is later explained as a fusion with—a *becoming of*—the Commander. The idea of *Retribution*, then—that sons have to discover their fathers, identify with them, and become fathers themselves—acts as a working out of the Oedipus complex and merges with the libertine's fateful meeting with his destiny in the Don Juan legend.

Tsvetaeva's Don Juan Cycle

Tsvetaeva explores the legend in the seven-poem cycle *Don Juan* (*Don Zhuan*, 1917), which engages both Pushkin and Blok in a dialogue on the theme. Throughout this study, I have noted that sexuality and seduction, the ostensible topics of the Don Juan legend, are gradually transformed into other foci in the course of its development. Tsvetaeva contributes to this pattern through a kind of "desexualization" of the Don Juan theme, in which the seduction narrative Pushkin presents is exchanged for a more spiritual interaction, reflecting the type of meeting Tsvetaeva imagined with the nineteenth-century poet.[25] In doing so, Tsvetaeva undermines the very premise of her admired predecessor, Blok, in his efforts to imagine a reconciliation of the sensual with the spiritual in Don Juan's meeting with Donna Anna.

The figure of Don Juan undoubtedly appealed to Tsvetaeva for his rebellion against convention, which I have described as typical of the legend and especially crucial in the Russian interpretation of the theme. As Simon Karlinsky writes about Tsvetaeva, "Her notion of rebellion was heroic and individualistic; her favorite heroes were the ones who raise themselves high above the crowd only to be ultimately vanquished by mediocrities: Joan of Arc, Napoleon, Byron, Pushkin, the False Dmitry, the Pugachev of Pushkin's *The Captain's Daughter*" (41). One could surely add Don Juan to this list, particularly in light of the Russian transposition of the theme, beginning with Pushkin's presentation of him as a poet symbolically defeated by a cruel, immobilizing force representing Tsarism. Moreover, the Don Juan legend resonates with other poetic myths Tsvetaeva adapts. Olga Hasty describes the Orpheus myth, with its configuration of Eros, poetry, and death, as a master narrative for her poetic inspiration (*Tsvetaeva's Orphic Journeys*). These categories apply equally well to the Don Juan legend, in which, as I have described, Eros is inextricable from artistry and connected to death as well.

As I discuss below, Tsvetaeva manipulates the usually dominant, aggressive, even violent Don Juan figure in keeping with her longing for passive, nondomineering men. As Jane Taubman explains, Tsvetaeva's ideal of an androgynous, asexual childhood shaped her relations with men. Needing a relationship in which she could feel stronger and more dominant than the man, she sought a gentle, nonthreatening male partner, and this motivated a great deal of her poetry, which often addressed a male other across a great distance, keeping the relationship on an otherworldly plane (27–29).

Tsvetaeva's personal relationships and sexuality perhaps also influence her presentation of the Don Juan theme. Her relationship with Sofia Parnok, which lasted from 1914 to 1916, inspired the cycle *Girlfriend* (*Podruga*), whose poems predict the end of their relationship. Still married to her husband, Sergei Efron, Tsvetaeva experienced the guilt of being in a love triangle and wanting to receive love from both partners without hurting either. She also had a brief affair with Osip Mandelstam in 1916, which bears on my discussion below of her vision of Don Juan. Although Mandelstam became infatuated with her and began to visit her in Moscow, Tsvetaeva envisioned instead a lofty, spiritual love and a relationship of brotherhood among poets (Taubman 60, 79).

Written between February and June of 1917, Tsvetaeva's Don Juan cycle belongs to the period of her maturation as a poet from roughly 1916 to 1920, when she wrote her two *Mileposts* (*Versty*) collections.[26] Tsvetaeva's poetry of this period features intense intertextuality and frequent coopting of other poets' styles and themes in order to shape her own voice, especially in the 1916 cycles *Poems to Blok* (*Stikhi k Bloku*) and *Poems to Akhmatova* (*Stikhi k Akhmatovoi*). Many of the poems explore sexual subversion, folk motifs, and otherworldly events. Stylistically, she uses multiple voices, often of uneducated speakers or other voices clearly different from her own. All of these characteristics can be seen in the Don Juan poems, which are composed of trochaic and other relatively simple meters. They do not cohere as a narrative, although Poems 1–2 and 3–4 seem to be linked as pairs. The cycle features a series of fantastic encounters between different female personae and a Don Juan who has suddenly appeared in the Russian winter, with a focus on moments of recognition and realization of identity.[27]

Moreover, the cycle reflects what many critics view as the dominant theme of her poetic career: her attempt to overcome the restrictions of her gender. As Alyssa Dinega puts it, Tsvetaeva "devotes her entire life and creative opus to a ceaseless hunt for some viable resolution to the riddle of how a woman can attain the status of pure, ungendered, human greatness" (4). Her antagonistic relationship with Briusov from the beginning of her career represented a challenge to the authority of the male establishment: rather than beginning her poetic career by publishing individual lyrics, and seeking Briusov's (or some other male poet's) "sponsorship," Tsvetaeva boldly debuted her first collection, *Evening Album* (*Vechernii al'bom*, 1910) without the assistance of a mentor.[28] Her well-known behavior during Briusov's 1921 "Evening of Poetesses" represents another example of this quest to overcome gender restrictions. Tsvetaeva wore a deliberately unfeminine overcoat with a leather belt and gray felt boots. In response to Briusov's comment in his introductory remarks that women could only write of love, she read poems praising the White Army (in front of an audience of Red Army soldiers). The Don Juan theme, as it turned out, provided fertile ground for her pursuit of this quest, and Tsvetaeva's allusions to Pushkin's and Blok's texts in particular in her cycle shed light not only on her rewriting of the legend, but also on the way in which she employs the subject to reshape her poetic identity and develops her views on the broader role of the poet.

Pushkin's questioning of traditional marriage and male-female relations undoubtedly interested Tsvetaeva, given her lifelong rebellion against the expectations held up for women, and especially female poets. As Diana Burgin and Stephanie Sandler point out, Tsvetaeva describes Pushkin as a liberating male in her 1913 poem "Meeting with Pushkin" ("Vstrecha s Pushkinym").[29] In the poem, Tsvetaeva imagines her predecessor speaking to her as one poet to another rather than condescending to her or treating her as a mere object of sexual desire. I argue that the theme of poetic self-realization through transgressing and transcending gender boundaries in the Don Juan cycle stems in part from Pushkin's *Stone Guest*. Tsvetaeva does not follow Pushkin's plot in these poems, and her language and imagery actually recall Blok's more than Pushkin's. Nevertheless, the cycle also contains key thematic links to *The Stone Guest*. In particular, Pushkin's reinvention of Don Juan as a poet, his reevaluation of gender roles in the play, and the hero's marked obsession with death all influence Tsvetaeva's own exploration of the same themes.

Tsvetaeva blurs traditional gender roles of the legend in various ways as well. Although in some of her poetry she obscures gender by omitting the past tense forms of verbs that would give it away, this cycle contains several references, such as "I lived" (zhila) in the first poem, "I brought" (prinesla) in the second poem, and "I was smart" (ia byla umna) in the fifth, that allow us to establish a female voice throughout the cycle. The marking of gender here emphasizes the reversal of traditional roles. In the first poem, the female speaker orders Don Juan to wait for her, presumably for a tryst (a command Don Juan himself usually makes). By swearing on "my sweetheart and my life" (Zhenikhom i zhizn'iu), the girl seems to take on masculine, Don Juan-like attributes, namely exaggerated expressions of sincerity and willingness to betray her lover to be with him. In doing so, she asserts her sexual and romantic freedom.

At this time, Tsvetaeva was fascinated by Pushkin, Napoleon, Pugachev, and other extraordinary historical figures as well as seducers such as the real-life libertine Casanova and the fictional Carmen. She arranges a meeting between Don Juan and his feminine counterpart, Carmen, in the third and fourth poems. The third poem announces this meeting: "At this very hour Don Juan of Castile / Met Carmen" (V etot samyi chas Don-Zhuan Kastil'skii / Povstrechal— Karmen). The fourth poem describes the meeting between Don Juan and Carmen in a minimalist dialogue. Tsvetaeva undermines the reader's expectation of a romantic affair, however, in lines 5–6, in which Carmen claims not to like Don Juan and only possibly to recognize him. In this manner, she also undermines

Don Juan's powers of seduction by suggesting that he has his equal in another, imaginary world.

Tsvetaeva takes Pushkin's transformation of Don Juan into a poetic seducer as her starting point, but she also makes him vulnerable and even somewhat emasculated. In his travels to Russia, Don Juan has reached an inhospitable and fatal place, in which his erotic power cannot save him from death. In the first poem, the speaker, apparently a peasant girl, regrets that in her homeland there is "nowhere to kiss" (negde tselovat'), that there are "no fountains" (net u nas fontanov), and that "the well has frozen" (zamerz kolodets; 334). In this manner, Tsvetaeva translates the actions of Pushkin's Commander, whose entrance prevents Don Juan from consummating his love for Anna by immobilizing him in his "stony grip," into new images of the deadening of life forces (water, lovemaking, etc.). For this reason, she proclaims that Don Juan will not like Russia: "My land does not become you" (Krai moi ne k litsu; 335). In the concluding lines of the first poem, Don Juan's erotic qualities are barely recognizable: "Ah, in your bearcoat / It would be hard to even recognize you, / If it weren't for your lips / Don Juan!" (Akh, v dokhe medvezh'e / I uznat' vas trudno, /Esli by ne guby / Vashi, Don-Zhuan!; 335).[30]

The violence against Don Juan comes not only from the Russian climate and environment, but also from its Orthodox religion: "A u bogorodits—Strogie glaza" (And our mothers of God—have stern eyes; 335). The deathly imagery of inclement weather and Orthodox Christianity is developed further in the second poem:

> For a long time in the foggy dawn
> A snowstorm wept.
> Don Juan was laid
> In his snowy bed.
>
> There is neither a thundering fountain,
> Nor ardent stars . . .
> On Don Juan's chest
> Lies an Orthodox cross.
>
> Долго на заре туманной
> Плакала метель.
> Уложили Дон-Жуана
> В снежную постель.
>
> Ни гремучего фонтана,
> Ни горячих звезд . . .

На груди у Дон-Жуана
Православный крест.

Tsvetaeva's images here recall Blok's "The Steps of the Commander" but reverse its genders: instead of Donna Anna sleeping with her arms crossed, it is Don Juan with an Orthodox cross on his chest; the sleeping Don Juan also recalls a traditional fairy tale representation of a woman. While emphasizing the inhospitality of the Russian environment, Tsvetaeva continually contrasts it with Don Juan's Spanish homeland, which the "hot stars" and later, in this second poem, the "Sevillian fan" (sevil'skii veer—perhaps that of Carmen) symbolize. This contrast helps create a sympathetic image of Don Juan that descends from Pushkin's character, whom some critics view more as a victim of a stultifying Tsarist society than an incorrigible sinner receiving just retribution.

As Michael Makin points out, Tsvetaeva's description of Don Juan's deathly fate in this cycle is mysteriously ambiguous: "Has some Russian she-devil taken revenge on Don Juan, radically revising (in favour of markedly female vengeance) the traditional accounts of his end?" he asks. "Nothing would be more typical of Tsvetaeva's treatments of such sources, but the poem gives only an equivocal answer" (55). The idea of a vicious, vengeful femme fatale destroying Don Juan certainly resonates with Tsvetaeva's *Carmen* cycle, written just a month after this one. These two poems focus on violent gestures: Carmen's figurative ripping out of Don Jose's heart, her biting of her own lip and tasting of blood, and her death, as she holds her chest where she's been stabbed. The interpretation of Carmen as an enchanting but violent agent of death (rather than as an object of worship, as in Blok's 1914 *Carmen* cycle) would seem to align with Tsvetaeva's portrait of Don Juan's fate here. Elena Zemskova suggests that Tsvetaeva rejected the idea that Don Juan could ever repent or that Donna Anna could save him. Thus, Tsvetaeva contradicts the idea of the feminine as a salvational force, both by removing Donna Anna and by having Don Juan meet his fate at the hands of Carmen instead of the Commander, as in Pushkin and Blok. In doing so, she reads the legend in a completely different manner from Blok in particular.

Tsvetaeva's attitude to real-life seductive male figures, however, suggests other possible ways to read the exchanges between Don Juan and the female personae in the cycle. Her relations with her fellow poets Blok and Boris Pasternak in particular were marked by indirect communication that seemed designed to foster spiritual, nonerotic exchanges from afar. The famous account of Tsvetaeva sending her daughter to give Blok a copy of her cycle dedicated to him, rather than introducing herself in person, indicates her need to maintain physical distance from the poet. As Dinega notes, Tsvetaeva deliberately wanted to approach

Blok not as a woman, but as a disembodied poet, a pure voice (36). Her pattern of correspondence with Pasternak from afar while avoiding in-person meetings and distancing herself from him when his communications became romantic in nature similarly evinces this need for separation.

Tsvetaeva, in the various personae she assumes in this cycle, seems to take on a similar role in relation to Don Juan. At times she seems to come close to him sexually, as in the aforementioned concluding lines of the first poem. However, in most cases she rejects him as a romantic partner or conquest. Her announcement in the second poem that she will help Don Juan see feminine beauty by bringing him her heart ("I will bring you my heart tonight" / Ia tebe segodnia noch'iu / Serdtse prinesu) opposes erotic fulfillment, as the heart represents her inner rather than external beauty. Her exclamation "Your list is complete, Don Juan!" (Vash spisok—Polon, Don-Zhuan!) recalls Pushkin's and Blok's interpretations of the hero's conquests not as mere debauchery, but as evidence of a desperate search for an ideal woman. Tsvetaeva's gesture to Don Juan suggests a similarly final but de-eroticized encounter. In Pushkin's account, Don Juan's obsession with Anna is triggered by a glimpse of her heel under the widow's garment. Tsvetaeva in effect substitutes a spiritual body part for Pushkin's physical, sensual one. The voiding of Eros also suggests a resolution to Blok's conundrum, the despair over the impossibility of integrating sexual passion with spiritual loftiness. Here, Tsvetaeva seems to suggest that a higher, more spiritual love that she can offer Don Juan, one that transcends Eros, will finally complete his quest. In this regard, Tsvetaeva may be suggesting an otherworldly meeting, not unlike her search for "poet-brothers," which included dead poets such as Pushkin and Byron along with living contemporaries such as Blok, Pasternak, and Mandelstam. In the case of Blok in particular, whom she revered as a Christlike martyr, death releases the poet from suffering and assures him immortality.

The third poem, similarly, rejects the traditional seduction narrative of the Don Juan legend: "Ah, aren't you tired / Of loving me? You are practically a skeleton / And I am almost a shadow" (Akh, uzhel' ne len' / Vam liubit' menia? Vy—pochti ostov, / Ia—pochti chto ten'). By pointing to Don Juan's and her shared proximity to the other world (a skeleton and a shadow), she not only questions the value of an erotic encounter but also suggests their linkage in death or some sort of afterlife. This impression is strengthened two stanzas later in the speaker's self-identification as Carmen. Whereas Carmen heralds only death in Blok's cycle, here she also seems to offer a form of liberation. Overall, the poem conveys Tsvetaeva's view of herself as a poetic figure in relation to Don Juan. By contemplating a meeting with him in death, she posits both herself and him as metaphysical beings who connect in an otherworldly way. She even suggests that she is more advanced than Don Juan, since he is still contemplating conquests, while she sees beyond him into death and challenges him to go farther.

Tsvetaeva's fascination with Don Juan, then, recalls some of the very same elements that Pushkin and Blok transformed most from their Western European predecessors. As in Pushkin's play and Blok's "The Steps of the Commander," her Don Juan's destruction does not involve supernatural vengeance for sin. Instead she evokes his mysterious fate, recalling the outcomes Pushkin and Blok each sensed for themselves and projected onto their heroes. Her transformation of their portrayals of gender and eroticism advances her goal of fashioning a poetic persona for herself that can be defined not so much as an assertion of powerful femininity, but as a female poet rather than poetess, who exists on the same plane as male poets through the dissolution of her gender and sexuality. In reversing Blok's positioning of active male seducer and passive female seducee, Tsvetaeva suggests an interchangeability of agency between the sexes. In the case of Pushkin, she departs from her predecessor on the question of eroticism. Pushkin characterizes Donna Anna's awakening sexuality as a potentially redeeming force, both for her and for Don Juan. For Tsvetaeva, however, eroticism is something to be voided as part of her search for a higher form of poetic kinship. Tsvetaeva, through her poetic personae, invites Don Juan to extinguish his erotic drive and to accept the necessity of death for exceptional people of both genders in order to attain spiritual transformation. Thus, if *The Stone Guest* demonstrates the tragic frustration of personal regeneration, and "The Steps of the Commander" depicts the impossibility of redemption due to the failure to reconcile sexual passion and loftier love, Tsvetaeva's cycle points the way to an exchange of earthly love and desire for immortality on a higher, transcendent plane.

Gumilev's *Don Juan in Egypt*

Following Tsvetaeva's poetic dialogue with Blok and Pushkin, I turn back slightly chronologically to Gumilev's play *Don Juan in Egypt* (*Don Zhuan v Egipte*, 1912), which offers a more irreverent view of the legend. Gumilev's interest in the Don Juan theme in turn differs from that of Blok and Tsvetaeva. Despite his involvement in numerous affairs, including during his marriage to Akhmatova, Gumilev's identification with the Don Juan figure proceeds from a sense of inferiority and unattractiveness. As his student Nikolai Otsup describes him, "Considering himself ugly, he tried that much harder to pass for a Don Juan, putting on a show of bravado and stretching the truth. His playacting, his notion that the poet appealed more to women's hearts than other men, his affectation as romantic and attractive, but dangerous—these are traits that Gumilev to the end of his days never got rid of. . . . Gumilev was a Don Juan out of zeal, from a desire to extinguish his timid, gentle, sensitive nature" (184). Gumilev also identified with Don Juan as a traveler and adventurer. His wanderlust since his youth, his frequent voyages to Africa, during which he hunted wild animals and experienced food and water shortages, and his enthusiastic military service in World War I must have attracted him to a legendary figure who is continually exiled, travels constantly, faces danger frequently, and is always ready to defend his honor.

If Tsvetaeva's cycle offers a kind of rebuttal to Blok through its emasculation of the Don Juan figure, and her use of the legendary seducer to gesture toward purely intellectual and spiritual rather than erotic relations among poets, Gumilev's play involves a distinct stylistic contrast to Blok's Symbolism. As the coleader of the Acmeist school in the early 1910s, along with Gorodetsky, Mandelstam, and Akhmatova, Gumilev established a new approach to poetry. He viewed poetic creation more as a craft than a revelation of otherworldly truth: the Acmeists saw themselves as a "guild of poets" in the tradition of Medieval guilds of craftsmen. Rejecting the mystical narratives and gestures of Blok and other Symbolists, Gumilev focuses on clarity of expression, concrete objects, and earthly reality rather than the other world in his poetry. This leads to a more concrete focus on Don Juan, with a clearer narrative, and at the same time, with a certain distance and humorous approach to the legend. His focus contrasts both with the ethereal, richly suggestive tapestry of "The Steps of the Commander" and with the otherworldly sphere of Tsvetaeva's encounter with Don Juan.

Like Blok and Bal'mont, Gumilev explores the Don Juan theme through more than one genre, contributing a short lyric poem and a play to the literature. His 1910 "Don Zhuan," a poem in sonnet form from the cycle *Pearls* (*Zhemchuga*), represents a sharp departure in many respects from the Pushkinian model, and in this section, I will offer some brief comments on this poem before focusing on Gumilev's play.[31]

In "Don Zhuan," Gumilev, using the first person, presents an "arrogant dream" of behaving like a Don Juan, "always kissing new lips" (vsegda lobzaia novye usta) and then exchanging this life for Christian repentance.[32] In this manner, he recalls the Tirso play, with Don Juan's refrain of "Plenty of time for that" (repentance) whenever he is reproached for his debauchery and pranks. Gumilev in effect imagines a Don Juan who is able to fulfill his promise of eventually repenting, and thus experiencing the best of both worlds: the time to enjoy sensual delights, and the opportunity to atone for them. In the last three lines, however, typically of the sonnet form, he creates a sharp break from the rest of the poem:

I remember that I, a superfluous atom,
Never had children from any woman
And never called any man my brother.

Я вспоминаю, что, ненужный атом,
Я не имел от женщины детей
И никогда не звал мужчину братом. (501)

This sudden insight substitutes for Don Juan's customary realization that his time is up and he is being called to account for his transgressions. Gumilev replaces the dramatic entrance of the statue with a psychological insight: that Donjuanism has simply made his life empty, preventing him from enjoying the deeper relationships of brotherhood and paternity. Like Akhmatova, who replaces the statue with the historical reality of the Stalinist terror as the agency of punishment in her *poema* (see below), Gumilev voids the legend of its otherworldly, supernatural element. He goes even further, though, in the sense that he focuses purely on emotional regrets: retribution arrives in this world via human psychology, rather than in the traditional Christian afterlife of Tirso and other early Don Juan writers. In this manner, Gumilev, as an Acmeist, rejects Blok's grand, otherworldly, metaphysical narrative, focusing instead on the palpable. Given that Gumilev presents this life as a dream ("My dream is arrogant and simple" / Moia mechta nadmenna i prosta), Donjuanism becomes a kind of nightmare, consisting of a banal cycle of excess sensual pleasure followed by equally excessive repentance. He thus transforms the moral focus of the original play, in which Don Juan's debauchery can be redeemed by repentance or at least marriage and monogamy. For Gumilev, the exaggerated embrace of monklike Christianity, no less than the serial seductions, leads to a kind of sterility; they are two sides of the same coin. Donjuanism is critiqued not just for its licentiousness, but also for its extreme approach to life that prevents a person from forming simple human relationships.

Gumilev's *Don Juan in Egypt* offers an entirely different, and less critical, take on Donjuanism than the poem. This play has received relatively little scholarly attention. Sam Driver refers to it as "a partly facetious and altogether unusual reworking of the theme" (326). As part of Gumilev's vision of Donjuanism, however, it contains various motifs that connect it not only to his other work, but also to contemporary Silver Age writers and Pushkin's *Stone Guest*. To briefly summarize the plot, Don Juan comes out of the rubble of hell and enters into a rivalry with Leporello, who has become a professor, dean, and scholar of Egyptology after his master's death. Don Juan and his former servant battle for the affections of Miss Poker, a young American woman who has come to Egypt with her father. Don Juan eventually runs off with her, and Leporello admits that, despite his scholarly accomplishments, he would rather be Don Juan's servant again.

By contrast with longer plays on the Don Juan theme by Russian writers such as Alexei K. Tolstoy, Bezhetsky, and Mordvin-Shchodro in the late nineteenth and early twentieth centuries, which reflect the influence of Hoffmann's 1813 story, Gumilev's one-act play recalls Pushkin's little tragedy, both in form and motifs.[33] Gumilev could expect his audience to recognize in his play aspects of Pushkin's approach to the Don Juan legend, such as its brevity, the cast of only four characters (Don Juan, Leporello, an American pork seller named Mr. Poker, and his daughter), the focus on specific motifs of the legend, and the omission of other episodes and characters that typically appear in the narrative. More significantly, Gumilev's version can be seen as a series of humorous reworkings of the legend through the prism of Pushkin's innovations. As Göbler notes, the playful opening of *Don Juan in Egypt*, with the hero's questions "How strange! Where am I? What kind of dream is this?" (Kak stranno! Gde ia? Chto za bred?), immediately signals that what follows should not be taken too seriously and that the continuation of Pushkin's play is a comic, parodic one (75).

Like Blok and Tsvetaeva, Gumilev focuses on the theme of resurrection, evoked at the very beginning of the play. However, unlike these poets, Gumilev's resurrection is a literal one, taking place in real life rather than in the deathly beyond. Don Juan's seemingly endless energy is so great that he is able to overcome the bounds of hell. And, like Tsvetaeva's Don Juan, who appears in Russia, Gumilev's poet-hero is moved to an exotic location, in this case one that reflects his author's fascination with Africa, to which he traveled four times.[34] The sense of imaginative relocation of seemingly incongruous nations and nationalities is emphasized by the American father and daughter visitors whom Don Juan meets upon escaping the rubble.

What is especially imaginative about Gumilev's recasting is the relationship between Don Juan and the Commander and the organization of the triangular relationships in the play. Early on, we find out that the Commander has also gone to hell, recalling Pushkin's stage direction that they descend together. Gumilev emphasizes this connection with Don Juan's description of his trip to hell in tandem with the Commander: "We flew to the depths / Like two birds that have been shot" (My sleteli v glubinu / Kak dve podstrelennye ptitsy; 269). Since Gumilev's Don Juan recalls his adventures with Anna and the Commander, the play serves as a kind of "afterlife" of Pushkin's little tragedy, not to mention a continuation of all the other works that end with Don Juan's descent to hell. The fact that he has returned intent on further seductions ("I have not kissed anyone in so long . . ." / Ia tak davno ne tseloval . . .) underscores his resilience as a legendary and literary figure: the Commander's punishment represents a mere interruption of his normal, unending course of seductions and rivalries. Moreover, the Commander, who is tormented in hell while Don Juan hides, shares Don Juan's sinfulness; the two figures take on the same interchangeability that I argue they have in Pushkin's play.

Gumilev, interestingly, departs from most previous Don Juan artists by exploring Leporello in greater depth. Since Leporello is the American girl's fiancé, Gumilev invents a new rivalry that doubles and parallels the conflict between Don Juan and the Commander in *The Stone Guest*. He has rearranged the traditional love triangle of the Don Juan legend by making Leporello the Commander, reimagined as a statue-like expert in petrification characterized by his knowledge of ancient learning and his rigidity and unattractiveness. In this sense, Gumilev projects his own features, which he saw as unattractive, onto Leporello as well as Don Juan. Don Juan tries to dissuade Miss Poker from marrying Leporello by using language similar to that of Pushkin's Don Juan with Anna: a plea for her to exchange a deathly state for a more life-affirming one. In Pushkin's play, as I discuss in chapter 1, Don Juan tries to tempt Donna Anna away from her mourning rituals to begin a romance with him that would free her to explore emotions and sensations other than devotion to a dead man. Gumilev's Don Juan, similarly, warns Miss Poker against Leporello, insisting that there is something in her nature that demands someone more vital:

> He'll lock you in a dark crypt
> Of clamorous words and beaten-up feelings.
> No, you have a fire in your blood,
> You'll put aside this caprice . . .

> Он заключит вас в темный склеп
> Крикливых слов и чувств изжитых.
> Нет, есть огонь у вас в крови,
> Вы перемените причуду . . . (275)

Don Juan, in turn, paints a contrast with himself, offering a poetic recitation that evokes nature and freedom:

> I love you! Let's go! Let's go!
> Do you know how roses smell,
> When you sniff them together?

And dragonflies resound in the sky?
Do you know how wondrous is the field,
How translucent the milky fog,
When a friend leads you into it
For pleasure, at an appointed hour?
Victorious love
Will crown us without crowns
And turn our blood into a flame
And our rapturous babble into song.
My horse is the most magnificent of horses.
He's white as snow and quite majestic,
When he starts to gallop, the thunder
Of his hooves resounds to glory. (276–77)

Я вас люблю! Уйдем! Уйдем!
Вы знаете ль, как пахнут розы,
Когда их нюхают вдвоем
И в небесах звенят стрекозы.
Вы знаете ль, как странен луг,
Как призрачен туман молочный,
Когда в него вас вводит друг
Для наслаждений, в час урочный.
Победоносная любовь
Нас коронует без короны
И превращает в пламя кровь
И в песню—лепет исступленный.
Мой конь—удача из удач,
Он белоснежный, величавый,
Когда пускается он вскачь,
То гул копыт зовется славой. (276–77)

Don Juan, then, plays the same role here as in *The Stone Guest*, freeing a woman from the tyranny of a bloodless, gloomy, older man while at the same time drawing her into his own sphere. Leporello has become older and is associated with the ancient history of Egypt, which here symbolizes a lifeless past, as the action takes place in the middle of a sarcophagus-filled vault on the Nile. Gumilev stresses Leporello's maturation and aging; in contrast, Don Juan returns from hell in the same state as when he entered it. Leporello himself notes this: "Life hasn't changed him" (Ne izmenila zhizn' ego). However, unlike Pushkin's play, *Don Juan in Egypt* is not a tragedy, and the whole exchange takes place on a more lighthearted plane. Despite Miss Poker's initial, amusing protests—"I don't want to! No, I don't want to! Oh, my dear, my dear!" (Ia ne khochu! . . . / Net, ne khochu! O milyi, milyi!)—she eventually departs with Don Juan, leaving Leporello to resign himself to his loss and wish that he could be Don Juan's servant again. After all, as Karpiak remarks, Leporello is not comfortable with his role to begin with: "Outside the myth Leporello's life is meaningless and cannot endure. He wears his bookish erudition and precarious fame like an ill-fitting cloak" ("The Sequels to Pushkin" 85). Moreover, Gumilev evaluates Don Juan from a greater distance than Blok, who identifies with the figure. His Don Juan may be a poetic seducer in the tradition of Pushkin, but he is not quite as inventive, as Gumilev deliberately attributes to him passé, clichéd rhymes such as *rozy* and *strekozy* ("roses," "dragonflies") and *krov'* and *liubov'* ("blood," "love") as he attempts to persuade the gullible Miss Poker to leave Leporello for him.

As mentioned above, Gumilev's play, like Tsvetaeva's cycle, features the theme of the exotic: Don Juan is in Egypt, and he is incongruously in the company of a father and daughter from Chicago, a juxtaposition that adds humor to the play. But unlike Tsvetaeva's Don Juan, who is incapable of surviving in a foreign land, Gumilev's returns from hell to pursue exactly the same activity in Egypt, and with the first girl he meets, that he had in various other countries before meeting the Commander. The implication is that the Don is eternal and indefatigable, unstoppable even by death and easily able to resume his seductions in an unfamiliar land, and this makes him an object of envy. Gumilev's poetic and dramatic contributions to the Don Juan legend, then, offer two polarized points of view: one condemning Donjuanism not so much from the moral as from the psychological standpoint, and the other reexploring Pushkin's depiction of Don Juan as liberator in addition to captivator of women.

Akhmatova: Don Juan and the Haunting of the Past

The final Silver Age writer I will discuss in this chapter, Akhmatova, has already been referenced several times in this study in connection with her 1947 essay "Pushkin's *The Stone Guest*."[35] In that seminal piece, Akhmatova links Pushkin not only to Don Juan, himself a lyric poet who has been reborn in love, but also to the jealous Commander, forced to witness his widow being seduced by a younger man as Pushkin feared would happen after his own death. Pushkin, for Akhmatova, thus transforms the Don Juan legend by suffusing it with his own personality and intimate concerns, as a poet, lover, and future husband. Committed to avoiding any moralizing in this retelling of the Don Juan tale, Pushkin instead creates a highly original, personal allegory of his own experience, real and anticipated.

For all Akhmatova's insights into Pushkin and his little tragedy, as Sandler argues, the essay describes Akhmatova herself as well as Pushkin. In "Pushkin's *Stone Guest*," the middle-aged Akhmatova reconstructs her own earlier life as a "gay sinner of Tsarskoe Selo" and her later waning popularity, recalling Pushkin's own situation as he entered his thirties.[36] Moreover, Akhmatova, according to Sandler, is also writing about Gumilev, a "Don Juan" before marriage whom she would like to bring back to life (reincarnated as the Commander); thus, she attributes to her ex-husband the same multiplicity of roles that Pushkin, according to her, assigns to his protagonists in his autobiographical working-out of his destiny ("The Stone Ghost").

Nor is Akhmatova's exploration of the Don Juan theme confined to "Pushkin's *Stone Guest*."[37] Several critics have interpreted *Poem without a Hero* (*Poema bez geroia*) as a retelling of the Don Juan legend, and I examine their research and attempt to build on their observations of Akhmatova's references to the legend in her *poema* below. In brief, I claim, synthesizing the views of previous critics, that Akhmatova rather unexpectedly manages in this work to identify in some way with all three protagonists of Pushkin's love triangle: Don Juan, the Commander, and Donna Anna.

Poem without a Hero alludes to various versions of the Don Juan legend. The title itself hints at the beginning of Byron's *Don Juan*: "I want a hero . . ." For her epigraph, Akhmatova uses a line from *Don Giovanni*, "You will stop laughing before dawn" (Di rider finirai / Pria dell' aurora), quoting what the Commendatore says to Don Giovanni in the graveyard scene as the libertine relates to Leporello an adventure of seducing a girl. The *poema* also recalls Vsevolod Meyerhold's production of Molière's *Don Juan* in 1913, the year in which *Poem without a Hero* is set, and closely engages Blok's "The Steps of the Commander." It is clear that Akhmatova is rethinking the Don Juan legend in terms of her personal life here too, as Sandler notes that she does in her essay, and indeed, *Poem without a Hero*'s various references to the Spanish legend can profitably be read in light of her observations in "Pushkin's *The Stone Guest*."

Significantly, the *poema* also represents the working out of a real-life Don Juan-like love triangle involving Akhmatova's married friend Olga Glebova-Sudeikina, an actress, and her two admirers at the time, Blok and the younger poet and officer Vsevolod Kniazev, who shot himself because of his unrequited love for Glebova-Sudeikina in 1913. All three participants in the love triangle are incorporated into the plot of the *poema*. Glebova-Sudeikina is identified with a painting of Donna Anna from "The Steps of the Commander." Akhmatova quotes several times from Kniazev's poetry in *Poem without a Hero* and also incorporates him into the Don Juan plot. The line "I am ready to die" (Ia k smerti gotov) can be attributed to him but can also be read as a response to the Commander's challenge in "Steps of the Commander": "You invited me to supper. /I've come. Are you ready?" (Ty zval menia na uzhin. /Ia prishel. A ty gotov?).[38] In this sense, Kniazev acts the role of Don Juan in Akhmatova's *poema*, punished by Blok as the Commander. However, the comment "God will punish those who made him suffer," reportedly spoken at Kniazev's funeral by his mother, casts the young poet—or at least forces avenging his death—as being on the side of the punishing Commander figure. Earlier in the chapter, I mentioned Akhmatova's and her contemporaries' perceptions of Blok as both a Don Juan and a Commander figure, and he is portrayed as both in *Poem without a Hero*. Thus, Akhmatova creates a dual role for both male antagonists—Blok and Kniazev—in this portrayal of a real-life drama.

Akhmatova's poem, set in 1913 but written during the period 1940–62, serves in part as a memorial to the poets with whom she had close relations in the 1910s; these include Blok, Gumilev, Mandelstam, and others. Blok, as mentioned, plays a particularly important role in the *poema*. Anna Lisa Crone views *Poem without a Hero* as a dramatization of the loss of a hero through the demise of Don Juan, a reading of the Don Juan legend through "The Steps of the Commander," and an allegory for events in Blok's life. Noting the use of doubling in the *poema*, Crone suggests conclusions similar to the ones I have drawn earlier in this chapter about Blok's poem. Akhmatova shows both Don Juan and the Commander failing to arrive, or perhaps being canceled out in a quick confrontation (Crone 152–53), which, as I would argue, reflects the similar disappearance together of the two antagonists at the end of Pushkin's play. As Crone speculates, both Don Juan and the Commander could be the "invited guest" or the "guest from the future" that Akhmatova refers to in Chapter 1: "Don Juan and the Commendatore are two sides of the same poet, Blok" (154). On a larger scale, these two internal forces within Blok prevent him from enduring as a leading poet, and—along with other leading poets such as Gumilev and Mandelstam—Blok is emblematic of the resignation of many poets in the face of the October Revolution and the horrors of Stalinism. Akhmatova, like her double Glebova-Sudeikina, is left alone, "widowed" by the leading poets who preceded her in death. Crone's analysis thus implies Akhmatova's identification, as narrator of the *poema*, with her namesake in Pushkin's and Blok's Don Juan works: she is abandoned by both suitors/collaborators and writes as a widow decades later.

For Wendy Rosslyn, Akhmatova's identification is very different. Rosslyn interprets *Poem without a Hero* as a recasting of the Don Juan legend from a feminized perspective. Akhmatova, in her reading, presents herself as a Don Juan-like, sinful figure who is being punished by the horrors of the True Twentieth Century (i.e., the one starting with the Bolshevik Revolution). She prepares supper for a guest, senses that her end is at hand, and sees her mysterious visitor emerge from the grave, knock on her door, and beckon to her, which recalls Don Juan's behavior in relation to the statue in various retellings of the legend. Alluding to her own promiscuity and that of other poets in the early 1910s, Akhmatova suggests that she and other women such as Glebova-Sudeikina, whom she refers to as her "double," are just as culpable as males: "when Akhmatova feminises the Don Juan figure she does not allot Don Juan's attributes to women alone, but points out that they are, in potential at least, part of human nature in general, and are thus as often to be found in women as in men" (Rosslyn 110). She claims that Akhmatova incorporates the Commander's role as well, as a kind of retribution in this world rather than the next. Akhmatova views herself, according to Rosslyn, as being punished by her experiences under Stalinism, and reflects on her conscience accordingly. To an extent, she also argues that parts of all three protagonists can be seen in Akhmatova herself: "The traditional characters of the Don Juan myth are internalised and, within one single character, play out a drama in which the unthinking immorality of youth is severely condemned by maturity, which consciously accepts the retribution meted out to it, as a means of purgation and atonement" (118). Yet she argues that "there is no character in the poem who functions as Donna Anna" (114).

Nevertheless, despite Akhmatova's critical comments on Donna Anna in her notes for revisions to her *Stone Guest* essay,[39] I would argue that one can also identify her as an Anna figure. The author portrays herself at various points—though not throughout the *poema*—in a passive position of waiting for or mourning someone. In Chapter 1 of Part I, she is seen awaiting the "guest from the future" (gost' iz budushchego; 552/134),[40] the hero who is called to "center stage" (Geroia na avanstsenu! ; 553/135), and "the guest from behind the mirror" (gost' zazerkal'nyi; 554/136). The possible identities of these people range, as various critics have discussed, from Blok to Gumilev to Kniazev and others, but her position in relation to them seems to be the same, one of expectation and eagerness to see the person, perhaps recalling Don Juan's eagerness to interact with the Commander in *The Stone Guest*.[41] Toward the end of this chapter, Akhmatova refers to herself being spoken to as a widow by an unknown male:

> *I hear a whisper: "Farewell! It's time!*
> *I will leave you alive,*
> *But you will be my widow,*
> *You—Dove, sister, light of my life!"* (554)

Слышу шепот: "Прощай! Пора!
Я оставлю тебя живою,
Но ты будешь моей вдовою,
Ты—Голубка, солнце, сестра!" (136)

Later, in Part II, she refers to herself weeping for the dead in a passage that recalls Anna mourning the dead Commander:

> I can't get clear of this motley trash;
>   Here's old Cagliostro acting the fool—
>   Elegant Satan himself,
> Who won't weep for the dead with me,
>   Who doesn't know what conscience means,
>   And why conscience exists. (568)

> Не отбиться от рухляди пестрой,
>   Это старый чудит Калиостро—
>   Сам изящнейший сатана,
> Кто над мертвым со мной не плачет,
>   Кто не знает, что совесть значит
>   И зачем существует она. (151)

This very act of mourning her past, as it turns out, actually links the author to the Commander as well. Rosslyn, I believe, is correct in describing Akhmatova as a kind of "internal Commander," punishing herself for her past sins. But another Commander-like feature can be seen in her return to a past life. Just as the Commander rises from the dead to avenge his past, Akhmatova presents herself as returning to her youthful period of gaiety, embodied in the year 1913, as though returning from beyond the dead. In keeping with this role, Akhmatova also characterizes herself several times with images of stoniness and hardness that recall the Commander.

> Seized by unbounded anxiety,
>   I myself, like a ghost in the doorway,
>   Guard my last vestige of peace.
> And I hear the insistent bell,
>   And I break into a cold sweat,
>   I turn to stone, I freeze, I burn . . . (550)

Нету меры моей тревоге,
Я сама, как тень на пороге,
Стерегу последний уют.
И я слышу звонок протяжный,
И я чувствую холод влажный,
Каменею, стыну, горю . . . (131)

Elsewhere, her claim "I am more iron than they" (Ia sama pozheleznei tekh; 551/132) similarly hints at the Commander's hardness. Akhmatova haunts her own past, as a wiser, chastened, more experienced version of herself who has come to understand the deathliness of the other world, that of the True Twentieth Century.

Beyond Akhmatova's embodiment of herself as all three protagonists of Pushkin and Blok's love triangle, one can see *Poem without a Hero* as a kind of synthesis of Silver Age attitudes toward Don Juan. Blok's interest in the Commander as a force of retribution clearly plays a significant role in Akhmatova's portrait of her milieu in 1913, and she reads Pushkin's play in this manner as well.[42] Although there are no direct references to Tsvetaeva's and Gumilev's Don Juan works, one can also find parallels with these versions. Like Tsvetaeva, for instance, Akhmatova rejects the idea of woman as savior found in Hoffmann's story, and, to some extent, in Pushkin's play. Instead, like Tsvetaeva, Akhmatova emphasizes the equality of masculine and feminine roles by cataloguing the dissoluteness of men and women alike. And it is also possible to see a variant of Gumilev's patented "exoticism" in Akhmatova's retelling of the legend. Where Gumilev sets his play in Egypt, Akhmatova creates a cluster of Don Juans from various versions and also links the legendary libertine to several other historical and fictional figures, such as Casanova and Faust. She describes him as part of a gallery of masked figures, drawn from various cultures and time periods:

" . . . Now I've decided to sing your praises,
    You New Year's rogues!"
This one is Faust, that one Don Juan,
    Dappertuto, Jokanaan,
        And the most modest one—the northern Glahn
            Or the murderer Dorian Gray . . . (550)

Вас я вздумала нынче прославить,
    Новогодние сорванцы! »
        Этот Фаустом, тот Дон Жуаном,

Дапертутто, Иоканааном,
Самый скромный—северным Гланом,
Иль убийцею Дорианом (132)

In this manner, Akhmatova consolidates various views of Don Juan and adapts the legend for her particular autobiographical and historical circumstances.

If the Silver Age presents an extremely diverse range of Don Juan portraits, one can say nonetheless that several of them, at least, are unified through the influence of Pushkin. Once again, in Blok and Akhmatova in particular, we see the uncanny linking of Don Juan with the Commander, a motif that I have characterized as one of Pushkin's great innovations in the legend. Moreover, in the case of Silver Age poets, Blok's "The Steps of the Commander" becomes an important subtext along with Pushkin's play, as Tsvetaeva clearly interprets Don Juan in opposition to Blok, and Akhmatova makes him a character in her own retelling of the legend. In the following chapter, I turn to Soviet and post-Soviet retellings of the Don Juan legend, traveling forward several decades to late and post-Soviet plays, novels, and novellas in order to explore how the Don Juan figure is adapted to a very different cultural and political context.

4

Soviet and Post-Soviet Don Juans

FEW WRITERS DEALT with Don Juan, or any other foreign archetype, in the Stalinist period. Literature of the time was not particularly open to foreign models; instead it attempted to invent and develop its own, particularly Soviet types, which were then imitated in successive Socialist Realist novels. As Göbler notes, the Don Juan theme was a dangerous one to undertake in light of Stalinist cultural restrictions, first, because of the supernatural element, and second, because in most instantiations the legend lacks a positive hero (201). And Soviet commentators themselves judged the legend as irrelevant following the Bolshevik victory: As Boris Kisin writes in 1930, "After the October Revolution, the problem of Donjuanism in its pure ... form naturally lost its social acuteness" (364).

The one exception to the general lack of Don Juan works during the Stalinist period is Samuil Aleshin's 1947 comedy *At That Time in Seville* (*Togda v Sevil'e*), which in any case was not performed until the 1960s. Aleshin takes the rather unusual approach of portraying Don Juan as a woman whose true gender has been disguised by her father so that she could avoid being sent to a monastery, and who has appeared in Seville, in masculine disguise, to escape the women who chase her in hopes of being seduced by the legendary libertine. The Commander, who discovers Don Juan's feminine identity, confesses his love for her, which is reciprocated, and they devise a plan that will allow the Commander to escape his marriage to Donna Anna and be with Don Juan. Valerian Revutsky traces Aleshin's portrait of Don Juan as a woman back to several preceding versions: those of Pushkin, Alexei K. Tolstoy, and Lesia Ukrainka, each of whom, he argues, advances the effect of feminine principles on Don Juan. He describes Aleshin's Don Juan as "an artist of love, a realisation and sublimation of Pushkin's Laura, the 'female counterpart' of Don Juan" (91). Where Pushkin reveals traits of Donjuanism in women, Aleshin explores the possibility of feminine traits in his Don Juan, who eschews seduction of women.[1]

Aleshin's very focus on the Don Juan legend in the wake of World War II was unusual, and as Robert Karpiak points out, his presentation of Don Juan as a transvestite, along with the racy eroticism of *At That Time in Seville*, was quite audacious for a Soviet playwright (*Don Juan in Slavic Drama* 348–49). This play was an outlier, though, and not until the Thaw, and the "youth prose" of writers such as Vasily Aksenov, did writers once again start to explore the kinds of references to earlier literature and foreign culture that have so deeply impacted Russian literature in most periods, and to write in what may be considered a consciously intertextual manner, especially incorporating Western sources. Moreover, in the 1960s, as in the West, the Soviet Union underwent a sexual revolution that opened up greater understanding of and sympathy for nonstandard sexual behavior. The Don Juan theme, with its focus on promiscuous sexuality, could more easily be explored in this period.

The final chapter will be devoted to examining three of the many writers who dealt with the Don Juan phenomenon in the late twentieth and early twenty-first centuries in light of postmodernist and other trends of Russian literature during this period. Venedikt Erofeev and Vladimir Kazakov, absurdist writers working on the theme in the 1980s, find different ways to subvert readers' and viewers' expectations of what is by then a well-worn legend, each using Pushkin as their reference point. They do so in ways that are recognizably postmodernist, including skepticism of grand narratives (in Erofeev's case, undermining the Soviet narrative of creating a perfect society, and in Kazakov's case, questioning the very concept of stable reality), ironic play with previous styles, and humorous self-referentiality. Liudmila Ulitskaya, though not considered a postmodern writer by most critics, finds different ways to play with her readers' expectations of the legend in several of her works of the 1990s and 2000s, clothing it in the *byt*, or everyday existence, of ordinary Soviet life.

In all three of these cases, the writers' use of the Don Juan theme represents a reaction to political, social, and sexual repression of the late Soviet period. Erofeev's and Kazakov's forms of rebellion can be framed in terms of dissidence, as they each refract Donjuanism through political aspects of Soviet culture. In fact, despite each writer's focus on Don Juan figures, the act of seduction itself becomes minimized in their works, and the focal point shifts to other concerns. The Don Juan theme's ostensible focus on the erotic, as in Tirso's original play, turns out to be either a device, as in Erofeev's play, or completely irrelevant, as in Kazakov's cycle. Ulitskaya, by contrast, presents a kind of erotic "dissidence": her use of the Don Juan figure in particular represents a rebellion against sexual repression. The Don Juan-like characters of her oeuvre (both male and female) all challenge the notion of traditional marital relationships as the only viable option, and through them, she underscores the authenticity that can be gained through sexual freedom.

Writing about the Don Juan figure in the late Soviet period can thus be seen as a form of cultural dissidence. However, Erofeev and Kazakov, each in his own way, question the simple binary opposition of official culture versus dissident culture, and this is unusual in their highly politicized cultural milieu. The intensely political focus of Soviet literature and the arts, brutally enforced during Stalinism, lasted long after this era ended in 1953. Thaw-period gestures such as Vladimir Pomerantsev's call for "sincerity" in literature and the rehabilitation of Mikhail Zoshchenko and Akhmatova, who had been censured for subjective writing, undoubtedly created new opportunities for greater individualism of perspective in Soviet literature. Nevertheless, they did not signify any sort of widespread retreat from the political since Thaw writers often focused on exposure of the preceding quarter-century's atrocities. Alexander Solzhenitsyn's momentous exposé of the GULAG system, beginning in 1962 with *One Day in the Life of Ivan Denisovich*, passionately engages this political tragedy. Opposition to Socialist Realism actually tended to reinforce its political focus through its very reversal of Stalinist values. As Mark Lipovetsky points out, even if Youth Prose writers such as Aksenov and Iuz Aleshkovsky critiqued Stalinism, "the authors of this fiction create their own myth in its image: the mirror image of the Soviet myth, recapitulating its structure entirely and illustrating extra-artistic discourse ('anti-Soviet,' liberal-democratic, dissident) in the exact same way" (*Postmodernist Fiction* 122–23). Conceptualist (or Sots-Art) writers and painters, in parodying the Soviet myth, similarly recreated it. As Boris Groys argues, "the attentive observer of the Soviet cultural scene in the 1960s and 1970s gradually became aware that all attempts to overcome Stalin's project on either the individual or the collective level resulted in fateful reproductions of it" (79–80).

Nevertheless, the post-Stalinist period also opened up new possibilities for avoidance of Soviet reality in art and society alike. Alexei Yurchak, in his study of the last Soviet generation, notes a general rejection of politics by certain writers as well as many ordinary citizens in the decades leading up to the fall of the Soviet Union. Distinguishing between "clear truths" and "deep truths," Yurchak cites Sergei Dovlatov's comment that the poet Iosif Brodsky "lived not in a proletarian state, but in a monastery of his own spirit" (127). Brodsky did not oppose the Soviet state so much as ignore it, preoccupied as he was with inner truths. And if Brodsky rejected Soviet politics as a matter of instinct, the group of underground artists known as the "Mit'ki," as Yurchak demonstrates, did so quite provocatively (238–43). By avoiding newspapers, television, and even such everyday activities as shopping, the Mit'ki sealed themselves off from Soviet reality in an effort to follow their own ritual of boiler room jobs, poetry, drinking, and friendship. Erofeev and Kazakov, in many respects, represent this alternative approach to Soviet reality and culture, and as I argue, the Don Juan theme creates special opportunities for them to attempt to find a "third way" to express their rebellion against their cultural environment. For Erofeev, mapping out the similarities between Don Juan and the Commander, seeming opponents, accomplishes the task of questioning the opposition between the stultifying, tyrannical Soviet authorities and the supposed agents of liberation, the dissidents. Kazakov, by contrast, erases the opposition by deliberately avoiding political questions altogether.

Erofeev's *Walpurgis Night, or the Steps of the Commander*

Erofeev's 1985 tragedy reworks the Don Juan legend, largely via Pushkin's *The Stone Guest*, primarily for the purpose of addressing the poet's position in the Soviet Union.[2] The story of a dissolute serial lover and dueler who is ultimately punished for his brazen rebellion against divine and human laws does not seem at first glance to relate to the "Venichka" myth established in Erofeev's magnum opus, *Moscow-Petushki* (1970), which for the critic Mikhail Epstein is characterized by alcoholism without blissful intoxication, lack of documents or permanent residence, exclusion from universities and workplaces, and shunning everyday activities and social conventions in favor of a search for a higher reality, among other elements ("Posle karnavala" 6–8). As it turns out, however, Venichka's holy foolishness actually bears surprising parallels to the Spanish legend. Don Juan is equally lawless and vagrant, exiled literally and figuratively to the outer fringes of society, and embodying a similar series of contradictions. Despite Don Juan's legendary immorality, Hoffmann and others have perceived him as far more than a mere womanizer. His erotic desires, from this point of view, are serious in intent and not purely frivolous, much like Venichka's drinking, the purpose of which is to reach a loftier spiritual state rather than carnivalesque intoxication (Epstein, "Posle karnavala" 12). Just as Venichka derives no satisfaction from his prodigious consumption of alcohol, Don Juan is never content with any of his endless series of female conquests. Both legends, one may argue, juxtapose the sacred and the profane, and the earthly and the spiritual; the holy fool meets the worldly libertine in the space of paradoxical opposition.

The plot of *Walpurgis Night* revolves around an alcoholic poet, Lev Isakovich Gurevich, who is brought into a Soviet mental hospital on the eve of May Day. The central conflict of the tragedy, as Naum Leiderman and Mark Lipovetsky point out, is a linguistic one (Vol. 2, 512). Erofeev contrasts the absurd but inventive wordplay of Gurevich and the other patients with the doctor's reified official language and the profanity-laced tirades of a ruthless orderly known as "Borenka the Thug" (Boren'ka Mordovorot). During the Act I interrogation, Gurevich frustrates the doctor with his propensity for playful, digressive answers and improvised lyrics; the doctor repeatedly demands that he stop talking in "Shakespearean iambs." He is then sent to Ward 3, where a colorful cast of patients recites parodic improvisations on contemporary Soviet discourse ranging from propaganda (ward monitor Prokhorov) to utopian plans for the construction of an ideal Communist society (Serezha Kleinmikhel') to village prose (Vova). Upon Gurevich's entrance, Prokhorov is holding a mock trial for the inmate Mikhalych, who, he claims, "betrayed the Motherland in thought and intention" (201).[3] The trial is interrupted by rounds conducted by Boren'ka and the nurse Tamarochka. Their sadistic, physically violent behavior provokes Gurevich into punching Boren'ka, who in response paralyzes him by throwing him against a bed frame and kicking him in the side. The orderly then mockingly invites Gurevich to the staff's May Day celebrations later that evening. Gurevich accepts and plots revenge with Prokhorov. He seduces the nurse Natalie, an ex-lover whom he suspects of having an affair with Boren'ka, in order to gain access to a supply of what turns out to be poisonous methyl alcohol. After bringing the alcohol back to the ward, Gurevich mixes drinks for the patients and leads them in a May Day celebration that results in their dying off, one by one.[4] The tragedy ends with the enraged Boren'ka ferociously beating the blind, dying Gurevich.

In terms of contemporary Russian reality, the plot most directly reflects the Soviet phenomenon of incarcerating dissidents in mental hospitals by fabricating illnesses. "Confidentially speaking," the doctor explains to Gurevich, "in the recent past we have begun to hospitalize even those who, at first glance, don't have a single visible syndrome of psychic disturbance. But surely we shouldn't forget about those patients' capacity for involuntary or carefully premeditated dissimulation. These people, as a rule, do not commit a single antisocial or criminal act for their entire lives, and there isn't even the smallest hint of nervous disorder, but they are dangerous precisely for this reason and need to be subject to treatment" (190). Erofeev captures the prisonlike atmosphere of the typical Soviet mental hospital as well, complete with the routine employment of vicious orderlies like Boren'ka, many of whom had criminal records.

On a literary intertextual level, the first part of the title indicates the Witches' Sabbath of the Faust legend, with Gurevich's poisonous drinks acting as a magical, deathly spell. The mental hospital setting recalls the psychiatric clinic in Mikhail Bulgakov's reworking of Goethe's *Faust* in *The Master and Margarita*, as well as Chekhov's story "Ward no. 6," with its brutal overseer Nikita. Petr

Vail' and Alexander Genis characterize Gurevich as a kind of apocalyptic Biblical prophet, foretelling the destruction of the world at the hands of the Soviet Union. Without minimizing the importance of these subtexts, I would argue that the Don Juan legend alluded to by the "steps of the commander" in the title is most crucial in holding together the play's plot and dramatic conflict. Erofeev ostensibly associates Boren'ka with Don Juan and Gurevich with the Commander. The orderly's request, "Gurevich! If you don't rot away this evening from sulfide, I ask you to visit me for supper" (209), clearly parallels the Don's legendary invitation to the stone monument. Further, Prokhorov alludes to Boren'ka necking with Tamarochka and describes him as Natalie's boyfriend, thereby portraying the orderly as a womanizer. Gurevich's furious reaction to the rumored affair with Natalie, which she coquettishly denies, catalyzes his entire plan for revenge. In an exchange with her at the end of Act III, he refers to himself as an instrument of vengeance against Boren'ka and the hospital, as he announces his intention to accept the invitation.

> *Natalie*: You know what you are in for, right?
> *Gurevich*: I do.
> The bastard found someone to play Don Juan with.
> The thug and you. Oh, no, I just can't stand it.
> Well, wait and see, quite soon, at Dawn, this Boar
> Will hear the fateful steps of the Commander! (222)

As Leiderman and Lipovetsky remark, however, the opposition is more complicated, since Erofeev splits up the roles of Don Juan and the Commander by attributing elements of each to both Gurevich and Boren'ka (Vol. 2, 515). In this manner, Erofeev takes his cue from Pushkin's similar attribution of elements of himself to both antagonists. It is Boren'ka who plays the role of the statue in the end, dragging the poet to his death. Moreover, Boren'ka represents the establishment, keeping Gurevich in place as he tries to rise from his seat during the doctor's interrogation of him. Gurevich's ruse of pretending to seduce Natalie in Act III in order to grab her keys to the supply closet while embracing her casts him in the role of a Don Juan-like seducer-trickster, as do Natalie's teasing reproaches about his past lover Lucy.[5] Moreover, these links extend far beyond simple plot correspondences. Erofeev's treatment of the Don Juan legend therefore raises several questions. Why does he combine Don Juan and the statue in each of his principal combatants, following Pushkin's example? How does *Walpurgis Night* engage Pushkin's concern with the poet's struggle against authority in *The Stone Guest*? What does Donjuanism signify for Erofeev as a creative artist and legendary figure in his own right?

Walpurgis Night takes Pushkin's conception of a poetic Don Juan, and the opposition between poet and authority, as a starting point.[6] Many of the observations of Kropf and Herman on the creative artist's need for constant self-reinvention and Pushkin's rigidity versus mobility construct apply equally to Gurevich in *Walpurgis Night*. His Don Juan-like desire for freedom of motion, in the literal and poetic senses, is encapsulated in the following, oft-quoted comment to the doctor regarding the Soviet Union: "I, for one, like it here very much. The only thing I don't like is the law against vagrancy. And disrespect for the Word" (186). Like Don Juan, Gurevich is associated with disguises and dubious identity, as reflected in the doctor's suspicions when he states his name: "Gurevich, you say. And how can you confirm that you are really Gurevich, and not . . . Do you have any documents on your person?" (182). Gurevich does not carry any and appears to have no fixed residence or employment either, recalling the fluidity of Don Juan (between both different lands and female conquests) rather than the fixed, unmoving Commander, with whom he associates himself in his Act III conversation with Natalie.[7]

If Gurevich's insistence on his right to freedom of motion may be read into the first element of Soviet society he lists in the above section, then his hatred of "disrespect for the Word" refers to his related need for creative poetic freedom, as witnessed by his compulsively playful, generative language. During the doctor's interrogation, Gurevich moves spontaneously from topic to topic, at one point in effect "traveling" verbally between geographical locations (from the Hindu Kush to Samoa to Karakorum). The doctor's condescending reference to Gurevich as an "unfettered seafarer" (vol'nyi moreplavatel') reinforces the connection between this verbal activity and the unrestricted spatial mobility that Pushkin's Don Juan, who refuses to stay in exile, requires (183). Erofeev frequently emphasizes the seductive, Don Juan-like effect of Gurevich's poetry on others through stage directions indicating laughter and applause from Natalie, and even the audience, in response to his improvisations. Both of the poet's objections thus entail a desire for movement and self-reinvention, in contrast to Soviet society's inherent inertia. To achieve this freedom, Gurevich, like Don Juan, creates an alternative set of rules for himself, organizing Ward 3 as a space for the free verbal creativity that is discouraged by the official order. Essentially, Don Juan's endless love affairs, travels, and exiles are transformed into a nomadism of the imagination in *Walpurgis Night*. Kropf's aforementioned comment on the state's difficulty fixing Don Juan in a stable identity could also describe Erofeev's protagonist, who continually frustrates the doctor's efforts to record his name, medical history, degree of loyalty to the Soviet Union, and other such information that would establish bureaucratic order. As Rebecca Reich argues, Gurevich is employing the strategy, common among citizens in the post-Stalinist Soviet Union, of simulating madness for practical purposes (such as avoiding criminal prosecution or military conscription), which similarly works against the goals of the state. Gurevich's half-Russian, half-Jewish status, which the doctors and other characters frequently comment upon, underscores his status as an outcast and a marginal, indefinable figure.

Gurevich's erotic encounter with Natalie in Act III further associates him with Don Juan, despite some obvious distortions from typical conquest scenes in previous retellings. For instance, the "seduction" takes place without any opposition whatsoever from Natalie. Moreover, the motive behind it is different. Although Don Juan's assertion to Anna in Scene 4 of *The Stone Guest* that "in loving you, I've come to love the good" (Vas poliubia, liubliu ia dobrodetel'; 91/168) may or may not be genuine, his motives clearly center on sexual passion. In *Walpurgis Night*, though, Gurevich's erotic advances themselves are a façade, masking his actual goal of attempting to gain access to the alcohol in the storeroom. These alterations exemplify Erofeev's pattern of playing with the boundary between parody and seriousness. For Epstein, carnival in Erofeev's works is often reversed into "trans-irony," where the ironic, carnivalesque debasing of an object or text folds back over itself, once again producing a sincere perspective ("Posle karnavala" 13–16). Thus, although Erofeev parodies the typical Don Juan seduction by minimizing its difficulty and replacing erotic love with alcohol as the desired end result, these distortions serve a serious purpose as well. Gurevich's alcoholism (like that of Erofeev and his other protagonists) may be viewed similarly to Don Juan's philandering as a kind of serial behavior. One alcoholic experience leads inevitably to another, just as Don Juan's sexual encounters follow each other in an unending chain.[8] The lists of vodkas recited by Gurevich and other patients in effect parallel Leporello's catalogue of his master's conquests in *Don Giovanni*. Erofeev does not so much parody the Don Juan legend, then, as substitute a new obsession that ultimately fulfills a similar function. In this sense, the alcoholism so integral to Erofeev's writings and world view is easily equatable with traditional Donjuanism.

Just as Erofeev attributes many traits of Donjuanism to Gurevich, he conversely allows Boren'ka to be perceived as a Commander-like figure of vengeance as well as a Don Juan. In Act I, the orderly lurks behind Gurevich during the entire interrogation, ready to carry him off at the doctor's command. At one point, he "comes up to [Gurevich] slowly, from behind, and waits for a signal to drag him off by the scruff of the neck" (189) and shortly afterward "lowers Gurevich back into the chair with well-practiced hands" (190). The emphasis on Boren'ka's steps—he constantly paces back and forth—hints at the Commander's motion indicated in the title of the play. These movements, along with Boren'ka paralyzing Gurevich with blows, kicks, and sulfide injections, mark the orderly as an "immobilizer" in the sense that Kropf and Herman consider Pushkin's Commander to be. Boren'ka's omnipresence and extraordinary physical strength suggest some of the same terror-inducing, uncanny, demonic qualities that Jakobson observes in Pushkin's portrayals of statues (5), although Erofeev in other respects depicts him as a Don Juan figure. Linda Hutcheon characterizes postmodern art as taking recognizable structures and defying our expectations of their arrangement: "it uses and abuses, installs and then subverts, the very concepts it challenges" (3). Erofeev accomplishes something along these lines in his rearrangement of the Don Juan and Commander roles. His parody by distortion acknowledges the past of the legend while simultaneously undermining our preconceived notions of it.[9]

Natalie is presented in a similarly ambiguous manner. Erofeev indicates both typical Russianness and the Spanish origins of the legend in his stage directions, noting of her appearance, dress, and motions that "all of this smacks of Slavic calm and gentleness, but also of Andalusia" (187).[10] As with the two antagonists, Erofeev gives her traits of two characters, Anna and Laura, from *The Stone Guest*. Her salvational role in relation to Gurevich recalls that potentially played by Donna Anna with Don Juan, although again Erofeev transfers it from the erotic to the alcoholic sphere. When Natalie offers Gurevich a drink, he thanks her profusely:

O Natalie! I yearn for it completely!
As resurrection, not as recreation. (216)

The lofty tones of this expression of gratitude resemble Don Juan's outpouring to Donna Anna after she has granted him a visit:

Angel Donna Anna!
May God comfort you as much as you today
Have comforted one suffering and unhappy. (83)

Ангел Дона Анна!
Утешь вас бог, как сами вы сегодня
Утешили несчастного страдальца. (158)

At the same time, Natalie acts as a poetic "apprentice" to Gurevich much as Laura does with Don Juan in Pushkin's little tragedy, imitating his use of blank iambic pentameter during their dialogue in Act III. In fact, it is Natalie who actually initiates the iambs, after which Gurevich completes her pentameter and starts another, almost in the form of a musical duet:

Gurevich (wearily): Natalie?
Natalie: I knew for sure that you would come, Gurevich.
  But wait—what's wrong?
Gurevich: I'm beaten up a bit—
  But Tasso's at Leonora's feet once more! (212)

In this manner, Erofeev replicates Pushkin's portrayal of a rival poetess. Gurevich's poetic invention not only amuses and enraptures Natalie but also inspires her to flirtatious poetic games of her own. Her coy comment, "And how's your Lucy?" (A kak tvoia Liusi? ; 221) in response to Gurevich's jealousy of Boren'ka parallels Laura's justification of her numerous lovers in *The Stone Guest*, previously referenced in chapter 1 ("What about you, skirt-chaser?" / А ты, повеса? 79/152).

Erofeev's splitting up of all three major characters reveals a considerably broader interpretation of Donjuanism than its original meaning—the seduction of numerous women—permitted. For him, it is an essentially ambivalent quality that may consist of positive or negative traits, and it is far from limited to sexual conquests. Gurevich's everchanging poetic lists and improvisations represent its lofty, creative possibilities, but Boren'ka's supposed advances toward Natalie and his crude, murderous behavior are equally emblematic. At the same time, Erofeev creates a new level of ambiguity by interrogating Pushkin's notion of the poet's role in light of his own political and cultural context. If Pushkin, according to Kropf and Herman, portrays Don Juan as a fellow artist who requires the freedom and mobility to change his role with each new performance, Erofeev continually critiques the poetic unaccountability of Gurevich and the other Ward 3 inmates. Gurevich's attempts to create a space for poetic freedom and transport them all into a higher spiritual sphere ends tragically, because this freedom comes at the cost of their lives. However, the tragedy lies not so much in the fact that Gurevich and the other inmates eventually lose their linguistic struggle against the doctor and staff as in their ultimate complicity with the authorities: their striving toward this higher freedom leads only to a recreation of the same tyranny they presumably are opposing.

The tribunal conducted against Mikhalych by Prokhorov in Act II, for example, at first glance parodies Soviet show trials and KGB interrogations. Prokhorov's speeches, woven together from various propaganda clichés, may be characterized as an accurate reflection of Soviet speech of the time, replete with empty words signifying nothing. The realism of the proceedings, though, goes beyond the actual words used. The tribunal, particularly because of its placement in the play right after the doctor's Act I interrogation and immediately preceding Boren'ka and Tamarochka's rounds in Act II, reproduces a great deal of the terror of these events. By tying Mikhalych up with towels and bed sheets, Prokhorov and Alekha deprive him of his mobility, just as Boren'ka does with Gurevich. The very real physical violence, confirmed by Mikhalych's roars of pain, renders the parodic game serious. Significantly, Prokhorov, who is a ward monitor and therefore a liaison to the staff, frequently employs profanities and verbal abuse with the other inmates, though not as often or crudely as Boren'ka and Tamarochka do. His obscene comments to Kolia and Stasik and his command to Alekha to "get Vovochka out of here" during the tribunal could be read simply as annoyance at their nonsensical rambling (201). In light of the doctor's disgusted attempts to get rid of Gurevich at the end of Act I, though, they come across more as similar efforts to control and restrict creative play with language.

Erofeev, then, indicates an alarming similarity of content, if not intent, in the language of the authorities and the would-be dissidents. As with Baudrillardian simulacra, it is difficult to distinguish between the "real" show trial and its parodic "image." When Mikhalych is ordered to say his prayers before his punishment, they turn out to be a series of Soviet patriotic slogans:

I'd gladly lose an arm and hand for Moscow, dearest Motherland;
Moscow is the world's true center, the greatest city you could enter;
Go to the Kremlin for just a while, it'll fashion your mind in the proper style. (197)

While these "prayers" meet with sarcasm from Prokhorov, Mikhalych's more alcoholically oriented, "politically correct" list in Act IV elicits the monitor's approval:

Moscow, Moscow, what a town, terrific place to knock one down;
The ill may fast, the sober pray, but it doesn't reach God's ear, no way;
Tea and coffee taste too boring, have some vodka in the morning. (233)

The fact that these clichés basically sound the same as the earlier ones, albeit with different subject matter, underscores the actual conformity of the ostensibly subversive ideology: Mikhalych merely substitutes alcoholic slogans for patriotic Soviet ones without changing the form.

The antisemitism exhibited by the doctor in his interrogation, and by Tamarochka and Boren'ka throughout the play, similarly finds a reflection in Prokhorov's absurd story of a Jew scaring off local wildlife in Act II.

As soon as a Jew appears, there's no more calm, and a tragic story begins. My late gramps told me: their forest was packed with deer. What do you call them? Roe deer—too many to shake a stick at. And the pond was chock full of white swans, and a rhodo-den-dron bloomed on the shore. And then a doctor by the name of Gustav came to the village . . . Well, maybe not exactly Gustav, but definitely a Yid. And what came of this? It's not me telling you, it's my gramps. Until this Gustav appeared, there were so many hares in the area that you could literally trip over them, you'd slip and fall . . . Well, for starters all the hares went, then the roe deer—no, he didn't shoot them, they disappeared by themselves. (200)

Although one could easily interpret this passage as a parody of Soviet anti-semitism, it takes on a more ominous character in light of Prokhorov's other comments. His Act V accusation that Gurevich cannot live without scheming, a trait he associates with the poet's Jewishness, reveals that the monitor to a great extent shares rather than opposes the staff's antisemitic attitude.[11] His parodies embody the unfettered creativity of Donjuanism, but because of their resonance with the authorities' terrorizing behavior, they expose a more deathly aspect of it as well.

This phenomenon of parody doubling back on itself can be seen with Gurevich as well as Prokhorov. From the beginning, Erofeev undercuts his hero's Don Juan-like use of language and his opposition to the hospital staff even as he seems to be presenting it as a viable alternative to official authority. In the list of characters, Gurevich is placed between Prokhorov ("monitor of Ward 3 and dictator of Ward 2") and Alekha ("nicknamed the dissident, Prokhorov's weapon-bearer"; 181). This positioning of the protagonist between a "dictator" and a "dissident" immediately signals Gurevich's paradoxical situation, as does the very fact that the dissident in question is a weapon-bearer for the dictator. Dissidence, or rebellion, always proves to have as its flip side a certain conformity to dictatorship and authority. This paradox in fact reflects one of the most striking features of the Don Juan legend. The hero functions as both rebel and tyrant, opposing convention but also bending women and men alike to his personal will. Gurevich, too, demonstrates both of these seemingly contradictory traits. Despite his alliance with his fellow Ward 3 "rebels," he actually shows a pattern of vacillation between sympathy and disdain for them in the course of the play. On the one hand, he protests their incarceration to Natalie: "They're all quite normal, all your people here. Cephalopodic mollusks, simply children. They're not insane, they're just a bit confused" (218). However, he just as frequently displays a disgust that grows especially palpable when the inmates misinterpret his poetic pronouncements.

Late in Act V, he complains: "Shush! Drunken fools! You don't understand anything of my inspired vision! You've mixed everything up" (250).

In this sense, Gurevich reflects Erofeev/Venichka's hatred of the common man, or the Nietzschean herd.[12] His perspective can be characterized as a type of totalitarian elitism that is unwilling to accommodate other positions. Like Prokhorov, Gurevich cuts short the lists and creative efforts of the other inmates, just as the doctor does with him in Act I. As Prokhorov reads aloud Serezha Kleinmikhel"s absurd utopian list of fifteen cultural homes, institutes, stadiums, and so on, he remarks: "How long will this torture drag on? No more drinks for Serezha" (232).[13] Gurevich also suggests that alcohol be withheld from Komsomol Secretary Pashka Eremin, tells Alekha to give Prokhorov "a little beating" after the monitor's statement that he would like the Poles to be punished for outdoing the Russians in "historical hatred for the Yids," and guides the inmates in compiling a parodic plan for the Soviet Union to destroy enemy peoples (247). In Bakhtinian terms, Gurevich monologizes the inmates' ideologies, synthesizing them through acceptance or rejection into his own vision. In method, if not in spirit, Gurevich's vision replicates the total dominance of the Soviet status quo represented by the staff, with its refusal to allow for dialogically competing points of view.[14]

Poetic Donjuanism fails because in its attempt to allow for rebellious creativity it merely generates its own brand of conformity. Epstein's hopeful description of a future culture that acts as "a laboratory where creative possibilities are tested" and a "totality of alternatives, rooted in human freedom" at first seems to be realized to an extent in Ward 3, with its diverse ideologies and forms of poetic invention, but these hopes are dashed by Gurevich's eventual homogenization of the various discourses (Epstein, *After the Future* 289). Ward 3, led by Gurevich and Prokhorov, does not end up serving as a haven against the ruling powers; it substitutes a different set of values, but with a similar result.

The play's ostensible opposition between the Gurevich-led inmates and the hospital staff is therefore only an apparent one. Ultimately, Erofeev analogizes Gurevich and Boren'ka, showing that the Soviet henchman and the dissident poet are equally destructive, and that both in effect function as immobilizing Commanders. The implication, if one applies this insight to the legend as a whole, is that Don Juan and the Commander are essentially one and the same. The Commander's deathlike stagnancy is embedded from the beginning in Don Juan's seeming creative freedom and mobility, to be revealed with the poet's invocation of his own death. And Don Juan's rebellion against an oppressive society, likewise, simply leads to the employment of similar tyrannical methods. The linguistic play that Gurevich offers as a possible antidote to the staff's reified official language turns out to be both deadly and homogenizing. "Yes, I had a scheme," he says, defending himself against Prokhorov's accusations: "To unite the loners. To pacify the wicked . . . to give them a little joy . . . to bring dawn into the twilight of these souls, sentenced here till the end of their days" (253). His attempt to use the Word and poetic Donjuanism to bring the ward into a "higher unity," though, merely speeds up the slow process of death already being conducted in the ward by the staff. It is no coincidence that Gurevich names Georges d'Anthès and Nikolai Martynov as his poetic influences. Although this identification with the killers of Pushkin and Lermontov (approved writers of the Soviet canon) can be viewed alongside his recitation of Nikolai Nekrasov, another officially condoned poet, as a mockery of the doctor's limited understanding, it also underscores his status as an agent of the death of poetry, his own and that of other Ward 3 inmates.

Erofeev's direct reference to Blok's "The Steps of the Commander" in his title signals Gurevich's failure to achieve a salutary effect with his poetry. On the most basic level, the title indicates Erofeev's interest in steps as a symbol of Don Juan's fate and relentlessly approaching destruction. If the motionless, forbidding quality of the statue serves as the impetus for Pushkin's title, then the steps of Blok's poem seem especially significant for Erofeev in view of the constant pacing, walking, and running back and forth by various characters in *Walpurgis Night*, as well as Gurevich's overt reference to his own steps. In Erofeev's tragedy, Blok's steps, like the Commander/Don Juan dichotomy in Gurevich and Boren'ka, work both ways. Gurevich takes his steps toward Boren'ka, but as a result of Prokhorov's scream, Boren'ka, along with the rest of the hospital staff, marches toward him, too. However, Erofeev also develops Blok's notion of Don Juan's betrayal. For Blok, the Commander's steps signify an inescapable destiny: Don Juan's punishment for betraying the Beautiful Lady, and thus also his poetic ideal. In *Walpurgis Night*, Don Juan's inevitable downfall is similarly tied to the betrayal of a poetic ideal, since his use of poetry for deadly purposes marks him as complicit with the establishment. Poetic Donjuanism, given a positive valence by Pushkin, reverts to a negative quality in Erofeev's tragedy, via Blok, as it fails to overcome restrictive authoritarian structures.

On the one hand, this failure demonstrates the fact that Soviet power, with its draconian attempts to document and control every detail of its citizens' activity, punishes its Don Juans even more strictly than the tsarist regime did. Erofeev shows that official Soviet culture has an incredible "gripping" power, overtaking and paralyzing poets (like himself) who try to escape from its clutches, much as the Commander, eventually, freezes and destroys the elusive, eternally rebellious Don Juan.[15] Soviet culture's grip prevents subversive art from achieving any real effect. However, the inability of poetic Don Juans to counter the prevailing ideology comes just as much from within as from without. Erofeev may be commenting on contemporary Russian poetry as a whole during the early 1980s, as many of the inmates' poetic improvisations in *Walpurgis Night* reflect trends of this period. One of these is Alekha's verbatim recitation of the last poem in Dmitry Prigov's cycle "The Image of Reagan in Soviet Literature" (1983):

> We'll get up with nothing on.
> We'll get up, the world's no more.
> Money's gone.
> Truth is gone.
> All the sacred things are gone.
> Reagan is in Syria! (249)[16]

> Завтра встанем в неглиже,
> Встанем-вскочим: свету-нету,
> Правды нету,
> Денег нету,
> Ничего святого нету, —
> Рейган в Сирии уже!

Much of the poetic absurdity of Gurevich and his wardmates resonates with that of Conceptualists like Prigov, who sought to reveal the emptiness of Soviet clichés by exposing their banality. Conceptualist poetry, Epstein remarks, aims to "demonstrate the depletion and deadening of language itself" and to reveal socialist ideological slogans as simulacra, signifiers without signifieds (*After the Future* 32). In keeping with Hutcheon's understanding of postmodernism as "a contradictory phenomenon, one that uses and abuses, installs and then subverts, the very concepts it challenges" (3), Conceptualism deals with the historical past by simultaneously undermining it ironically and inscribing it into itself. Erofeev, though, seems to doubt the capacity of contemporary poetry to achieve a sufficient distance from the Soviet reality, culture, and clichés it parodies.

This incapacity stems from the poet's own limitations. Paradoxically, despite Gurevich's articulacy and continuous improvisation, his poetic recitations are somewhat methodical. Instead of changing or developing markedly over the course of *Walpurgis Night*, the same tone, style, and delivery are repeated with every audience. Even in the most intimate situation, alone with Natalie, Gurevich parodies the same Nekrasov poem he parodied in Act I, "Who

Is Happy in Russia?" ("Komu na Rusi zhit' khorosho?"). Moreover, his most amusing, inventive verbal gestures grow stale and routine through sheer repetition by the end of the tragedy. In the beginning of Act I, for instance, Gurevich invokes Descartes to try to subvert the doctor's interrogation. After several more references to Descartes in the course of the play, however, the citations become so predictable that late in Act V, Prokhorov responds to one such phrase with the question "René Descartes?" (242). Gurevich's poetic tools—iambic pentameter, parodic quotation, wordplay—become habitual, even if the actual content changes. Ironically, his poetic inventiveness turns out to be as banal and mechanical, in its own way, as the profanities and Sovietisms of Boren'ka and the doctor and as destructive and tyrannical as the staff's physical violence. Pushkin's Don Juan represents a celebration of poetry's endless variety, despite the creator's tragic position in relation to society. As Herman points out, the poet has the consolation that even if his art is dying and unappreciated in Russia, he can still create and try to overcome immobility. Erofeev, though, argues that there is no longer even any possibility of variety. Don Juan's endless improvisations and self-recreations turn out to be nothing but repetitive self-parodies, leaving a sense of poetry having exhausted itself. For Herman, Pushkin's Don Juan is actually undone by his own poetic invocation of the Commander. As he puts it, "the Don Juan play enacts the metaphysical drama of poetry as Pushkin sees it: in his creativity, the poet inexorably conjures to life entities that cannot help but hamper his mobility" (21). But in Erofeev's tragedy, poetry *itself* is a destructive and ultimately sterile phenomenon, a Commander that destroys Don Juan and the entire ward.[17]

Erofeev's depiction of Donjuanism through Gurevich also indicates the death of his own legend as a poet, artist, and eccentric.[18] This death is symbolized by Gurevich's inarticulate roaring at the end, which stands in such sharp contrast to his earlier eloquence, as Boren'ka deals him repeated blows. In this scene, Erofeev seems to follow Mozart and Da Ponte, who reduce Don Giovanni's former expressivity to deathly, awful roars as he descends to hell, rather than Pushkin, who allows Don Juan to cry out the name of his beloved as he collapses. As with the terrifying silence at the conclusion of *Moscow-Petushki*, the end of *Walpurgis Night* highlights a poet's inability to speak. This ending is made even more poignant by the fact that the play was written around the time when Erofeev became aware of his throat cancer, because of which he was eventually able to speak only through the aid of a mechanical device pressed to his throat. Given the fact that Gurevich clearly represents many of Erofeev's values, the author may be acknowledging a certain failure in his own "poetic" creation and alcoholic lethargy to effectively combat Soviet ideology, and even a type of complicity with it on his part. Vladimir Murav'ev remarks that Erofeev, far from being a dissident, functioned "in Soviet reality like a fish in water" (94) and was well aware of his dependence on the Soviet Union.[19] In fact, Erofeev even felt the need to advance the legend of his identity as a holy fool figure by distorting biographical facts pertaining to such incidents as his expulsion from the university.[20] For all his individual rebellion, Erofeev may have recognized the tendency of this freedom to double back on itself, negating its original impulse by simply becoming a different form of totalitarianism.

Erofeev thus recasts Pushkin's discovery of an essential identity in two legendary roles that are usually seen as opposing forces in a new political context. In *Walpurgis Night*, the ambiguity of Donjuanism is connected with a broader statement concerning how the struggle against a reified power and its language system inevitably leads to the substitution of relations similar to those the rebel is supposedly trying to combat. This ambiguity clarifies Don Juan's own dual function as a rebel and tyrant. Don Juan may be rebelling against a restrictive society, but the alternative way of life he creates, far from simply striving to assert itself as a viable ideology, violently subjugates those around him. He forces everyone to accept his personal arrangement of the world through his tools of seduction and murder, the very tools that Gurevich, in effect, employs to achieve his own "higher vision."[21] Through his exploration of Donjuanism in *Walpurgis Night*, Erofeev takes a bleaker, more pessimistic position than Pushkin on the role of the poet and the failure of poetry, and in doing so, he questions the value of his own legend-in-formation as well.

Kazakov's *Don Juan* Cycle

Neo-avant-garde writer Vladimir Kazakov's cycle *Don Juan* (*Don Zhuan*, 1983) has several features in common with Erofeev's play, which it preceded by two years. Like Erofeev, Kazakov uses the foreign, centuries-old legend to question the reality of his time period, largely through poetic wordplay. However, where Erofeev's nightmarish vision of the Soviet mental hospital cum prison undermines the Soviet insistence that they were creating a perfect society, Kazakov uses verbal tricks to obscure reality itself, thus reinforcing the unreal state of time and place indicated by the very juxtaposition of the Don Juan legend with Russian language and culture. And if Erofeev ultimately makes an intensely political statement about poetry, Kazakov's brand of postmodernism is deliberately apolitical as he actively avoids any association between the Don Juan theme and contemporary Soviet political reality. One gets the impression that his plays could just as easily have been written in the 1960s, or indeed, before or after the Soviet Union.

Kazakov's effort to create a "private" literature that completely avoided Soviet politics and everyday reality is rooted, similarly to Erofeev's writing, in a lifelong career of nonconformism. He was expelled from two institutions of higher education in the 1950s, after which he drifted for years, spending time in such remote regions of the Soviet Union as Chukotka and Kolyma, and working as a teacher, gold panner, sailor, and woodcutter, among other professions. Beginning in the early 1960s, he wrote poetry, plays, and novels, but he was not officially published in Russia until after his death: his works were known mostly through German translations in Western Europe and *tamizdat* editions in Russia.

Although Kazakov did not formally belong to any group, he can be considered part of the neo-avant-gardist revival of the 1950s and '60s (also including Gennady Aigi and Viktor Sosnora), which attempted to resuscitate Futurist and Oberiu (Association of Real Art) experiments of the first half of the century. These writers followed Velemir Khlebnikov in their use of neologisms, palindromes, semantic ellipses, and other *zaum* (trans-sense) techniques. However, they did not share the Futurists' program for reinventing language in order to shape new political structures. Kazakov's language, like that of Daniil Kharms, aims for the breakdown rather than the creation of meaning. As Bertram Müller puts it, "Kazakov's world is ruled not by order and comfort, but by chaos and threats" (7). His works feature frequent motifs of physical pain, imprisonment, and flight. They can be seen as offering "poetic escape" from a torturous world not by remaking it, but by destroying all forms of order and logic through puns, nonsense, alogic, and incongruous combinations. A couple of examples of this destruction of logic can be seen in the 1969 poems "Multiplication Tables" ("Tablitsa umnozheniia"), a series of equations with incorrect or nonexistent solutions, and "Wonderful crossed-out quatrain" ("Prekrasnoe zacherknutoe chetverostishie"), which consists simply of four lines crossed out. Both of these poems illustrate Kazakov's characteristic approach of deliberately voiding possible meanings and humorously undermining readers' expectations.

Kazakov and other neo-avant-gardists also differed from Futurist and Oberiu writers, as they did from most of their late twentieth-century contemporaries, in their apoliticism. Occupying a space outside of both official and dissident literature, their status at the time was less than central. As Leiderman and Lipovetsky write, "The neo-avant-garde of the 1950s-60s was clearly marginal not only with respect to official ideology, but also the cultural 'Thaw' as a whole" (Vol. 1 376–77). The Futurist poets Velemir Khlebnikov and Vladimir Mayakovsky, each in his own way, predicted and celebrated revolutionary upheaval. And although Kharms's destruction of traditional causal relations goes way beyond political references, there is no doubt that his works reflect the violence, arrests, and disappearances that had become a deadly norm in the 1930s. Kazakov's works, by contrast, are far more difficult to contextualize in relation to his milieu, since he deliberately avoids describing Soviet politics or *byt*. If there is anything "political" about his works, it is a rejection of the very issues that both official and dissident figures considered important and an exclusive focus on aesthetic and philosophical concerns. "Having programmatically disclaimed all political commitment," Renate Lachmann writes regarding Kazakov's preface to his 1970 novel *Mistake of the Living* (*Oshibka zhivykh*), "this Muscovite author can hardly be taken for an ideological dissident; he is, however, without doubt an aesthetic one" (315).

In his Don Juan cycle, Kazakov chooses a theme that, especially in light of its traditional Russian treatment, would seem to demand some sort of Soviet political contextualization, as Erofeev provides in his play. Instead of drawing political resonance from the legendary Don's criminal rebellion against authority, though, Kazakov uses nonsense and paradox to parody some of the most central elements of the legend: the theme of exile, the notion of poetry as a form of seduction, duels as expressions of a desire for vengeance, and the Don's struggle with authority. His application of the absurd to the Don Juan theme allows him to inject new comic valence into the legend where other Russian treatments had deemphasized this element. However, Kazakov's deliberate emptying out of all possible political references itself serves as a serious statement on the role of poetry in relation to politics. Kazakov ultimately reinterprets Don Juan as a symbol of escape from political and everyday reality, and even the Soviet milieu itself, into a cerebral, poetic world of imagination. In doing so, he outlines a new solution to what Groys, characterizing the avantgarde both before and after Stalinism, describes as "the impossibility of breaking the closed circle of the dominant Soviet ideology" (107). If other avantgarde artists paralleled the state, to a degree, in their totalizing impulse, then Kazakov reworks the Don Juan legend in such a way as to escape this complicity by completely avoiding any political references.

Compared to Pushkin's *The Stone Guest*, which in a concise form preserves much of the traditional Don Juan narrative, Kazakov's reworking is deliberately looser, more episodic, and at all times whimsically absurd. His cycle includes four short plays titled *Don Zhuan*, *Dinner at Cordova* (*Obed v Kordove*), *Dinner at the Escurial* (*Obed v Eskuriale*), and *The Last Duel* (*Poslednii poedinok*), as well as an epilogue. In the first play, Don Juan meets a nobleman (referred to simply as "Kavaler") and a group of robbers who seek to capture him. He disguises himself by pretending that he is also searching for Don Juan. *Dinner at Cordova* takes place following a duel in which Don Juan has killed an unnamed opponent. He and Leporello are stopped by armed guards and an officer. They escape by claiming that Don Juan has already been caught. Don Juan then enters into a conversation on poetry with a nobleman named Don Ignatio and his wife, Donna Irina, until the officer returns, saying that the traces of Don Juan have led him there. Don Juan claims to be a poet named Vladimir Kazakovsky and is released. *Dinner at the Escurial* takes place in the Madrid palace of a King Sancho, who is ordering his police chief to find Don Juan. This time, Don Juan disguises himself as a Portuguese alchemist, promises to invent gunpowder, and converses about poetry with the king, the queen, and her lady in waiting. In *The Last Duel*, Don Juan and Leporello discuss lunch plans on the road between Barcelona and Madrid before stopping at a tavern where four noblemen are talking about poetry. They are joined by a Don Valentin and his sister, Donna Matreshechka. Don Juan introduces himself as Don Khuan (as opposed to the Don Zhuan they are seeking), flirts with Matreshechka, and sings her an Andalusian romance. He is then challenged to a duel by Don Valentin and the first nobleman, who turns out to be the author. Finally, in the epilogue, the officer and guards again attempt to arrest them, and Don Juan and Leporello fight with them until they flee. The cycle concludes with Don Juan again singing and accompanying himself on the guitar.

This summary of Kazakov's plays displays various recognizably postmodernist devices. The very fact that it is a cycle, rather than a single play, highlights the notion of serialism that is so important to Brodsky, Il'ia Kabakov, Vladimir Sorokin, and other Russian writers associated with postmodernism. Serialism is also reflected in the various lists that characters construct in *Walpurgis Night*.[22] Another feature of the cycle is its playful, self-referential quality, underscored by Don Juan's claim (alongside other lies and disguises) to be Vladimir Kazakovsky. The plays—like Kazakov's oeuvre in general—comprise a pastiche of several incongruent styles. These include a Kharmsian type of alogic built on disrupting causal connections, Futurist neologisms, and puns in the style of writers such as Gogol and Bely. This mixture of styles and influences continually works toward the destruction of traditional language and logic. Kazakov employs these devices throughout the cycle to parody familiar elements of the Don Juan legend: the pairing of the hero with Leporello, duels, attempts to seduce women, and flight from authority. He therefore destabilizes the legend's narrative impulse with Don Juan's inexorable path to damnation or some other form of destruction. From play to play, the episodes Kazakov describes have an aimless character and lack the sense of urgency found in other Don Juan versions, since it does not seem to matter what happens to the hero.

Many of Kazakov's absurdities parody Pushkin's version of the legend in particular. The passage in *The Last Duel* in which Kazakov intersperses Don Juan's reminiscences of Donna Yulia with Leporello's suggestions for dinner serve as one example:

> *Leporello*: Then tell me, for love of Jupiter, what you would prefer: suckling pig with kasha or mutton with kasha.
> *Don Juan*: I recall Donna Yulia. What an astonishing gaze she had!
> *Leporello*: I'd prefer mutton.
> *Don Juan*: It wasn't a gaze, but a kind of divine midnight, streaming from her eyes.
> *Leporello*: With kasha. (178)[23]

This passage clearly evokes Don Juan's reminiscences to Leporello in *The Stone Guest* of his deceased lover Inez's features:

> *Don Juan*: I found strange pleasure
>   In gazing at her sorrowful eyes
>   And death-pale lips. It's strange.
>   You apparently didn't think she was
>   A beauty. And in fact, there wasn't
>   Much beautiful about her. Her eyes,
>   Just her eyes. And her glance . . . I've never seen
>   Another glance like that. (68)

> *Дон Гуан*: Странную приятность
>   Я находил в ее печальном взоре.
>   Ты, кажется, ее не находил
>   Красавицей. И точно, мало было
>   В ней истинно прекрасного. Глаза,
>   Одни глаза. Да взгляд . . . Такого взгляда
>   Уж никогда я не встречал. (139)

Kazakov reworks Pushkin's description of Inez's eyes and gaze by mixing them with incongruous images ("divine midnight, streaming from her eyes"). By doing so, he parodies the wistful, elegiac tone introduced by Pushkin into Don Juan's character. He also parodies the Don's improvisational, conversational style in the Pushkin passage (the ellipses after "And her glance" indicate his search for words). Kazakov's reference to Donna Yulia is a non sequitur in the first place since Don Juan responds to Leporello's prosaic concerns with completely unrelated material. Kazakov thus creates ironic distance from Pushkin's romanticization of Don Juan.

However, the absurdist reworking does not parody Pushkin's transference of his elegiac style to his hero simply to make fun of it. Kazakov considered Gogol and Dostoevsky his favorite writers, along with Khlebnikov and his idol, Alexei

Kruchenykh, and it is clear that his relationship to the classics is one of admiration rather than the scorn frequently expressed by the Futurists. Here and elsewhere in the plays, Kazakov in fact continues Pushkin's project by implicitly comparing his own identification with Don Juan to the nineteenth-century poet's. He develops Pushkin's notion of Don Juan's desire to improvise creatively through seductive poetry and to avoid categorization, and he transforms it into the impulse to disappear into one's own world, escaping politics and even logical meaning altogether. Thus, even as Kazakov parodically dismantles the classic Russian Don Juan text, he simultaneously uses it as a means of exploring the role of the Russian poet, replaying a similar situation but highlighting its new context. In this sense, his treatment exemplifies the "repetition with critical distance" that Hutcheon describes as characteristic of postmodern parody (26).

Other motifs Kazakov selects from the legend similarly reveal his indebtedness to Pushkin and the Russian tradition of representing Don Juan as a poet. Don Juan and Leporello wander through different parts of Spain, with several scenes taking place on the road and others in a tavern (a temporary stopping point on the road). The road motif, of course, is a staple of the legend, as the Don is often in exile or fleeing capture. Linked with wandering, exile, and flight motifs, it is also a cornerstone of the broader Russian poetic tradition, whether one thinks of exiled poets Pushkin and Lermontov, émigrés such as Brodsky and Tsvetaeva, poet-wanderers (Khlebnikov and Kazakov himself), or simply the poetic desire to reshape oneself constantly, which Pushkin inscribes into his Don Juan. Indeed, the "wandering" of Kazakov's plays is as much a poetic as a geographical journey on the part of Don Juan. The hero's constant (though absurd) escapes from trouble are fully consonant with Kazakov's poetic style and mission in general, with its theme of flight from reality. If Erofeev's play exiles the hero to the fringes of society in the mental hospital in which he is incarcerated, Kazakov's hero exists in a different type of marginalized society: the endless road. In addition to its setting, Kazakov's cycle contains several references to the road within the action of the plays. A group of robbers whom Don Juan and Leporello find at a tavern can be heard toasting the road:

1st robber: I suggest a toast to the wide road!
2nd robber: And I, to the wide merchant caravan.
3rd robber: And I, to Hegel as the pioneer of the wide road in philosophy.
4th robber: But couldn't I suggest a toast to Kant as the widest caravan in all of merchant philosophy! (145)

This series of toasts, of course, displays Kazakov's characteristic alogical juxtapositions (e.g., "the widest caravan in all of merchant philosophy"). At the same time Kazakov also emphasizes the notion of mental flight by interconnecting philosophy with the road, as a kind of retreat from the concrete to the cerebral. Unlike in *The Stone Guest* (and other Don Juan texts), Kazakov's physical road does not lead anywhere in particular. If Pushkin's protagonist, for instance, has clear goals—return to his native Madrid, the seduction of Donna Anna—Kazakov's Don Juan and Leporello drift aimlessly from point to point on a road that has no concrete destination, no beginning or end.

The theme of Don Juan's capture is similarly highlighted throughout the play but divested completely of its usual urgency. Authority figures such as the knight whom Don Juan and Leporello meet in the first play, the officer in *Dinner at Cordova*, and the Spanish king in *Dinner at the Escurial*, have repeated opportunities to bring Don Juan to justice. As in other versions of the legend, Don Juan continually avoids capture through lies and disguises. But since the escape in Kazakov's plays takes the form of a series of distractions through puns, paradoxes, and illogical statements, the very idea of capture is rendered ridiculous. In *Dinner at the Escurial*, for instance, when Don Miguel announces to King Sancho that he has found a trace of Don Juan (who is in fact present in the room), the king simply tells him to look for more traces. The combination of the first names "Miguel" and "Sancho" appears to refer to *Don Quixote*, another work that takes place largely on the road and concerns the dominance of the imaginary over reality. At the same time, Kazakov also disappoints the expectations of a reader seeking to make a connection between the Don Juan legend (or *Don Quixote*) and Soviet politics. In *The Stone Guest*, Don Juan's references to the king protecting him from exile in the little tragedy inevitably bring to mind comparisons to Pushkin's complex relationship with Nikolai I: in Kazakov's text, however, no similar implications can be found. Although the notion of Don Juan's arrest could easily call forth potential connections to Soviet reality, Kazakov deliberately avoids following up on this possibility, instead dissolving the idea of search and arrest into absurdity.

Throughout the cycle, Kazakov also parodies the traditional device of disguises that Don Juan uses (in *Don Giovanni*, for example, by trading places with Leporello, and in Pushkin's play, by pretending to be a monk). In the first play, when a Sevillian nobleman announces that he seeks vengeance on Don Juan for seducing his sister and killing her husband in a duel, the disguised Don Juan responds that he wants to avenge the villain for pawning his only watch. The following exchange takes place when the nobleman tries to find out how to recognize Don Juan:

> *Don Juan*: There's one sure clue: he resembles me like two drops of water. So much so that in every mirror I glance into, I see Don Juan. . . .

Cavalier: But, in that case, how can we distinguish you from your double?
Don Juan: The thing is that there is one, but only one, distinction between us. Don Juan, when he lies, never blushes, whereas I, when I happen to lie, blush like a girl.
Cavalier: But you blushed just now, precisely like a girl!
Don Juan: Precisely because I'm not Don Juan.
Cavalier: Hmm . . . But doesn't that mean you lied to me?
Don Juan: How could I be lying if I blushed? After all, if I hadn't blushed, I'd be Don Juan and not myself.
Cavalier (after reflecting): Yes, everything in my head is all mixed up from all this thirst for revenge. (143)

By offering up this version of the famous paradox whereby a Cretan claims that all Cretans are liars, Kazakov parodies the ideas of vengeance and disguise. Once again, however, the parody folds back to reveal a serious purpose. The play with Don Juan's identity may signify Kazakov's desire to shape his own persona, frustrate expectations, and avoid being categorized at all costs, echoing characteristics of Pushkin's Don Juan. In *The Last Duel*, Kazakov similarly plays with this notion of disguise in the following exchange between Don Juan and Don Valentin:

Don Juan (bowing): I'm as happy as you. My name is Don Juan. And this is my loyal servant, Leporello.
Don Valentin: Don Juan?! Are you sure you aren't Don Zhuan?
Don Juan: If I were sure I were Don Juan, then I would have introduced myself as Don Theobald or even Don Vladimir. (183)

The comic device of disguise in Mozart/Da Ponte and Pushkin takes place concretely through changes of clothing and function. Kazakov, by contrast, moves Don Juan's deconstruction of his own identity to the verbal sphere as he simply invents other names he could attach to himself, additionally playing with the different possible spellings of his name.

In the same manner, Kazakov reworks the notion of Don Juan's exile and his flight from state power and individual vengeance. His Don Juan escapes not so much from a particular leader or authority as from the very idea of the political into the poetic, imaginative world. Kazakov's use of puns, paradoxes, and illogical statements dictates this transformation from the very beginning of the play. Asked by Don Juan during the first scene of *Don Zhuan* what the sense in duels is, Leporello responds: "I don't see any sense in duels. But I do see many duels in sense" (141). This kind of absurdity typifies Kazakov's attempt to subvert logic. Because it refers to duels, it also undermines one of the legend's most dramatic plot elements. It outlines a motion from action to philosophical play that is typical of the cycle, as Kazakov proposes an escape from the world of concrete action (duels) to that of the mind (sense). Similarly, according to Leporello, Don Juan's wallet is filled not with ducats (a tangible object), but sense:

> *Don Juan*: And about my wallet, I can also say, without blushing, that's it's also full.
> *Cavalier*: Of what?
> *Don Juan*: Leporello, what is it full of?
> *Leporello*: Sense.
> *Cavalier*: Yes, but mine is full of double ducats.
> *Don Juan*: Leporello, parry!
> *Leporello*: Sense is also double. (144)

By contrasting the ducats with sense, Leporello underscores Don Juan's intangible, philosophical realm. Don Juan's command for Leporello to "parry" the cavalier's "blow" also transfers the idea of dueling from the physical to the poetic arena.

At the end of the play, the dueling motif transforms into a metaliterary reference as the three robbers discuss the possibility of a confrontation with Don Juan:

> *1st robber*: If that's Don Juan, then it's the end for us.
> *2nd robber*: And if it's not?
> *3rd robber*: Then it's only the end of the play. (149)

The very threat of deathliness pervading the Don Juan legend, for his opponents as for himself, is avoided as literary play overcomes the seriousness of dueling. Thus Kazakov develops the continual improvisation of Pushkin's Don Juan by turning dueling into a play of philosophical and poetic musings. The idea of tangible, concrete actions leading to possible capture and death—the very "stoniness" of the Commander, which joins him together with Don Juan at the end of *The Stone Guest*—vanishes into the thin air of pure mental space. Later, Don Juan shows the power of words to unmake reality itself through negation, as he denies that the word "duel" even exists: "In Chinese, and in the other alchemical languages, such a word simply does not exist" (165). The poet has the power to undo reality itself through language.

Elsewhere in the cycle, Kazakov continually plays with contrasts between the poetic and the concrete. Don Juan compares the power of gunpowder and poetry in his conversation with the Spanish king and queen in *Dinner at the Escurial*, in his disguise as a Portuguese alchemist named Don Filipp Figueroa:

Queen: Don Filipp, what disturbs you more than gunpowder?
Don Juan: Your majesty, only poetry disturbs me. Gunpowder, to the contrary, only calms me. (165–66)

On the one hand, Don Juan seems to be making a purely playful response. However, Kazakov's comparison of poetry with gunpowder also underscores the explosive quality of poetry to undermine any sort of action, and its consequent superiority over physical reality.

The anachronisms of the plays, along with their apoliticism, also highlight Kazakov's attempt to escape everyday Soviet life as he continually rejects temporal Russian reality and politics for a timeless mental world. This device is typical of Kazakov's work: Lachmann, discussing the intertextuality of *Mistake of the Living*, defines its present as "the 'present' created by texts, all the texts that, from within his reading experience, and in his literary (but unofficial) memory, offer a cross section of the present, in other words, the present constituted by the semantic and cultural experience stored within all these texts" (316). Similarly, in the *Don Juan* cycle, Don Juan refers to Kruchenykh as the greatest living poet and Soviet poet Alexander Bezymensky as the best cook during a scene that takes place in medieval Spain. Several characters mention electric devices and shooting with guns at a time period supposedly before the invention of gunpowder. Although the plays therefore mix different times, they pointedly exclude 1980s Russia. They also either avoid direct Soviet political or cultural allusions or, in the case of Kruchenykh and Bezymensky, make them meaningless through juxtaposition with completely different time periods. The above references to two Soviet-era poets—one officially approved, the other rejected—contain a great deal of potential for political implications, but this potential is dissolved through absurdity. There is a great deal of cultural incongruence as well, mostly involving juxtaposition of Russian and Spanish names and titles: the female characters include Donna Irina, Donna Yulia, Donna Anastasiia, and Donna Matreshechka. The escape from the chronotope of Soviet reality takes place, therefore, through a pastiche of randomly combined temporal and cultural references as Kazakov intermingles eternal Russian reality with the space of the Don Juan legend, rendering both absurd.

The Don Juan cycle, like much of Kazakov's oeuvre, is thoroughly self-referential, but in a very different manner from Erofeev's use of his alter ego, Gurevich. Kazakov's metaliterary commentary on his own work and technique contributes to the dismantling of any possible political message rooted in Soviet reality. For one, it fashions an effective escape from everyday life into a personal, idiosyncratic mental space that is typical of postmodern writing.[24] In addition, Kazakov dismantles any possible serious message Don Juan, following the Russian tradition, might have as a poet-rebel. He does so partly by continually highlighting his own awkwardness as a writer. In *Dinner at the Escurial*, Don Juan calls a comment by the king "the usual Kazakoving" (obyknovennoe kazakovstvo; 167) and later refers to the author of the play as "talentless" (bezdarnyi; 192). In *The Last Duel*, Leporello comments on the difficult position in which the author has found himself in the act of creation: "He's looking for an effective denouement and not finding it" (172). Don Juan himself, at one point, steps out of the play and demands that the author change course: "Now I suggest the following: if the author does not—with a stroke of his pen—transport us right now to some tavern, and with a wallet stuffed full of ducats or at least doubloons, we'll refuse not only to speak, but also to go along this stony road" (179).

Such passages display Kazakov's playful tendency to undermine his own work and detract from the seriousness of his subject as well. However, they also emphasize his identification with the poetic Don Juan first introduced by Pushkin. When Don Juan, having referred to himself as "Vladimir Kazakovsky," is asked to read his poems, he acts as a kind of poetic seducer, along the lines of Pushkin's autobiographical Don (later it turns out that Kazakov is actually the first robber—also a poet). By inscribing parts of his poetic identity into his hero, à la Pushkin, Kazakov likens himself to a Don Juan who continually escapes from trouble through poetry, albeit that poetry comprises nonsensical lyrics and paradoxes that break down logic.

Kazakov similarly undermines any possible concreteness that the stage itself could provide by ensuring the plays' unperformability. He frequently includes linguistic devices that are impossible to represent on the stage. During *The Last Duel*, Don Juan and Leporello communicate using a series of ellipses:

Don Juan: Tell me, Leporello, what word do you think is the most boring?
Leporello: In my opinion, it's "................................"
Don Juan: And in my opinion, it's "................................"
Leporello: No, sir, the most boring word has not been invented. Otherwise, pronouncing it, I would have fallen over.
Don Juan: But you actually did almost fall over, pronouncing the word "............................"
Leporello: That was from hunger and unbearable thirst. (179)

Such conversations, deliberately impossible to put into action, call into question the reality of even something as concrete as the stage itself.

What, then, makes Donjuanism significant for an absurdist writer like Kazakov, and how does it relate to his all-pervasive theme of flight? The simple fact of the legend's popularity for Russian writers in the twentieth century seems an insufficient explanation. And as I have tried to suggest, although the legend's motifs of escape and capture immediately bring to mind associations with the Soviet political context, particularly in relation to writers, Kazakov's treatment, far from offering either overt or Aesopian allusions to Soviet reality, seems marked by a lack of political resonance.

This does not mean, though, that Kazakov has nothing to say about his literary milieu. Ultimately, the Don Juan legend, in its foregrounding of a striking paradox regarding the problem of rebel and authority, offers Kazakov a vehicle for representing his own situation as a writer. Don Juan ostensibly rebels against the legal and moral restrictions of his society through his seductions and duels. In doing so, however, he ends up creating a new type of tyranny that forces everyone with whom he interacts—men and women alike—to bend to his will. This paradox can also be seen as central to post-Stalinist art, with its opposition between official and dissident writers. Through his Don Juan character, Kazakov attempts to dismantle any type of stable meaning altogether and therefore escape the type of complicity Groys describes between the state and its rebel artists. He does so not only by avoiding the use of Soviet clichés (even via parody), but also by foregrounding poetic escape as the dominant ideology. He depicts a rebellion, therefore, against both authority *and* dissidence, by escaping, and poetically destroying, the very political truth that they both embrace.[25] Kazakov destroys oppositions through pure nonsense: his Don Juan does not try very hard to hide himself, and the authorities are equally willing to let him escape.

Avoidance of this opposition, of course, comes with its own dangers. As Groys points out, "the single utopia of the classical avantgarde and Stalinism has been replaced by a myriad of private, individual utopias, each of which, however, is thoroughly intolerant of all the others and especially of the people and the 'socialist realist kitsch' in which the people live" (78). While Kazakov's world is indeed a type of private (and narcissistic) utopia, in which language provides an escape from politics and ideology, it is difficult to consider it intolerant in this manner. For one thing, its emphasis is on play and humor; for another, it simply refuses to allow any blatantly political or religious ideology to enter the fray. It thus does not actually express any intolerance of "socialist realist kitsch" so much as simply ignore it.

Significantly, *Don Zhuan* contrasts noticeably with other works of Kazakov: if his early poetry and prose focus on pain and imprisonment, then these motifs seem unusually absent from this dramatic cycle. There are, of course, actual duels, but they are absurd, focusing on deliberate nonsense, obfuscation, and most of all, humorous ways to interpret the most "serious" situations. Written toward the end of Kazakov's career, the cycle seems to reflect the fulfillment of the escape he had yearned for as the Don and Leporello, far from being vanquished, ride off onto the eternal road singing and creating poetry. In this manner, Kazakov provides a unique solution to the problem of the Soviet artist who seeks to avoid politics. At the same time, he sheds new light on the Don Juan legend itself by uncovering its potential as an expression of purely aesthetic dissidence, in contrast to the kind of political dissidence described by Erofeev.

Ulitskaya's Don Juans

Contemporary writer Liudmila Ulitskaya's works feature numerous characters in multiple relationships as part of her broader examination of unorthodox sexual relations and marginalized people in Russian society. She does not explicitly refer to any of her characters as Don Juans, and it is thus a matter of judgment which of them should be discussed in light of this archetype. Moreover, unlike Erofeev and Kazakov, who focus throughout their respective works on the phenomenon of Donjuanism, Ulitskaya's use of this theme is less overt. In her early works *Sonechka* (1992) and *The Funeral Party* (*Veselye pokhorony*, 1997), Ulitskaya portrays serial lovers who, as painters, call to mind Pushkin's fascination with the intersection of sexuality and art; thus, although she explicitly refers neither to Donjuanism nor to Pushkin's *The Stone Guest*, these works seem to represent a continuation of this way of understanding the phenomenon of Donjuanism. In the later work *Sincerely Yours, Shurik* (*Iskrenne vash Shurik*, 2004), Ulitskaya offers a Don Juan figure but turns the elements of the legend upside down in creating a more realistic and—reflecting Pushkin's description of Donjuanism as I understand it—ultimately sympathetic character. In this section, I will contrast the ways in which each of these three works explores Donjuanism.

Unlike Kazakov and Erofeev, who clearly represent postmodern writers, Ulitskaya does not fit this categorization. "Unencumbered by the stylistic mimicry and postmodernist devices that many find alienating in works by Sorokin and Pelevin," Helena Goscilo writes, "her prose is straightforward and transparent, firmly welded to the heritage of nineteenth-century realism" (Foreword, xx). Despite the efforts of some critics to classify her as postmodern, Ulitskaya fits better into what Benjamin Sutcliffe and Elizabeth Skomp have described as a kind of "new sincerity" in late twentieth- and early twenty-first-century Russian literature.[26] For Sutcliffe and Skomp, this concept harks back to Pomerantsev's 1953 essay "On Sincerity in Literature" ("Ob iskrennosti v literature"), which announced a new Thaw aesthetics that privileged individual lives over the collective. Ulitskaya's emphasis on intelligentsia values of tolerance, inclusivity, and individual integrity similarly marks her as part of the "new sincerity" (Sutcliffe and Skomp 4).

Ulitskaya's works have also been discussed in the context of so-called "women's prose" (zhenskaia proza), which came to the fore in the 1980s and '90s and also includes Liudmila Petrushevskaya, Tatiana Tolstaya, Nina Sadur, and other female writers of the time. Although Ulitskaya follows Petrushevskaya in making *byt* (everyday life) a serious literary topic, she departs from these writers in key ways. Men's abusive sexuality, as Sutcliffe and Skomp point out, is a primary topic of writers such as Petrushevskaya and Sadur; Ulitskaya, by contrast, offers a more egalitarian view of male and female sexuality and a more optimistic account of the potential of bodily beauty and sexuality in general to contribute to human happiness.[27] This tolerance regarding what the late Soviet Union and post-Soviet Russia would consider unorthodox sexual relations informs her descriptions of male characters who could be considered Don Juan-like in their penchant for an endless variety of sexual experiences with multiple women.

In *Sonechka*, the title character's husband, Robert Viktorovich, embodies clear characteristics of a Don Juan. Ulitskaya's introduction of the character establishes the prototype: "He was a committed ladies' man and obtained a great deal of sustenance from the seemingly inexhaustible supply of women" (9).[28] Moreover, he has the geographical profile typical of Don Juans, his peregrinations having led him from Russia to France, Spain, the United States, and other places. Under Stalinism, he has spent time in prison and in exile; it is not until the early 1950s that he is able to return to Moscow and live within an artistic community that embraces him.[29] His commitment to serial relationships and remaining unmarried is so strong that by proposing to Sonechka, at the age of 47, he breaks a longstanding vow he has made never to marry. Thus, Ulitskaya finds a new way of conveying the notion of a serial quest ending in an ideal woman, as reflected in works of Hoffmann, Pushkin, and other Romantic texts about Don Juan. Sonechka's frankly asexual description, if anything, accentuates the degree of her lofty, spiritual state of humility and self-sacrifice, so important in the Russian tradition.[30] Robert sees her entirely in terms of fate, as he senses that his destiny is being accomplished by his being brought into contact with her. Gazing at her in the library, he senses that she has salvational power and wisdom (embodied in her full name, Sofia).

The fact that Robert is an artist invites comparisons to Pushkin's linking of prolific sexuality with aesthetic functions, and this linkage is borne out throughout the narrative. Robert and Sonechka's "courtship" is occasioned by art, as she helps him find French literature at their first meeting in the library where she works, and he presents her with a portrait of her, as part of his marriage proposal, when he returns two days later. Art becomes both a means of seduction and a wedding gift. As Ulitskaya shows later in the narrative, Robert's versatility as an artist matches his extensive sexual experience and geographical journeys: formerly a famous avantgarde painter, he survives by painting portraits of officials' wives, then crafts toys during their daughter Tania's childhood, and later earns a living constructing theater sets before returning to painting at the end of his life.

As in the Don Juan legend, Sonechka's appearance comes across as an unexpected but fated event; the same is the case with Jasia, who becomes Robert's last muse. Critics have noted that Ulitskaya takes a nonjudgmental tone with Robert's new relationship, as she does with numerous other unusual sexual relationships she portrays in her works. As Sutcliffe and Skomp argue, Ulitskaya's works hinge on the quality of "corporeality" (telesnost'), in which the body is inseparable from the mind, or spirit, and is equally important in defining human beings.[31]

This nonjudgmental quality, perhaps, conveys itself through Sonechka's own attitude toward the affair. First, there is her sense that the marriage, and the happiness it brings, is more than she deserves and had to end at some point. Second, she views Jasia as a gift for Robert:

> How right it is that he will have someone so young and beautiful at his side, so soft and clever, and as exceptional and outstanding as he is himself; and how well it has all turned out that life should bring about a miracle in his old age that has made him turn again to the most important thing about him, his painting, thought Sonechka. (57–58)

Far from being jealous of Jasia, as one might expect, she admires her and is happy for Robert; ultimately, she even unofficially adopts her as a second daughter.

Like his first meeting with Sonechka, Robert Viktorovich's encounter with Jasia seems fated; it is laden with significance and symbolism that go beyond the normal, all-too-common May-to-December relationship between an older man and a young girl. Tania first brings Jasia home on New Year's Eve, which marks their encounter as a kind of crossing of a symbolic boundary, and the beginning of a new life for both characters. Robert's first interactions with her, as with Sonechka, are linked to art: she first offers herself to him as he comes into her room at night to search for some gray paper. Later, Robert describes this encounter to himself as a kind of hallucination, as if he had happened on someone else's dream. Their affair takes place mostly at his studio. Ulitskaya creates a repetition of this experience that Robert notices, as he asks her to hold a roll of white paper as he leads Jasia into the studio for the first time: "'Hold this for a moment, please,' he said, shoving the roll of paper into her arms with a vague sense that something of the kind had occurred somewhere before" (53). The reminder of their first encounter, on New Year's Day, reinforces the uncanny aspects of the affair.

Most of all, Jasia, whose name means "clear," acquires special significance through her association with whiteness and translucence. The narrator first describes her as "transparent as an apothecary's gleaming flask" and with "a face as smooth as a new-laid egg" (38). From here follows an exhaustive series of explicit descriptions of her whiteness. Robert's lust is connected with this element of Jasia even as he tries to avoid her: "Now he allowed Jasia only into his peripheral vision, his eyes lingering stealthily on her tranquil whiteness while he melted into jelly on the fires of youthful lust" (52). Her whiteness inspires a year of creativity, amounting to 52 still lifes of white objects and portraits of Jasia. Robert's artistic inspiration is integrally linked to his sexual urges, and the affair is inseparable from the paintings.[32] As in Pushkin's play, where Don Juan's seduction of Anna consists of poetic recitations, Robert Viktorovich's interactions with Jasia are at the same time sexual and replete with aesthetic inspiration. In observing her, he lusts after her and at the same time is inspired to create art based on her. In this sense, he recalls Pushkin's Don Juan, inspired by Anna's foot to create the rest of her, as if he were a portrait painter.

Also similarly to Pushkin's Don Juan, who professes to be "reborn" through his love for Donna Anna, Robert Viktorovich experiences a rebirth in his interactions with Jasia (symbolically described as an egg, or giver of birth) as he undergoes an artistic revival in the throes of his affair with her. For Olga Livshin, the paintings, with their whiteness, represent a purification of Jasia, a cleansing of her past (providing sexual favors to survive), and even a recuperation of the modernist movement that was interrupted by Stalinism (8–9).[33] Moreover, Jasia is linked with the white (empty) canvas that he can paint on again, after years of not practicing this form of art. With her transparency, Jasia has no real self other than providing rebirth. With this character, at least, Ulitskaya presents women as fodder for artistic inspiration, but not as artists themselves.

However, Jasia is also connected closely with Robert Viktorovich's death. While indicating something pure about Jasia despite her own history of serial sexual encounters with men, Ulitskaya seems to be simultaneously alluding to Eastern associations of whiteness with death. Robert himself seems to be aware of this: "That face was the keynote from which everything else developed and grew, playing and singing the secret of the whiteness of dead things and the whiteness of things alive" (55). This association of Jasia with death is recalled later in the description of him in his coffin, in which his hands gleam with what he had called "the whiteness of dead things" (beloe-nezhivoe; 69).

In this sense, Robert Viktorovich, in his affair with Jasia, can be seen as pursuing an encounter with death (he dies in the act of having sex with Jasia). Ulitskaya portrays in Robert's love for Jasia the association of Eros and Thanatos typical of the Western romantic myth as described by de Rougemont. As with Don Juan, Robert's last erotic encounter is accompanied by deathly forces that he senses but cannot avoid, and in some way perhaps does not want to. Just as Pushkin's Don Juan is seeking some kind of encounter with death, Robert, too, appears to be attracted to Jasia's simultaneous lifelike and deathlike symbolism, which encompasses both the renewal of life and the closing of the circle of life through death. In this light it is significant that he starts painting her in mid-April (the time of Easter, a celebration of the renewal of life) and finishes a year later, with fifty-two pictures, one for every week of the year. The intersection of death and life is also perfectly embodied in the cerebral hemorrhage he experiences in the middle of the sexual act. In their relationship, art, Eros, and Thanatos are perfectly intermingled, in such a way as to affirm Ulitskaya's aforementioned nonjudgmental attitude when it comes to nonmonogamous sexual relationships and her awareness that love and human needs may express themselves in ways that cross the boundary of traditional morality.

In *The Funeral Party*, Ulitskaya again features an artist-seducer who comprises many of the aspects I have discussed in Don Juan figures, as she incorporates the theme into a tale of Russian émigré life in New York City. Donjuanism in this work revolves around a dying protagonist, Alik, who serves as the center of the novel: the action focuses entirely on him, as numerous friends and lovers come in and out of his apartment, caring for him in his last days. The funeral party near the end of *Sonechka* thus becomes the single plot point for this novel, which adumbrates a transition from life to death, celebrating Alik's life even as its end approaches. Ulitskaya's focus on the blurred line between life and death, the creative artist, and the intersections between art, sexuality, and death recall some of the main themes of the Don Juan legend.

Alik strikes the reader immediately with his resemblance to a Don Juan figure, in part simply for his lifelong attractiveness to women. "Since the day he was born," the narrator tells us, "women had always adored Alik" (27).[34] In this respect, he parallels Robert Viktorovich, for whom women have never been in short supply. Even more so than Robert, for whom Sonechka and Jasia somewhat controversially occupy equally central roles at the funeral party after his death, Alik is visited by a variety of women he has seduced, including his wife, Nina; his former lover Irina; and his former mistress Valentina; he has obviously had many other lovers as well. The women function as caretakers, though, and give Alik enjoyment in this role as well, as he approaches death: "Along with the weight of his body and the living flesh of his muscles, the reality of life was slipping away, which was why he took such pleasure in the half-naked women clinging to him from morning to night" (46).

Like Don Juan, Alik commits firmly to his way of life in the face of death: "I shall die an adulterer," he resolves (75). Alik has the gift of inspiring everyone (women and men) to like and surround him, and women compete over him. He is a trickster partly in his ability to improvise, to survive without planning, and to find ways to get what he wants from people through sheer persuasion, but he also fulfills this role through his ability to transcend the typical moral code without bringing about punishment or retribution. The motif of physical immobility from the Don Juan legend is noticeable here, but it is transformed into simple atrophying motion. Alik has been caught not by a supernatural force but by the most natural and irrevocable of all forces: death. But the death is in no way connected to retribution, and his deeds are not castigated in any way, just as Robert Viktorovich's Donjuanism and his affair with Jasia are presented without apparent judgment by the author.

Like Robert Viktorovich and the typical Don Juan figure, Alik has been all over the world, traveling as far as India, and is now dying far away from home in New York City. The narrator emphasizes the link between travel and conquest, noting that Alik treats the various places in which he lives like lovers: "He quickly made himself at home in new places, exploring their side-streets and dark spaces, their beautiful and perilous angles, like the body of a new lover" (92). He similarly evinces a knowledge of many languages, including Italian: he delights in listening to Goia, whom he has *not* seduced, reading aloud Dante (a fellow émigré and thus possibly an object of identification). The multiplicity and serialism in all areas (not just seduction) characterizing Alik thus recall that of the Don Juan legend.

Alik's art similarly recalls that of Don Juan figures like Pushkin's hero, for whom seduction and art are interrelated, and are a means of fighting deathly forces that would impose a closed, ossified quality onto artists and their artworks. Alik describes his paintings to the teenaged Maika as being about asymmetry, likening this stylistic quality to a fight against mortality: "Symmetry's death!" he exclaims (8). His artistic career, then, like Don Juan's improvisations in Pushkin's play, represents a struggle against the forces of death and ossification. For his still lifes, Alik uses bottles, evoking his love of drinking as a life force. Unprotective of his paintings, he allows them to live a free, unbounded artistic life in the public sphere. One of them, as he shows Valentina at the beginning of their affair, has been sold to a bar, which allows him to drink free for life. This passage recalls Pushkin's comparison of two different approaches to art in his little tragedy *Mozart and Salieri*, in which Salieri is horrified to hear a street musician "butchering" one of Mozart's famous arias, but Mozart is delighted to see that his music has penetrated the masses and become part of ordinary, everyday life.

Similarly, the forces of bohemianism that allow Alik to live a free and easy life correspond to crucial features of Donjuanism, some of which can be seen in the Erofeev and Kazakov works discussed previously in this chapter. Alik is an undocumented immigrant, living in the U.S. without proper papers, life insurance, or regular work. He does not even pick up his paintings after they are exhibited, depriving himself of a chance to make money from them, and generally dislikes forms and officials. His instinctual, strictly day-to-day way of life—the narrator notes that Alik improvises as he goes along instead of planning—recalls Pushkin's Don Juan as both artist and seducer, diverted even in the middle of his pursuit of Anna by the prospect of a reunion with Laura. Although Alik is dying at home in part simply because he prefers the procession of women to the atmosphere of a hospital, he also cannot go there with false papers. Like Erofeev's Gurevich and Kazakov's absurdist hero, Alik survives without a fixed identity. Even his name is unfixed and transitional: he is registered as Abraham officially, in his Soviet documents, but is called Alik, and that is what is listed in his American papers. His Judaism, as with the half-Jewish Gurevich, seems to play a role in this rootlessness and thus also makes him comparable to the Don Juan figure. The rabbi Menashe calls Alik a "captive," separated from the Torah and thus neither here nor there, not really a Jew, but not a Christian, more of a heathen.[35] His wife Nina's efforts to end this liminality by summoning a Russian Orthodox priest to convert him to Christianity essentially fail, as Alik deliberately asks for a rabbi as well as a priest to be in attendance and diverts the priest from his task by discussing beautiful women with him. Like both the proverbial Wandering Jew and the legendary Don Juan, Alik is without a home. This liminal state of being is reinforced, perhaps, by the circumstances of his homeland: at his death, he and his visitors are watching the 1991 breakup of the Soviet Union and Russia's transformation into a new nation.

Lastly, *The Funeral Party* features continual play with the boundaries between life and death, a distinct motif of the Don Juan legend hinging upon the

Commander's transition from inanimate to animate, from immobility in death to a strange afterlife as a peripatetic statue. Ulitskaya describes Alik in terms of a fusion of life and death. Neither dead nor alive, he occupies a transitional state in which "the bright, lively eyes and the dead body" are both apparent (45). Ulitskaya even compares the process of paralysis he undergoes to a transition to a work of art, albeit plaster rather than stone: "A sort of slow paralysis was consuming the last vestiges of his musculature, and his limbs lay meek and inert, like setting plaster" (4). Alik, similarly to Pushkin's Commander, comes to life from beyond the grave, declaring "I'm right here with you" (142) on the cassette that he has requested to be played at the party after his death, where he claims to be occupying a "strange third position" between life and death (145). However, Ulitskaya completely reverses the statue's ominous quality, creating an afterlife that serves as a celebration of the Don Juan figure, for all his moral vagaries. Alik achieves a "resurrection" of sorts through others' love for him (it is Maika who plays the cassette), and his spirit—with the celebration of alcohol, women, and art—impacts those who outlive him. Sexuality is completely separated from morality, though not human emotions like jealousy, resentment, and nostalgia, and it is shown functioning on the level of Alik's artistic, improvisatory, and "poetic" powers.

There is a key difference between Ulitskaya's portrayal of the Don Juan-like men in *Sonechka* and *The Funeral Party*, though, and it concerns other characters' perspectives on this figure. In *Sonechka*, neither of the women with whom Robert Viktorovich is involved objects to his behavior. Sonechka accepts his affair with Jasia and is only pleasantly surprised when he does not abandon her as a consequence; Jasia fully accepts the ménage-à-trois that results (Livshin correctly describes their relationship as polyamorous). In *The Funeral Party*, by contrast, Ulitskaya presents a female character, Irina Pirozhkova, one of Alik's former lovers, who expresses resentment of his Donjuanism. When she arrives at his apartment and he tells her that he is dying, she thinks: "you died for me long ago" (7). Irina has forgiven but not forgotten that while she gave birth to his daughter, Maika, he was making love to another woman. And while they listen to the cassette recording Alik made to be played after his death, Irina reproaches him mentally for not having been with her. Thus, Ulitskaya's perspective on the Don Juan figure is more qualified in this work, as she recognizes that despite Alik's charisma and ability to unite others, he has damaged other people's lives.

In her 2004 novel, *Sincerely Yours, Shurik*, Ulitskaya again employs a variation on the Don Juan theme, though very different from that of the previous two works I have discussed. Sutcliffe and Skomp explicitly refer to the protagonist, Shurik, as a Don Juan while noting the clear departure Ulitskaya makes from other instantiations of this hero: "In contrast to the usual representation of Don Juan, he strives not to debauch and destroy, but only to comfort and ease suffering" (65).[36] In this novel, Ulitskaya deliberately selects key elements of the Don Juan legend only to subvert them. These elements include Don Juan's serial adventures, which are less sought after than foisted upon him, the notion of an ideal woman whose appearance can end the sequence of adventures by supplying the lofty love that the hero unconsciously seeks, the force of Don Juan's desire, which is inverted (Shurik satisfies others rather than receiving pleasure), and the theme of Don Juan as a destructive figure, since Shurik is associated with death for several of these women. All of these qualities are in some way turned on their head, not, I would argue, as a function of postmodern parody so much as a means of undermining, through its application to ordinary life, the customary sense of purposefulness characteristic of Donjuanism.

Shurik's circumstances, perhaps, predispose him to a life of adventures with women, with whom he is surrounded from birth. The product of an affair between his mother, Vera Alexandrovna, and her longtime lover, Alexander Sigizmundovich, who dies in a car accident months before Shurik is born, he is brought up by his mother and grandmother, Elizaveta Ivanovna. He sees them as "winged angels," and they, for their part, view him in sacred terms for being part of the mysterious world of men: "Masculine life was a riddle to them, even a sacred mystery" (23). Shurik is cared for and watched over his entire young life: during a party that includes almost all the girls in his high school, Vera Alexandrovna and Elizaveta Ivanovna spy on them and exchange impressions on their worthiness for him.[37] Throughout the novel, Shurik lives with his mother and maintains an unusual attachment to her. When she suggests at one point that he get married, he whispers to her: "Verusia! Don't even think of it! I could only marry you. But there's no other such woman!" (411).

Shurik's sheer number and variety of sexual relationships, beginning in his teenage years, would seem to liken him to a Don Juan. The women with whom he interacts sexually range widely in various ways. They include girls his age, such as his schoolmate Lilia Laskina, who moves to Israel; the Kazakh Alia; and the suicidal Svetlana, who stalks him to keep track of his whereabouts. They also include older, more experienced women such as the "lioness" Faina Ivanovna, who demands that he accompany her after a party to her home, where she takes advantage of him; his boss, Valeria Adamovna, a disabled woman who longs for a child and has him impregnate her, with disastrous results; and Matil'da Pavlovna, a cat owner who poses nude for studio artists and gives Shurik his first sexual experiences. Shurik pursues all of these adventures unthinkingly, not concerning himself with the consequences. In his second encounter with Svetlana, she asks for his assistance during her illness, and he readily complies: "and to the girl Svetlana he brought medicine and showed sexual respect, which she so touchingly asked for . . ." (269–70). However, afterward, while she is weighing his every word and gesture, he is already forgetting about the adventure and in general seems incapable of making plans beyond the evening. In this manner, Shurik displays the thoughtlessness toward affairs that typifies the legendary Don Juan.

However, the reader quickly notices patterns that diverge from the traditional Don Juan plot. For one thing, Shurik does very little of the choosing: he is targeted by most of these women. Thus, Alia tries to sleep with him as often as possible (she keeps a running count of their sexual experiences), hoping that he will eventually marry her, thus enabling her to stay in Moscow and escape her Akmolinsk residence. This is not wholly foreign to the legend: Byron's Don Juan is first seduced by an older woman, Julia, and later becomes captive to a Sultan's wife. But Shurik's passivity exceeds even that of Byron's hero. At times, he simply falls into experiences by accident, as with Matil'da Pavlovna, whom he meets when he arrives at an address that he thinks is a friend's apartment but that turns out to be an art studio. His stereotypically feminine pliability also distinguishes him from all other Don Juan-like serial seducers.

What differs most from the typical Don Juan, though, is that Shurik not only gratifies all of the women's desires, but makes it a principle of his relations with them, doing it out of a sense of "pity" (zhalost') for them. When he accompanies the dwarf Zhanna home, he is more preoccupied with finding a toilet and then getting home to his mother's apartment than sex, but he feels pity for her and, as the narrator puts it, "pity won out" (303). The encounters are even described in an asexual manner, as when the narrator associates his "services" for Valeria with his upbringing by his grandmother: "He fulfilled his promise evenly, diligently, and conscientiously, as his grandma had taught him to fulfill all his obligations" (208). Sex for Shurik becomes more of a task or duty than a means of enjoyment; thus, paradoxically, Donjuanism, ostensibly for the purpose of obtaining sexual delight, becomes a generous means of *giving* (but not necessarily receiving) pleasure. Shurik even seems to enjoy the submissive aspect of this type of relationship. "You like it, I see, when you're commanded to do things? ," Valeria asks him at one point, and he responds: "Apparently. I've noticed that myself" (187). In fact, women are attracted by Shurik's very pliability. Hearing Shurik's explanation of his fictitious marriage to his friend from the institute, Lena Stovba, and his taking on of fatherhood duties to her daughter by another man is what first interests Valeria in him. Similarly, Alia hopes that his willingness to make this arrangement with Lena will enable him to marry her. Women are often drawn to him by his very attentiveness to other women, and thus experience the kind of mediated desire Girard describes, which is also found in other Don Juan texts.

For this reason, Sutcliffe and Skomp are correct to link Shurik with Jasia of *Sonechka*, for whom sexual favors are often described as a small act that she does not begrudge people. The key difference is that for Jasia, sexual favors are transactional in nature: they allow her to rise from poverty and homelessness to become the mistress of a well-known artist, and to find a secure home for herself. Shurik, however, gains nothing in particular from his "favors" other than the satisfaction of knowing he has granted them. Moreover, the very fact that Shurik shows the same solicitude to nonsexual partners (his mother and Lena's daughter, Maria) indicates that his feelings are completely asexual and consist more of sympathy for women as a gender than any desire to seduce. In this sense, however, Ulitskaya's Don Juan may be likened to Pushkin's, who even as he seeks out pleasure from women, paradoxically functions to free them from their restrictions and to bring out their own hidden desires for pleasure. Shurik simply takes this tendency to a new, hyperbolic level.

For all his aimlessness, however, Shurik recalls the Romantic Don Juan of Pushkin, Hoffmann, and others in that, as it turns out, he really does have an ideal woman, and that is Lilia. His interactions with her when she visits him during a layover in Moscow on her way from Paris to Tokyo clarify that she is the one woman who brings out desire in him and whom he can be said to love. The fact that he cries when she leaves for Israel, early in the novel, perhaps foreshadows the ending, in which he makes a key discovery about her. As the narrator describes it, everything seems to go from black-and-white to color around them as he makes love to Lilia in a Moscow hotel room: Everything without her, he decides, is a lie: "stupid translations, stupid service to lonely women" (434). Lilia, then, is the woman he has sought all his life, has longed for, perhaps, without knowing it while engaging in "love of pity" for so many other women. The tragedy of the novel, perhaps, is not only that it ends with her disappearance from his life for a second time, but that she does not share his renewed feelings of love for her. Thinking of how the thirty-year-old Shurik has grown older and fatter since their teenage years, and how he continues to live with his mother, she marvels at the strangeness of their sexual experience and seems amazed that he loves her to this day, finding him "awfully gentle and completely asexual. Somehow old-fashioned" (446). Don Juan has found his ideal but will presumably return to his old routine of passively distributing sexual favors to various women. Through Lilia, Ulitskaya critiques and ridicules Shurik as a Don Juan who has found an ideal but is too immature to capitalize on it and form a lasting relationship.

Similarly to Pushkin, whose Don Juan is attracted to death, Ulitskaya associates Shurik with the demise of several people. During a tryst with Lilia, he fails to visit his grandmother at the hospital in time and misses her death, for which he reproaches himself. Later, Shurik feels the same guilt when Valeria falls and loses the baby they conceived together. Despite the fact that her accident is in no way his fault, he feels that he somehow caused the misfortune. He thinks to himself: "What kind of monster am I! Why do so many bad things happen because of me? I never wanted any such thing!" (225). We do not learn Shurik's reaction to Svetlana's suicide, but we know that he feels responsible for her and is aware of her suicide attempts in his absence. Unlike most Don Juans, but like Pushkin's protagonist, who reminisces about his dead lover Inez, Shurik remembers former lovers, feels guilt for neglecting them, and often circles back to them.

Thus, the Don Juan figure serves as one of the various "types," along with holy fools, the mentally disabled, and various other characters marginalized in Soviet society who populate Ulitskaya's works. Her tolerance extends to the Don Juan type, as these figures are excused their sexual excesses either because they are linked to their artistry, as in the case of Robert Viktorovich and Alik, or because they have become good deeds, as with Shurik.

As my final thoughts for this chapter, I will note another important example of Donjuanism in Ulitskaya's works. As *Sincerely Yours, Shurik* demonstrates, her female characters are often more assertive and occasionally display healthier libidos than their male counterparts. In fact, Ulitskaya recasts Pushkin's Laura in various works. This type appears in her first novella, *Sonechka*, in which the title character's daughter Tania is described as maximally free in her sexual explorations, experiencing a purely physical enjoyment of her body: "emerging from the diversions of an extended childhood, she had a couple of years of dormancy during which she underwent the transition of puberty, before coming to an early recognition of which game exactly was preferred by grownups, and throwing herself into it with a confident awareness of her right to pleasure and the uninhibitedness of a personality that had never been repressed" (32). Tania plays with a succession of boys, beginning with Boris, whose math homework she copies, and then a series of other admirers. Interestingly, recalling Laura's musico-theatrical soirée in Scene 2 of *The Stone Guest*, Tania attracts boys with her flute-playing. Among these conquests are the pianist Vladimir and a guitarist and poet who calls himself Alesha Petersburg. After passing through an infatuation with the eighteen-year-old Polish janitor Jasia, and experiencing disappointment when she realizes her father is having an affair with her erstwhile friend, Tania follows Alesha to Leningrad, marries him, and eventually has two more "short-term husbands" (70).[38]

The promiscuous female can be found in Ulitskaya's latest work, the 2015 novel *Jacob's Ladder* (*Lestnitsa Iakova*) as well. Nora, the granddaughter of the eponymous hero Jacob Ossetsky and a theater set designer, engages in a string of conquests of young men during her teenage years. Following her initiation into sex with her eighth-grade classmate Nikita Tregubsky, after which she is expelled from school, she makes up her mind to take a purely physical, hedonistic approach to lovemaking: "she understood that love made a person defenseless and vulnerable, and that sex had to be kept separate from human emotions and relationships for reasons of personal safety" (66). Much like her counterpart Tania from *Sonechka*, she focuses purely on "the technical aspects of love," and begins a chain of conquests, each of which increases her feminine self-esteem. She even has a son, Yurik, with one lover, Vitia Chebotarev. Nevertheless, her string of love affairs continues until she meets the Georgian theater director Tengiz, who becomes a quasi-permanent lover. After Tengiz leaves her the first time, she acquires a once-a-week lover in Kolia, who demands nothing of her, but when she sees Tengiz again, she realizes that "she had reentered the basic condition of her existence" (109) and he seems to conclude her "list." In this sense, Nora's experience recalls that of Pushkin's Don Juan, who claims to be reborn in love, as she is surprised to experience genuine love for another person despite all the defenses she has built up against it. At the same time, her interactions with men also recall those of Laura, who chooses different men each night yet at the same time remains attached closely to Don Juan, whose poetry she sets to music and whom she calls "my faithful friend and fickle lover" (73). Nora and Tengiz, similarly, experience this type of intermittent return to former relations. Significantly, the erotic and artistic are intertwined as Tengiz and Nora work together with profound synergy on their theatrical productions as well.

Ulitskaya thus adapts Pushkin's interrelation of art and Eros in her works and at the same time assimilates his Laura figure into them by including avid female sexual experimenters who seduce a long line of men. The fact that she is a bestselling author in Russia who is also considered a "serious" writer and part of the canon of classic literature perhaps underscores the popularity of her exploration of serial love affairs among both sexes. It also shows that Donjuanism continues to inspire the Russian imagination and testifies to the durability of Pushkin's discoveries of the close relationship between artistic and erotic seduction, as well as the adaptability of Donjuanism to either sex.

Conclusion

To conclude this study, I will assess broader patterns of the Don Juan theme as it has developed in Russia over roughly two centuries and attempt to account for the fruitfulness of Pushkin's play for his compatriots before ending with a brief discussion of the impact of *The Stone Guest* on a non-Russian work. Examining the various texts influenced by Pushkin reveals a series of social, generic, aesthetic, and spiritual transformations in the Russian interpretation of the Don Juan legend during this period. These transformations represent responses to Pushkin's own recasting of the legend and his reworking of motifs from previous iterations.

One of the dominants Tirso de Molina establishes in the first written Don Juan text is the protagonist's simultaneous enjoyment of the perquisites of his class and his own rebellion against the social order that conferred upon him the advantages of the nobility. These noble privileges are equally emphasized in the two major versions of the Don Juan legend that Pushkin definitely knew well: Molière's play and Mozart/Da Ponte's opera. In *The Stone Guest*, Pushkin retains this dominant, underscoring Don Juan's aristocracy by emphasizing his close ties with the king, who, as he assures Leporello, exiled him out of affection and concern for his safety rather than as a punishment, and by depicting his firm adherence to the rules of dueling, an exclusively noble activity.

Gradually, however, Russian treatments of the legend reduce or minimize Don Juan's class status. Although Goncharov and Tolstoy, during the Realist period, maintain their heroes' nobility, they each link Donjuanism to the decline of this class, thus continuing the critique of the libertine's misuse of his social status that began with Tirso's play. In the late nineteenth and early twentieth centuries, these aristocratic heroes are replaced by characters of a lower status: Chekhov's banker Gurov; Blok's protagonists, who are representatives of a gentry that is even further on the decline than in the preceding century; and Don Juan figures who do not belong to any particular class (as in Tsvetaeva's cycle) or who represent the world of art more than any particular social stratum (as in Akhmatova's *poema*).

In Soviet and post-Soviet literature, this trend continues. Although Kazakov deliberately situates his noble and royal characters in an unspecified time, and Aleshin "travels back" to 1342 to determine the "truth" about Don Juan (i.e., that he is really a woman), many Soviet writers set their stories in the present day and erase the hero's nobility. Erofeev and Ulitskaya write, respectively, during and about a Soviet era that had eliminated the aristocracy and any notion of a "higher-born" class—ironically reversing traditional values by exalting proletarian birth—and they create Don Juans who have no social advantage whatsoever. In fact, by attributing Jewishness to their heroes, both writers link Don Juan to a people historically excluded from the nobility by their very birth. At the same time, the half-Jewish, half-Russian Gurevich of *Walpurgis Night* and fully Jewish heroes of Ulitskaya's works such as Robert Viktorovich of *Sonechka* and Alik of *The Funeral Party* embody both Donjuanism and the Wandering Jew archetype, thus emphasizing one important characteristic of the traditional Don Juan—his endless travels—even while omitting another—his noble status. During the Soviet and post-Soviet periods, then, Don Juan paradoxically becomes both more ordinary, through loss of noble status, and more "exotic," through identification with a second archetype featuring wandering and alienation. Thus, although Pushkin's emphasis on his protagonist's nobility does not prove crucial for all Russian writers, his autobiographically inspired emphasis on Don Juan's exile proves quite fruitful.

The gradual stripping away of Don Juan's upper-class origins in Russia is accompanied by a lowering of the generic level of the works, as the legendary seducer becomes fully prosaicized in the course of two centuries. *The Stone Guest* embodies this transition in itself, to an extent. By writing a tragedy, Pushkin makes use of the high category of the eighteenth-century Russian Neoclassical tripartite system of genres, and even maintains the Classical unities to a degree.[1] However, he uses blank iambic pentameter rather than the rhymed verse typical of tragedies up to that point. Moreover, as with *Eugene Onegin*, whose strict stanza form nevertheless allows for frequent snatches of conversation between characters and informal comments by the narrator, Pushkin incorporates colloquial speech into *The Stone Guest*, giving it a "medium" rather than "high" register. And while Alexei K. Tolstoy followed Pushkin's play with a lofty, rhymed verse drama two decades later, several subsequent nineteenth-century writers who explored the Don Juan theme turned to prose genres: the novel and short story. For Goncharov, Lev Tolstoy, and

Chekhov, the focus on the everyday and the absence of the supernatural dictated by Realist aesthetics shifts Don Juan's tragedy from metaphysical rebellion to a type of everyday banality, whether it be Raisky's and Vronsky's dilettantism or Gurov's inability, until he meets Anna Sergeevna, to establish meaningful relationships.

Although the various poetic treatments of the legend during the Silver Age would seem to signal a shift upward in terms of genre, some Don Juan works—such as Tsvetaeva's cycle, with its intimate, conversational language, and Gumilev's witty, irreverent verse play—find ways to counterbalance the loftiness of the genre. This lowering of register becomes even more pronounced in the Soviet plays of Erofeev (with his frequent use of coarse, profane language) and Kazakov (with his absurdism). The trend toward the exploration of Donjuanism via the realia of everyday life continues in the prose works of Ulitskaya, as well as other late- and post-Soviet writers who feature Don Juan-like characters: one example is Liudmila Petrushevskaya's "The Lookout Point" ("Smotrovaia ploshchadka," 1982), with its protagonist Andrei, who constantly brings his female conquests to Lenin Hills so that he can celebrate his victories over men and women from high up in Moscow. Such works, with their concrete locations and ordinary, recognizable character types, establish the legendary figure as a legitimately "prosaic" subject, participating in all the same types of ordinary rituals as everyone else.

The Don Juan legend in Russia also continues the gradual secularization that had already started with Molière's shift of focus from Christian damnation to skepticism and revelation of society's hypocrisy. Pushkin retains various religious elements of the legend: two of the play's four scenes take place in a monastery, and Don Juan pretends to be a monk in his first interactions with Donna Anna. However, at the same time, he continues the deemphasis of the legend's original religious purpose begun in Molière's play, in particular by replacing the traditional dispatching of the libertine to hell with interlocked protagonists who, as I argue, suggest a psychological confrontation of younger and older selves rather than the carrying out of divine vengeance. Like the ambiguity surrounding Don Juan's possible rebirth in love, Pushkin's intermingling of the sacred and secular creates a broad range of possibilities for further development. Don Juan and the statue's act of "falling through together" at the conclusion of *The Stone Guest* is reinvested with religious symbolism in *Anna Karenina*, as Anna's motion of falling to her knees before Vronsky after the consummation of their love and later, under the wheels of the train, is linked to the Biblical Fall. Chekhov, as part of his polemical reaction to Tolstoy's novel, in turn resecularizes his Anna character through Gurov's diminishing of her self-recriminations after their affair begins. Likewise, although Pushkin retains the element of the fantastic through the statue, he continues the ongoing deemphasis of the supernatural, condensing the statue's role and excluding the customary references to hell and repentance. Some subsequent Russian Don Juan works omit the fantastic altogether, either by dispensing with the Commander entirely (as do Tsvetaeva, Kazakov, and Ulitskaya), or by taking Pushkin's cue and transforming him into a manifestation of guilt or some other psychological preoccupation rather than a supernatural figure, as can be seen in the works of Tolstoy, Blok, Akhmatova, and Erofeev.

Silver Age writers, by contrast, incorporate conspicuous religious motifs: Blok transforms Donna Anna into the "Maiden of Light" (Deva sveta), Tsvetaeva visualizes Don Juan in the realm of Orthodox mothers of God, and Gumilev—albeit comically—portrays him ascending from hell. In none of these, however, does the issue of divine retribution play anything close to the role it played in Tirso's original version. Akhmatova, of course, portrays the Don Juans of her youth (including herself) as "sinners" receiving punishment from a real-life Commander, Stalin. But aside from Akhmatova's representation of the legend in this manner, most Don Juan writers working during the Soviet period continue the steady process of secularization. Kazakov's play, with its focus on the absurd, omits the Commander entirely, along with the question of vengeance. Erofeev, although he does include this figure, uses it to explore Pushkin's linking of him with Don Juan rather than in a religious sense. And by the turn of the twenty-first century, the issue of Donjuanism is completely disconnected from any notion of sinfulness. The narrative has been transformed from a metaphysical drama into an everyday, concrete story, and Don Juan has become an ordinary, down-to-earth persona. Thus, the overall arc of the Russian treatment of the theme is one of secularization, in which the focus turns to the psychological, personal, and (in many cases) autobiographical. As with the shift of genre described above, Pushkin's turn to a psychological characterization of the Commander in relation to Don Juan paves the way for this gradual secularization of the theme.

The theme of rebellion so integral to the Don Juan legend, on the other hand, remains constant throughout various periods in Russia. Pushkin develops this topos from Tirso, Molière, and Mozart/Da Ponte by encoding his personal revolt against the restrictions he suffered in Tsarist Russia, as a poet and creative thinker, into his play. This motif may in turn be seen in Lev Tolstoy's depiction of Anna's rebellion against social and gender restrictions; Tsvetaeva's resistance, expressed through her female protagonist, to both the charms of Don Juan and traditional women's roles in general; Gurevich's poetic rebellion in the context of his incarceration in a mental ward; and Ulitskaya's protagonists, male and female alike, who refuse to conform to sexual, artistic, or social expectations. Although this theme of rebellion does not begin with Pushkin by any means, he invests it with new energy, links it with artistic originality, and paves the way for succeeding artists to explore it in new contexts.

Throughout this series of transformations, Pushkin's linking of seduction with artistic processes, focus on gender relations and exploration of the possibility of Donjuanism in women, depiction of Don Juan's obsession with the Commander and uncanny urge to confront him, and portrayal of surprising identity between putative opponents provide multiple potential directions Russian writers could take in reworking the legend. By creating mysteries, deliberately fleshing out characters and plot situations just enough to allow for more than one possible interpretation without conclusively resolving them, he enables a stream of varying Don Juan interpretations to arise from the questions he leaves unanswered. These interpretations proceed in different directions, according to the artist involved. If Pushkin's awareness of female agency in seduction inspires celebration of female sexuality in Ulitskaya's works, for example, it generates horror of the same in Tolstoy's *Anna Karenina*. And just as Pushkin's revelation of identity between seeming opposites in Don Juan and the Commander creates the space for Blok to explore Oedipal conflict in *Retribution*, it alternatively leads to a critique of the intelligentsia in relation to Soviet power in Erofeev's play.

Moreover, Pushkin's play and the Russian works that follow it invite us to rethink our assumptions about the essence of the Don Juan legend. For one, not only does the apparently core element of divine punishment turn out not to be crucial for the expression of the Don Juan theme, but it also may have been less central even to Tirso's original play than it appears to be at first glance. Although *The Trickster of Seville* was intended to center on the tragedy of inexorable divine retribution, its secular "distractions" have consistently proven too alluring to both audiences and creative artists from the play's inception and have themselves become a focal point.[2] This ambivalence sets the stage for subsequent writers who play with this tension between the sacred and secular elements (such as Molière and Mozart/Da Ponte). By removing even what scaffolding of a religious tragedy was left in *Don Giovanni*, Pushkin transforms the encounter of Don Juan and the Commander into the discovery of past and future selves and possible rebirth in love. This omission of divine punishment is, of course, not unique to Russian transpositions of the Don Juan theme, as witnessed by Albert Camus's interpretation of Don Juan in *The Myth of Sisyphus* as a figure who has abandoned illusions of an afterlife to pursue joy in this life, and who knows that freedom entails rebellion against death and the commitment to one's personal values in the absence of a god or a priori meaning. The diverse variety of Russian approaches to the legend that omit the element of divine punishment, though, either by leaving the Commander and his statue out entirely or considerably changing their function, casts particularly robust doubt on its centrality to the legend.

Similarly, the Russian tradition inspired by Pushkin exposes the other core element in the legend, Don Juan's purported rampant sexuality, as illusory. This becomes clear from the very beginning in Pushkin's unmistakable transformation of the libertine into a hero whose pursuit of sex is inextricable from poetic improvisation. If, in Pushkin's hero as well his female counterpart, Eros is truly inseparable from artistic seduction, then the only solution—since the absence of art, for Pushkin, is unthinkable—is to accept rather than condemn the sexuality that makes us human, and that in any case is not a sinful trait to be isolated and eradicated, but an organic aspect of our being. This is the lesson Pushkin's Don Juan seems to have successfully taught Laura, tried to teach Inez, and attempted to convey to Anna as well. As I suggest throughout this study, Pushkin's inextricable and explicit linking of the sexual impulse with art creates a new pattern that influenced Goncharov, Tolstoy, Erofeev, and perhaps most of all, Ulitskaya in her description of such characters as Robert Viktorovich and Alik. At the same time, it suggests a model of a Don Juan who, for Kazakov in particular, may show no interest in sex whatsoever or who, for Ulitskaya in *Sincerely Yours, Shurik*, sees the sexual act as an act of compassion rather than a moment of erotic gratification. Turning back to Tirso's original play, we discover that sexual gratification there too is not so much the goal as are acts of trickery.

Thus, if the legend of Don Juan and his punishment by the statue would seem at first glance to boil down to sexuality and its consequences, Pushkin, like other great artists engaging the theme, demonstrates that it has much broader implications related to poetic creation, gender relations, and the conflict between generations, among other topics. The revelation of these new ways to look at the Don Juan theme, along with his lack of resolution of these topics, has opened it up to an incredibly wide range of responses in Russian literature.

But what about the little tragedy's impact outside of Russia? Pushkin's influence beyond his homeland, overall, has been relatively limited compared to that of Dostoevsky, Tolstoy, and Chekhov. Works such as British playwright Peter Shaffer's *Amadeus* (1979), inspired by *Mozart and Salieri*, and the Indian novelist and poet Vikram Seth's 1986 novel *The Golden Gate*, written in Onegin stanzas, testify to the considerable interest non-Russian writers have taken in his works. However, compared to subsequent nineteenth-century Russian writers, Pushkin's influence has been disproportionately felt at home rather than abroad, and this is as true of *The Stone Guest* as of the rest of his oeuvre. Given

Prosper Mérimée's prominent role in introducing the French public to Pushkin's works through his translations beginning in the 1840s, it is tempting to compare *The Stone Guest* with his novellas "Venus of L'ille" (1837) and *Souls in Purgatory* (1834) and look for possible influence. "Venus of L'ille" in particular contains notable parallels to *The Stone Guest*, since it revolves around a libertine who provokes a statue and winds up gripped in its cold embrace.[3] However, Pushkin's little tragedy was not published until 1839 (and Pushkin, for that matter, could not have read Mérimée's novella since he died early in 1837). Thus, while *The Stone Guest* and "Venus of L'ille" offer great potential for comparative analysis, there can be no question of direct influence by Pushkin.

However, *The Stone Guest* does directly impact a foreign writer closer to home in Lesia Ukrainka. Her 1912 play *The Stone Host* (*Kaminnyi hospodar*, also sometimes translated as *The Stone Master*), which she proudly proclaimed to be the first Don Juan text authored by a woman, offers a feminist interpretation of the legend in general, and Pushkin's play in particular.[4] As such, *The Stone Host* demonstrates Pushkin's impact on a foreign literature: Ukrainka, though a subject of the Russian Empire, ranks alongside Taras Shevchenko and Ivan Franko as a foundational Ukrainian nationalist writer.[5] *The Stone Host*, written the year before her death, can be linked to various earlier Don Juan versions, from her use of Tirso's location of Seville to her inclusion of a saintly, self-sacrificial woman to whom Don Juan is betrothed (Dolores, who resembles Elvira of Molière's play and Mozart/Da Ponte's opera). As Clarence Manning notes, Ukrainka's play also references Mérimée's fusing together of the stories of Don Juan Tenorio and Don Juan de la Maraña ("Lesya Ukrainka" 44).[6] She also freely mixes the names of traditional characters from different plays, taking the name Sganarelle for Don Juan's servant from Molière and the name Donna Anna (the Italian spelling) from *Don Giovanni*. But she borrows many plot elements, motifs, and themes from Pushkin's play as well, and *The Stone Host* may be interpreted as both developing these elements of *The Stone Guest* and ultimately offering a rejoinder to the Russian poet in some respects.

As in *The Stone Guest*, Ukrainka sets up a triangular rivalry between Don Juan and the Commander, Don Gonzago, who begins the play as Anna's fiancé, marries her, and is then killed by Don Juan in a duel. She emphasizes the stone motif even more than Pushkin, as Anna refers to Don Gonzago as a "stony mountain" due to his oppressive reliance on propriety (97).[7] Following Pushkin, who describes the Commander as jealously guarding Anna from the rest of the world and imprisoning her from beyond the grave in her mourning ritual, Ukrainka depicts Anna's irritation during her marriage at having to perform mourning rituals for various deceased relatives of her husband and describes their life together as dull and stifling.

Ukrainka's major transformation of *The Stone Guest* is her considerable development of Anna, who becomes the main protagonist of the play. Ukrainka wanted to create a "new woman" who would break free of stereotypical female roles and instead behave in a more active, rational, strong-willed fashion, thus taking on what were seen as masculine traits (Mihaychuk 104). Thus, if Pushkin's Anna represents an ingénue who experiences the first stirrings of curiosity about worldly life through her encounter with Don Juan, Ukrainka creates a more fleshed-out, complex heroine who genuinely searches for freedom from the beginning, is frustrated by Don Juan's weakness (he refuses to give up the ring that binds him to his fiancée Dolores), rejects him, and ultimately succumbs to the temptation of power. She marries the Commander to eventually become queen and serves as Don Juan's accomplice when he kills his rival (she pretends that thieves broke in and allows Don Juan to escape). As George Mihaychuk notes, Ukrainka reverses the traditional roles: while Don Juan starts off attempting to seduce Anna in the beginning of the play, it is she who ends up persuading him to take on the role of the Commander, à la Lady Macbeth, proposing marriage to him and leaving his declaration of love to her unreciprocated.[8] Ukrainka's "new woman" Anna breaks free of stereotypically female roles, embodying qualities such as rationality that are traditionally seen as masculine and seeking equality with both the Commander and Don Juan (Mihaychuk 104). She announces to Don Juan that even though he has destroyed other women's hearts, "The only one/ That remained safe and undestroyed is mine/Because I am your equal" (139). Don Juan himself notes her departure from typical female roles, telling her: "Till now, Anna, I have not known you. You're not like a woman, Your charms surpass by far the charms of women" (141). In this manner, Ukrainka grafts one of Pushkin's most significant innovations, his female counterpart to Don Juan, onto Anna's character but gives her a much more central role in the play than Laura has in *The Stone Guest*. At the same time, Ukrainka may have taken note of Donna Anna's own, perhaps unwitting (or unconscious) contribution to her own seduction in the little tragedy. If Pushkin's Anna experiences conflict between her growing desire for Don Juan and her duty to mourn her husband, Ukrainka attributes no such compunctions to her heroine and even characterizes her as a Don Juan-like manipulator. Moreover, Ukrainka emphasizes her heroine's superior intellect in comparison to Don Juan. For Jaroslav Rozumnyj, Ukrainka's Don Juan is a superficial thinker of limited intelligence and ethical principles who justifies his behavior toward women by claiming that he is helping them achieve self-fulfillment, something I have argued that Pushkin's Don Juan is doing. Could Ukrainka be engaging in a polemic against Pushkin (and perhaps other male Don Juan writers) who treat Don Juan as a potential liberator of women rather than their jailor?

Ukrainka's ending exemplifies both her awareness of Pushkin's striking departures in his finale and her creative development of their implications. Despite Don Juan's hesitation, Anna persuades him to put on the Commander's coat and then to take his sword, baton, and helmet. Looking in the mirror, he cries out, seeing the Commander's face instead of his own. The Commander then steps out of the mirror and kills Don Juan by placing his hand over his heart, upon which Anna falls at the Commander's feet. By dressing Don Juan in the Commander's outfit, Ukrainka's Anna makes the implied identity of the two figures in *The Stone Guest* explicit, as Pushkin's image of two opponents coming together in a stony handgrip is replaced by the image of a man seeing his transformation into another being in a mirror (which also takes place, in a more figurative sense, at the end of Chekhov's "The Lady with the Little Dog").

In addition to replicating Pushkin's identity of seeming opposites, though, Ukrainka adds another dimension by linking Donna Anna to the Commander as well. Several times, Don Juan refers to her as stony, just as they had each earlier described the Commander that way. When Anna refuses his offer to flee after the Commander's death, he tells her, "You are indeed stone, without soul or heart" (129). Thus, following Pushkin's linking of his two male protagonists, Ukrainka extends this chain of identities by showing the stoniness of the Commander passing itself along to Anna, too. As Mihaychuk argues, Anna as heroine must choose between two visions of happiness: the freedom Don Juan offers her and the embrace of power within society, which she ultimately not only chooses but "seduces" Don Juan into accepting (100–102). Although Mihaychuk connects this dichotomy to Molière's focus on his hero's attempt to live authentically, according to his nature and without succumbing to the hypocritical moralizing of society, one can also link it to Pushkin's examination—through his protagonists—of his own transition from libertine freedom to domestic stability, except that Ukrainka demonstrates that this evolution applies to men and women alike. In this manner, the gender exploration of Pushkin's play paves the way for a genuinely feminist take on the legend.

It remains to be seen whether other non-Russian writers will turn to *The Stone Guest* for its rich insights into the Don Juan theme. Regardless of Pushkin's future influence outside his homeland, the impact of his play on Russian literature, as I have argued, is widely diffused, variegated, and enduring. Ultimately, Pushkin takes his place alongside Tirso, Molière, Mozart/Da Ponte, and Hoffmann as a powerful interpreter of the Don Juan legend who in turn influences a series of artistic figures. If Hoffmann initiated a Romantic interpretation of Don Juan that predominated in the nineteenth century, however, Pushkin's influence, though unlike his German predecessor's largely relegated to his own homeland, persisted through two centuries, impacting writers of all types and in various genres. For this reason, the Don Juan legend owes a great debt to Pushkin. *The Stone Guest* refreshed the legend through the questions Pushkin asked about Donjuanism, art, and rivalry. It also generated a series of explorations, innovative in their own right, that enriched the Don Juan oeuvre in unexpected ways. And it is likely that, with Pushkin's ongoing influence, we have not seen the end of these explorations in Russian culture.

Notes

Introduction

1. In this passage and all other English citations of *The Stone Guest*, I am using Nancy Anderson's translation.
2. All Russian citations of *The Stone Guest* are of vol. 7 of A. S. Pushkin's complete works in Russian.
3. The choice of the heel, of course, underscores Don Juan's autobiographical nature, since Pushkin was a well-known foot fetishist who wrote about women's legs and feet in several works.
4. See Dmitry Darsky (55–58), Anna Akhmatova (*O Pushkine*), David Glenn Kropf, and David Herman on the poetic qualities of Pushkin's Don Juan.
5. As Jack Weiner notes, the play also draws on other sources, including Giacinto Andrea Cicognini's *The Stone Guest* (*Il convitato di pietra*, 1640s) and an early eighteenth-century German puppet show entitled *Don Juan and Don Pietro, or the Stone-Dead-Banquet* (*Don Juan und Don Pietro oder das Steinerne-Todten-Gastmahl*) (11–12).
6. Frank Göbler speculates that *Dom Juan*, unlike other plays of Molière, was not performed in the St. Petersburg theater founded in 1756 by Alexander Sumarokov, either because the play was considered unsuitable for Russian society or because the statue presented a supernatural element that did not fit in with Classicism (that is, it prevented the play from being considered part of either the high genre of tragedy or the low genre of comedy; 9).
7. Byron was actually better known—around the world as well as in Russia—for the *Eastern Tales*, *Childe Harold*, *Manfred*, and *Cain* than for *Don Juan*. Pushkin was one of the few Russians who appreciated *Don Juan*, which influenced *Eugene Onegin*, *Count Nulin*, *A Little House on Kolomna*, and—in Svetlana Klimova's view—*The Stone Guest*.
8. Vsevolod Bagno argues that the myth of Don Juan was already rooted in the Russian popular consciousness because of the presence of byliny (folk epics) about Alesha Popovich, a seducer of women, and Vasily Buslaev, who mocks the dead (150–59). Unlike in Western Europe, he claims, where one artist (Tirso) was needed to connect these two motifs, "Pushkin and A. K. Tolstoy had at their disposal a centuries-old, manifold tradition of the myth of Don Juan, which they put to brilliant use" (159).

9. As Andrew Wachtel points out, Dostoevsky's Pushkin Speech exemplifies a broader Russian impulse to perfect other cultures by translating them: "It became a given that Russia's manifest destiny was built not on any inherent quality of Russian culture itself but rather on its ability to absorb and perfect what it had taken from outside" (64).

10. Nikolai Gogol had earlier described Pushkin's genius in similar terms: "In Spain he is a Spaniard, with a Greek, a Greek—in the Caucasus—a free mountaineer" (834). Despite the fact that many Russians believed in the doctrine of the *vsechelovek* (panhuman), this concept actually originated in Germany, where thinkers such as Johann Gottfried Herder and the Schlegel brothers believed that the ability to embrace all cultures was unique to their nation.

11. Perhaps reacting to the attribution of Dostoevskian traits to characters such as Eugene Onegin and Tatiana Larina, W. J. Leatherbarrow writes dismissively, "There can be no doubt that much of Dostoyevsky's admiration for Pushkin was based upon a profound misunderstanding of that poet's significance" (370). As other commentators have pointed out, however, Dostoevsky's Pushkin Speech is the first instance of a type of criticism that would become characteristic of the Russian intelligentsia's approach to the poet. As Alexandra Smith observes, "The immediate response of contemporaries to the Pushkin Speech demonstrates that it contained a new form of synthesized national identity. It gave rise to a Pushkin myth that presents Pushkin's works and life in terms of his importance to the formation of a new national unity and in terms of creative engagement with European tradition" (126). Marina Kanevskaya interprets the speech as a quasi-fictional mythologization of Pushkin that paved the way for the "My Pushkin" genre utilized by Briusov, Tsvetaeva, and others in the twentieth century.

12. The origins of the Don Juan story are uncertain. As Leo Weinstein explains, three possible origins have been proposed but never conclusively proven: a real-life Don Juan Tenorio from the fourteenth century, an *auto sacramental* (a religious play from the fifteenth or sixteenth century), and a medieval folktale of a dead man who appears at the mocking invitation of a younger man (6–11). Throughout this study, I refer to the Don Juan story as a legend because it revolves around events that were thought to have happened at some point in human history.

13. See Singer (14–18) for a list of Don Juan–like characters before and during Tirso's time. As Dorothy Epplen MacKay argues, Tirso combines the fictional story of Don Juan based on earlier ballads with the folk motif of the double invitation. In Tirso's version, Don Juan invites the statue to supper, and the statue appears and extends the same invitation to Don Juan. At the second supper, the statue sends his guest to hell. Two plays compete for the status of first Don Juan drama: *Plenty of Time for That* (*Tan largo me lo fiáis*), discovered in 1878, which many critics think was written earlier, and *The Trickster of Seville*, which some argue was not written by Tirso.

14. As Boris Tomashevsky notes, Pushkin would have been aware of Tirso's play from Voltaire's commentary on Molière's *Don Juan*. However, it is unlikely that he read it, as it was not translated into Russian or French at the time, and Pushkin did not study Spanish until 1831 (286–87).

15. Robert Karpiak notes, however, that despite his didactic intent, Tirso created an object of admiration rather than an antihero, a figure whose joie de vivre and courage in the face of death inspired emulation ("Don Juan in Slavic Drama," 22–23).

16. All citations of Tirso's play are from Adrienne M. Schizzano and Oscar Mandel's translation.

17. This hint at Don Juan burning in the finale is not the only example of Tirso's use of foreshadowing. In Act III, Don Juan, promising Aminta that he will keep his word to her, unwittingly invokes his own doom:

Aminta: Call on God to damn you if you are untrue.
Don Juan: If I do not keep my word, let God send a man to ensnare and kill me.
[*Aside.*] A dead man, of course. God forbid he should be alive. (83)

18. The play clearly represents an attack on the foundations of Spanish society at all levels. This includes the Crown itself (the kings of Naples and Castile both prove incapable of bringing Don Juan to justice), along with the nobility that produces and is unable to protect itself against not only a seducer and trickster such as Don Juan, but other noblemen (e.g., his friend the Marquis de la Mota) who engage in the same pursuits. The critique extends to a peasantry that is too enamored of noble appearance and impressed by the aristocracy to prevent Aminta from being seduced by Don Juan. Although *The Trickster of Seville* is ostensibly set in the fourteenth century (one of the characters is the King of Castile, Alfonso XI, who ruled from 1312–50), it is deliberately anachronistic and clearly describes Tirso's early seventeenth-century society. In fact, Tirso seems to indicate that Spanish society of this era is stuck in old, medieval values that no longer have a useful function in the early modern age. As Catherine Connor writes: "The *burlador* Don Juan calls into question the distance between an idealized view of medieval patriarchy's cultural values and the evolution or degeneration of those values in the seventeenth century" (87).

19. Tirso's female portraits have been viewed alternately by critics as misogynistic or sympathetic toward women. "Regardless of social stature," Ruth Lundelius writes, women are "uniformly portrayed as weak, frail, and literally helpless in resisting their desires, even for what they know is sinful and dangerous" (13). Other critics, however, view Tirso as a critic of the patriarchy that enforces the social norms by which Don Juan benefits from his seductions. For Raymond Conlon, Tirso undermines the moral authority of both the *burlador* (trickster) and *burlados* (those whom he tricks: Octavio, the Marquis de la Mota, and Batricio) by attributing to them comments that underscore their fear of women's sexuality. And as Ann Davies remarks: "The inability of the men to resolve the problems posed by events in *Trickster* indicates fundamental weakness in patriarchy, as it is conceived by Tirso, and serves as a reminder that we should not necessarily take patriarchy at its own estimation" (162). J. Douglas Canfield agrees that the object of attack is the patriarchy rather than women—whether it be in the form of actual fathers and uncles or the king as symbolic father: the portrait of Don Juan "paradoxically reaffirms a system of shared power between men—at the expense of women and oppressed classes" (43). Susana Pendzik, who focuses not only on the main female figures but also on absent or underdescribed female characters such as the queen, whom Isabela serves as a lady in waiting, and the prostitutes Don Juan and De La Mota ridicule, argues that the real rebels of the play are women, and they are punished according to their degree of rebellion against conventional feminine roles. The fact that women in *The Trickster of Seville* may be seen as either rebelling against male

control or unfairly victimized by men (and not just Don Juan) points to the subversive qualities of Tirso's play.

20. See Simerka (226–27) for a list of Don Juan's moments of astonishingly eloquent language throughout the play.

21. Georges Gendarme de Bévotte, however, argues that despite the parallels between Molière's and Tirso's plays, it is more likely that Molière was relying on the two Italian plays, which were well-known in France, whereas *The Trickster of Seville* was not even well-known in Spain in 1665 (vol. 1, 80–81). The passages Molière seems to borrow from the Spanish play, he claims, are closer to the Italian and French models than the Spanish, and such traits as Don Juan's wickedness, irreligion, and tendency to base his misconduct on nature are found in the French pieces rather than Tirso's play; similarly, Tirso's religious gravity and his moral lesson on the brevity of life and the need to repent all disappear from Molière's version (vol. 1, 83–84). "If Molière knew the Trickster, which is improbable," he concludes, "it does not mean he was inspired by it. The immediate sources of *Festin de Pierre* were solely the Italian and French works that were competing for public favor in Paris from 1658–64" (84).

22. For a discussion of how Molière's play differs from those of Dorimon and de Villiers, see Wilton-Godberfforde.

23. Sganarelle's role of disapproving of his master's pranks, however, is much firmer and less ambivalent than Catalinón's role in *El Burlador*, as Robert Bayliss points out. Sganarelle, in his opening lines, tells the audience frankly what he thinks of Don Juan's behavior and expresses regret that he is bound by service to him to do things he would rather not. He tells the audience that Don Juan is, among other things, "the greatest scoundrel that ever walked the earth" (Molière 34–35).

24. Barbara Simerka argues, however, that in Tirso's play as well, Don Juan could be considered an atheist because of the association of this philosophy with immorality and depravity, and that skepticism had already at this point influenced writers in England, France, and even Spain. Moreover, analyzing Tirso's play along with Thomas Shadwell's *The Libertine* (1676), she expresses skepticism that the audience would have accepted both plays' ostensible moral that God's judgment cannot be ignored: "As the audience delights in the spectacle of smoke, fire, stage machinery, and the anticlimactic scenes that follow the Don Juans' deaths, it is uncertain that the statue's moral message could have much of an impact, or that the audience would see this as plausible proof of providential intervention" (230).

25. See Felicity Baker on the mixing of Classical motifs with Christian ones in the finale. Also see Roy Porter on the opera's reflection of the Enlightenment-era reevaluation of the Augustinian theology of original sin in favor of a sense of a benevolent deity, along with the notion of sexuality as desirable, socially positive, and a source of health.

26. For a discussion of these versions, see Smeed 45–63.

27. See Weinstein 96–103; Smeed 75–90.

28. As Sarah Wright remarks, "Zorrilla's version is the one that holds sway in Spain" (9). As she demonstrates, the "unification of extremes" in Zorrilla's hero influences subsequent Spanish interpreters of the theme, such as Rafael María Liern and Miguel de Unamuno y Jugo (12–13). Weinstein suggests that the "happy ending" of Don Juan's salvation is at least partly responsible for the greater popularity of Zorrilla's version

(128). Part of the enjoyment of Zorrilla's play, however, arguably stems from our knowledge of Tirso's original ending, and the contrast the later playwright makes with the traditional version. See Mandrell (92–111) for a discussion of how Zorrilla both includes and thematizes the inclusion of Tirso's play in his own rewriting of his precursor's work.

29. In another variation of the "rehabilitation" theme, Prosper Mérimée's novella *Souls in Purgatory* (1834) incorporates the legend of Miguel Mañara Vincentelo de Leca, who lived from 1626 or 1627 to 1679, into the Don Juan tale. Mañara led a dissolute, Don Juan-like life in his youth but had a vision of his own funeral and repented, turning thereafter to a saintly life. Mérimée creates a character named Don Juan de Maraña who combines features of Miguel Mañara and Don Juan Tenorio. Alexandre Dumas the Elder, O. V. de Lubicz-Milosz, and other writers have also relied on this legend of a converted Don Juan in their works. See Weinstein 104–18.

30. Robert Karpiak positions Pushkin's play as the last of the classic, Tenorio line, while the Russian poet's French contemporary, Prosper Mérimée, turns the legend in a new direction by popularizing the historical figure Don Miguel de Mañara. De Mañara, who reportedly saw a performance of Tirso's play and claimed to be the real Don Juan, embarked on a path of debauchery before reforming and devoting his life to penance and charity. This reinterpretation of the Don Juan legend makes explicit for the first time the potential, perhaps already present in Tirso's original version, for Don Juan to reform. As Karpiak acknowledges, however, Pushkin's ambiguous portrayal of Don Juan, who may or may not reform, already gestures toward this figure: "If, on the other hand, the hero of Kamennyi gost' is indeed converted by true love; if his renunciation of donjuanism is genuine, then he emerges the prototype of the Romantic Don Juan on the road to redemption and salvation, anticipating the interpretations of Dumas and Zorrilla" (Don Juan in Slavic Drama 69).

31. It is unknown whether Pushkin's conceptions of Don Juan and Donna Anna were influenced by Hoffmann's story. Pushkin was reading Hoffmann during a time of keen interest in the German author's tales in France, between 1826 and 1829 (Clayton 277, 287), and he might well have read Hoffmann's "Don Juan." However, Karpiak argues that Pushkin's *The Stone Guest* was only minimally influenced by Hoffmann's story, and indeed, the Russian poet's conception of these characters differs greatly from that of his German predecessor ("The Crisis of Idealism" 128).

32. Karpiak, for instance, notes: "Even in the secondary episodes of seduction Don Juan almost invariably pursues women pledged to obedience, subservience, or allegiance to some form of male authority, be it father, husband, lover, fiancé, or God" ("Lesia Ukrainka's 'The Stone Host' and 'the Don Juan Myth'" 253).

33. This is the last of Rank's writings from a psychoanalytic perspective, before he abandoned its tenets; as such it represents a transitional work.

34. In this regard, Rank's interpretation recalls Carl Jung's description of Donjuanism as a typical effect of the mother complex on a son, who "unconsciously seeks his mother in every woman he meets" (85).

35. Lacan wrote specifically on Donjuanism in one of his seminars. As Brian Robertson demonstrates, Lacan was highly influenced by the British psychoanalyst Joan Riviere's work *Womanliness as a Masquerade* (1929). Riviere argues in this book that women apply coquettishness to mask deep-seated penis envy and to neutralize the

anxiety they feel in rivalry with men. Lacan twists this negative formulation into a positive expression of women's erotic superiority and astonishingly elevates Don Juan to the status of ideal male lover because he bears a looser relation to the fetish object than ordinary men have. "Don Juan," he claims, "is a woman's dream" (Lacan, *Anxiety* 192). Leporello's "Catalogue Aria" is actually a comprehensive list of fetishes in which every woman can find a place. She has no need to condescend to Don Juan's level of desire, to situate herself in his framework of masculine fantasy, because any woman can be his ideal. There is no risk of becoming an erotic absolute in his eyes because every conceivable masculine fetish is reduced to the same level. Thus, "his 'prestige' as an ideal lover consists precisely in his uncanny ability to take the pesky question of desire out of the game" (Robertson 143). When a woman feels she is the object at the center of a desire, she takes flight, but with Don Juan there is no reason to do so.

36. Moreover, in a very concrete sense, Don Juan validates Lacan's distinction between need and desire, as his desire is in no way based on need.

37. This impulse is different from Freud's death instinct, which forms in opposition to the sex drive. In both the Tristan and Isolde and the Don Juan legends, Eros and Thanatos seem to be inextricably linked.

38. Interestingly, Connell cites the conquistadors, who were in full force when Tirso wrote his Don Juan play, as perhaps the first group to be defined as a masculine cultural type. The conquistadors, like Don Juan, were displaced from customary social relationships, and presented special challenges to state control (187).

39. In Tirso's play, the King of Naples, as Isabela tries to explain her situation to him following Don Juan's visit, turns his back on her and, when she asks him to turn his face to her, leaves the room.

40. For a much earlier Western discussion of Russian Don Juans (Pushkin's *The Stone Guest* and A. K. Tolstoy's *Don Juan*), see Manning ("Russian Versions of Don Juan").

41. Manning, in fact, refers to Onegin as "a disillusioned Don Juan" ("Russian Versions of Don Juan" 485) and also compares Pechorin to Don Juan (491).

Chapter 1. The Artist-Seducer as Liberator

1. Pushkin denied writing this poem for years but confessed to its authorship to Tsar Nikolai I in 1828.

2. See Lotman's classic essay "The Decembrist in Everyday Life" on the rebels' cultivation of "seriousness as a norm of behavior" (79). Despite these oppositions between Pushkin and the Decembrists, Emily Wang correctly notes that the two groups (libertines and Decembrists) shared key common ground, too. Each group formed a kind of emotional community that served as a refuge from the strictly coded court life.

3. As Paul Debreczeny shows, Pushkin's exaggerated reputation as a revolutionary during his lifetime stems in large part from the emotional impact of his unpublished poetry on the Decembrists and other listeners, who often spread his ideas by circulating inaccurate, distorted copies (5–13).

4. Nemirovsky also notes Pushkin's interest in French poet Évariste de Parny's combination of eroticism, political overtones, and anticlericalism (48).

5. As Debreczeny notes, Pushkin started this journal in part because he was having difficulty finding venues for his own work (121).
6. Although Pushkin didn't write *The Stone Guest* until 1830, he got the idea for it several years earlier. Stepan Shevyrev claimed that Pushkin was planning to write it in 1826, and it is included in a list of ten plays he intended to write that dates no later than 1827 (Tomashevsky 283–84). The origin of the idea thus closely follows his visit with Nikolai and his subsequent disillusionment with his reign.
7. Dmitry Blagoi characterizes *Don Giovanni* as the immediate source for Pushkin's little tragedy, with Molière's play also providing crucial material (*Sotsiologiia tvorchestva Pushkina* 215). Other scholars identify different sources as primary for Pushkin. Gendarme de Bévotte, for instance, argues that Pushkin was inspired by de Villiers's play *The Stone Guest* (*Festin de Pierre*), which includes the character Don Alvar, and which had been known for a long time in Russia (vol. 2, 15–16). Boris Tomashevsky, though he acknowledges the importance of *Don Giovanni*, considers Molière's play the main source for *The Stone Guest*, noting that another of the little tragedies, *The Miserly Knight*, also takes a subject from Molière (*The Miser*). He notes that Pushkin did not invent his play's title but derived it from Val'berkh's translation of Molière's title, *Don-Zhuan, ili Kamennyi gost'* (*Don Juan, or The Stone Guest*), for the production that was being performed in 1816 and from Canobbio's ballet of the same title. He also notes that Molière's play was the only Don Juan text known to Pushkin from his youth and that Pushkin would have read Germaine de Staël's complimentary remarks on the play in *On Germany*. He also mentions various motifs that Pushkin relies on (but in some cases, transforms substantially) from Molière's play, including the Commander's death half a year before the play begins, the danger of revenge by the family of the Commander, Don Juan's return from exile, and the invitation to the statue (281–99). Nemirovsky cites Pierre Choderlos de Laclos's *Dangerous Liaisons* as a crucial source (222–24). See also David Shengold's convincing argument that Victor Hugo's *Hernani*, which premiered in February 1830, may have been an important source for Pushkin. For the reasons I give above, I find *Don Giovanni* to be the most crucial source text for Pushkin.
8. As Akhmatova notes, his wealth is referred to only once in Pushkin's play, while it is central in Molière's and Mozart/Da Ponte's works (92).
9. For example, as Nemirovsky points out, Pushkin's omission of the warnings that the hero receives in the works of Tirso, Molière, and Mozart/Da Ponte indicates the desire to emphasize that his Don Juan knows that the statue is coming to punish him (219).
10. One may argue that this move is prefigured to some extent in *Don Giovanni*, in which Don Ottavio tells Donna Anna, after her father is slain by Don Giovanni in a duel, that he will be both husband and father to her.
11. This character is presumably an allusion to Petrarch's Laura, but here the inspiration appears to work in reverse. Whereas Laura de Noves inspired Petrarch's sonnets, in *The Stone Guest*, it is Don Juan whose poems inspire Laura to compose musical settings. Svetlana Klimova suggests, however, that Pushkin took the name Laura from Lord Byron's poem *Beppo* (338).
12. Boris Gorodetsky argues that Laura is brought into the plot to make a more effective contrast with Anna, to underscore how distinct Don Juan's feeling for her is compared to his feelings for other lovers.

13. Don Juan's very pursuit of Laura indicates the continual, self-reproducing nature of desire and Lacan's distinction between desire and need. He does not "need" Laura, but simply desires her (she is not even his main object of seduction, as he has already decided to woo Donna Anna).

14. These comments represent another autobiographical linking of Don Juan with Pushkin, who flirted with atheism as a young poet and was himself frequently accused of being godless.

15. The version this ending recalls the most is actually not Molière's or Mozart/Da Ponte's, but Tirso's (which Pushkin probably did not read), in which Don Juan sinks in the tomb together with Don Gonzalo's statue.

16. See his June 15, 1880, letter to Yulia Abaza, in which he points out that the reader cannot decide whether the ghost of the Countess arose from Hermann's imagination or whether he did have contact with another world (*Polnoe sobranie sochinenii* 192). Tzvetan Todorov, writing on the fantastic much later, defines it similarly in terms of this irresolution: "The fantastic, as we have seen, lasts only as long as a certain hesitation: a hesitation common to the reader and character, who must decide whether or not what they perceive derives from 'reality' as it exists in the common opinion" (41).

17. As Gasparov points out, Pushkin's Don Juan list represents a stylization of himself as the famous libertine. His writing down of these names recalls Don Giovanni's recordkeeper Leporello rather than the seducer himself, who would never have written such a list (49).

18. As Akhmatova notes, Leporello's comment that Don Juan should have stayed in exile recalls the advice Pushkin received to stay in Mikhailovskoe and write poetry rather than return from exile, as he was tempted to do (94).

19. All citations of Pushkin's letters are from *The Letters of Alexander Pushkin: Three Volumes in One*, translated by J. Thomas Shaw.

20. As Karpiak notes, this position, which he terms the "moral regeneration theory" and traces to Belinsky, became almost an official position in Soviet Pushkin criticism (*Don Juan in Slavic Drama*, 66–68). As he also points out, however, non-Russian critics did not subscribe to this theory, and were more skeptical that Don Juan truly reforms (68–72).

21. See also Walter N. Vickery, who finds the lack of resolution to this ambiguity a weakness of the play: "believe in Don Juan's sincerity we must, not merely because of the extrinsic evidence offered by Pushkin's biography, but because, without this belief, *The Stone Guest* loses much of its point" (*Alexander Pushkin* 97).

22. See also the same critic's earlier *Sotsiologiia tvorchestva Pushina*, 218–19.

23. To my knowledge, Blagoi is the earliest critic to propose this linking of Eros and Thanatos as Pushkin's major contribution to the Don Juan legend, noting that "the theme of *The Stone Guest* is the convergence of love and death" (*Sotsiologiia tvorchestva Pushkina* 219) and that Don Juan is "attracted by the special piquancy [ostrota] of raptures of love 'in the presence of the dead,' in the face of death, at its very point of no return" (*Sotsiologiia tvorchestva Pushkina* 222).

24. There is no evidence, however, of a criminal past for Pushkin's Don Juan, who, as two characters acknowledge, slew the Commander honorably in a duel. At the time duels were tacitly accepted rituals.

25. Todd views this as characteristic of Russian aristocratic society of the early nineteenth century, noting that "participation in the social whirl required considerable adaptability and a large repertoire of roles" (33).

26. It is for this reason, Herman argues, that Pushkin includes the character of Laura, who "seduces" her audience with her songs; Pushkin invites the reader to admire the power of art and the seduction inherent in it. "The figure of Laura," Herman writes, "provides Pushkin with a lever to pry the Don Juan myth out of the moralizing ruts it has been running in" (14).

27. Lotman notes the reference to this work in *Eugene Onegin* (*Pushkin* 558).

28. See Nemirovsky (222–24) for a detailed discussion of the links between *Dangerous Liaisons* and *The Stone Guest*. As Nemirovsky argues, "Don Juan's true goal turns out to be not the seduction of Donna Anna, but a sacrilegious challenge to the heavens," which recalls Valmont's desire to take Mme. de Tourvel away not just from her husband but also from God (223).

29. Pushkin's appreciation of Staël and her writings is well documented. Tomashevsky notes that Pushkin read her works in 1817–19 and probably knew both her novels (*Delphine* and *Corrine*), "Considerations on the French Revolution," "On Germany," and "10 years in exile" (19–20, 31–32), and Lotman notes that her conversations were passed along to Pushkin orally (338–39); Hilde Hoogenboom, however, notes that Volume 3 of the copy of *Delphine* in Pushkin's library was uncut (537). In addition to the reference to Delphine as one of Tatiana's models in *Eugene Onegin*, Pushkin includes an epigraph from Staël's *Considerations of the French Revolution*; there are various other references to Staël in that novel (see Lotman, *Pushkin*, passim). Pushkin's incomplete prose work *Roslavlev* (1831) features Staël as a character who is emulated by the female protagonist.

30. In a letter to her confidante, her sister-in-law Louise, Delphine writes, "The fact is, a woman's life is over when she does not marry the man she loves" (98).

31. In an 1827 article, for instance, Pushkin complains about women's indifference to poetry and ascribes it to their inability to appreciate the Russian language; he thinks poetry fails to penetrate their souls: "Look how they sing modish romances, how they distort poetry" (qtd. in Guber 29).

32. Her proposed title was "Notes by the Own Hand of the Russian Amazon Known Under the Name of Alexandrov"; Pushkin changed it to "The Memoirs of N. A. Durova" (*Letters* 794).

33. See also Todd's discussion of Tatiana's creativity as hostess of her Petersburg salon (129–30).

34. Pushkin briefly (and witheringly) refers to his former lover Anna Kern's translation of Sand's *André* in an 1835 letter to his wife (*Letters* 726).

35. Oleg Zaslavsky argues that Don Alvar (the Commander) and Inez's husband are in fact one and the same, and that this explains why the duel was fought: Don Juan was avenging Alvar's killing of Inez in retaliation for her affair (156).

36. Don Juan's reproach and Laura's retort resonate with Valmont's comment in *Dangerous Liaisons*: "Oh women, women! Can you complain if we deceive you? Every act of treachery we commit we have learned from you" (240).

37. The parallels between Laura and Anna, in fact, are quite striking. Laura does not believe that Don Juan went straightaway to see her after arriving in Madrid, just as

Anna is skeptical that Don Juan finally loves a woman. Just as Laura warns Don Juan to avoid being seen when he brings the dead body of Don Carlos outside her house, Anna urges Don Juan to hide when they hear the sound of the approaching Commander. Herman remarks that introducing Laura in Scene 2 paves the way for the reader or viewer to accept Don Juan morally (14), but I would argue that it is just as possible that Pushkin wants to underscore similarities between the two women and to encourage the reader to look for signs of Donjuanism in Anna as well as Laura.

38. From today's perspective, of course, Don Juan's treatment of Anna could appear to be harassment, since he ignores her importunations to leave. Nevertheless, we see her gradually become increasingly interested in Don Juan throughout the scene.

39. See Helena Goscilo ("Feet Pushkin Scanned") on Pushkin's use of the foot (nozhka) in various poetic works to stimulate the poetic imagination. She views the presentation of this image as characteristic of Pushkin's preference for metonymy and synecdoche in his poetry.

40. As Kropf notes, the cemetery serves as a symbol of both death and rebirth. "Saint Anthony's Monastery," he writes, "is the site of both: the 'cemetery' of Don Juan's sweet moments of the past. But it is also the place where, encountering death in the widow Donna Anna, he begins the becoming that will distance death and offer him a kind of rebirth" (27–28).

41. This trait, of course, finds a reflection in Pushkin's own disparaging remarks to women he loved, such as Anna Kern, about their husbands.

42. Felicity Baker demonstrates that Da Ponte interweaves Christian and pagan references in the libretto, taking motifs from Dante's *Divine Comedy* as his starting point. One example is Leporello's comment in the finale that his master's soul was dragged by demons to the realm of Persephone and Pluto (80). In the previous century, Molière had already secularized the legend to a great extent by turning his hero into a skeptic and deemphasizing the terror of the supernatural reflected in Tirso's version in favor of an exposé of the hypocrisy of Don Juan's society.

43. Moreover, the use of the verb *provalivaiutsia*, instead of the more logical *spuskaiutsia*, arguably places the Commander on the same level as Don Juan as he is taken by surprise by the series of events, rather than positioning him as a purposeful administrator of long-awaited justice.

44. The overture, which begins in D Major, returns to that key at the end, as does the opera's final ensemble, generally omitted in the nineteenth century.

45. Besides Dargomyzhsky's opera, *The Miserly Knight, Mozart and Salieri*, and *A Feast in the Time of Plague* were also transposed, respectively, by Sergei Rachmaninov, Nikolai Rimsky-Korsakov, and Cesar Cui. See Emerson ("Little Tragedies, Little Operas") and Taruskin 325–28.

46. Dargomyzhsky died shortly before finishing *The Stone Guest*. Following its completion by Cesar Cui and orchestration by Nikolai Rimsky-Korsakov, the opera was premiered at the Mariinsky Theater in St. Petersburg in 1872.

Chapter 2. Don Juan in Everyday Life

1. Robert Karpiak has pointed out that, although Janko Lavrin and Alexei Veselovsky see the influence of Hoffmann's story on *The Stone Guest*, there is only minimal evidence for it in the play (the story first appeared in French in 1829, the year before

Pushkin wrote the play, and in Russian in 1833, three years after) ("The Crisis of Idealism" 128). More likely, Pushkin created his own independent Romantic reconceptualization of the hero, who as a Romantic poet and exile from the capital is clearly fashioned after himself.

2. This is particularly the case since, even before Pushkin's play, Byron's *Don Juan*, and the behavior associated not only with Byron's works but with his actual life, had long been imitated in Russian society.

3. Quotations from Alexei K. Tolstoy are from the compilation *Don Zhuan russkii*, edited by A. V. Parin. Translations here and elsewhere in the chapter are mine if not otherwise specified.

4. In the original 1862 edition, Satan claims Don Juan's soul, but the spirits rescue him, and he retires to a monastery to expiate his sins. However, Tolstoy substituted a different ending in 1867, in which Don Juan does not repent and is killed by the statue. As Karpiak notes, Tolstoy reverts from the "Mañara tradition" of Mérimée and Zorrilla back to the "classic" ending of the Tenorio line (*Don Juan in Slavic Drama*, 117–20).

5. Bezhetsky, for instance, describes Don Juan's supernatural punishment as a rumor, while in reality, he is killed by assassins' knives. See Karpiak, "The Crisis of Idealism" and *Don Juan in Slavic Drama*, 217–73.

6. See Karpiak, *Don Juan in Slavic Drama*, 273.

7. See Paperno, *Chernyshevsky and the Age of Realism*, especially 28–36.

8. The novel was originally titled *The Artist* (*Khudozhnik*) or *The Artist Raisky* (*Khudozhnik Raiskii*), when Goncharov was planning a more traditional psychological novel. As E. A. Krasnoshchekova points out, the eventual title was chosen to convey the same negative associations with nihilism as other anti-nihilist novels such as Dostoevsky's *Devils* (*Besy*), Alexei Pisemsky's *Troubled Seas* (*Vzbalamuchennoe more*), Vsevolod Krestovsky's *The Flock of Panurge* (*Panurgogo stado*), Viktor Askochensky's *The Asmodeus of Our Time* (*Asmodei nashego vremeni*), and Lev Tolstoy's play *The Infected Family* (*Zarazhennoe semeistvo*). See Krasnoshchekova, *Goncharov* 378.

9. As Vsevolod Setchkarev points out, *The Precipice* led to an "anti-Goncharov campaign" as leftwing critics such as Mikhail Saltykov-Shchedrin and Alexander Skabichevsky saw it as an antiradical novel even though the plot involving Mark Volokhov was only one aspect of it (240). Viktor Burenin, however, praised Raisky as a new type: "The talented artist Raisky represents just as general and complete a type as Oblomov" (qtd. in Krasnoshchekova, *Goncharov* 380).

10. See, for example, Milton Ehre, 233–63. As Ehre comments, "*The Ravine* has the 'pasted' quality Goncharov described: a number of scenes and characters are not related or related only incidentally to the plot" (257).

11. It is unclear which philosopher he is referring to. Perhaps it is Hippocrates, to whom is attributed the aphorism "Art is long, life is short" (Ars longa, vita brevis).

12. Elsewhere in his oeuvre, in the essay "Notes on Belinsky's Personality" ("Zametki o lichnosti Belinskogo" 1874), Goncharov characterizes Belinsky's passionate embrace of one writer after another (Pushkin, Lermontov, Gogol, Dostoevsky, etc.) as a kind of Donjuanism. He describes the way each writer would "seduce" Belinsky, in light of the critic's ardent, single-minded championing of what he perceived to be socially relevant literature, only to disappoint him later, leading to another "infatuation" in an endless

cycle: "One idol followed another almost nonstop" / Idoly sledovali pochti neprestanno odin za drugim (Goncharov, *Literaturno-kriticheskie stat'i* 205).

13. All translations of *The Precipice* are by Laury Magnus and Boris Jakim, adjusted where necessary.

14. As several commentators have pointed out, Volokhov can be seen as a double of Raisky. See, most recently, Krasnoshchekova, "Oblomovets" 159–60.

15. As E. N. Stroganova points out, Goncharov's oeuvre in general contains numerous Pygmalion allusions. For Stroganova, Goncharov simplifies the Pygmalion myth in *The Precipice* from his more complex use of it in *Oblomov*. That novel contains gender reversal of the myth, as Olga is attempting to transform Oblomov and wake him up from his slumbers into real life; at the same time, Olga is also compared to a statue (Galatea), and Oblomov plays a role in awakening her as well. In *The Precipice*, the reworking is more straightforward. See also Masing-Delic, "A Change in Gender Roles."

16. Krasnoshchekova argues that Goncharov describes Raisky and Volokhov as a unity, a combined eternal type that appears in all generations, embodying laziness, inactivity, and incapacity for practical work ("Oblomovets" 159). As she notes, "In *The Precipice*, the dilettante Raisky's 'infamous laziness' and the nihilist Volokhov's 'frantic activity' appear to be two faces of a person suffering from Oblomovitis, representing Goncharov's most well-known depiction of the national mentality" (166).

17. All quotations of *Anna Karenina* are from Rosamund Bartlett's translation.

18. On the first possible critical direction, see Helena Goscilo, who argues that Stiva, along with Vronsky and Vasenka Veslovsky, embodies the libertine archetype rooted in Ovid's *Art of Love* ("Tolstoy, Laclos, and the Libertine"). For Julie Buckler, the reference to the opera signals Tolstoy's interest in how theatrical roles and conventions structure the characters' lives (164–77). As she notes, Tolstoy planned to have his heroine view a performance of Mozart's opera in an earlier draft, which also indicates the importance of the theme for *Anna Karenina*. Finally, Ian Saylor, connecting *Don Giovanni* to Tolstoy's epigraph, notes the connection between sensuality and the punishment it calls forth in both the opera and novel.

19. All quotations of Da Ponte's libretto are from Norman Platt and Laura Sarti's translation.

20. Mozart referred to *Don Giovanni* as an *opera buffa*, and following the D minor finale in which Don Giovanni is sent to hell, he concludes with a final sextet in D Major, "Questo è il fin di chi fa mal, e de' perfidi la morte alla vita è sempre ugual," which delivers the moral of the opera. Throughout the nineteenth century, though, as I have noted, this finale was customarily omitted, and the opera was interpreted as a tragedy.

21. These were not, of course, the only two Don Juan texts Tolstoy could have referred to: he surely knew Molière's *Don Juan*, Byron's *Don Juan*, and perhaps other retellings as well. However, I find that the works of Mozart and Pushkin—especially their common focus on the connection between eroticism and its repercussions—bear the closest relation to Tolstoy's concerns in *Anna Karenina*.

22. See, especially, his remarks on Richard Wagner's music dramas and *Gesamtkunstwerk* theory in *What is Art?* 101–12.

23. Tolstoy's mention of Turgenev in this letter indicates his awareness of the cult of *Don Giovanni* that, as I mentioned, had engulfed Russia in the 1850s. Pauline Viardot-

Garcia's manuscript of the opera was linked to Pushkin's version of the Don Juan theme: in 1861, Turgenev and Louis Viardot (her husband), translated *The Stone Guest* and *Mozart and Salieri* into French. Tolstoy's desire to share his impressions with Turgenev thus likely confirms his intimate understanding of both Mozart and Da Ponte's and Pushkin's versions of the Don Juan theme, and the differences between them.

24. In an oft-cited March 25, 1873, letter to Nikolai Strakhov shortly after beginning work on the novel, Tolstoy claims to have derived several characters and plot elements from Pushkin's 1828 fragment beginning "The Guests Were Arriving at the Dacha," which he reports reading along with *The Belkin Tales, The Captain's Daughter*, and the unfinished story "Egyptian Nights." Such works of Pushkin, as Boris Eikhenbaum explains, offered Tolstoy a model of the stylistic concision and clarity he was seeking in the early 1870s (132–33). And already during *Anna Karenina's* serial publication, commentators such as Dostoevsky and Vasily Avseenko noted the central role of *Eugene Onegin*, especially in relation to the novel's adultery plot. For Eikhenbaum, "Tolstoi's Anna is a kind of reincarnation of Tatyana, contemplated by Pushkin himself in fragments of a planned novel" (131).

25. In a rare reference to the little tragedies, V. A. Zhdanov and E. E. Zaidenshnur point out that Levin quotes Walsingham from *A Feast in the Time of Plague* (821). Also, in two early drafts of *Anna Karenina*, a young diplomat in a drawing room, asked to say something evil and funny, responds: "it's said that evil and funny do not mix" (Govoriat, chto zloe i smeshnoe nesovmestimy), a witty paraphrase of Salieri's comment in *Mozart and Salieri* that "evil and genius do not mix" (Genii i zlodeistvo dve veshchi nesovmestnye).

26. In this sense, *The Stone Guest* plays a similar role as a subtext to *Eugene Onegin*, which is nowhere mentioned explicitly in Tolstoy's novel but clearly impacts *Anna Karenina*.

27. Numerous commentators have pointed out that *Don Giovanni*, as a result of its episodic subject, lacks the unity and taut structure of *The Marriage of Figaro* and other Mozart operas. However, Da Ponte, using Giovanni Bertati's libretto to Giuseppe Gazzaniga's early 1787 opera as a starting point, tightens up the plot considerably, for example by reducing the female roles from four to three. Donna Anna's thirst for vengeance, combined with Giovanni's spurned lover Elvira's continual pursuit of him, unites the opera more closely around the theme of personal revenge than Da Ponte's predecessors had. See Edward Forman, "Don Juan before Da Ponte" 27–44.

28. As Helena Goscilo points out, Tolstoy draws on the archetypal libertine depicted by Laclos in *Dangerous Liaisons* for his characterization of Vronsky. In my interpretation, Tolstoy refers more specifically to the particular Don Juan subset of this archetype elaborated by Mozart/Da Ponte and Pushkin ("Tolstoy, Laclos, and the Libertine").

29. See Buckler (168) and Goscilo, "Tolstoy, Laclos, and the Libertine" 411.

30. See de Sherbinin 649.

31. More recently, Tatiana Kuzmic, interpreting the novel in terms of homosociality, argues that despite the fleshiness/fleshlessness opposition between Vronsky and Karenin, they each participate in reinforcing Anna's essentially functionless role by their shared refusal to interact or acknowledge one another's importance. Anna, frustrated "at being stuck between two passive men," tries to goad each of them into action and

eventually punishes both of them for their failure to act by forcing them into a meeting at Karenin's house (and later, of course, by committing suicide) (8).

32. See Ustiuzhanin 68–83; Herman 18–21.

33. This parallels Vronsky's experience, as stated earlier; however, to an extent, the same could be said of Anna. Although Tolstoy's account of Anna and Karenin's relations before the events of the plot is notoriously sparse, his brief explanation in Part V of the circumstances that brought them together reveals it to be an arranged marriage (much like that of Donna Anna to Don Alvar). One can infer that this marriage brought Anna a degree of comfort, along with respect for Karenin, but not passionate love, which she apparently experiences for the first time with Vronsky.

34. In this connection, Tolstoy picks up on a crucial "falling motion" in *The Stone Guest*. Donna Anna's fall into a faint at the end of the play is followed soon after by the stage direction of Don Juan and the statue interlocking as they descend. However, Tolstoy links Anna's motion downward onto the tracks, implicitly, with her previous moral Fall: the consummation of her affair with Vronsky, when she slips downward physically, giving him the impression that he has murdered her as he stands above her.

35. In the nursery, Dolly notes that Anna seems unaccustomed to visiting her daughter Annie, and that she does not know how many teeth she has. And while playing lawn tennis later with Anna, Vronsky, and their guests, she dislikes the "general unnaturalness of grownup people playing a children's game alone without children" and feels that "she was acting in a theatre with actors who were better than she was" (637).

36. For Amy Mandelker, however, this dismissiveness of the woman question does not make Tolstoy an archconservative regarding women's roles in marriage and society. She argues that Tolstoy's rejection of the woman question actually radicalizes it as he argues against the institution of marriage itself. As she puts it, Tolstoy "exposes the cult of domesticity for what it often becomes in a bad marriage: an oppression of women and a denial of her selfhood perpetuated by the myth of the glories of maternity and housekeeping" (53).

37. See, for example, Gary Saul Morson, who argues that Anna's suicide results from the romantic, novelistic narrative she constructs for herself, reinforced by her fatalism and belief in omens (118–39). Vladimir Golstein attributes "Peter Pan Syndrome" to Anna, noting her refusal to take responsibility or learn from her mistakes: "the pity and sympathy that Tolstoy feels for Anna and with which he obviously infects us, should not blind us to the essentially childlike nature of her responses to her moral predicament" (205).

38. Translations of *The Kreutzer Sonata* are by Michael R. Katz, in *Tolstoy's Short Fiction*.

39. The translations of "The Lady with the Little Dog" are Rosamund Bartlett's, from *About Love and Other Stories*.

40. As Kataev also points out, Chekhov produced many "Don Juan" characters, starting early in his career. Kataev lists the title character of his early play *Platonov* (1878), Kamyshev of "The Shooting Party" ("Drama na okhote," 1884), Panaurov in "Three Years" ("Tri gody," 1895), Shternberg in "Lights" ("Ogni," 1888), and Dorn in *The Seagull* (*Chaika*, 1896) (108). One might also mention "Anna on the Neck" ("Anna na shee," 1895), in which the young, newlywed protagonist, Anya (another Anna), married

to the much older Modest Alekseevich, flirts with the more attractive Artynov, whom the narrator refers to as a "notorious Don Juan" (*Anton Chekhov's Selected Stories* 318).

41. According to Karpiak, the name Don Juan can be found at least 40 times in Chekhov's dramas, stories, and personal writings ("Don Juan 'in the Russian Manner'" 240).

42. Noting the various anthroponymic associations between Chekhov's characters in *Platonov* and previous Don Juan versions, Karpiak argues that Chekhov creates a uniquely Russian version of Don Juan in this play.

43. In this light it may be significant that, like Donna Anna, Anna Sergeevna is childless. With her single child in eight years of marriage to her husband, Anna Karenina similarly seems trapped in a sexless marriage, or at least one that does not yield the expected fruit (Tolstoyan families and, indeed, nineteenth-century families in general typically had multiple children).

44. As Caryl Emerson points out, Chekhov writes several other stories—including "Anna on the Neck" and "About Love"—that similarly depict a married "Anna" considering or partaking in infidelity ("Chekhov and the Annas").

Chapter 3. Don Juan in the Silver Age

1. As Irina Paperno demonstrates in her study of Chernyshevsky, this reciprocal shaping of life and art takes place in the Realist period as well.

2. However, as Vsevolod Bagno argues, the influence of *The Stone Guest* can be seen in Bal'mont's translation of Tirso's play. For instance, Don Juan's monologues and his seductions of Tisbea and Aminta are loftier and more eloquent than in the Spanish play, and Pushkin's vocabulary, stylistics, and imagery are present throughout the translation (418–21).

3. All translations in this chapter are mine unless otherwise specified.

4. Moreover, Blok acted the part of Don Juan in *The Stone Guest* as a young man, and also read monologues from A. K. Tolstoy's *Don Juan* (Gorchakov 357).

5. Blok can be linked to Pushkin in his love of prostitutes. In Pushkin's case, though, prostitutes were only one type of women, among many, whom he appreciated.

6. Presto notes Blok's ambivalence about family life and generational continuity. Blok concluded that the artist must abandon "hearth and home" and wander (22). As she also points out, the idea of domesticity was distinctly alien to the Symbolists in general, few of whom had children and most of whom traveled a great deal.

7. Blok was most likely also reluctant to consummate their marriage because of his syphilis. His lack of sexual attention to Liubov' Dmitrievna proved quite unsatisfactory to her. She eventually "seduced" Blok in fall 1904, more than a year after they were married. They had brief, unsatisfactory encounters, which ended in spring 1906. On Blok's probable syphilis, see Matich (106–11) and Masing-Delic, "Black Blood."

8. Kornei Chukovsky, however, does not agree with such characterizations of Blok's face as statue-like: he describes it as being "in a state of intense yet barely noticeable perpetual motion" (26).

9. Although Liubov' Dmitrievna eventually rejected Bely after his lengthy infatuation for her, this love triangle can be likened to the one in Pushkin, in which Don Juan (played by Bely) nearly has an affair with Anna (Liubov' Dmitrievna), and Blok is the Commander.

10. This fascination is particularly characteristic of the modernist era; it can be seen, for instance, in Bely's *Petersburg*. As Rolf Hellebust writes, "Dualities (for example, East vs. West in the person of Apollon Apollonovich) rupture and bleed into one another in a confutation of any reconciliation" (496).

11. As poet-flâneur, Blok often depicts motion in his poetry, showing the hero walking or following someone. This is true of both "The Steps of the Commander" and *Retribution*. It gives the Don Juan theme as he develops it here a different sense, that of a man following or in search of something or someone (as opposed to, say, the invitation of the statue to supper, which requires the statue to come to him).

12. Blok famously described his poetic inspiration as musical, which supports the notion of an operatic as well as theatrical element in this poem.

13. Anna Lisa Crone comments that much of "The Steps of the Commander" can be read as Anna's dream (150).

14. See also Gorchakov's interpretation of this image as a reference to *Hamlet*.

15. This image of Anna recalls Liubov' Dmitrievna, whom Blok viewed as spiritually asleep.

16. This is also true of Blok's well-known 1908 poem "Of Valor, Noble Deeds, and Glory" ("O doblestiakh, o podvigakh, o slave"), which features a similar fusion of dream and reality.

17. See Jakobson's well-known essay on Pushkin's statue myth as expressed in *The Stone Guest*, "The Bronze Horseman," and "The Tale of the Golden Cockerel." The footsteps also recall Pushkin's *Bronze Horseman*, with the heavy steps of the steed chasing Evgeny, as he hears: "The rumble of thunder—A heavy, sonorous gallop"/ Kak budto groma grokhotan'e—Tiazhelo-zvon'koe skakan'e.

18. Moreover, Anna herself—if we think of Liubov' Dmitrievna, who, like Blok, had affairs during their marriage—falls short of the "Maiden of Light" ideal.

19. Donjuanism can thus be seen as a generational reproduction of traits, or what Max Nordau and other fin-de-siècle thinkers would call "hereditary taint." Interestingly, one can see this not only in Blok, but also in other versions of the Don Juan legend. In *Anna Karenina*, Vronsky appears to inherit his Donjuanism from his mother, who has a reputation for scandalous affairs.

20. Nevertheless, Blok was overjoyed when Liubov' Dmitrievna gave birth in 1908 to a boy named Mitia, conceived with another man, and looked forward to bringing him up; he was devastated when the baby died after ten days.

21. This scene reverberates with psychoanalytical associations. In *Totem and Taboo*, Freud speaks of the longing the sons, once they have successfully banded together to kill their father, feel for the murdered figure. Blok's description of his poetic persona's fear that the father could return, perhaps, implies a concealed admiration and longing for him.

22. Irene Masing-Delic interprets this gesture as the poet's acknowledgment of his inner similarity with his father ("Black Blood" 141).

23. *Ozloblennye*, which can mean "hostile" or "embittered," also implies inimical feelings toward his son. Schumann is an appropriate choice of composers to reference here: a "poetic" composer of fragmentary, programmatic, deeply autobiographical piano pieces, he is somewhat analogous to Blok himself.

24. Dmitrienko notes the connection between Pobedonostsev here and the Commander in "Steps of the Commander," as the phrase "Chernyi, tikhii, kak sova, motor"

(A black car, quiet as an owl) recalls the description "Pobedonostsev nad Rossiei / Proster sovinye kryla" (Pobedonostsev stretched his owl's wings over Russia; 55–56).

25. See, for instance, her poem "Meeting with Pushkin" ("Vstrecha s Pushkinym").

26. The cycle also coincides with the February revolution and the unrest that followed in Russia. Although Tsvetaeva experienced the revolution and ensuing famine in Moscow (and rejected it politically), she does not allude to them directly in this cycle, in contrast to the way Molière, Mozart/Da Ponte, and other Don Juan writers have likened the hero to social and political rebels. Anna Saakiants, in fact, argues that Tsvetaeva uses such fantastic subjects to retreat into a "theatrical" world as an escape from reality (119); Lily Feiler, by contrast, argues that Tsvetaeva asserts her own type of romantic, heroic rebel in these poems (along with the cycles on Stenka Razin and Carmen of that year) against the vulgar, violent mass rebellion taking place around her (82–83).

27. In "My Pushkin" ("Moi Pushkin"), Tsvetaeva characterizes Pushkin similarly, referring to his "African shoulders loaded down and overpowered with all the Russian snows" (37–38).

28. See Irina Shevelenko (15–18) and Olga Peters Hasty, *How Women Must Write* (117–18).

29. Burgin describes Tsvetaeva's Pushkin as "a Pushkin who answered most of her own creative and personal needs for a true, undying, transgressive Russian poet" (95). Sandler comments on Tsvetaeva's interpretation of Pushkin as a poet who does not sexualize her or press her to be his muse, but frees her to act as a poet in her own right (*Commemorating Pushkin*, 231–32).

30. This reference to Don Juan's lips potentially links the erotic with the artistic because of their dual function: the lips could be kissing or speaking seductive words.

31. Karpiak aptly describes the poem as describing the Classical, Romantic, and modern Don Juans in its respective stanzas ("The Sequels to Pushkin" 80–81).

32. Gumilev's archaic and lofty language, such as "lobzaia" for kissing and "usta" for lips, here distances Don Juan from Russia in the 1910s, locating him in an exotic, foreign locale. In a sense this is typical of the Don Juan legend, going back to Tirso's play, which is set two centuries in the past.

33. Karpiak calls it a continuation of Pushkin's little tragedy, pointing out that Gumilev amplifies the bold, Classical Don Juan of the first quatrain of his poem in the play ("The Sequels to Pushkin" 82).

34. See Matlaw and Walker on Gumilev's fascination with Africa.

35. This essay did not appear in print until 1958, but Akhmatova read it to leading Pushkin scholars before its publication.

36. I follow the practice of other contemporary critics in keeping "gay" in the translation, even though nowadays the word is seldom used to connote cheerfulness.

37. In criticism, Akhmatova also discusses *The Stone Guest* in her 1936 essay "Benjamin Constant's *Adolphe* in Pushkin's Work" and in a 1961 essay in the journal *Questions of Literature* (*Voprosy Literatury*).

38. The line "I am ready to die" can also be attributed to Osip Mandelstam, who reportedly said it to Akhmatova in 1934.

39. Akhmatova, in notes for a revision of her *Stone Guest* essay, writes: "For Don Juan, Donna Anna is an angel and savior, but for Pushkin, she is a very coquettish, curious and fainthearted woman, and a sanctimonious hypocrite" (163).

40. In this and all other references to Akhmatova, I am referring to Judith Hemschemeyer's English translation first, followed by the Russian original.

41. This could be seen as a characterization of Don Juan, who awaits—at different points—Donna Anna and the Commander. However, it also recalls Anna's position of awaiting Don Juan's visit to her house.

42. Crone suggests that Akhmatova may have come to see the theme of retribution in Pushkin through her reading of "The Steps of the Commander" (148). As I discuss in Chapter 1, I find different motives behind the statue's destruction of Don Juan in *The Stone Guest*.

Chapter 4. Soviet and Post-Soviet Don Juans

1. Aleshin is not the first writer to cast doubt on Don Juan's traditional ultramasculine persona. During the period of "Tenoriomania" in Spanish letters in the 1920s-30s, coinciding with the reception of Freudian psychoanalysis and the rise of feminism in Spain, Miguel de Unamuno y Jugo, José Ortega y Gasset, and various other writers, critics, and medical doctors debated Don Juan's sexuality and psychology. Endocrinologist Gregorio Marañón, in "The Psychopathology of Don Juan" (1924), critiqued Don Juan's childlessness and empty, sterile sexuality, viewing him as effeminate and possibly bisexual. In the 1929 essay "Don Juan's Old Age," he reinterpreted him as homosexual. See Wright 52–83. Aleshin, of course, could not have known of this debate.

2. In the title of his play, Erofeev, interestingly, connects the Faust and Don Juan legends. However, in contrast to writers like Christian Grabbe, who evoke the Romantic view of Don Juan as a Faust-like striver for the lofty, he connects the Don Juan legend to the Witches' Sabbath of Goethe's tragedy, which takes place in a section titled "Walpurgis Night."

3. This and subsequent in-text parenthetical citations refer to Venedikt Erofeev, *Ostav'te moiu dushu v pokoe: Pochti vse*. All translations are mine and Tatiana Tulchinsky's, with occasional slight modifications from the published version.

4. The question of whether Gurevich knows that the alcohol is poisonous is never conclusively resolved. He claims not to have realized it until the inmates started to die, denying Prokhorov's accusations that he plotted it from the beginning.

5. In this sense, Gurevich fits well into the discussion of tricksters in Soviet literature by Lipovetsky, who focuses on their marginality, liminality, lack of stable character, artistic gestures, and most of all, transgression of the social order. As Lipovetsky writes, "Transgression—i.e., the breaking of boundaries and reversal of social and cultural norms—is the most important device of the trickster" (*Charms of the Cynical Reason* 34).

6. Erofeev alludes to Byron as well as Pushkin and Blok on Don Juan. In Act I, when asked by the doctor which parent he prefers, Gurevich responds: "I'd have to say my dad. When we swam across the Hellespont . . ." (183). This comment hints at Byron, who swam the Hellespont and "fathered" a Don Juan novel of his own. Following the parallel to its logical conclusion, if Gurevich's father swam the Hellespont, then he is the "son" (Don Juan) of that man.

7. These habits, of course, also characterize Erofeev himself (see "Neskol'ko monologov o Venedikte Erofeeve," especially the entries by Galina Erofeeva, Vladimir Murav'ev, and Ol'ga Sedakova). Gurevich's lack of steady employment and the fact

that his principal occupation is obviously that of a poet may also hint at Brodsky's famous trial, in which he was accused of lacking professional authorization to be a poet. Brodsky, who migrated from job to job and at one point was incarcerated in Kashchenko Psychiatric Hospital in Moscow for a month, parallels Gurevich in striking ways. Erofeev seems to liken the dissident poet in general to a Don Juan, at least in the sense of vagrancy and marginality.

8. Given postmodern art's fascination with enumerations and series (among Russian works of this time, Vladimir Sorokin's line and the endless list of names, products being sold, and topics of conversation in *The Queue* and Lev Rubinstein's repetitive, numbered card catalogues come to mind), Don Juan's serial behavior and almost obsessive need for lists may be the most specifically contemporary aspect of the legend.

9. See Epstein ("Posle karnavala") and Lipovetsky, *Russian Postmodernist Fiction*, on Erofeev's particular brand of postmodernism.

10. By using the name Natalie more often than the Russian Natalia, Erofeev may be obliquely referring to Pushkin's wife. Pushkin addressed Natalia Goncharova as "Natalie" in his letters to her before their wedding, all of which were in French (after their wedding, he wrote to her solely in Russian).

11. Elsewhere in the play, Prokhorov eulogizes the Jewish people and announces that he and Alekha are taking pro-Israeli positions, having chased the Israelis themselves out of these positions. Although this seemingly contradictory, absurd attitude resembles postmodern travesty, it is also grounded in the phenomenon of alternating praise and denigration that antisemitism often features.

12. See Konstantin Kustanovich 145–47. Erofeev's critique of Gurevich's elitism recalls Andrei Siniavsky's critique of the intelligentsia's support of Boris Yeltsin in the early 1990s. See *The Russian Intelligentsia*.

13. This character's name most likely alludes to Petr Andreevich Kleinmikhel' (1793–1869), a military officer and administrator who oversaw numerous construction projects under Nikolai I. Serezha's absurd utopian plans, which include a "House for the Love and Health of Sick Astronauts" and a "House of Love for One's Mom More Than You Can and As Much," parody the grandiose titles of many of Petr Kleinmikhel''s projects, such as "Hall of Industry" and "House of the Patriotic Institute."

14. Various critics have discussed *Moscow-Petushki* as a dialogic work. See for example Lipovetsky, *Russian Postmodernist Fiction* 66–82. One may easily argue, though, that Venichka's doubles and interlocutors are nothing more than projections of his mind and that his narrative is therefore in fact extremely solipsistic and closed off to true dialogue. In a sense, both the *poema* and *Walpurgis Night* contrast dialogic and monologic possibilities within themselves. In the play, Erofeev offers Ward 3 as a possible space for coexistence of multiple points of view but then synthesizes them into Gurevich's vision, thus destroying any sense of true interaction.

15. Erofeev was invited to Paris for treatment of his throat cancer but was denied permission by the Soviet authorities. His internal exile, or lack of motion, may therefore have contributed to the worsening of his condition and his eventual death. See Ryan-Hayes 4.

16. The original poem can be found in Prigov 263.

17. Nowhere can this be seen more vividly than in the actual function of Gurevich's poetry. His solemn promise to Prokhorov in Act II that he will destroy Boren'ka and

the rest of the staff portends revenge, presumably in part through poetic means. And Gurevich does indeed charm Natalie through his improvisations, both in Act I and later in Act III. His exchange of glances with Prokhorov at the end of Act III, implying that their whispered plans (unclear to the reader/viewer) in the previous act are progressing, sets up an expectation of a dramatic confrontation between him and Boren'ka that never takes place. Instead, Gurevich and his wardmates drink until the early morning, and he only attempts to take his "steps of the commander" toward Boren'ka when he is already blind and nearly paralyzed. The drinking that substitutes for an actual confrontation is accompanied by a feast of verbal improvisation on the part of Gurevich and his allies.

18. Rebecca Reich, however, offers a different opinion on this topic in a recent interpretation of the play. She intriguingly argues that Gurevich, who is simulating madness, loses sight of the dividing line between his feigned, theatrical madness and real insanity and therefore cannot be held responsible for his destructive actions (198). Moreover, she views Erofeev as reevaluating his own "mask of madness" in this play and thus avoiding his hero's fate: "By erecting a more resilient boundary between an insanity that is theatricalized and an insanity that is real, the implied authorial persona who emerges through *Walpurgis Night* uses his own mask to affirm his sanity" (212).

19. Erofeev's interview in *Kontinent*, in which he claims: "I love my country . . . I love everything in it," similarly indicates that he could not have flourished anywhere else ("Neskol'ko monologov" 95).

20. As Guy Houk explains, Erofeev claimed he was expelled for seditious writings, but the charge against him may have simply been laziness and delinquency. Houk argues that Erofeev's withering parody of Evgeny Evtushenko in the character Evtiushkin in *Moscow-Petushki* actually serves as an attempt to distance himself from a contemporary whom he saw as a conformist in an effort to make his stance as a dissident figure more credible than it was in reality. It may also be that Erofeev recognizes a certain inherent banality in the very idea of a sacred holy fool. As Prokhorov remarks about Alekha in Act II, "Of course you know that every Russian village has a fool . . . Without a single fool, what kind of Russian village would it be?" (Ty ved' znaesh': v kazhdom rossiiskom selenii est' pridurok . . . Kakoe zhe eto russkoe selenie, esli v nem ni odnogo pridurka?; 207). Yet the holy foolishness in this case consists of nothing more than discharging mucus at people. In this sense, as with Gurevich's poetry, Erofeev seems to acknowledge not only the destructiveness of the holy foolishness he himself partakes of, but its clichéd, banal, ubiquitous quality as well.

21. Gurevich's blindness reinforces his failure through its associations with Oedipus. Unlike in Sophocles's *Oedipus at Colonus*, though, Erofeev's prophetic figure gains no new insight along with his condition.

22. See Vyacheslav Kuritsyn 59. To a great extent, this serialism also characterizes the Don Juan legend itself: the Don keeps a famous book of his conquests, listing the women of various nationalities whom he has seduced.

23. All translations of Kazakov's play are mine.

24. At the same time, it also recalls *Don Quixote*, which appears to be another of Kazakov's intertexts.

25. This recalls other trends in late Soviet culture, such as Conceptualism in Russian art. Artists such as Erik Bulatov, Prigov, and Il'ia Kabakov sought to avoid identifying

with either official Soviet or avantgarde ideology. See Daniil Leiderman on "shimmering" ("The Strategy of Shimmering").

26. Other critics of Russian and world literature have characterized the "new sincerity" as a broader trend, equivalent in meaning to post-postmodernism. For Mikhail Epstein, it is "an experiment in resuscitating 'fallen,' dead languages with a renewed pathos of love, sentimentality and enthusiasm" (Epstein, Genis, and Vladis-Glover 146).

27. Sutcliffe and Skomp 18–22. Ulitskaya dismisses "women's prose" as an "antifemale" term, and distances herself from feminism as well.

28. Translations of *Sonechka* are by Arch Tait.

29. For Robert Viktorovich's models in real-life avantgarde painters, see Salys 453–54.

30. Sonechka's character, like her name, recalls Dostoevsky's Sonia Marmeladova, who embodies a similar spiritual purity and functions as Raskolnikov's savior, much as Sonechka, in a more secular manner, does for Robert Viktorovich.

31. This viewpoint, as Sutcliffe and Skomp point out, is a reaction against both the Soviet New Man prototype, with its division between body and soul, and its privileging of firm, virile, youthful male bodies and the perestroika-era concept of traumatized, scarred bodies found in the works of Petrushevskaya.

32. For Rimgaila Salys, "Robert's painterly study of whiteness is simultaneously an allegory for his attempts to understand femininity," and his fifty-two paintings testify to his ultimate failure to do so (459).

33. See also Christina Parnell, who connects whiteness to the Symbolist conception of the coming of the Divine Sophia (316).

34. Translations of *The Funeral Party* are by Cathy Porter.

35. To some extent, Alik's undefined religious status recalls that of Ulitskaya, an ethnic Jew who converted to Orthodoxy and considers herself both Christian and Jewish. It also anticipates the linking of Judaism and Christianity in the protagonist of *Daniel Stein, Interpreter* (2006), a Polish Jew who converts to Catholicism and becomes a monk in Israel.

36. Translations of *Sincerely Yours, Shurik* are mine.

37. As Natalia Olshanskaya puts it: "His mother and grandmother have made sure that he would grow up kind and friendly, and it is with a mixture of friendliness, detachment and lust that he responds to numerous sexual opportunities and demands from various women around him. He is at their service and at their mercy, without ever being able to follow his own desires or his personal feelings, if he has any" (146).

38. Tania's infatuation with Jasia appears to be homoerotic, but also involves a kind of identification (she imitates Jasia's gait). She experiences jealousy when she discovers that Robert and Jasia are having an affair, but only because she was not in on the secret.

Conclusion

1. Only the unity of time, by which all action should take place within one day, is violated. Don Juan, in hiding after his duel with Don Carlos, watches Donna Anna for several days before speaking to her.

2. This may reflect a certain ambivalence on the part of Tirso himself, a monk writing plays and enjoying a worldly life despite his sacred vocation.

3. *Souls in Purgatory*, on the other hand, invokes the Don Juan legend but approaches it very differently from the way Pushkin did: Mérimée focuses on Don Juan de Maraña (based on a historical character) rather than on Don Juan Tenorio, and he announces this distinction from the beginning. In contrast to Don Juan's possible rebirth in love in Pushkin's play, Mérimée's Don Juan is moved by a vision of his own funeral procession to confess his sins and become a monk.

4. Ukrainka wrote that she was proud to have written the first Ukrainian Don Juan text and also the first Don Juan text by a woman: "finally our literature has a Don Juan of its own, not translated, but original in that it was written by a woman" (qtd. in Mihaychuk 92–93). Karpiak notes, however, that Armand Singer's magisterial compendium of Don Juan texts does include one preceding work by a female writer, Anna Quidling Akerhielm's four-act play *Don Juan Tenorio* (Sweden, 1909), which Ukrainka was almost certainly unaware of.

There is some disagreement on the extent of Pushkin's influence on Ukrainka. Soviet critics tended to emphasize the importance of *The Stone Guest*, noting that Ukrainka had it on hand while writing *The Stone Host*; other critics have pointed to different influences, and more importantly, to Ukrainka's thoroughly original revision of key parts of the legend, such as her unique portrait of the hero, her strengthening of the figure of Donna Anna, and her addition of another female character, Dolores, who embodies faith, devotion, and Don Juan's victimization of women. Mihaychuk emphasizes Ukrainka's debt to Molière; Oleksandr Pronkevich, by contrast, views the play as a rewriting of Tirso's play, with Don Juan as the *burlador* and Anna as a *burladora*, a female version of the trickster who is Don Juan's equal. I fully acknowledge both the importance of other, non-Pushkinian sources and her originality—indeed, the use of other Don Juan sources, unavoidable in any case, does not impinge on a given text's originality. I maintain, however, that Pushkin's interest in gender relations on the one hand attracted Ukrainka's attention and on the other offered several opportunities for expansion, development, and even argumentation with this particular source.

5. Indeed, *The Stone Host*, despite its Spanish setting, can easily be (and has been) interpreted in terms of Ukrainka's struggle—along with many other writers of her time—to fight for the propagation and development of Ukrainian culture despite the various Tsarist prohibitions of Ukrainian cultural expression. Manning, in fact, interprets Ukrainka's contrast of Madrid, with its rigidity and disregard for the individual, and Seville, a more cultured, humane setting, as an implicit parallel of the Russian regime's crushing of Ukrainian civilization, referring to *The Stone Host* as part of "a long series of works by Lesya Ukrainka which under a literary form depict the Ukrainian opposition to the Russian Empire and set forth an ideal of human dignity which is consonant with that of Western Europe and not with that of the Great Russians" (47). Moreover, it represents the spirit of rebellion that pervades her oeuvre and likely made the Don Juan theme so relevant for her. "The Promethean spirit, the myth of titanic struggle and rebellion which pervades her work at every stage," writes Karpiak, "bears a remarkable kinship to the theme of courage, freedom, and defiance of authority so inalienable from the classical conception of Don Juan" (Karpiak, "Lesia Ukrainka" 250).

6. Donna Anna introduces Don Juan to her guests in the final scene as "Señor de Maraña, Marquis de Tenorio" (135).

7. Translations of *The Stone Host* are by Vera Rich (Bida).

8. See, for example, Karpiak, who notes that Ukrainka creates a parallel between Lady Macbeth, who directs Macbeth's actions, and Donna Anna, who does not kill her husband herself but serves as Don Juan's accomplice (Karpiak, "Lesia Ukrainka" 258). If anything, though, Ukrainka's Donna Anna is even more strong-willed and ruthless than her Shakespearean model. Lady Macbeth, like her husband, experiences guilt over her role in his murder of Duncan. Sleepwalking after a nightmare about the murder, she cries, "Out damned spot," and "All the perfumes of Arabia will not sweeten this little hand." Donna Anna, by contrast, experiences no such guilt.

Works Cited

Akhmatova, A. A. *O Pushkine. Stat'i i zametki.* Leningrad: Sovetskii pisatel', 1977.
Akhmatova, Anna. *The Complete Poems of Anna Akhmatova.* Translated by Judith Hescheymeyer. Boston: Zephyr Press, 2014.
Akhmatova, Anna. *Sobranie sochinenii v 6 tomakh.* Vol. 3. Moscow: Ellis Lak, 1998.
Alexandrov, Vladimir. *Limits to Interpretation: The Meanings of "Anna Karenina."* Madison: University of Wisconsin Press, 2004.
Anderson, Nancy K. "The Weight of the Past: The Stone Guest." In *The Little Tragedies*, 156–81. New Haven, CT: Yale University Press, 2000.
Austen, John. *The Story of Don Juan: A Study of the Legend and the Hero.* London: Martin Secker, 1939.
Austin, J. L. *How to Do Things with Words.* 2nd. ed. Cambridge: Harvard University Press, 1975.
Bagno, V. E. *Rossiia i Espaniia: obshchaia granitsa.* St. Petersburg: Nauka, 2006.
Baker, Felicity. "The Figures of Hell in the Don Giovanni Libretto." In *Words about Mozart: Essays in Honour of Stanley Sadie.* Edited by Dorothea Link with Judith Nagley, 77–106. Woodbridge: Boydell Press, 2005.
Bal'mont, K. D. "Don-Zhuan." In *Don Zhuan Russkii*, 497–500. Moscow: Agraf, 2000.
Bal'mont, K. D. "Tip Don-Zhuana v mirovoi literature." In *Don Zhuan Russkii*, 512–45. Moscow: Agraf, 2000.
Bayliss, Robert. "Serving Don Juan: Decorum in Tirso de Molina and Molière." *Comparative Drama* 40.2 (Summer 2006): 191–215.
Belinskii, V. G. *Sobranie sochinenii v trekh tomakh.* Vol. 3. Moscow: Gosudarstvennoe izdatel'stvo khudozhestvennoi literatury, 1948.
Bethea, David. *The Superstitious Muse: Thinking Russian Literature Mythopoetically.* Boston: Academic Studies Press, 2009.
Bévotte, Georges Gendarme de. *La Légende de Don Juan: Son Évolution dans la Littérature du Romantisme a l'Époque contemporaine.* 2 vols. Paris: Librairie Hachette, 1929.
Bida, Constantine. *Lesya Ukrainka: Life and Work. Selected Works.* Translated by Vera Rich. Toronto: University of Toronto Press, 1968.

Blagoi, Dmitrii. *Sotsiologiia tvorchestva Pushkina: Etiudy*. Moscow: Federatsiia, 1929.
Blagoi, Dmitrii. *Tvorcheskii put' Pushkina*. Moscow: Sovetskii pisatel', 1967.
Blok, Aleksandr. *Izbrannye proizvedeniia*. Leningrad: Lenizdat, 1970.
Blok, Aleksandr. *Zapisnye knizhki, 1901–1920*. Moscow: Khudozhestvennaia literatura, 1965.
Buckler, Julie. *The Literary Lorgnette: Attending Opera in Imperial Russia*. Stanford, CA: Stanford University Press, 2000.
Burgin, Diana. "Tsvetaeva's Three Pushkins," In *Two Hundred Years of Pushkin*, vol. 1, 91–103. Edited by Joe Andrew and Robert Reid. Amsterdam: Rodopi, 2003.
Canfield, J. Douglas. "The Classical Treatment of Don Juan in Tirso, Molière, and Mozart: What Cultural Work Does It Perform?" *Comparative Drama* 31.1 (Spring 1997): 42–64.
Chaikovskii, P. I. [Petr Tchaikovsky] *Muzykal'no-kriticheskie stat'i*, edited by V. V. Iakovlev. Moscow: Gosudastvennoe muzykal'noe izdatel'stvo, 1953.
Chekhov, Anton. "The Lady with the Little Dog." *About Love and Other Stories*. Translated by Rosamund Bartlett. New York: Oxford University Press, 2004, 167–83.
Chekhov, Anton. *Anton Chekhov's Selected Stories*. Edited by Cathy Popkin. New York: W. W. Norton, 2014.
Chekhov, Anton. *The Early Plays*. Translated by Carol Rocamora. Lyme, NH: Smith and Kraus, 1999.
Chukovsky, Korney. *Alexander Blok as Man and Poet*. Translated by Diana Lewis Burgin and Katherine Tiernan O'Connor. Ann Arbor: Ardis, 1982.
Cixous, Hélène, and Catherine Clément. *The Newly Born Woman*. Translated by Betsy Wing. Minneapolis: University of Minnesota Press, 1986.
Clayton, J. Douglas. "*Povesti Belkina* and the Commedia Dell'Arte: Callot, Hoffmann, and Pushkin." *Russian Literature* 40 (1996): 277–92.
Conlon, Raymond. "The *Burlador* and the *Burlados*: A Sinister Connection." *Bulletin of the Comediantes* 42.1 (Summer 1990): 5–22.
Connell, R. W. *Masculinities*. 2nd ed. Berkeley: University of California Press, 2005.
Connor, Catherine. "Don Juan: Cultural Trickster in the *Burlador* Text." In *New Historicism and the Comedia: Poetics, Politics, and Praxis*, 83–109. Edited by José A. Madrigal. Boulder, CO: Society of Spanish and Spanish-American Studies, 1997.
Costlow, Jane T. "'Oh-là-là' and 'No-no-no': Odintsova as Woman Alone in *Fathers and Children*." In *A Plot of Her Own: The Female Protagonist in Russian Literature*, 21–32. Edited by Sona Hoisington. Evanston: Northwestern University Press, 1995.
Crone, Anna Lisa. "Blok as Don Juan in Axmatova's "Poèma bez geroja." *Russian Language Journal* 35.121/122 (Spring–Fall 1981): 145–62.
Dalton, Margaret. *A. K. Tolstoy*. New York: Twayne Publishers, 1972.
Dargomyzhskii, A. S. [Alexander Dargomyzhsky] *Avtobiografiia. Pis'ma. Vospominaniia sovremennikov*. St. Petersburg: Gosudarstvennaia akademicheskaia filarmonia, 1922.
Darskii, Dmitrii [Dmitry Darsky]. *Malen'kie tragedii Pushkina*. Moscow: Nauka, 1915.
Davies, Ann. "Don Juan and Foucauldian Sexual Discourse: Changing Attitudes to Female Sexuality." *European Studies* 17: 1 (2001): 159–70.
Davydov, Sergei. "'Strange and Savage Joy': The Erotic as a Unifying Element in *The Little Tragedies*." In *Alexander Pushkin's Little Tragedies: The Poetics of Brevity*, 89–105. Edited by Svetlana Evdokimova. Madison: University of Wisconsin Press, 2003.

Debreczeny, Paul. *Social Functions of Literature: Alexander Pushkin and Russian Culture*. Stanford: Stanford University Press, 1997.
De Rougemont, Denis. *Love in the Western World*. Princeton: Princeton University Press, 1983.
De Sherbinin, Julie. "The Dismantling of Hierarchy and the Defense of Social Class in 'Anna Karenina.'" *The Russian Review* 70: 4 (October 2011): 646–62.
De Staël, Germaine. *Delphine*. Translated by Avriel H. Goldberger. DeKalb: Northern Illinois University Press, 1995.
Dinega, Alyssa. *A Russian Psyche: The Poetic Mind of Marina Tsvetaeva*. Madison: University of Wisconsin Press, 2001.
Dmitrienko, S. F. "O problematike stikhotvoreniia A. A. Bloka 'Shagi komandora.'" In *Aleksandr Blok i mirovaia kul'tura: Materialy nauchnoi konferentsii 14–17 marta 2000 goda*, 48–62. Velikii Novgorod: Novgorodskii gosudarstvennyi universitet, 2000.
Dostoevskii, Fedor [Fyodor Dostoevsky]. *Polnoe sobranie sochinenii* Vol. 30, part 1. Leningrad: Izdatel'stvo "Nauka," 1988.
Dostoevsky, Fyodor. *A Writer's Diary*. Translated by Kenneth Lantz. Evanston: Northwestern University Press, 1993.
Driver, Sam. "Nikolaj Gumilev's Early Dramatic Works." *Slavic and East European Journal* 13.3 (Autumn 1969): 326–47.
Ehre, Milton. *Oblomov and His Creator: The Life and Art of Ivan Goncharov*. Princeton: Princeton University Press, 1973.
Eikhenbaum, Boris. *Tolstoi in the Seventies*. Translated by Albert Kaspin. Ann Arbor, MI: Ardis, 1982.
Emerson, Caryl. "Chekhov and the Annas." In *Life and Text: Essays in Honour of Geir Kjetsaa on the Occasion of his 60th Birthday*, 121–32. Edited by Erik Egeberg, Audun J. Morch, and Ole Michael Selberg. Oslo: Meddelelser, University of Oslo, 1997.
Emerson, Caryl. "Little Tragedies, Little Operas." In *Alexander Pushkin's Little Tragedies: The Poetics of Brevity*, 265–89. Edited by Svetlana Evdokimova. Madison: University of Wisconsin Press, 2004.
Epstein, Mikhail. "Posle karnavala, ili vechnyi Venichka." In *Ostav'te moiu dushu v pokoe (pochti vse)*, 3–30. Moscow: Kh. G. S., 1995.
Epstein, Mikhail N. *After the Future: The Paradoxes of Postmodernism and Contemporary Russian Culture*. Translated by Anesa Miller-Pogacar. Amherst: University of Massachusetts Press, 1995.
Epstein, Mikhail N., Alexander A. Genis, and Slobodanka M. Vladiv-Glover. *Russian Postmodernism: New Perspectives on Russian Culture*. New York: Berghahn Books, 1999.
Erofeev, Venedikt. *Ostav'te moiu dushu v pokoe (pochti vse)*. Moscow: Kh. G. S., 1995.
Erofeev, Venedikt. "Walpurgis Night, or 'The Steps of the Commander.'" Translated by Alexander Burry and Tatiana Tulchinsky. *Toronto Slavic Quarterly* 9 (Summer 2004).
Evdokimova, Svetlana. "The Anatomy of the Modern Self in The Little Tragedies." In *Alexander Pushkin's Little Tragedies: The Poetics of Brevity*, 106–46. Edited by Svetlana Evdokimova. Madison: University of Wisconsin Press, 2003.
Everist, Mark. "Enshrining Mozart: *Don Giovanni* and the Viardot Circle." *Nineteenth-Century Music* 25 (2001): 165–89.

Fainberg, Margarita. "'Shagi komandora' v sud'be Aleksandra Bloka." *Zvezda* 11 (2004): 208–17.
Feiler, Lily. *Marina Tsvetaeva: The Double Beat of Heaven and Hell.* Durham: Duke University Press, 1994.
Felman, Shoshana. *The Scandal of the Speaking Body: Don Juan with J. L. Austin, or Seduction in Two Languages.* Stanford, CA: Stanford University Press, 2002.
Finke, Michael C. *Seeing Chekhov: Life and Art.* Ithaca: Cornell University Press, 2005.
Firestone, Shulamith. *The Dialectic of Sex: The Case for Feminist Revolution.* New York: Morrow, 1970.
Forman, Edward. "Don Juan before Da Ponte." In *W. A. Mozart: Don Giovanni* (Cambridge Opera Handbooks), 27–44. Edited by Julian Rushton. Cambridge: Cambridge University Press, 1981.
Freud, Sigmund. *Totem and Taboo.* New York: W. W. Norton, 1950.
Freud, Sigmund. "The Uncanny." In *Psychological Writings and Letters*, 120–53. New York: Continuum, 1995.
Freud, Sigmund. "A Very Special Type of Choice of Object Made by Men." In *The Freud Reader*, 387–94. Edited by Peter Gay. New York: W. W. Norton, 1995.
Frolova, Nina et al, "Neskol'ko monologov o Venedikte Erofeeve." *Teatr* 9 (1991): 74–116.
Gasparov, Boris. "Don Juan in Nicholas's Russia (Pushkin's *The Stone Guest*)." In *The Don Giovanni Moment: Essays on the Legacy of an Opera*, 47–60. Edited by Lydia Goehr and Daniel Herwitz. New York: Columbia University Press, 2006.
Girard, René. *Deceit, Desire, and the Novel: Self and Other in Literary Structure.* Translated by Yvonne Freccero. Baltimore: Johns Hopkins University Press, 1965.
Göbler, Frank. *Don Juan in der russichen Literatur.* Berlin: Frank & Timme, 2020.
Gogol', N. V. [Nikolai Gogol]. *Polnoe sobranie sochinenii*, Vol. 8. Moscow, 1952.
Golstein, Vladimir. "Anna Karenina's Peter Pan Syndrome." In *Leo Tolstoy*, 197–217. Edited by Harold Bloom. Philadelphia, PA: Chelsea House, 2003.
Goncharov, I. A. *Literaturno-kriticheskie stat'i i pis'ma.* Leningrad: Khudozhestvennaia literatura, 1938.
Goncharov, I. A. *Sobranie sochinenii*, Vol. 5. Moscow: Gosudarstvennoe izdatel'stvo khudozhestvennoi literatury, 1959.
Goncharov, Ivan. *The Precipice.* Translated by Laury Magnus and Boris Jakim. Ann Arbor: Ardis, 1994.
Gorchakov, G. N. "Po povodu stikhotvoreniia A. Bloka 'Shagi komandora.'" *Russian Literature* 39 (1996): 329–58.
Gorodetskii, B. P.; [Boris Gorodetsky]. *Dramaturgiia Pushkina.* Moscow: Izdatel'stvo Akademii Nauk SSSR, 1953.
Goscilo, Helena. "Feet Pushkin Scanned, or Seeming Idée Fixe as Aesthetic Credo." *The Slavic and East European Journal* 32.4 (Winter 1988): 562–73.
Goscilo, Helena. "Foreword." Sutcliffe and Skomp. xi–xxiii.
Goscilo, Helena. "Tolstoy, Laclos, and the Libertine." *The Modern Language Review* 81.2 (April 1986): 398–414.
Gozenpud, Avram. *Russkii opernyi teatr XIX veka (1857–1872).* Leningrad: Muzyka, 1971.

Grabbe, Christian. "Don Juan and Faust: A Tragedy in Four Acts." Translated by Maurice Edwards. In *The Theatre of Don Juan: A Collection of Plays and Views, 1630–1963*, 331–97. Edited by Oscar Mandel. Lincoln: University of Nebraska Press, 1963.
Grigoryan, Bella. "The Poet Turned Journalist." *Pushkin Review* 18/19 (2015–16): 61–84.
Groys, Boris. *The Total Art of Stalinism: Avant-Garde, Aesthetic Dictatorship, and Beyond*. Translated by Charles Rougle. Princeton: Princeton University Press, 1992.
Guber, P. K. *Don-Zhuanskii spisok Pushkina: Glavy iz biografii s 9-iu portretami*. St. Petersburg: Izdatel'stvo "Petrograd," 1923.
Gumilev, N. S. "Don Zhuan." In *Don Zhuan Russkii*, 501. Moscow: Agraf, 2000.
Gumilev, N. S. *Don Zhuan v Egipte: Odnoaktovaia p'esa v stikhakh*. In *Don Zhuan Russkii*, 268–78. Moscow: Agraf, 2000.
Gusev, N. N., and A. B. Gol'denveizer. *Lev Tolstoi i Muzyka. Vospominaniia*. Moscow: Gos. muz. izd. , 1953.
Hasty, Olga Peters. *How Women Must Write: Inventing the Russian Woman Poet*. Evanston: Northwestern University Press, 2019.
Hasty, Olga Peters. *Pushkin's Tatiana*. Madison: University of Wisconsin Press, 1999.
Hasty, Olga Peters. *Tsvetaeva's Orphic Journeys in the Worlds of the Word*. Evanston: Northwestern University Press, 1996.
Hellebust, Rolf. "The Real St. Petersburg." *The Russian Review* 62 (October 2003): 495–507.
Herman, David. "Don Juan and Don Alejandro: The Seductions of Art in Pushkin's *Stone Guest*." *Comparative Literature* 51.1 (Winter 1999): 3–23.
Hoffmann, E. T. A. *Tales of Hoffmann*. Edited by Christopher Lazare. New York: Grove, 1946.
Hoogenboom, Hilde. "Sentimental Novels and Pushkin: European Literary Markets and Russian Readers." *Slavic Review* 74.3 (Fall 2015): 553–74.
Houk, Guy. "Erofeev and Evtushenko." In *Venedikt Erofeev's "Moscow-Petushki": Critical Perspectives*, 179–95. Edited by Karen Ryan-Hayes. New York: Peter Lang, 1997.
Hutcheon, Linda. *A Poetics of Postmodernism: History, Theory, Fiction*. New York: Routledge, 1988.
Jackson, Robert Louis. "On the Ambivalent Beginning of Anna Karenina." In *Semantic Analysis of Literary Texts*, 345–52. Edited by Eric de Haard, Thomas Langerak, Willem G. Weststeijn. Amsterdam: Elsevier, 1990.
Jakobson, Roman. *Pushkin and His Sculptural Myth*. Translated by John Burbank. The Hague: Mouton, 1975.
Jung, Carl. *The Archetypes and the Collective Unconscious*. Translated by R. F. C. Hill. New York: Pantheon Books, 1959.
Kanevskaya, Marina. "Poet-Prophet-Wanderer: The Image of Pushkin in Dostoevsky's Pushkin Speech." In *Collected Essays in Honor of the Bicentennial of Alexander Pushkin's Birth*, 53–74. Edited by Juras T. Ryfa. Lewiston: Edwin Mellen Press, 2000.
Karlinsky, Simon. *Marina Cvetaeva: Her Life and Art*. Berkeley: University of California Press, 1966.
Karpiak, Robert. "The Crisis of Idealism: E. T. A. Hoffmann and the Russian Tradition of Don Juan." In *Crisis and Commitment: Studies in German and Russian Literature in*

Honour of J. W. Dyck, 127–39. Edited by John Whiton and Harry Loewen. Waterloo: University of Waterloo Press, 1983.

Karpiak, Robert. "Don Juan in Slavic Drama." Ph. D. diss., University of Ottawa, 1977.

Karpiak, Robert. "Don Juan 'in the Russian Manner': Chekhov's *Platonov* as Poetic Myth." In *Cultural Link: Kanada-Deutschland*, 239–51. Edited by Beata Henn-Memmesheimer and David G. John. Ingbert, Germany: Röhrig Universitätsverlag, 2003.

Karpiak, Robert. "Lesia Ukrainka's 'The Stone Host' and 'the Don Juan Myth.'" *Anniversary Collection of the Ukrainian Free Academy of Sciences in Canada* (1976): 249–61.

Karpiak, Robert. "The Sequels to Pushkin's *Kamennyi Gost'*: Russian Don Juan Versions by Nikolai Gumilev and Vladimir Korvin-Piotrovskii." In *Studies in Honour of Louis Shein*, 79–92. Edited by S. D. Cioran, W. Smyrniw, G. Thomas. Hamilton, ON: McMaster University, 1983.

Kataev, Vladimir. *Literaturnye sviazi Chekhova*. Moscow: Izdatel'stvo moskovskogo universiteta, 1989.

Kazakov, Vladimir. *Izbrannye sochineniia*, Vol. 2. Moscow: Gileia, 1995.

Kazakov, Vladimir. *Sluchainyi voin: Stikhotvoreniia 1961–1976: Poemy, dramy, ocherk "Zudesnik."* Munich: Verlag Otto Sagner, 1978.

Kierkegaard, Søren. *Either/Or: A Fragment of Life*. Translated by David F. Swenson and Lillian Marvin Swenson. Princeton: Princeton University Press, 1949.

Kisin, B. "Don-Zhuan." *Literaturnaia entsiklopediia*, Vol. 3. Izdatel'stvo kommunisticheskoi akademii, 1930. 349–64.

Kliger, Ilya. "Resurgent Forms in Ivan Goncharov and Alexander Veselovsky: Toward a Historical Poetics of Tragic Realism." *Russian Review* 71 (October 2012): 655–72.

Klimova, Svetlana. "Byron, Pushkin and Russian *Don Juans*." In *Aspects of Byron's "Don Juan,"* 336–46. Edited by Peter Cochran. Newcastle upon Tyne: Cambridge Scholars, 2013.

Krasnoshchekova, E. A. *Goncharov: Mir tvorchestva*. St. Petersburg: Izdatel'stvo "Pushkinskogo fonda," 2012.

Krasnoshchekova, E. A. "Oblomovets, udarivshiisia v nigilizm," *I. A. Goncharov. Materialy Mezhdunarodnoi nauchnoi konferentsii, posviashchennoi 195-letiiu so dnia rozhdeniia I. A. Goncharova: Sbornik statei russkikh i zarubezhnykh avtorov*. Edited by A. V. Lobkareva, I. V. Smirnova, E. B. Klevogina. Ulyanovsk: Nika-Dizain, 2008.

Kropf, David Glenn. *Authorship as Alchemy: Subversive Writing in Pushkin, Scott, Hoffmann*. Stanford: Stanford University Press, 1994.

Kuritsyn, Vyacheslav. "Postmodernism: The New Primitive Culture." In *Re-Entering the Sign: Articulating New Russian Culture*. Edited by Ellen E. Berry and Anesa Miller-Pogacar. Ann Arbor: Ardis, 1995.

Kustanovich, Konstantin. "Venichka Erofeev's Grief and Solitude: Existential Motifs in the *Poema*." In *Venedikt Erofeev's 'Moscow-Petushki': Critical Perspectives*, 123–51. Edited by Karen Ryan-Hayes. New York: Peter Lang, 1997.

Kuzmic, Tatiana. "The Mind, the Body, and the Love Triangle in *Anna Karenina*. *Tolstoy Studies Journal* 19 (2007): 1–14.

Labrecque, Nathalie. "La Relation: Don Juan—Anna, Chez Pouchkine et Blok." *Études Slaves et Est-Européennes* 19 (1974): 86–98.

Lacan, Jacques. *Anxiety: The Seminar of Jacques Lacan, Book X*. Translated by A. R. Price. Maiden, MA: Polity Press, 2016.
Lacan, Jacques. *Écrits: A Selection*. Translated by Alan Sheridan. New York: W. W. Norton, 1977.
Lachmann, Renate. *Memory and Literature: Intertextuality in Russian Modernism*. Minneapolis: University of Minnesota Press, 1997.
Laclos, Pierre Choderlos de. *Dangerous Liaisons*. Translated by Helen Constantine. London: Penguin, 2007.
Leatherbarrow, W. J. "Pushkin and the Early Dostoyevsky." *Modern Language Review* 74.2 (April 1979): 368–85.
Leiderman, Daniil. "The Strategy of Shimmering in Moscow Conceptualism." *Russian Literature* 96–98 (2018): 51–76.
Leiderman, N. L., and M. N. Lipovetskii. *Sovremennaia russkaia literatura, 1950–1990-e gody*. 2 vols. Moscow: Akademiia, 2003.
Levitt, Marcus C. *Russian Literary Politics and the Pushkin Celebration of 1880*. Ithaca, NY: Cornell University Press, 1989.
Lipovetsky, Mark. *Charms of the Cynical Reason: The Trickster's Transformation in Soviet and Post-Soviet Culture*. Brighton, MA: Academic Studies Press, 2011.
Lipovetsky, Mark. *Russian Postmodernist Fiction: Dialogue with Chaos*. New York: Routledge, 1999.
Livshin, Olga. "Two Kinds of Non-Monogamy: Lyudmila Ulitskaya on the Sensual and Spiritual Love with Multiple Partners." Unpublished manuscript.
Llewellyn Smith, Virginia. *Anton Chekhov and the Lady with the Dog*. London: Oxford University Press, 1973.
Lotman, Iu. M. *Pushkin: Biografiia pisatelia. Stat'i i zametki 1960–1990. "Evgenii Onegin": Komentarii*. St. Petersburg: Iskusstvo-SPB, 1995.
Lotman, Iu. M. "The Decembrist in Everyday Life." Translated by C. R. Pike. In *The Semiotics of Russian Culture*. Jurij Lotman and Boris A. Uspensky, 71–123. Edited by Ann Shukman. Ann Arbor: Michigan Slavic Contributions, no. 11: 1984.
Lundelius, Ruth. "Tirso's View of Women in *El Burlador de Sevilla*." *Bulletin of the Comediantes* 27.1 (Spring 1975), 5–14.
MacKay, Dorothy Epplen. *The Double Invitation in the Legend of Don Juan*. Stanford: Stanford University Press, 1943.
MacKinnon, Catharine. "Feminism, Marxism, Method, and the State: An Agenda for Theory." *Signs: A Journal of Women in Culture and Society* 7.3 (Spring 1982): 515–44.
Makin, Michael. *Marina Tsvetaeva: Poetics of Appropriation*. New York: Oxford University Press, 1993.
Mandel, Oscar, ed. *The Theatre of Don Juan: A Collection of Plays and Views, 1630–1963*. Lincoln: University of Nebraska Press, 1963.
Mandelker, Amy. *Framing "Anna Karenina": Tolstoy, the Woman Question, and the Victorian Novel*. Columbus, OH: The Ohio State University Press, 1993.
Mandrell, James. *Don Juan and the Point of Honor: Seduction, Patriarchal Society, and Literary Tradition*. University Park: The University of Pennsylvania Press, 1992.
Manning, Clarence Augustus. "Lesya Ukrainka and Don Juan." *Modern Language Quarterly: A Journal of Literary History* 16 (1955): 42–48.

Manning, Clarence Augustus. "Russian Versions of Don Juan." *PMLA* 38.3 (Sept. 1923): 479–93.
Masing-Delic, Irene. "Black Blood, White Roses: Apocalypse and Redemption in Blok's Later Poetry." In *Shapes of Apocalypse: Arts and Philosophy in Slavic Thought*, 134–52. Edited by Andrea Oppo. Brighton, MA: Academic Studies Press, 2013.
Masing-Delic, Irene. "A Change in Gender Roles: The Pygmalion Myth in Jane Austen's *Emma* and Ivan Goncharov's *Oblomov*." In *Exotic Moscow under Western Eyes: Essays on Culture, Civilization and Barbarism*, 19–41. Boston: Academic Studies Press, 2009.
Matich, Olga. *Erotic Utopia: The Decadent Imagination in Russia's Fin-de-Siècle*. Madison: University of Wisconsin Press, 2005.
Matlaw, Ralph. "Gumilev, Rimbaud, and Africa: Acmeism and the Exotic." In *Proceedings of the 6th Congress of the International Comparative Literature Association*, edited by Michel Cadot, 653–59. Stuttgart: Kunst und Wisse, E. Bieber, 1975.
Messerschmidt, James. *Hegemonic Masculinity: Formulation, Reformulation, and Amplification*. Lanham: Rowman & Littlefield, 2018.
Michelet, Jules. *Love*. N.p. : Andesite Press, 2017.
Mihaychuk, George. "Molière's *Don Juan* and Ukrainka's *The Stone Master*: Freedom, Authenticity and the Other." In *Text and Presentation*, edited by Graley Herren, 92–109. Jefferson, NC: McFarland & Company Publishing, 2017.
Millett, Kate. *Sexual Politics*. Garden City, New York: Doubleday, 1970.
Molière. *Don Juan and Other Plays*. Oxford: Oxford University Press, 2008.
Mochulsky, Konstantin. *Aleksandr Blok*. Translated by Doris V. Johnson. Detroit: Wayne State University Press, 1983.
Morson, Gary Saul. *"Anna Karenina" in Our Time: Seeing More Wisely*. New Haven, CT: Yale University Press, 2007.
Mozart, Wolfgang Amadeus. *Don Giovanni* (*Opera guide 18*). Translated by Norman Platt and Laura Sarti. London: John Calder, 1983.
Müller, Bertram. "Zagadochnyi mir Vladimira Kazakova." *Sluchainyi voin: Stikhotvoreniia 1961–1976. Poemy, dramy, ocherk "Zudesnik."* Munich: Verlag Otto Sagner, 1978. 5–13.
Nemirovsky, Igor.' *Pushkin—Liberten i Prorok*. Moscow: Novoe literaturnoe obozrenie, 2018.
Olshanskaya, Natalia. "From a Faltering Bystander to a Spiritual Leader: Rethinking the Role of Translators in Russia." In *Transfiction: Research into the Realities of Translation Fiction*, edited by Klaus Kaindl and Karlheinz Spitzl, 141–55. Amsterdam: John Benjamins Publishing Company, 2014.
O'Neil, Catherine. *With Shakespeare's Eyes: Pushkin's Creative Appropriation of Shakespeare*. Newark: University of Delaware Press, 2003.
Otsup, Nikolai. "Nikolai Stepanovich Gumilev." *Nikolai Gumilev v vospominaniiakh sovremennikov*, 182–99. Moscow: Vsia Moskva, 1990.
Ovid. *The Art of Love*. Translated by Rolfe Humphries. Bloomington: Indiana University Press, 1957.
Paperno, Irina. *Chernyshevsky and the Age of Realism: A Study in the Semiotics of Behavior*. Stanford: Stanford University Press, 1988.
Paperno, Irina, and Joan Delaney Grossman, eds. *Creating Life: The Aesthetic Utopia of Russian Modernism*. Stanford: Stanford University Press, 1994.

Parin, A. V., ed. *Don Zhuan russkii*. Moscow: Agraf, 2000.
Parnell, Christina. "Hiding and Using Sexuality. The Artist's Controversial Subject in Modern Russian Women's Literature." In *Gender and Sexuality in Russian Civilisation*, edited by Peter Barta, 311–24. London: Routledge, 2001.
Pendzik, Susana. "Female Presence in Tirso's *El Burlador de Sevilla*." *Bulletin of the Comediantes* 47.2 (1995): 165–81.
Peschio, Joe. *The Poetics of Impudence and Intimacy in the Age of Pushkin*. Madison: University of Wisconsin Press, 2012.
Petrushevskaya, Ludmilla. *Immortal Love: Stories*. Translated by Sally Laird. New York: Pantheon Books, 1995.
Porter, Roy. "Libertinism and Promiscuity." In *Don Giovanni: Myths of Seduction and Betrayal*, 1–19. Edited by Jonathan Miller. New York: Schocken, 1990.
Postnov, O. G. *Estetika I. A. Goncharova*. Novosibirsk: Nauka, 1997.
Presto, Jenifer. *Beyond the Flesh: Alexander Blok, Zinaida Gippius, and the Symbolist Sublimation of Sex*. Madison: University of Wisconsin Press, 2008.
Prigov, D. A. *Sovetskie teksty. 1979–84*. St. Petersburg: Izdatel'stvo Ivana Limbakha, 1997.
Pronkevich, Oleksandr. "*The Stone Host*, Ukrainka's 'Spanish' Play." *Kyiv-Mohyla Humanities Journal* 8 (2021): 16–32.
Pushkin, A. S. *Polnoe sobranie sochinenii*. Vol. 7: Dramaticheskie proizvedeniia. Akademiia Nauk SSSR, 1948.
Pushkin, Alexander. *The Letters of Alexander Pushkin*. Translated by J. Thomas Shaw. Madison: University of Wisconsin Press, 1967.
Pushkin, Alexander. *The Little Tragedies*. Translated by Nancy K. Anderson. New Haven, CT: Yale University Press, 2000.
Pyman, Avril. *The Life of Alexander Blok*. Vol. 2. Oxford: Oxford University Press, 1979–80.
Rank, Otto. *The Don Juan Legend*. Translated by David G. Winter. Princeton: Princeton University Press, 1975.
Rassadin, Stanislav. *Dramaturg Pushkin. Poetika. Idei. Evoliutsiia*. Moscow: Iskusstvo, 1977.
Rayfield, Donald. *Anton Chekhov: A Life*. Evanston: Northwestern University Press, 1997.
Reich, Rebecca. *State of Madness: Psychiatry, Literature, and Dissent after Stalin*. Ithaca: Cornell University Press, 2018.
Revutsky, Valerian. "A New View of Don Juan: Samuel Alyoshin's Comedy 'At That Time in Seville.'" *The Slavonic and East European Review* 44 (1966): 88–97.
Robertson, Brian. *Lacanian Antiphilosophy and the Problem of Anxiety: An Uncanny Little Object*. New York: Palgrave Macmillan, 2015.
Rosslyn, Wendy. "Don Juan Feminised." In *Symbolism and After: Essays on Russian Poetry in Honour of Georgette Donchin*, 102–21. London: Bristol Classical, 1992.
Rozumnyj, Jaroslav. "Conflicting Ideals in Lesia Ukrainka's *Stone Host*." *Canadian Slavonic Papers* 15.3 (Autumn 1973): 382–89.
Ruch'evskaia, Ekaterina. *Pushkin v russkoi opere: Kamennyi gost' Dargomyzhskogo, Zolotoi petushok Rimskogo-Korsakova*. St. Petersburg: Kompozitor, 2012.
Ryan-Hayes, Karen, ed. *Venedikt Erofeev's "Moscow-Petushki": Critical Perspectives*. New York: Peter Lang, 1997.

Saakiants, Anna. *Marina Tsvetaeva: Stranitsy zhizni i tvorchestva (1910–1922)*. Moscow: Sovetskii pisatel', 1986.
Salys, Rimgaila. "Ljudmila Ulickaja's Sonecka: Gender and the Construction of Identity." *Russian Literature* 70 (2011): iii, 443–66.
Sandler, Stephanie. *Commemorating Pushkin*. Stanford: Stanford University Press, 2004.
Sandler, Stephanie. "The Stone Ghost: Akhmatova, Pushkin, and Don Juan." In *Literature, Culture, and Society in the Modern Age: In Honor of Joseph Frank*, edited by Edward J. Brown, Lazar Fleishman, Gregory Frieden, and Richard D. Shupach, 35–49. Stanford: Stanford University Press, 1992.
Saylor, Ian. "Anna Karenina and Don Giovanni: The Vengeance Motif in Oblonsky's Dream." *Tolstoy Studies Journal* 8 (1995–96): 112–16.
Schönle, Andreas. "Gender Trial and Gothic Thrill: Nadezhda Durova's Subversive Self-Exploration." In *Gender and Sexuality in Russian Civilisation*, edited by Peter Barta, 55–70. London: Routledge, 2001.
Sears, Theresa A. "'A Man with No Name': A Contrarian Reading of One Version of Don Juan in the Twenty-First Century." *Bulletin of the Comediantes* 55.2 (2003): 97–116.
Setchkarev, Vsevolod. *Ivan Goncharov: His Life and Works*. Wurzburg: Jal-Verlag, 1974.
Shengold, David. "Adding to the 'Guest' List: Hugo's *Hernani* and Pushkin's Don Juan." *Slavic Review* 58.2 (Summer 1999): 329–36.
Shevelenko, Irina. *Literaturnyi put' Tsvetaevoi: Ideologiia, poetika, identichnost' avtora v kontekste epokhi*. Moscow: Novoe literaturnoe obozrenie, 2015.
Simerka, Barbara A. "Eros and Atheism: Providential Ideology in the Don Juan Plays of Tirso de Molina and Thomas Shadwell." In *Echoes and Inscriptions: Comparative Approaches to Early Modern Spanish Literatures*, edited by Barbara A. Simerka and Christopher B. Weimer, 220–33. Cranbury, NJ: Associates University Presses, 2000.
Singer, Armand E. *The Don Juan Theme: An Annotated Bibliography of Versions, Analogues, Uses, and Adaptions*. Morgantown: West Virginia University Press, 1993.
Sinyavsky, Andrei. *The Russian Intelligentsia*. Translated by Lynn Visson. New York: Columbia University Press, 1997.
Smeed, J. W. *Don Juan: Variations on a Theme*. London: Routledge, 1990.
Smith, Alexandra. "Pushkin as a Cultural Myth: Dostoevskii's Pushkin Speech and its Legacy in Russian Modernism." In *Dostoevskii's Overcoat: Influence, Comparison, and Transposition*, edited by Joe Andrew and Robert Reid, 123–47. Amsterdam: Rodopi, 2013.
Stelleman, Jenny. "The Legend and the Self: The Stone Guest and Don Guan." *Russian Literature* 52 (2002): 493–510.
Stroganova, E. A. "Mif o Pigmalione v romannoi trilogii I. A. Goncharova." In *I. A. Goncharov. Materialy Mezhdunarodnoi nauchnoi konferentsii, posviashchennoi 195-letiiu so dnia rozhdeniia I. A. Goncharova: Sbornik statei russkikh i zarubezhnykh avtorov*, edited by A. V. Lobkareva, I. V. Smirnova, E. B. Klevogina, 215–21. Ulyanovsk: Pechatnyi dvor, 1998.
Sutcliffe, Benjamin, and Elizabeth Skomp. *Ludmila Ulitskaya and the Art of Tolerance*. Madison: University of Wisconsin Press, 2015.

Taruskin, Richard. *Opera and Drama in Russia as Preached and Practiced in the 1860s.* Ann Arbor: UMI Research Press, 1981.
Taubman, Jane A. *A Life through Poetry. Marina Tsvetaeva's Lyric Diary.* Columbus, OH: Slavica, 1989.
Tirso de Molina. "The Playboy of Seville, or Supper with a Statue." Translated by Adrienne M. Schizzano and Oscar Mandel. In *The Theatre of Don Juan: A Collection of Plays and Views, 1630–1963,* edited by Oscar Mandel, 47–99. Lincoln: University of Nebraska Press, 1963.
Todd, William Mills III. *Fiction and Society in the Age of Pushkin: Ideology, Institutions, and Narrative.* Cambridge, MA: Harvard University Press, 1986.
Todorov, Tzvetan. *The Fantastic: A Structural Approach to a Literary Genre.* Translated by Richard Howard. Ithaca: Cornell University Press, 1973.
Tomashevskii, B. V. [Boris Tomashevsky]. *Pushkin i Frantsiia.* Leningrad: Sovetskii pisatel', 1960.
Tolstoi, L. N. [Lev Tolstoy, Leo Tolstoy]. *Polnoe sobranie sochinenii.* Moscow: Gos. izd-vo khudozh. lit-ry, 1928–58.
Tolstoy, Leo. *Anna Karenina.* Translated by Rosamund Bartlett. Oxford: Oxford University Press, 2016.
Tolstoy, Leo. *Tolstoy's Letters.* Translated by R. F. Christian. London: Athlone Press, 1978.
Tolstoy, Leo. *Tolstoy's Short Fiction.* Translated by Michael R. Katz. New York: Norton, 2008.
Tolstoy, Leo. *What is Art?* Translated by Richard Pevear and Larissa Volokhonsky. London: Penguin, 1995.
Tsvetaeva, Marina. *Moi Pushkin.* Moscow: Sovetskii pisatel', 1967.
Tsvetaeva, Marina. *Sobranie sochinenii v 7-kh tomakh,* vol. 1. Moscow: Ellis Lak, 1994.
Ulitskaia, Liudmila. [Liudmila Ulitskaya]. *Iskrenne vash Shurik: Roman.* Moscow, Eksmo, 2004.
Ulitskaya, Ludmila. *The Funeral Party.* Translated by Cathy Porter. New York: Schocken Books, 1999.
Ulitskaya, Ludmila. *Sonechka: A Novella and Stories.* Translated by Arch Tait. New York: Schocken Books, 2005.
Ustiuzhanin, Dmitrii. *Malen'kie tragedii A. S. Pushkina.* Moscow: Khudozhestvennaia literatura, 1974.
Vail, Petr, and Aleksandr Genis. "Vo chreve machekhi." *Grani* 139 (1986), 137–50.
Vickery, Walter N. *Alexander Pushkin.* New York: Twayne Publishers, 1970.
Vickery, Walter N. "Hamlet and Don Juan in Blok: 'Shagi komandora.'" *International Journal of Slavic Linguistics and Poetics* 25 & 26 (1982): 465–76.
Wachtel, Andrew. "Translation, Imperialism, and Self-Definition in Russia." *Public Culture* 11.1 (1999): 49–73.
Walker, Gwen. "Songs of Africa: The Native Voice in Four Poems by Nikolai Gumilev." *Ulbandas Review* 7 (2003): 73–106.
Wang, Emily Ambrose. "Civic Feeling: Pushkin and the Decembrist Emotional Community." Ph. D. diss., Princeton University, 2016.
Wanner, Adrian. "Aleksandr Blok's Sculptural Myth." *The Slavic and East European Journal* 40.2 (Summer 1996): 236–50.

Wasiolek, Edward. *Tolstoy's Major Fiction*. Chicago: University of Chicago Press, 1978.
Watt, Ian. *Myths of Modern Individualism: Faust, Don Quixote, Don Juan, Robinson Crusoe*. Cambridge: Cambridge University Press, 1996.
Weiner, Jack. *Mantillas in Muscovy: The Spanish Golden Age Theater in Tsarist Russia, 1672–1917*. Lawrence: University of Kansas Publications, 1970.
Weinstein, Leo. *The Metamorphoses of Don Juan*. Stanford: Stanford University Press, 1959.
Williams, Bernard. "Don Juan as an Idea." In *The Don Giovanni Moment: Essays on the Legacy of an Opera*, edited by Lydia Goehr and Daniel Herwitz, 107–18. New York: Columbia University Press, 2006.
Wilton-Godberfforde, Emilia. "Molière's Dom Juan: The Trickster Transformed." In *Adaptation: Studies in French and Francophone Culture*, edited by Neil Archer and Andreea Weisl-Shaw, 55–66. Oxford: Peter Lang, 2012.
Wright, Sarah. *Tales of Seduction: The Figure of Don Juan in Spanish Culture*. London: Tauris Academic Studies, 2007.
Yurchak, Alexei. *Everything Was Forever, Until It Was No More: The Last Soviet Generation*. Princeton: Princeton University Press, 2005.
Zaslavskii, Oleg. [Oleg Zaslavsky]. "'Uznal ia pozdno': Skrytaia predystoriia v 'Kamennom goste.'" *Toronto Slavic Quarterly* 43 (Winter 2013): 149–79.
Zemskova, Elena. "'Don-Zhuan' Mariny Tsvetaevoi: 'Dialog' s Pushkinym," *Toronto Slavic Quarterly* 36 (Spring 2011): 305–12.
Zhdanov, V. A., and E. E. Zaidenshnur. "Istoriia sozdaniia romana 'Anna Karenina'." In L. N. Tolstoi, *Anna Karenina: Roman v vos'mi chastiakh*, 803–33. Moscow: Nauka, 1970.
Zirin, Mary. "A Woman in the 'Man's World': The Journals of Nadezhda Durova (1783–1866)." *Revealing Lives: Autobiography, Biography, and Gender*. Edited by Susan Gorag Bell, Marilyn Yalom, and Lillian S. Robinson, 43–51. Albany: SUNY Press, 1990.
Žižek, Slavoj. *The Plague of Fantasies*. New York: Verso, 1997.

Index

Abaza, Yulia, 202n16
Acmeism, 132, 133
Adamovich, Georgii, 5
Aigi, Gennady, 161
Akerhielm, Anna Quidling, *Don Juan Tenorio*, 216n4
Akhmatova, Anna, 5, 17, 18, 26, 36, 38, 39, 52, 58, 104, 105, 106, 111, 131, 137, 138, 146, 195n4, 201n8, 202n18, 211n35, 211n37, 211n38, 211n39; *Poem without a Hero*, 27, 106, 109, 133, 138–43, 186, 188, 212n41, 212n42
Aksenov, Vasily, 144, 146
Aleshin, Samuil, 5; *At That Time in Seville*, 144–45, 186, 212n1
Aleshkovsky, Iuz, 146
Alexander II (Tsar of Russia), 120
Alexandrov, Vladimir, 93
Alfonso XI (King of Castile), 197n18
Anderson, Nancy, 52, 195n1
Andreev, Vadim, 5
Angiolini, Gasparo, 4
Annin, Alexander, 5, 25
anti-Semitism, 154–55, 213n11
apocalypse, 6, 27, 106, 117, 124
Arzamas literary society, 30
Askochensky, Viktor, *The Asmodeus of Our Time*, 205n8
atheism, 29, 198n24, 202n14
Austen, John, 13

Austin, John, *How To Do Things with Words*, 13
Avseenko, Vasily, 207n24

Bagno, Vsevolod, 195n8, 209n2
Baker, Felicity, 198n25, 204n42
Bakhtin, Mikhail (dialogism), 156, 213n14
Bal'mont, Konstantin, 5, 104, 107, 117, 132, 209n2; "Don Juan," 26, 108–9; "The Don Juan Type in World Literature," 26, 107–9
Baudrillard, Jean, 154
Bayliss, Robert, 198n23
Beethoven, Ludwig van, 95, 118
Beketova, Alexandra, 118, 119, 120
Belinsky, Vissarion, 37, 202n20, 205–6n12
Bely, Andrei, 105, 111, 163, 209n9; *Petersburg*, 210n10
Benjamin, Walter, 109
Bertati, Giovanni, 14, 207n27
Bethea, David, 37
Bezhetsky, Alexei, 5, 70, 107, 134, 205n5
Bezymensky, Alexander, 169
Blagoi, Dmitry, 38, 52, 55, 201n7, 202n22, 202n23
Blok, Alexander, 5, 26, 27, 104, 105, 107, 109–111, 125, 127, 129–30, 132, 138, 139, 140, 209n4, 209n5, 209n6, 209n7,

Blok, Alexander (*continued*)
  209n8, 209n9, 210n18, 210n19,
  210n22; *Carmen*, 129; "I Foresee You,"
  114; *Notebooks*, 109; "Of Valor, Noble
  Deeds, and Glory," 210n16; *Poems
  about a Beautiful Lady*, 116; *Retribution* (cycle), 112; *Retribution* (narrative
  poem), 26–27, 28, 106, 109, 111, 112,
  117–24, 143, 185–86, 188, 189, 210n11,
  210n20, 210n21, 210n22, 210n23, 210–
  11n24; "The Scythians," 122; "The
  Steps of the Commander," 26, 28,
  106, 109, 110, 111–17, 125, 126, 129,
  130, 131, 132, 134, 138–39, 142, 143, 157,
  185–86, 188, 210n11, 210n12, 210n13,
  210n14, 210n16, 210n17, 210–11n24,
  212n42, 212n6; *The Twelve*, 122
Blok, Alexander L'vovich (father),
  117–24
Blok, Liubov' (née Mendeleeva) (wife),
  105, 109, 110, 111, 112, 209n7, 209n9,
  210n15, 210n18
Bonaparte, Napoleon, 4, 125, 127
Brik, Lilia, 105
Brik, Osip, 105
Brodsky, Iosif, 146, 163, 212–13n7
Briusov, Valerii, 5, 104, 105, 107, 126,
  196n11
Buckler, Julie, 206n18, 207n29
Bulatov, Erik, 214–15n25
Bulgakov, Mikhail, *The Master and
  Margarita*, 148
Bulgarin, Faddei, 31
Burenin, Viktor, 205n9
Burgin, Diana, 127, 211n29
Byron, George Gordon (Lord), 4, 119,
  120, 125, 130, 195n7, 212n6; Byronic
  hero/Byronism, 74–75; *Beppo*, 201n11;
  Don Juan, 4, 68, 76, 138, 181, 195n7,
  205n2, 206n21

Camus, Albert, *The Myth of Sisyphus*,
  189–90
Canfield, J. Douglas, 23, 24, 197–98n19
Canobbio, Carlo, 4, 201n7
Carmen, 27, 127–28, 129, 130

carnival, 151
Casanova, Giacomo, 127, 142
Cathars, 21
Catholicism, 9, 15, 215n35
Cervantes, Miguel de, *Don Quixote*, 166,
  214n24
Chekhov, Anton, 5, 25, 28, 98, 190, 208–
  9n40, 209n41; "About Love," 209n44;
  "Anna on the Neck," 208–9n40,
  209n44; "The Lady with the Little
  Dog," 25, 26, 28, 67, 69, 70, 71, 81,
  96–103, 106–7, 185–86, 187, 193,
  209n43; "Lights," 208–9n40; *Platonov*, 97–98, 208–9n40, 209n42;
  The Seagull, 208–9n40; "The Shooting Party," 208–9n40; "Three Years,"
  208–9n40; "Ward no. 6," 148
Chernyshevsky, Nikolai, 45, 60, 71,
  209n1; *What is To Be Done?*, 71, 79
Christ, Jesus, 113
Chukovsky, Korney, 209n8
Cigognini, Giacinto Andrea, *The Stone
  Guest*, 13, 195n5
Cixous, Hélène, 22, 45, 79
Clayton, J. Douglas, 199n31
Conceptualism, 146, 158, 214–15n25
Conlon, Raymond, 197–98n19
Connell, R. W., 22, 200n38
Connor, Catherine, 197n18
Constant, Benjamin, *Adolphe*, 211n37
Copernicus, Nicolaus, 123
Costlow, Jane, 102
Counter-Reformation, 5
Crone, Anna Lisa, 139, 210n13, 212n42
Cui, Cesar, 204n46; *A Feast in the Time
  of Plague*, 204n45

Da Ponte, Lorenzo, 4, 14, 206n19,
  207n27; also see *Don Giovanni*
  (Mozart)
Dalton, Margaret, 70
damnation, 9, 10, 33, 57, 163, 187
D'Annunzio, Gabriel, *The Pleasure*,
  107
Dante, 177; *The Divine Comedy*, 204n42
D'Anthès, Georges, 32, 37, 157

Index

Dargomyzhsky, Alexander, 26, 72; *The Stone Guest*, 26, 28, 60–67, 72, 100, 204n45, 204n46
Darsky, Dmitry, 39, 195n4
Davies, Ann, 197–98n19
Davydov, Sergei, 39
De Sherbinin, Julie, 207n30
Debreczeny, Paul, 200n3, 201n5
Decembrists, 29–30, 32, 200n2, 200n3
Deleuze, Gilles, 41, 102
Delmas, Liubov', 109
Del'vig, Anton, 31
Descartes, Rene, 159
Dinega, Alyssa, 126, 129–30
dissidence (Soviet), 145–47, 155–56, 159–60, 172, 212–13n7, 214n20
Dmitrienko, S. F., 117, 210–11n24
Dobroliubov, Nikolai, 71, 74
dominant (Jakobson), 8, 17, 185
Don Quixote, 5
Dorimon (Nicolas Drouin), *The Stone Guest*, 13, 198n22
Dostoevsky, Fyodor, 6, 101, 110, 119, 164, 190, 196n11, 202n16, 205–6n12, 207n24; *The Brothers Karamazov*, 107; *Crime and Punishment*, 215n30; *Devils*, 205n8; "Pushkin Speech," 6, 36, 196n9, 196n11; *White Nights*, 110
Dovlatov, Sergei, 146
Driver, Sam, 133
Druzhin, Alexander, 60
Dumas, Alexandre (the Elder), 199n29
Durova, Nadezhda, 45–46; *The Cavalry Maiden*, 45–46; *The Memoirs of N. A. Durova*, 203n32

Efron, Sergei, 126
Ehre, Milton, 205n10
Eikhenbaum, Boris, 30, 207n24
Emerson, Caryl, 204n45, 209n44
Enlightenment, 15
Epstein, Mikhail, 147, 151, 156, 158, 215n26
Erofeev, Venedikt, 5, 146, 147, 169, 212–13n7, 213n15; *Moscow-Petushki*, 147, 159, 169, 213n14, 214n20; *Walpurgis Night, or the Steps of the Commander*, 27, 145, 146, 147–60, 162, 163, 165, 172, 178, 186, 187, 188, 190, 212n2, 212n4, 212n5, 212n6, 212–13n7, 213n10, 213n11, 213n12, 213n13, 213n14, 213–14n17, 214n18, 214n20, 214n21
Erofeeva, Galina (wife), 212–13n7
Esenin, Sergei, 5
Espronceda, Jose de, *The Student of Salamanca*, 107
Evdokimova, Svetlana, 57
Everist, Mark, 4
Evtushenko, Evgeny, 214n20
exile, 5, 17, 23, 29, 30, 31, 36, 43, 57, 76, 106, 110, 123–24, 132, 147, 150, 162, 165, 166, 167, 173, 185, 186, 201n7, 202n18

Fainberg, Margarita, 112
False Dmitry I, Tsar of Russia, 125
Faust legend, 5, 16, 28, 142, 148, 212n2
Feiler, Lily, 211n26
Felman, Shoshana, 11, 13
feminism, 22, 212n1
Filosofova, Anna, 71, 119
Finke, Michael, 96
Firestone, Shulamith, 22
flâneur, 109–10, 210n11
Fonvizin, Denis, 101
Forman, Edward, 207n27
Franko, Ivan, 191
Freud, Sigmund, 18, 200n37, 212n1; *Totem and Taboo*, 18–19, 118, 210n21; "The Uncanny," 19, 56–60, 62–63; "A Very Special Type of Choice of Object Made by Men," 118
Futurism (Russian), 161, 165

Gartung, Maria (née Pushkina), 84
Gasparov, Boris, 32, 37, 51, 202n17
Gazzaniga, Giuseppe, *Don Juan Tenorio*, 14, 207n27
Gendarme de Bévotte, Georges, 198n21, 201n7
Genis, Alexander, 149
Giliberto, Onofrio, *The Stone Guest*, 13
Gippius, Zinaida, 5, 105; "Otvet Don-Zhuana," 105–6

Index

Girard, René, 20–21, 78, 86, 182
Glebova-Sudeikina, Olga, 138, 139, 140
Glinka, Mikhail, 62; *Ruslan and Liudmila*, 62–63
Gluck, Christoph Willibald, 4
Göbler, Frank, 24, 26, 134, 144, 195n6
Goethe, Johann Wolfgang von, 68; *Faust*, 68, 70, 148, 212n2
Gogol, Nikolai, 31, 60, 163, 164, 196n10, 205–6n12
Goldenveizer, Alexander, 83
Golstein, Vladimir, 208n37
Goncharov, Ivan, 5; *An Ordinary Story*, 73; "Ivan Savich Podzhabrin," 73, 205n11; "Notes on Belinsky's Personality," 205–6n12; *Oblomov*, 73, 74, 205n9, 206n15, 206n16; *The Precipice*, 25, 26, 28, 67, 69, 70, 72–81, 86, 96, 100, 106–7, 185, 186–87, 190, 205n8, 205n9, 205n10, 206n14, 206n15, 206n16
Gorchakov, G. N., 112, 116, 210n14
Gorodetsky, B. P. (Boris Pavlovich), 53, 201n12
Gorodetsky, Sergei, 111, 132
Goscilo, Helena, 86, 172, 204n39, 206n18, 207n28, 207n29
Gozenpud, Avram, 62
Grabbe, Christian, *Don Juan and Faust*, 16, 68, 212n2
Grech, Nikolai, 31
Green Lamp literary society, 30
Grigoryan, Bella, 31
Griboedov, Alexander, 74; *Woe from Wit*, 74–75, 101
Grigor'ev, Apollon, 60
Groys, Boris, 146, 162, 171
Guattari, Felix, 41, 102
Guber, Petr, 45
GULAG, 146
Gumilev, Nikolai, 5, 25, 26, 104, 107, 117, 138, 139, 140, 211n34; "Don Zhuan," 132–33, 211n30, 211n31, 211n32; *Don Juan in Egypt*, 27, 109, 131, 132, 133–37, 142, 187, 188
Gusev, Nikolai, 83

Hasty, Olga Peters, 44, 47, 125, 211n28
hegemonic masculinity, 22–23, 43
Hellebust, Rolf, 210n10
Herder, Johann Gottfried, 196n10
hereditary taint, 118, 210n19
Herman, David, 17, 38, 42, 57, 150, 152, 153, 159, 195n4, 203n26, 203–4n37, 208n32
Hippocrates, 205n11
Hoffmann, E. T. A. (Ernst Theodor Amadeus), 5, 14, 25; "Don Juan, or a Fabulous Adventure that Befell a Music Enthusiast on His Travels," 15–16, 17, 25, 35–36, 68, 69–70, 107, 108, 110, 111, 142, 147, 173, 182, 193, 194, 199n31
Hollywood, 21
holy foolishness, 147, 160, 214n20
homosexuality, 212n1
homoeroticism, 215n38
Hoogenboom, Hilde, 203n29
Houk, Guy, 214n20
Hugo, Victor, *Hernani*, 201n7
Hutcheon, Linda, 152, 158, 165

Jackson, Robert Louis, 93
Jakobson, Roman, 8, 58, 123, 152, 210n17
Jews (and Jewish identity), 151, 154–55, 178, 186, 213n11, 215n35
Joan of Arc, 125
Jung, Carl, 199n34

Kabakov, Ilya, 163, 214–15n25
Kanevskaya, Marina, 196n11
Karamzin, Nikolai, 36, 101
Karlinsky, Simon, 125
Karpiak, Robert, 25, 26, 69, 70, 144, 196n15, 199n30, 199n31, 199n32, 202n20, 204–5n1, 205n4, 205n5, 205n6, 209n41, 209n42, 211n31, 211n33, 216n4, 216n5, 217n8
Kataev, Vladimir, 96–97, 208–9n40
Kazakov, Vladimir, 5, 146, 147, 160–62; *Don Juan*, 27, 28, 145, 146, 147, 160–72, 178, 186, 187, 188, 214n24; *Mistake of the Living*, 162, 169; "Multiplica-

tion Tables," 161; "Wonderful crossed-out quatrain," 161
Kern, Anna (née Poltoratskaya), 203n34, 204n41
Kharms, Daniil, 161, 163
Khlebnikov, Velemir, 161, 164
Kierkegaard, Søren, 14, *Either/Or*, 14
Kisin, Boris, 144
Kleinmikhel', Petr, 213n13
Kliger, Ilya, 78
Klimova, Svetlana, 195n7, 201n11
Kniazev, Vsevolod, 138, 139, 140
Knipper-Chekhova, Olga, 97, 98
Krasnoshchekova, Elena, 205n8, 206n14, 206n16
Krestovsky, Vsevolod, *The Flock of Panurge*, 205n8
Kropf, David Glenn, 17, 41, 53, 57, 102, 150, 152, 153 195n4, 204n40
Kruchenykh, Alexei, 164–65, 169
Kuritsyn, Vyacheslav, 214n22
Kustanovich, Konstantin, 213n12
Kuzmic, Tatiana, 207–8n31
Kuzmin-Karavaeva, Elizaveta, 111

Labrecuqe, Nathalie, 117
Lacan, Jacques, 20; desire, 20, 41–42, 200n36, 202n13; Donjuanism, 199–200n35; "Name of the Father," 20, 122
Lachmann, Renate, 162, 169
Laclos, Pierre Choderlos de, *Dangerous Liaisons*, 43–44, 203n28, 203n36, 207n28
Leatherbarrow, W. J., 196n11
Leiderman, Daniil, 214–15n25
Leiderman, Naum, 147, 149, 161
Lermontov, Mikhail 28, 157, 205–6n12; "Death of a Poet," 60; *Demon*, 120; *A Hero of Our Time*, 28, 74, 200n41
Leskov, Nikolai 28; *Lady Macbeth of the Mtsensk District*, 28, 71
Levitt, Marcus, 60
libertinage, 6, 10, 29–31, 32, 41–42, 82, 86–87, 206n18, 207n28
Liern, Rafael María, 198–99n28

Lipovetsky, Mark, 146, 147, 149, 161, 212n5, 213n14
Livshin, Olga, 175, 179
Longinov, Mikhail, 60
Lope de Vega, 7
Lotman, Yuri, 21, 38, 39, 43, 45, 200n2, 203n27, 203n29
Lubicz-Milosz, O. V. de, 199n29
Lundelius, Ruth, 197–98n19

MacKay, Dorothy Epplen, 196n13
MacKinnon, Catharine, 22
Makin, Michael, 129
Mañara Vicentelo de Leca, Miguel, 199n29, 199n30, 205n4
Mandelker, Amy, 208n36
Mandelstam, Osip, 126, 130, 139, 211n38
Mandrell, James, 11–12, 20, 198–99n28
Manning, Clarence, 191, 200n40, 200n41, 216n5
Marañón, Gregorio, 212n1
Martynov, Nikolai, 157
Masing-Delic, Irene, 206n15, 209n7, 210n22
Matich, Olga, 105, 209n7
Matlaw, Ralph, 211n34
Mayakovsky, Vladimir, 105, 161
Mérimée, Prosper, 190–91; *Souls in Purgatory*, 191, 199n29, 199n30, 216n3; "Venus of L'ille," 191
Messerschmidt, James, 22–23
Meyerhold, Vsevolod, 138
Michelet, Jules, 45; *L'amour*, 45
"Mighty Handful" (moguchaia kuchka), 61, 64
Mihaychuk, George, 192, 193, 216n4
Mikhailov, Mikhail, 45, 71
Millett, Kate, 22, 45
misogyny, 45, 98–100, 203n31
Mit'ki, 146–47
Mochulsky, Konstantin, 113, 116, 117–18
modernism, 103, 175, 210n10
Molière (Jean-Baptiste Poquelin), *Don Juan, or the Stone Guest*, 4, 12–14, 17, 21, 25, 33, 35, 38, 39, 42, 63, 70, 111, 138, 185, 187, 188, 189, 191, 193, 195n6, 196n14,

Molière (Jean-Baptiste Poquelin) (*continued*)
198n21, 198n22, 198n23, 201n7, 201n8, 201n9; *The Miser*, 121, 201n7, 202n15, 204n42, 206n21, 211n26, 216n4
Mordvin-Shchodro, Alexander, 5, 70, 107, 134
Morson, Gary Saul, 208n37
Mozart, Wolfgang Amadeus, 4, *Don Giovanni*, 14–16, 17, 18, 19, 21, 22, 25, 26, 28, 29, 33–34, 35, 38, 39, 41, 42, 54, 56–57, 58, 62, 63, 68, 69, 70, 73, 77, 81–84, 90, 92, 94, 107, 111, 123, 138, 151, 159, 166, 167, 185, 188, 189, 191, 193, 200n35, 201n7, 201n8, 201n9, 201n10, 202n15, 202n17, 204n42, 204n44, 206n18, 206n20, 206–7n23, 207n27, 207n28, 211n26; *The Magic Flute*, 14; *The Marriage of Figaro*, 14, 207n27
Müller, Bertram, 161
Murav'ev, Vladimir, 159–60, 212–13n7

Nabokov, Vladimir, 5
Napoleonic Wars, 45–46
Nekrasov, Nikolai, 157; "Who Is Happy in Russia?," 158–59
Nemirovsky, Igor', 30, 35, 200n4, 201n7, 201n9, 203n28
Neo-Classicism, 15
Nietzsche, Friedrich, 156
nihilism, 73, 74, 77, 78, 79, 205n8
Nikolai I (tsar of Russia), 6, 31, 32, 166, 200n1, 201n6, 213n13
nobility (class), 8, 13, 23–24, 33, 72, 81, 185–86, 197n18
Nordau, Max, 210n19

OBERIU (Association for Real Art), 161
Oedipal conflict, 18, 118, 123, 124
Olenina, Anna, 31
Olshanskaya, Natalia, 215n37
O'Neil, Catherine, 47
Ortega y Gasset, José, 212n1
Ostup, Nikolai, 5, 131
Ovid, 43; *Art of Love*, 43, 206n18; *Metamorphoses*, 77–79

Paperno, Irina, 71, 105, 205n7, 209n1
Parnell, Christina, 215n33
Parnok, Sofia, 125–26
Parny, Evariste de, 200n4
Pasternak, Boris, 129–30
patriarchy, 11, 18, 22, 24, 74, 76, 77, 197n18, 197–98n19
Pelevin, Viktor, 172
Pendzik, Susana, 197–98n19
Peschio, Joe, 30
Peter I (Tsar of Russia), 4, 32
Petrarch, 201n11
Petrovskaya, Nina, 105
Petrushevksaya, Liudmila, 173, 215n31; "The Lookout Point," 187
Pisarev, Dmitry, 60
Pisemsky, Alexei, *Troubled Seas*, 205n8
Pobedonostsev, Konstantin, 123, 210–11n24
Polevoi, Nikolai, 31
Pomerantsev, Vladimir, 146, 173
Porter, Roy, 198n25
postmodernism, 145, 152, 163, 170, 172, 180, 213n8
Postnov, Oleg, 75
Presto, Jenifer, 105–06, 209n6
Prigov, Dmitry, 158, 214–15n25; "The Image of Reagan in Soviet Literature," 158
Pronkevich, Oleksandr, 216n4
Przybyszewski, Stanislav, 107; *Homo sapiens*, 107
Pugachev, Emilian, 125, 127
Purgold-Molas, Alexandra, 64
Pushkin, Alexander, 5, 24, 25, 60, 125, 127, 130, 157, 195n3, 196n11, 200n2, 202n17, 202n18, 203n29, 203n31, 203n32, 203n34, 204n40, 204n41, 205–6n12, 207n24, 209n5, 211n27, 213n10; *The Belkin Tales*, 207n24; *The Bronze Horseman*, 32, 117, 210n17; *The Captain's Daughter*, 125, 207n24; "Conversation between a Bookseller and a Poet," 32; *A Feast in the Time of Plague*, 204n45, 207n25; "The Guests Were Arriving at the Dacha," 42,

Index

207n23; "Egyptian Nights," 207n24;
Eugene Onegin, 28, 44, 47, 74, 121,
186, 190, 196n11, 200n41; 203n27,
203n29, 203n33, 207n24, 207n26; *The
Gabrieliad*, 30, 32, 200n1; "I'm Here,
Inezilia," 64–66; *The Miserly Knight*,
201n7, 204n45; *Mozart and Salieri*,
178, 190, 204n45, 206–7n23, 207n25;
"Ode to Liberty," 29; *Poltava*, 46;
"The Queen of Spades," 36, 202n16;
Roslavlev, 203n29; *Ruslan and Liudmila*, 32; *The Stone Guest*, 3–4, 5–7,
12, 13, 14–15, 16–18, 19, 21, 22, 24,
25–28, 29–67, 68–69, 70, 71, 72, 73,
74, 76–81, 82–94, 95, 96–98, 100–103,
104, 106, 107, 109, 110, 111, 113–14,
115–16, 120, 122, 123, 124, 126, 127,
128, 129, 130, 131, 134, 135, 136, 137–38,
140, 141, 142, 143, 144, 147, 149, 150,
151, 152, 153, 157, 159, 160, 162, 163,
164, 165, 166, 167, 168, 170, 172, 173,
174, 175, 177–78, 179, 182, 183, 184,
185, 186, 187, 188, 189, 190, 191, 192,
193, 195n8, 199n30, 199n31, 200n40,
201n6, 201n7, 201n8, 201n9, 201n10,
201n11, 201n12, 202n13, 202n14,
202n15, 202n18, 202n20, 202n21,
202n23, 202n24, 203n26, 203n35,
203n36, 203–4n37, 204n38, 204n40,
204n41, 204n43, 204–5n1, 206–7n23,
207n26, 208n32, 208n34, 209n43,
209n2, 209n4, 209n9, 211n33, 211n39,
212n41, 212n42, 212n6, 215n1, 216n3,
216n4; "The Tale of the Golden
Cockerel," 210n17; "The Village," 29;
"To the Young Widow," 36
Pushkina, Natalia (née Goncharova),
31–32, 36–37, 45, 57, 97, 213n10
Pushkina, Olga (sister), 31
Pushkina, Sofia (cousin), 31
Pygmalion, 72, 77–79, 80, 206n15
Pyman, Avril, 109, 110, 118

Rachmaninov, Sergei, *The Miserly
Knight*, 204n45
Radzinsky, Edvard, 5

Rank, Otto, *The Don Juan Legend*, 19,
199n33, 199n34
Rassadin, Stanislav, 38, 39, 58, 115
Rayfield, Donald, 96
Realism, 6, 26, 60–61, 66–67, 68–69,
70–72, 81, 84, 86, 87, 97, 102, 103,
104, 105, 106, 187, 209n1
Reich, Rebecca, 150–51, 214n18
Renaissance, 5
Revolution (Russian), 106, 116, 117, 124,
139, 144, 211n26
Revutsky, Valerian, 144
Richardson, Samuel, 44
Rimsky-Korsakov, Nikolai, 62, 204n46;
Mozart and Salieri, 62, 204n45
Riviere, Joan, *Womanliness as a Masquerade*, 199–200n35
Robertson, Brian, 199–200n35
Romanticism, 16, 17, 18, 26, 33, 60–61,
67, 68, 84, 86, 103, 105, 110
Rosslyn, Wendy, 139–40, 141
Rostopchina, Evdokiia, 5
Rougemont, Denis de, 21, 39, 90, 176
Rousseau, Jean-Jacques, 44
Rozumnyj, Jaroslav, 192
Rubinstein, Lev, 213n8
Ruch'evskaia, Ekaterina, 62
Russian Orthodoxy, 128–29, 178, 188,
215n35
Ryan-Hayes, Karen, 213n15

Saakiants, Anna, 211n26
Sadovskaya, Ksenia, 110
Sadur, Nina, 173
Salys, Rimgaila, 215n29, 215n32
Saltykov-Shchedrin, Mikhail, 205n9
Samoilov, David, 5
Sand, George, 45, 47, 203n34
Sandler, Stephanie, 127, 138, 211n29
Saylor, Ian, 206n18
Schlegel, August, 196n10
Schlegel, Friedrich, 196n10
Schönle, Andreas, 46
Schumann, Robert, 118, 122, 210n23
Sears, Theresa, 8, 23
Sedakova, Ol'ga, 212–13n7

serialism, 110, 111, 151, 163, 177, 180, 213n8, 213n22
Setchkarev, Vsevolod, 205n9
Seth, Vikram, *The Golden Gate*, 190
Severianin, Igor', 5
Shadwell, Thomas, *The Libertine*, 198n24
Shaffer, Peter; *Amadeus*, 190
Shakespeare, William, 47, 71; *Hamlet*, 210n14; *Macbeth*, 191, 217n8; *Othello*, 47
Shaw, George Bernard, 14; *Man and Superman*, 107
Shcheglova, Valentina, 109
Shcherbina, Nikolai, 5
Shengold, David, 201n7
Shevchenko, Taras, 191
Shevelenko, Irina, 211n28
Shevyrev, Stepan, 201n6
Silver Age, 5, 6, 26–27, 103, 104–7, 109, 142, 143, 187, 188
Simerka, Barbara, 198n20, 198n24
Singer, Armand, 196n13, 216n4
Sinyavsky, Daniil, *The Russian Intelligentsia*, 213n12
Skabichevsky, Alexander, 205n9
Skomp, Elizabeth, 172–73, 174, 179–80, 182, 215n27, 215n31
Smeed, John, 198n26, 198n27
Smith, Alexandra, 196n11
Smith, Marie, 36
Smith, Virginia Llewellyn, 98
Sobańska, Karolina, 51–52
Socialist Realism, 144, 146, 171
Solov'ev, Vladimir, 105, 106; *Short Tale of the Antichrist*, 106
Solzhenitsyn, Alexander, 146; *One Day in the Life of Ivan Denisovich*, 146
Sophocles, 214n21
Sorokin, Vladimir, 163, 172; *The Queue*, 213n8
Sosnora, Viktor, 5, 161
Staël, Germaine de, 44, 201n7, 203n29; *Delphine*, 44, 203n29, 203n30
Stalin, Iosif, and Stalinism, 27, 106, 133, 139, 140, 144, 145, 146, 162, 171, 173, 175, 188

Stasova, Nadezhda, 71
Stelleman, Jenny, 58–59
Strakhov, Nikolai, 207n24
Stroganova, E. N., 206n15
Sukhotin, Mikhail, 93
Sumarokov, Alexander. 195n6
superfluous man, 72, 73, 74
Sutcliffe, Benjamin, 172–73, 174, 179–80, 182, 215n27, 215n31
Symbolism, 105, 108, 132

Taubman, Jane, 125, 126
Taruskin, Richard, 61–62, 204n45
Tchaikovsky, Petr, 4, 61
Tenoromania, 212n1
Thaw (period), 146, 173
Tirso de Molina (Gabriel Téllez), 215n2; *The Trickster of Seville and the Stone Guest*, 7–12, 13, 14, 15, 16, 17, 18, 19, 23, 24, 25, 29, 33, 35, 38, 42, 56, 63, 68, 70, 72, 84, 104, 107, 108, 111, 124, 133, 145, 185, 188, 189, 190, 191, 193, 195n8, 196n13, 196n14, 196n15, 197n17, 197n18, 197n19, 198n20, 198n21, 198n23, 198n24, 198–99n28, 199n30, 200n38, 200n39, 201n9, 202n15, 204n42, 209n2, 211n32, 216n4
Todd, William Mills III, 31, 203n25, 203n33
Todorov, Tzvetan, 202n16
Tolstaya, Maria, 83
Tolstaya, Sofia (née Behrs), 45
Tolstaya, Tatiana, 173
Tolstoy, Alexei K. (Konstantinovich), 5, 25; *Don Juan*, 25, 26, 69–70, 107, 134, 144, 186, 195n8, 200n40, 205n3, 209n4
Tolstoy, Lev, 5, 45, 190, 206–7n23, 207n24; *Anna Karenina*, 22, 26, 28, 67, 69, 70, 71, 72, 81–94, 95, 96, 97–103, 106–7, 111, 117, 185, 186–87, 188, 189, 190, 206n18, 206n21, 207n24, 207n25, 207n26, 207n28, 207–8n31, 208n33, 208n34, 208n35, 208n36, 208n37, 209n43, 210n19; *The Infected Family*, 205n8; *The Kreutzer Sonata*, 24, 94–96, 97, 98–103; *What*

is Art?, 206n22; "Why Do Men Stupefy Themseslves?," 96
Tomashevsky, Boris, 196n14, 201n6, 201n7, 203n29
triangulation (love triangles), 11, 18, 20–21, 26, 32, 55, 69, 73, 81, 82, 84, 89–90, 102, 105, 134–35, 207–8n31, 209n9
tricks (*burlas*)/tricksters, 7, 10, 11, 12, 23, 24, 29, 30, 75, 149, 177, 212n5, 216n4
Tristan and Isolde legend, 21, 200n37
Trubnikova, Maria, 71
Tsvetaeva, Marina, 5, 26, 104, 105, 106, 196n11, 211n26, 211n29; *Carmen*, 129, 211n26; *Don Juan*, 27, 28, 109, 125–31, 132, 134, 137, 142, 143, 186, 187, 188; *Evening Album*, 126; *Girlfriend*, 125–26; "Meeting with Pushkin," 127, 211n26; *Mileposts*, 126; "My Pushkin," 211n27; *Poems to Akhmatova*, 126; *Poems to Blok*, 126; *Sten'ka Razin*, 211n26
Turgenev, Ivan, 71, 72, 83, 206–7n23; "Diary of a Superfluous Man," 74; *Fathers and Children*, 101–2; "Hamlet of the Shchigrovsky District," 71; *Nest of the Gentry*, 74; *Rudin*, 74

Ukrainka, Lesia, 216n5; *The Stone Host*, 144, 191–93, 216n4, 216n5, 216n6, 217n8
Ulitskaya, Liudmila, 25, 27, 28, 145, 172–84, 186, 187, 188, 189, 215n27, 215n35; *Daniel Stein, Interpreter*, 215n35; *The Funeral Party*, 27, 172, 176–79, 186, 190, 215n35; *Jacob's Ladder*, 27, 184; *Sincerely Yours, Shurik*, 27, 172, 179–83, 190, 215n37; *Sonechka*, 27, 172, 173–76, 177, 179, 183, 186, 190, 215n29, 215n30, 215n38
Unamuno y Jugo, Miguel de, 198–99n28, 212n1
Ushakova, Elizaveta, 36
Ustiuzhanin, Dmitry, 38, 52, 208n32

Vail', Petr, 148–49
Val'berkh, Ivan, 4, 201n7
Viardot, Louis, 206–7n23

Viardot-Garcia, Pauline, 4, 206–7n23
Viazemskaya, Vera, 45
Viazemsky, Petr, 45
Vickery, Walter, 116, 202n21
Villiers, Claude Deschamps, Sieur de, *The Stone Guest, or the Criminal Son*, 4, 13, 198n22, 201n7
Volokhova, Natalia, 109
Voltaire, 196n14
Vorontsov, Mikhail, 30
Vorontsova, Elizaveta, 24, 30
Vul'f, Evpraxiia, 46

Wachtel, Andrew, 196n9
Wagner, Richard, 206n22
Walker, Gwen, 211n34
Wang, Emily, 200n2
Wanner, Adrian, 113–14, 117
Wasiolek, Edward, 89–90
Watt, Ian, 5, 8
Weiner, Jack, 195n5
Weinstein, Leo, 11, 14, 15, 16, 196n12, 198n27, 198–99n28, 199n29
Williams, Bernard, 15
Wilton-Godberfforde, Emilia, 13, 198n22
woman question (Russia), 42–47, 62–66, 71–72, 79, 81, 92, 103, 208n36
women's prose (zhenskaia proza), 173, 215n27
Wright, Sarah, 198–99n28, 212n1

Yeltsin, Boris, 213n12
Yurchak, Alexei, 146–47

Zaidenshnur, E. E., 207n25
Zaitsev, Boris, 70
Zaslavsky, Oleg, 203n35
Zemskova, Elena, 129
Zhdanov, V. A., 207n25
zhiznetvorchestvo, 105–6
Zhukovsky, Vasily, 31
Zirin, Mary, 46
Žižek, Slavoj, 20
Zorrilla, José, *Don Juan Tenorio*, 16, 68, 104, 110, 111, 198–99n28, 199n30
Zoshchenko, Mikhail, 146

Publications of the Wisconsin Center for Pushkin Studies

Realizing Metaphors: Alexander Pushkin and the Life of the Poet
DAVID M. BETHEA

The Pushkin Handbook
EDITED BY DAVID M. BETHEA

Legacies of the Stone Guest: The Don Juan Legend in Russian Literature
ALEXANDER BURRY

*The Uncensored "Boris Godunov": The Case for Pushkin's
Original "Comedy," with Annotated Text and Translation*
CHESTER DUNNING WITH CARYL EMERSON, SERGEI FOMICHEV,
LIDIIA LOTMAN, AND ANTONY WOOD

Alexander Pushkin's "Little Tragedies": The Poetics of Brevity
EDITED BY SVETLANA EVDOKIMOVA

Taboo Pushkin: Topics, Texts, Interpretations
EDITED BY ALYSSA DINEGA GILLESPIE

Tragic Encounters: Pushkin and European Romanticism
MAKSIM HANUKAI

Pushkin's Tatiana
OLGA HASTY

*Lyric Complicity: Poetry and Readers in the Golden Age
of Russian Literature*
DARIA KHITROVA

Derzhavin: A Biography
VLADISLAV KHODASEVICH; TRANSLATED AND WITH AN
INTRODUCTION BY ANGELA BRINTLINGER

The Poetics of Impudence and Intimacy in the Age of Pushkin
JOE PESCHIO

The Imperial Sublime: A Russian Poetics of Empire
HARSHA RAM

The Unlikely Futurist: Pushkin and the Invention of Originality in Russian Modernism
JAMES RANN

How Russia Learned to Write: Literature and the Imperial Table of Ranks
IRINA REYFMAN

Challenging the Bard: Dostoevsky and Pushkin, a Study of Literary Relationship
GARY ROSENSHIELD

Pushkin and the Genres of Madness: The Masterpieces of 1833
GARY ROSENSHIELD

Pushkin's Rhyming: A Comparative Study
J. THOMAS SHAW

A Commentary to Pushkin's Lyric Poetry, 1826–1836
MICHAEL WACHTEL